The Letters of
Douglas Oliver and J. H. Prynne

1967–2000

Edited with an introduction
and notes by Joe Luna

The Last Books
Amsterdam and Sofia, 2022

Published in 2022 by The Last Books,
Amsterdam and Sofia

www.thelastbooks.org

Introduction and notes © Joe Luna 2022
Letters and appendices © the authors 2022

Design, typesetting, and editorial
assistance by Phil Baber

Composed in LL Bradford, designed by
Laurenz Brunner

Printed and bound in Estonia by
Tallinna Raamatutrükikoda

Every effort has been made to clear the
necessary permissions; any omissions
will be rectified in future reprints

ISBN 978-94-91780-18-9

Contents

Introduction   vii

Note on the Text   xix

Abbreviations   xxi

The Letters of Douglas Oliver and J. H. Prynne   23

Appendices

A Reviews from the *Cambridge News*   169
   Douglas Oliver

B Transliteration of Runic Inscription   174
   J. H. Prynne

C What the Plants Can Tell Us   175
   Douglas Oliver

D Defunct Tokens: Review of Prynne's 'Marzipan'   188
   Douglas Oliver

E Letters to Liu Xiang-jun   190
   J. H. Prynne

Bibliography   199

Index   204

Introduction

This volume contains most of the letters exchanged between the poet, novelist, and journalist Douglas Oliver (1937–2000), born to Scottish parents but raised and educated in England, and the English poet J. H. Prynne (b. 1936). More than three-quarters of the correspondence is included, spanning thirty-three years of the poets' friendship and reciprocal influence, with the selection favouring exchanges pertaining to each poet's oeuvre over shorter notes and communiqués, though a representative selection of these is also included. The letters have been transcribed from two archival collections held by the libraries of each poet's alma mater: the J. H. Prynne Papers in the Cambridge University Library, and the Douglas Oliver Archive in the Albert Sloman Library at the University of Essex. The vast majority of the letters are transcribed from Prynne's archive, with material from Oliver's papers filling in the gaps where possible. Prynne's practice since the 1960s has been to preserve copies of letters sent to his correspondents, and his archive contains a near-complete record of his letters to Oliver, as well as substantial documentation of their professional and poetical relationship, from reading lists to job references. Oliver's archive preserves certain letters and documents from Prynne but very few copies of letters sent the other way, almost all of which are preserved in Prynne's papers. A small minority of letters were unavailable to this edition by default: of more than six hundred pages in Prynne's record of the correspondence, ten remain closed to the public on the basis of the confidential or sensitive information therein.

Prynne's name will likely be more familiar to readers than Oliver's. His work is the subject of a large and varied body of scholarly, journalistic, and anecdotal criticism and appreciation, his poems have been translated into half a dozen European languages, as well as Chinese, and his collected *Poems* is in its third edition. Prynne's public presence is often characterized as a divisive one, and he is often represented as being championed by an academic few and maligned, or ignored, by sundry others. There is some truth to this critical commonplace: lavish praise has been plucked for *Poems*' blurbs, whilst certain critics have been tirelessly dismissive, often in the national media. But the narrative of a 'divisive' Prynne obscures more than it clarifies. It caricatures the range of critical-academic writing about his poetry as an unreflective fandom, and it imagines two, and only two, ways of responding to his poetry. A more accurate narrative of Prynne's influence on postwar British poetry would begin by tracing it through the small press and underground scenes of literary production of the 1960s to the 1980s, and reflecting on his four decades of teaching work at the University of Cambridge. The correspondence with Oliver represents one distinct, complex strand of this influence. It also further illuminates the wider literary cultures (of publication, dissemination, and exchange) in which Oliver and Prynne were caught up, and which they, in turn, helped to foster. Oliver, for his part, despite receiving more public accolades for his poetry during his lifetime than most other British poets of his generation, including Prynne and all their mutual, immediate circle, is barely known in the UK beyond a handful of poets, writers, and scholars of Anglophone late modernism. Most of his books are out of print, although a new *Selected Poems* (Shearsman, 2020) indicates some resurgence of interest. There exist a small number of critical essays on his work and reminiscences of his person. He is best known in the United States as the second husband of the American poet Alice Notley, his second wife, whom he married in 1988, and with whom he coedited the journals *Scarlet* (1990–1) and *Gare du Nord* (1997–9). Oliver's vocational life was far more varied than Prynne's, though teaching literature became a staple of his career from the mid-1970s onwards; he held teaching positions in the UK and in France, and taught occasionally in North America. His life and work are held in a high regard and generous affection out of all proportion to his humble position in the present cultural constellation.

From at least the 1970s onwards, various critical distinctions have sought to map the social commitments and aesthetic priorities of British poetry since 1945. The 'British Poetry Revival', in Eric Mottram's coinage, refers to the writing, publication, and circulation practices of a heterogeneous generation of poets in the 1960s and 1970s whose rejection of the staid conservatism of postwar English letters and influence by modern American verse forms constitute a core of shared practice, however great the differences between the poets in question. Association with the British Poetry Revival has settled into a critical shorthand used to distinguish any number of poets from those standard-bearers of national literary culture represented by the Laureateship and the editorial practices of the major presses and journals. Whilst the relationship between 'mainstream' and 'experimental' or 'avant-garde' has been endlessly complicated and problematized in recent years, in terms of the poetry publishing world of the 1960s it is perfectly serviceable. To think of Oliver and Prynne as Revival poets, then, is an inadequate generalization, but one that serves the important purpose of situating them within, and against, the major currents of English verse practice and publication that supplied the contexts of their writing and publishing at the time of their first contact. As Mottram recalled in the early 1990s, poetry that departed significantly from the spiritual and imperial nostalgia of 'the 1950s Axis of Conquest–Fraser–Larkin', 'existed largely unrecognized by the literary establishment, that is the big controlling presses, the universities and schools, and the reviewing fraternity'.[1] When they met in 1967, both Oliver and Prynne were firmly unrecognized, in Mottram's sense. By the mid-sixties, Prynne had turned his back on his 1962 collection, *Force of Circumstance*, published by Routledge and Kegan Paul, and was centrally involved in the wildly ambitious, collective experiment of *The English Intelligencer* (on which more below). Oliver, who had published a handful of poems in the early 1960s, was eager to discover alternative modes of exchange and publication to those he had hitherto sought out.[2] Both poets were part of a movement that had no centre and no single defined programme of operation, but which in all its variousness was deeply invested in the reinvention of the idioms and registers of English-language poetry and its public function, and which responded not just to the innovations of European and American modernism, but to vast stretches of poetical history, from Marcus Manilius to Ma Rainey.

Oliver and Prynne maintained a remarkably consistent correspondence from the time of their first meeting up until Oliver's death from cancer in 2000. Between 1970 and 1995 barely a year goes by without some contact, and most years see a steady stream of letters back and forth, including exchanges that develop a momentum which impels each correspondent to reply within days of each other. When Oliver initiated the correspondence by writing to Prynne in the summer of 1967, both were living and working in Cambridge, Prynne as director of studies in English at Gonville and Caius College, Oliver as a reporter with the *Cambridge News*. Both were at formative stages in their writing careers, though as Oliver's first letter indicates, Prynne was already well enough established among the local poets to be recommended to Oliver as a particularly 'informed' interlocutor.[3] The poems that each had already published would remain deliberately uncollected into what became their oeuvres; both were seeking through correspondence and exchange to deepen their understanding of their art and its possibilities. Oliver, as he recalls in his memoir, would read his poems in the town's 'university venues', where he likely met some or all of the poets he names as his close associates at the time: Anthony Barnett, Andrew Crozier, John James, and Wendy Mulford.[4] The 'Intelligencer circle' that Oliver mentions in his first letter, which he would have learnt about from these poets, refers to the contributors to, and recipients of, the poetry worksheet *The English Intelligencer* (1966–8), of which Crozier was the founding editor, James a consistent recipient, and Prynne a regular contributor. Prynne also mimeographed the *Intelligencer*'s sheets and sent them out to subscribers from Caius. That the barely elder but decidedly more academic Prynne was sought out by the autodidact Oliver ('didn't get to university', he writes[5]) speaks equally to Prynne's reputation for pedagogical acumen and to the wider culture of largely homosocial coterie poetics

1 Eric Mottram, 'The British Poetry Revival, 1960–75', in *New British Poetries: The Scope of the Possible*, ed. Robert Hampson and Peter Barry (Manchester: Manchester University Press, 1993), 15–50 (23, 15).

2 Oliver's four first published poems ('The Ordeal of Conversation', 'Dance It', 'Before Suicide', and 'One Man and His Dove') appeared in *Ambit*, no. 5 (Summer 1960): 13–15.

3 Oliver to Prynne, 31 August 1967.

4 Oliver, *Whisper 'Louise': A Double Historical Memoir and Meditation* (Hastings: Reality Street, 2005), 54.

5 Oliver to Prynne, 31 August 1967.

and politics upon which the *Intelligencer* was founded, and through which its conversations and conflicts played out.

Whereas Prynne had been engaged in scenes of literary production and dissemination, both local and cross-Atlantic, at least since his first contact with the American poet Charles Olson in 1961, Oliver established himself among the local poets and the wider *Intelligencer* circle quickly, wrote reviews of their books for the *Cambridge News*, began at least one other lifelong correspondence with another of the *Intelligencer*'s editors, Peter Riley, and in 1969 published his first book, *Oppo Hectic*, with Andrew Crozier's Ferry Press. The energies of collective exchange that impelled the *Intelligencer* and that were the creative crucible for much of Prynne's poetry of the mid- to late 1960s were thus not absent from Oliver's growth as a poet in this period, despite his never being a recorded recipient of the worksheet. The relative paucity of letters between Oliver and Prynne in the late 1960s after Oliver's initial approach (no reply from Prynne is preserved in either archive) speaks more to the frequency with which they were able to see and talk to one another during this period, whether in Prynne's College rooms or in their favoured pub, the Panton Arms, than it does to a lack of contact. Prynne, Oliver recalled, 'would give me free tutorials and the first "booklist" I'd ever had'.[1] Prynne's archive includes one of these lists, as well as cuttings of Oliver's reviews of Prynne's, Peter Riley's, and John James's books in the *Cambridge News*. These are the textual ephemera of an evolving set of relationships that straddled the *Intelligencer*'s own shifting community of poets, and which carried, diversified, and extended its emphasis on composition-through-exchange into the myriad publications, little magazines, and correspondences that flourished after its dissolution. The *Intelligencer* emphasized collective correspondence as the lifeblood of poetic community; its afterlives play out through the critical pressures and spontaneous freedoms of private correspondences with a public, if embattled, sense of ethical vocation. This is the terrain of the exchanges selected for this volume.

Prynne greeted Oliver's entry into the small but teeming hive of poetic production and discussion in Cambridge with enthusiasm and not a little teacherly zeal. Prynne's correspondence with Olson throughout the 1960s was petering out, leaving in its wake a sense of profound disappointment for that which Prynne felt to have been left unsaid and unwritten by them both, and for the unrealized conditions of poetical community that he felt, by 1967, 'we uniquely should already have had'.[2] During the same period that Prynne was mourning the loss of this felt potential, the 'idealized continuum of practice and criticism' to which the *Intelligencer* aspired rose and fell as a possibility of committed praxis, for Prynne as for others in the circle.[3] Oliver, with his intellectual enthusiasm and journalist's sense of humanist pragmatism, must have been a breath of fresh air. Both were omnivorous readers whose priority was to establish the relationship

---

[1] Oliver, *Whisper 'Louise'*, 54.

[2] Prynne to Olson, 15 October 1967, in *The Collected Letters of Charles Olson and J. H. Prynne*, ed. Ryan Dobran (Albuquerque: University of New Mexico Press, 2017), 222.

[3] See Alex Latter, *Late Modernism and The English Intelligencer* (London: Bloomsbury, 2015), 73 and passim.

between what they read and how they wrote; both read each other's poetry with a commitment to disclosing the intellectual and social ramifications of their thought and practice. Each publicly and privately advocated for the other's work, and in Prynne's case, for Oliver's character and professionalism, as indicated by the references he provided for Oliver throughout the latter's career. Oliver's public and private critical appreciation of Prynne's work, although influential among their fellow poets, remains largely unexplored in the scholarship on Prynne, whilst Prynne's readings of Oliver's poetry and prose in the correspondence unfold, explore, and contest his arguments and ambitions with an attention to detail that far exceeds, in scope and intent, the small body of scholarship on Oliver's work. What is striking about the detailed consideration of each other's writing in the correspondence, beyond its indication of extraordinary mutual appreciation, is the impression it gives of each poet figuring out the terms of their relationship both to the major currents of Anglo-American modernism and postmodernism, and to the immediate present as something their poetry must consistently encounter, claim, and respond to. This imperative is everywhere apparent, from enthusiastic reports of readings attended and books read, to snide dismissals of the New York School, to improvised sketches of the linguistic coordinates of contemporary selfhood, to reflections on party-political strategy and policy, geopolitical dynamics, and environmental devastation. Early on in the correspondence, this imperative is lent a grammar of exuberant fellow feeling that sets the basic tone for the lengthier and more reflective later letters: 'And when are you coming down again or when are we going to meet or what lies ahead you name it did you say spring?'[1]

Between 1970 and the 1990s, Oliver's shifting locales—from Cambridge, to Paris, to Coventry, to Brightlingsea, to Paris again, to New York, and finally back to Paris—contrast vividly with Prynne's virtually undisturbed residence in Cambridge and employment at Caius until his retirement in 2003. Oliver's first move to France came directly in the wake of the personal tragedy that profoundly affected his subsequent thought and writing: the cot death of his son Tom, born with Down syndrome, in November 1969. The death is not mentioned in the extant correspondence with Prynne, though its influence can be felt throughout as a subtext informing the major lines of debate and disputation that characterize the letters of the following three decades. Tom, to whom Oliver referred in his poetry, prose, and correspondence by the racist epithets *mongol* and *mongoloid*, is repeatedly named and figured in Oliver's mature poetry as an emblem of essential human goodness that both underlies and transcends the contemporary left's striving for social justice. The failure of the left to acknowledge and embrace the radical, humane, and universal simplicity which Tom's brief life and disability exemplified for Oliver is identified explicitly in his major works of the 1970s

1 Prynne to Oliver, 10 January 1972.

and 1980s as a profound moral and spiritual deficit, one that poetry could, and should, identify and attempt to ameliorate. In an oeuvre that returns again and again to movements for, and histories of, socialist, communist, and anarchist transformation, from Uruguayan urban guerrillas to British trade unionism, Oliver returns just as persistently to Tom, writing him into the work as the beatific progenitor of a moral ideal mystically in excess of the most radical political and social aspirations of the century. Oliver's figuration of Tom is both a work of mourning and a critical leverage of that mourning against the failings of the contemporary and historical left, chief among which, for Oliver, were the strains of righteous, dogmatic fervour exemplified by the post-1968 intellectualism of the student left (which he encountered first-hand as a journalist in Cambridge), and later the inability of the British Labour Party to produce a viably electable alternative to the Conservatism that defined British political life from 1979 until very nearly the end of his life.

Tom's influence also galvanized for Oliver his self-reflexive critique of the poetic voice and vocation. In his correspondence with Peter Riley, shortly after Tom's death, Oliver is explicit about his son's example and its effect on his thinking about literary labour. Describing in 1970 the nascent composition of his novel *The Harmless Building* (1973), Oliver refers to his motivation as 'an unease about my previous poetic structures', and describes his effort to elaborate in the novel's prose 'their dishonesty, their techniques at hiding inadequacy, their essential falseness, which is the falseness of most such attempts in present-day society'.[1] Tom is the wellspring of this desire. 'For two years', he writes, 'I had a mongol son whose lack of intelligence did not one whit affect his ability to give pleasure (if only we were excellent enough to accept that gift unaffectedly)'.[2] Tom's example illuminated for Oliver both his own unthought poetical predilections, and his suspicions about his contemporaries' work; Tom's 'stupidity' and his 'gift' throw into relief the intellectual posturing which Oliver saw as stymying the work of the poets with whom he otherwise felt the most natural comradeship: 'So why are all the left-wing poets intellectual snobs? Why are their structures so carefully cemented so that no one should see through the gaps? Why are they so concerned to tell other people <u>exactly</u> how it is? Why are they the heroes of their own poems all the time?'[3]

The letter explicitly takes aim at 'left-wing' American poets, but the poetry that Prynne was writing when he and Oliver first met might well be characterized in these same terms: the poems of *Kitchen Poems* (1968) and *The White Stones* (1969) are certainly intellectual, exhortative, and meticulously structured. Throughout the 1970s Oliver and Prynne develop a rapturous mutual appreciation, and as their trust in each other builds, so too does their willingness to define their priorities in relation to each other's praxis. The major exchanges in the 1980s and

[1] Oliver to Riley, 31 December 1970. Douglas Oliver Archive, the Albert Sloman Library, University of Essex (hereafter cited as DOA), box 9.

[2] Ibid.

[3] Ibid.

1990s thus come increasingly to emphasize, on Oliver's side, the ethical imperatives that require admitting into poetic discourse the inadequacies of the speaking voice, imperatives that stem, ultimately, from Tom. Oliver's explanations and defences of his approaches to both theoretical and poetical work often valorize what he calls his 'crudity' as a moral and political necessity, even as he maintains a consistent solidarity, drawn from assiduous close reading, with what he understands to be the motivations for Prynne's more discursively complex experimentalism.

Prynne, who in 1966 had written the line 'I draw blood whenever I open my stupid mouth', was no stranger to the inadequacies of the speaking voice.[1] But his lyric subject in this period is historically emblematic, not personally responsible; it vocalizes the philologically inflected desire for a 'community of wish' and, often in the same poem, laments the inadequacies of such a desire, its desperate insecurity in a world of universal alienation and consumerism.[2] Prynne's poetry of the following three decades shifts decisively away from the lyric voice as even a structure of subjective signification, however self-reflexive and ethically exacting, and towards a setting, or dispersal, of the lyric impulse amongst the discourses and dictions of political, economic, and ideological power. Oliver's readings of this later work are full of admiration for its careful adumbration of the processes of thought and feeling, its reflection of an exploitative reality, and its implied critique of the pitfalls of modern selfhood. But Oliver is more often than not wary of these techniques, and tends to cast his own practice in terms of a more demotic approach to the political, social, and moral questions which are the bread and butter of the correspondence. Likewise, after the extraordinary assertions of mastery and brilliance with which he greets *The Harmless Building*, and his co-conspiratorial sympathy with Oliver's poetry of the 1970s, Prynne's relationship to Oliver's work becomes more and more bifurcated between a critique of its absolutizing tendencies and an unwavering assertion of basic common purpose. This purpose came to be understood by each poet in terms of the ethical mandate of social and intellectual responsibility that developed into the mutual organon of their widely varying practices. It is most clearly expressed in the later letters because the correspondence is, in part, a record of each poet discovering in the other's work an essential component of their own, and, in the course of doing so, clarifying their sense of poetical vocation in the light of each other's contribution. It is this sense of shared endeavour that underlines Prynne's claim, during a period of debate about the ethics of poetic speech, that 'what is at question in our exchanges is clearly non-fundamental, being an issue of projective outwork and backflow rather than difference at source'.[3] In some ways this is a presumptive statement, rigged with a kind of rhetorical revision of the stakes themselves. But it is also the expression of a fiercely valuable connection that is again and again confirmed

[1] 'Concerning Quality, Again', in Prynne, *Poems* (Hexham, UK: Bloodaxe Books, 2015), 82–3 (82). The poem was first circulated in *The English Intelligencer* in November 1966.

[2] The phrase 'community of wish' appears in 'Moon Poem' (*Poems*, 53–4 (53)). For a reading of the phrase in the context of the poem's circulation in *The English Intelligencer*, see Latter, *Late Modernism*, 95–6.

[3] Prynne to Oliver, 19 June 1994.

and mutually reiterated, tacitly or explicitly, across an often-disputative correspondence.

The trust in their connection—underwritten by the generic entitlement of two white men speaking (or writing) to each other—also affords each poet the freedom to write offensively, whether in scornful asides or through casual stereotyping. Both exhibit a Francophobia with regards to continental thought and theory shared by the most snobbish exponents of English rationalism, as well as by sceptical currents on the British left. Prynne's narratives of his experiences in China—and his letters to his student Liu Xiang-jun—can be as uncomfortably paternalistic as Oliver's insistence on the 'crudity of [his] approach as a merit' can be crudely fetishistic.[1] Oliver's discussion of Haitian Voodoo, whilst earnestly studious, clumsily conflates socio-religious representation with pathology when he refers to 'the similarly between, say, Baron Samedi, and some mental patients'.[2] The casual sexism legible in Prynne's correspondence with Olson in the 1960s is raised to a pitch of considered misogyny in his correspondence of the 1980s, with Oliver as in his letters to his lifelong friend, the American poet Edward Dorn. The more obnoxious elements of Prynne's letters are often received by Oliver with a rather graceful indulgence, as when Oliver takes up Prynne's tone-deaf phrase 'the near-autistic mutilations of phantom selfhood' as a way to characterize those aspects of the self of most importance and interest to him, or when a remark about sentimentalism and (in pejorative scare quotes) its 'womanliness' elicits from Oliver a frank admission of his heartfelt attraction to the word and all that it means for him.[3] Beyond the poets' capacity for unreflective, or indeed reflective, offensiveness, Prynne is also given to an epistolary impressionism that can sometimes leave Oliver impatient at the former's 'cryptic imagery';[5] it is fair to say that Oliver's insistence on the distinctions between his work and Prynne's, more and more on display in the later letters, is clearly born of some frustration with Prynne's tendency to read these distinctions as themselves the secondary byproducts of longstanding mutual convictions. The two were capable of winding each other up as much as they were of inspiring each other to rethink the terms and terminology of their practice.

Many of these terms are drawn from the poets' extensive reading habits. The reading referred to in the letters encompasses a wide range of subjects, disciplines, and texts, including economics, anthropology, phenomenology, linguistics, the natural sciences, political theory, and the daily papers, as well as poetry, poetics, and the contemporary novel. That the two poets—one an academic, the other an autodidact—maintained heterogeneous reading habits is no great surprise. That such varied and interdisciplinary reading should be undertaken by the poets explicitly with a view to its direct bearing on the composition and meaning of their poetry, however, is an indication of the extent to which

---

1 Oliver to Prynne, 13 November 1982. Two of Prynne's letters to Liu Xiang-jun are printed in appendix E.

2 Oliver to Prynne, 24 January 1978.

3 Prynne to Oliver, 30 December 1977, and Oliver to Prynne, 24 January 1978; Prynne to Oliver, 30 November 1987, and Oliver to Prynne, 10 December 1987.

4 Oliver to Prynne, 30 November 1982.

at least one strand of high modernist praxis had become an indispensable necessity for some in their generation, since the appeal of idiosyncratic and polysemous research as a condition of poetic composition has a distinct heritage in the work of Pound and Olson. In the early 1960s, Prynne had acted as transatlantic research assistant for Olson during the composition of the latter's sprawling *Maximus Poems*, and the scholarly sources of Prynne's own poems of the 1960s and 1970s are well documented, sometimes in the poems themselves. Oliver rarely names his sources in-text, although the last, brief chapter of *The Harmless Building*, 'Illustration of a Thought from Scheler', points to the influence of German phenomenology which was to deepen through Oliver's reading of Husserl and Heidegger while a mature student at the University of Essex from 1972 to 1975. What emerges in the correspondence of the 1970s especially, in addition to the sheer breadth of the poets' reading matter, are the ways in which they negotiate the potential meaning-making processes of their work in relation to the data absorbed through their reading, each seeking to reconfigure, syncretize, and make use of such data, by analogy or more imaginative cross-pollination. This kind of working out, in anticipation or retrospection, entails both epistemological and technical considerations, as when Prynne suggests that 'any use' in his poetry of an astronomical textbook he is presently reading 'will certainly not be mere extrapolated figuration', since such an approach would simply dress up science in metaphor rather than incorporate its assumptions into the original practice of poetical thought; or when Oliver replies by invoking the catastrophe theorist Christopher Zeeman's 'analysis of human behaviour' to help clarify the narrative topology of *The Harmless Building*. 'Wisdom', writes Prynne, 'is good because it is functionally interfused with what we do'; outside of this purposive imperative, lacking the dynamics of prosody or reflexive attention to its public utterance, 'it is a boring white noise'.[1]

Perhaps surprisingly, given Prynne's literal tutoring of Oliver, Oliver's influence is legible in Prynne's mature poetry in a way that Prynne's is not in any of Oliver's. Prynne's *The Oval Window* (1983), the title of which names the vestibule between the middle and inner ear, is a work of assemblage composed largely through the arrangement and splicing together of various texts, including articles from *The Times*, a surgical textbook, and ninth-century Chinese lyrics, to construct a narrative of Thatcherite privatization and a synesthetic dream of escape therefrom. The poem quotes from and alludes to Oliver's *The Diagram Poems* (1979) on at least two occasions. *The Diagram Poems* narrates the misadventures of the Uruguayan urban guerrillas the Tupamaros, and in doing so develops a sympathetic critique of the insurgents' means and ends that is also a moral rejoinder to the country's Western observers. The poems weave together accounts of the Tupamaros' radical insurgency with appeals to an inaudible

[1] Prynne to Oliver, 18 January 1972, and Oliver to Prynne, 21 January 1972.

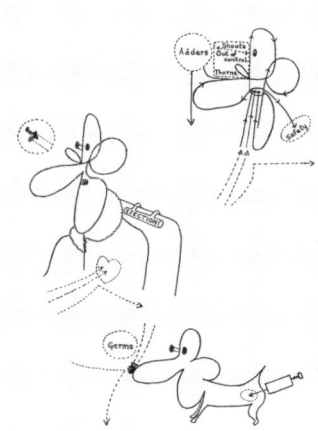

An early (1972) version of the 'P.C.' diagram from Oliver's *The Diagram Poems*, preserved in Prynne's papers.

'lost child's voice [that] breaks in my throat' with a Keatsian 'softness unheard'; this voice

> should speak softly but undyingly
> across a land silvery with democracy
> and glistening with wheat, trembling at the spoken
> kindness [...]¹

It is Tom's voice; and we, like the Tupamaros, are immune to it: 'we let the voice break in our throats' just as Oliver felt unable to 'accept [Tom's] gift unaffectedly'. *The Diagram Poems*' term for our capacity to acknowledge the human kindness that is obstructed by our refusal of its existence is 'ear knowledge'. *The Oval Window* takes up this complex image as theme. It nominates audibility as a threshold onto a radical alterity, signified in part by the codified symbolism of centuries-old Chinese song, although the terms of such alterity (whether political, social, metaphysical, or imaginary) are never defined in *The Oval Window* with anything like the earnest, elegiacal exhortation that they are in Oliver's 'land silvery with democracy'. Instead, the physiology of emphatic humanity designated by Oliver's 'ear knowledge' is threaded through *The Oval Window*'s lyric topography of privatized selfhood, a technique which calls attention to the moral urgency of Oliver's work even as it is relativized by Prynne's strident dialectics. The basic tenor of *The Oval Window* is visionary lament, but the quotation of and allusion to Oliver's work come in moments that figure a threshold of possibility beyond systemic domination and moral disintegration, as if to borrow from Oliver a fleeting note of wholesale, transformative optimism. In the years leading up to the composition of *The Oval Window*, Oliver and Prynne corresponded at length about Oliver's experimental research on the sounds and stresses of spoken poetry, a subject that must have at least galvanized, and very likely strongly inspired, the direction of Prynne's poetry in the early 1980s.

Whilst not as audible in the diction and prosody of Oliver's poems, Prynne's influence on Oliver's thinking about poetical language was profound and lifelong. This is especially true of the period from 1967 to 1975, when the correspondence resembles a collaborative research project as much as an exchange of ideas, with each poet referring to their work as part of a mutual, responsive, and ongoing project that includes the work of other poets on the 'Anglo team' (Prynne's phrase) who formed or were adjacent to the *Intelligencer* circle, as well as the work of Edward Dorn.² Prior to the composition of *The Oval Window*, Prynne's interest in the thresholds and borderline states of the body dates back at least to *Wound Response* (1974), a book that was as rapturously received by Oliver as *The Harmless Building* had been by Prynne two years prior. Figuring the book as a proleptic reply to the 'question' of his own *In the Cave of Suicession* (1974), Oliver writes that '*Wound Response* is the finest response

---

1 Oliver, *The Diagram Poems* (London: Ferry Press, 1979), n.p.

2 Prynne to Oliver, 10 January 1972.

I could have imagined', and that '[w]hat you [...] give me is poetry-as-knowledge, as though there were any other kind, of value' (the audibly Olsonian rhythm of Oliver's gratitude refers implicitly to Olson's poetics as another shared field of inspiration).[1] Oliver would remain especially and deeply attached to Prynne's 'Of Movement Towards a Natural Place', published in *Wound Response*, for his whole life, studying the poem and its stress-distributions by recording himself speaking it aloud, and publishing an essay on it in Tim Longville's *Grosseteste Review*.[2] In his correspondence with Peter Riley, in the 1970s as in the 1990s, Oliver politely demurs from Riley's exasperation at the obscurity of Prynne's poetry, writing in 1977 that Prynne 'is still the Englishman to look to, in my estimation', and in 1993 that 'Jeremy's recent writing [...] seems motivated by concerns very close to my own heart', in terms of what Oliver saw as Prynne's criticism of Western individualism.[3] Incorporating as much esoteric mystery and Romantic enthusiasm as Poundian high modernism, it is the vibrant tenet of 'poetry-as-knowledge' that constitutes one essential continuum of each poet's solidarity with the other's practice, whilst the questions of what kind of knowledge, how to get it, and what to do with it, come to be answered very differently indeed. Oliver's last letter to Prynne is a moving testimony to this solidarity. Handwritten when he was woozy from the fentanyl he was taking to ease his pain, it expresses his great pleasure in the recent publication of Prynne's collected *Poems* (1999), and in the fact of Prynne's meeting and reading with Edward Dorn shortly before Dorn's death on 10 December 1999. The letter is signed off with an explicit declaration of Oliver's 'intense loyalty to the cogency of your own work'.[4]

Prynne's reply reached Oliver in Paris weeks before Oliver's death on 21 April 2000. Prynne attended and spoke at Oliver's memorial service, held in the British Institute on 27 April. A meeting to remember Oliver was held in Swedenborg Hall, London, on 22 October 2000, and *A Meeting for Douglas Oliver and 27 Uncollected Poems* was collectively published shortly thereafter, by Wendy Mulford, Peter Riley, and Nigel Wheale (Street Editions, Poetical Histories, and Infernal Methods). Oliver's archive was donated to the University of Essex by Alice Notley and opened to the public in 2001.[5] Prynne's archive is part of a larger archive of poets associated with Cambridge held in the Cambridge University Library, cataloguing work on which is ongoing.[6] Oliver's 1987 collected poems, *Kind*, is still in print and available from Allardyce, Barnett, Publishers, as is his posthumously published double historical memoir, *Whisper 'Louise'*, from Reality Street. The majority of Oliver's extensive and varied post-1987 poetic output, for which he received some extraordinary public plaudits, is out of print. The latest edition of Prynne's *Poems* is published by Bloodaxe Books and is widely available.

---

[1] Oliver to Prynne, 11 September 1974.

[2] A revised version of this essay, drafted for, but finally omitted from, Oliver's *Poetry and Narrative in Performance* (Houndmills, UK: Macmillan, 1989), is printed in appendix C.

[3] Oliver to Riley, 5 January 1977 and 21 November 1993. DOA, box 9.

[4] Oliver to Prynne, 16 February 2000.

[5] A summary of the archive's contents can be accessed at http://libwww.essex.ac.uk/archives/oliver.htm.

[6] The J. H. Prynne Papers are listed and summarized at https://archivesearch.lib.cam.ac.uk/repositories/2/resources/13497.

I wish to extend my profound gratitude to Alice Notley, Anselm Berrigan, Edmund Berrigan, and J. H. Prynne for their generous and enthusiastic encouragement of, and assistance with, this project from its inception. Sincere gratitude is also due to John Wells, senior archivist at the Cambridge University Library, and to Lucy McCaul, special collections and archives coordinator at the University of Essex, whose assistance in the archives has been invaluable.

This volume is dedicated to my grandmother Sheila Chamberlain, whose letters have meant so much to me.

JOE LUNA

Brighton, 2022

Note on the Text

The editorial principles of this edition are based on the desire to flesh out the historical, intellectual, and social contexts of the letters without overburdening them with extraneous information. Names, journals, poems, books, philosophical and theoretical terms, and major and minor historical events, personages, and authorships have been noted, with reference where possible (through archival confirmation or bibliographic inference) to the poets' own reading.

Citations and explanatory notes have been provided for the frequent references each poet makes to reading matter, although if the author and title of the text are clear from the letter this information reappears only in the bibliography. When no edition of a modern text is indicated or possible to identify, first editions are deferred to. Quotations and interpolations from unidentified reading matter are noted and the texts identified where possible.

Both poets often quote or interpolate lines of poetry (each other's and canonical) in their letters as a matter of discursive and conversational course; where these are unidentified, details have been provided in the notes to make explicit the underlying connections assumed and rhetorically relied upon. Silent quotations and interpolations from canonical texts, the publication details of which are irrelevant to the point at hand (e.g., from Wordsworth's *Prelude* or Dante's *Inferno*), are identified only in the notes and do not appear in the bibliography.

Historical explanatory notes provide indications of the political and social movements frequently named and alluded to. Interpretation of the ways in which the poets' reading matter, and indeed the correspondence itself, shaped their work, is almost entirely absent from the notes so as not to impose a narrative upon them; for the same reason, reference to the scholarship on Oliver and Prynne is avoided unless it was felt to be especially pertinent to the discussion at hand.

Oliver was a far more biographically minded poet than Prynne has ever been. Autobiography is an essential element in his work, and he takes up the genre in a number of different forms across his oeuvre, from Dantesque prosimetrum to the 'double memoir' of himself and the nineteenth-century Communard Louise Michel. This material is helpful for elaborating in the notes the indications of Oliver's changing vocational practices and social scenes. No such material exists for Prynne, but since his working life is a rare constant among his contemporaries, this presents fewer difficulties than it would have done in Oliver's case.

Prynne is the more rhetorically abstruse of the correspondents. Particularly dense, nested references in his letters have been extrapolated and explained as concisely as possible, though the notes do not gloss either Prynne's or Oliver's letters unless to explain the particular relevance of a passage to a subject of the correspondence itself.

Obvious misspellings, slips of the pen, and typing errors have been silently corrected. Stylistic spellings (e.g., Prynne's use of *shew* for *show*) have been preserved. Single and double quotation marks, and their placement relative to other points of punctuation, have been regularized in line with the principles set forth in the *Oxford Manual of Style* (2002). Double hyphens (frequent in the typewritten letters of the 1960s to the 1980s) have been converted to em dashes. Other punctuation has been preserved, as have underlines and italics. Line breaks have been preserved in dedications, inscriptions, and where judged to be deliberate or significant.

The placement of dates, addresses, and signatures has been regularized. Dates in letter headings have been expanded (e.g., '26.9.74' becomes '26 September 1974') and, where necessary, reformatted according to the European convention of *day month year* (e.g., 'Thu, Apr 14, 1994' becomes '14 April 1994'). Where a date was only partially given by one of the poets, the missing element is supplied in the form of an editorial insertion.

Both Oliver and Prynne occasionally use square brackets in their letters; editorial emendations and insertions are therefore italicized [*like so*]. Words that could not be deciphered with certainty are enclosed in square brackets and preceded by a question mark [*?like so*]. Marginalia and interlinear insertions of fewer than three words have been silently incorporated into the text. Longer marginalia are incorporated and enclosed in braces {like so}. Ellipses in the text are from the original letters and should not be read as editorial omissions.

Abbreviations

The following abbreviations have been used in the notes:

CAAS Douglas Oliver, 'Douglas Oliver, 1937–', *Contemporary Authors Autobiography Series* 27 (1997): 242–61.
DOA Douglas Oliver Archive, the Albert Sloman Library, University of Essex.
ICS Douglas Oliver, *In the Cave of Suicession* (Cambridge: Street Editions, 1974).
PNP Douglas Oliver, *Poetry and Narrative in Performance* (Houndmills, UK: Macmillan, 1989).
STSW J. H. Prynne, *Stars, Tigers and the Shape of Words* (London: Birkbeck College, 1993).
TVTH Douglas Oliver, *Three Variations on the Theme of Harm: Selected Poetry and Prose* (London: Paladin, 1990).

When not otherwise indicated, all references to 'Prynne's papers' or 'Prynne's archive' refer to MS Add.10144, temporary files 240–6, 352, 553. The record of the correspondence preserved in Oliver's archive is stored in DOA, box 9; all references to 'Oliver's papers' or 'Oliver's archive' indicate the relevant box number when referring to other items.

The Letters of
Douglas Oliver and J. H. Prynne

1967–2000

31 August 1967   59 Tavistock Road
                                                           Cambridge

Dear Mr. Prynne,

   I've got to a stage in poetry where I feel an informed judgement would greatly help. From what I have heard about the 'Intelligencer' circle your opinion of my work would be one to value.[1]

   If you can spare time to look at the poems I have enclosed I should be very pleased.[2] No reason why you should, of course; so if you're too busy don't hesitate to send them back.

   But I'd very much like to come and discuss them with you, for close and frank criticism would do me good. I'm a journalist with the 'Cambridge News' and have only rarely encountered poets whose opinion mattered to me (didn't get to university).[3]

   Next week I hope to be free most evenings, the two weeks after that most afternoons. The forthcoming by-election may mess about with my free time a bit, but I am sure I could fit in with any suggested date.

   I apologise for coming out of the blue at you.

      Yours sincerely,

            Douglas Oliver

P.S. As 'Illustrations' makes clear, I hope, I've never been to India.[4]

[*19 August 1969*]

[*Prynne sent photocopies of eight illustrations from the second book (on the ligaments and muscles) of Andreas Vesalius's* De humani corporis fabrica *(1543), introducing them with the following note:*]

THE FIRST EIGHT TABULAE FROM THE DE CORPORIS HUMANI FABRICA LIBER SECUNDUS OF ANDREAS VESALIUS GATH-ERED INTO A WHIFF OF MORTALITY FOR DOUGLAS OLIVER ESQ TUESDAY 19TH AUGUST 1969

[*Prynne also included the following extract from John Donne's sermon 'Preached at Lincolns Inne':*]

> I must have this body with me to heaven, or else salvation it self is not perfect; And yet I cannot have this body thither, except as <u>S. Paul</u> did his, <u>I beat down this body</u>, attenuate this body by mortification; <u>Wretched man that I am, who shall deliver me from this body of death?</u> I have not body enough for my body, and I have too much body for my soul; not body enough, not bloud enough, not strength enough, to sustain my self in <u>health</u>, and yet body enough to destroy my soul,

---

1 Oliver refers to *The English Intelligencer*, a 'privately circulated poetry worksheet […] which ran over three series comprising nearly forty individual issues from January 1966 to April 1968'. Neil Pattison, Reitha Pattison, and Luke Roberts, eds., *Certain Prose of* The English Intelligencer, 2nd rev. ed. (Cambridge: Mountain, 2014), i. Oliver was never a (recorded) recipient of, or contributor to, the worksheet. In a late autobiographical essay, Oliver identifies 'Prynne, John James, Wendy Mulford, [Crozier, and] Anthony Barnett' as his principle literary interlocutors in the late 1960s. See 'Douglas Oliver, 1937–', in *Contemporary Authors Autobiography Series* 27 (1997): 242–61 (248) (hereafter cited as *CAAS*). For a full-length scholarly study of the *Intelligencer* and its place in the broader history of modernist coterie poetics and politics, see Latter, *Late Modernism*.

2 Oliver enclosed typescripts of 'Indian Sequence' (comprising five poems), 'Jealous Mother', and 'Sampler (Dr. John Dee)'. 'Indian Sequence' was revised and expanded into a seven-poem sequence, retitled 'Jain Sequence', and collected in *Oppo Hectic* (London: Ferry Press, 1969); see Oliver, *Kind* (London: Agneau 2 / Allardyce, Barnett, 1987), 23–31. 'Sampler (Dr. John Dee)' is an earlier version of a poem, 'Dr. Dee and the Angels', contained in a photocopied typescript of *Oppo Hectic* preserved in Prynne's papers; the poem is not included in the Ferry Press *Oppo Hectic* or in *Kind*. 'Jealous Mother' is unpublished and does not appear in the typescript.

3 'My real education began when the *Cambridge Evening News* signed me on to handle agriculture and general news. I slid off agriculture, stayed for nearly six years, and ended up running my own book page, writing in-depth news features, and the leaders.' Oliver, *Whisper 'Louise'*, 52. Among Oliver's book reviews (for what was then the *Cambridge News*) are three which address Prynne's poetry: 'Pioneer in Poetry' (10 August 1968), review of *Kitchen Poems* (London: Cape Goliard Press, 1968) and *Day Light Songs* (Pampisford, UK: R Books, 1968); 'Poetry in Paperback' (21 February 1969), which includes a review of *Aristeas* (London: Ferry Press, 1968); and 'Rewarding Poetry' (13 June 1969), review of *The White Stones* (Lincoln, UK: Grosseteste Press, 1969). These reviews are reproduced in appendix A. On 3 October 1968, Prynne wrote to the *News*'s editor, Keith Whetstone, praising Oliver's literary journalism, as indicated by Whetstone's reply (dated 5 October 1968) preserved in Prynne's papers.

4 'Illustrations', the first poem of the sequence later published as 'Jain Sequence'.

and frustrate the grace of God in that miserable, perplexed, riddling condition of man; sin makes the body of man miserable, and the remedy of sin, mortification, makes it miserable too; If we enjoy the good things of this world, Duriorem carcerem praeparamus, wee doe but carry an other wall about our prison, an other story of unwieldy flesh about our souls; and if wee give our selves as much mortification as our body needs, we live a life of Fridays, and see no Sabbath, we make up our years of Lents, and see no other Easters, and whereas God meant us Paradise, we make all the world a wildernesse.[1]

JOHN DONNE, Fifty Sermons, 19

---

22 August 1969 Gonville and Caius College
  Cambridge

Here is one of those lists, unneeded and probably unuseful as well. You might shred it into your soup or tuck it into your driving licence, to have handy when next you're stopped by our men in blue.
  JHP

[*On a separate sheet of Caius notepaper, Prynne included the following bibliography:*]

Paul Schilder, The Image and Appearance of the Human Body (London, 1935)
M. Merleau-Ponty, The Phenomenology of Perception, trans. C. Smith (London, 1962)
C. Bernard, An Introduction to the Study of Experimental Medicine, trans. H. C. Greene (New York, 1957)
S. Fisher & S. E. Cleveland, Body Image and Personality (New York, 2nd rev. ed., 1968)
E. Mason, Internal Perception and Bodily Functioning (New York, 1961)

---

9 January 1972[2] 44 Carlyle Road
  Cambridge

Dear Doug,

I returned from a dutiful and underheated visit to a pair of grandparents to find your note with the special green label fading unsuccessfully on the doormat. And to discover from John (more or less) that you have been here twice: which is trying since I especially want to see you before Wainbody gets its damp little brackets around your 'way of life'.[3] It would be good to talk, there is really a lot in the air which could come down in arrows if we got the chance to gnash at it for a while.

I saw John yesterday for the first time after Innocents' Day and he lent me The Harmless Building.[4] I have just finished reading it and I need to write at once because I am struck by how

---

[1] John Donne, *Fifty Sermons, Preached by That Learned and Reverend Divine, John Donne, Dr in Divinity, Late Deane of the Cathedrall Church of S. Pauls London. The Second Volume* (London: Printed by Ja. Flesher for M. F. J. Marriot and R. Royston, 1649), 158–9.

[2] Most of this letter and its two postscripts were published in *Grosseteste Review* 6, nos. 1–4 (1973): 152–4.

[3] John James (1939–2018), British poet. 'Wainbody', Prynne refers to Oliver's address in Coventry, 188 Wainbody Avenue. Oliver moved to Coventry with his family in October 1971, having taken a job with the *Coventry Evening Telegraph*.

[4] Oliver, *The Harmless Building* (London and Pensnett: Ferry Press and Grosseteste Review Books, 1973), at this point still in typescript, to which Prynne's page numbers refer. The equivalent page numbers of the first edition, followed by those of the revised reprint in *Three Variations on the Theme of Harm* (London: Paladin, 1990) (hereafter cited as *TVTH*), are given in square brackets. A page of notes on Oliver's novel is preserved in Prynne's papers.

decisively good it is, I mean really powerfully and toughly so. It was exhilarating to work with because it was so closely crosswoven and under control. That kind of intellective deliberateness goes for maximum vigilance in the arena, all the tendons under multiple stress, it absolutely is fine. I had to go very carefully indeed over the surface transformations, following the jolts of body syntax from the synthetic identities of person as subject, ready for skew pieces of affect, wary for quickened wits: it is rare & truly exciting to be asked for that kind of attention and to find it then taken up & used. Prompted by your stay near Versailles I started with a Cartesian mind–body manifold, extended into a continuous 3-space along the memory/intuition/expectation timeline;[1] this produced a three-dimensional endocrine hypersurface forming the world tube of the 'novel'. From page 2 [6; 113–14] up to the end of Chapter 10 I took as récit, page 1 [5–6; 113] and Chapters 11 to 15 as texte, what follows as hors-texte; with interoceptive transformations of the co-ordinates.

But of course that would just ('just') be a French roman. What you have done is quite beyond that in saturnine tenderness, a novel deeply curled in around the experience of good. The ethic vector is violent and discontinuous, developing schizophrenia of the body-percept and the embedding of will within larger spiritual bodies, but also revealing absolute moments of truth. 'The flaw in goodness is also a wound in your image of your body.'[2] At first I thought the penultimate sentence on page 184 [141; 252] was an impurity, but then I realised it was a calculated risk, and it is the risk throughout which I find profoundly moving.[3] Going right through to where the heart would be if the reader could afford that golden idea-rhyme; I think of Iris Murdoch's paper on 'The Idea of Perfection' in her new book The Sovereignty of Good. The thematic relation between récit and texte partakes of mimetic sentimentalism; but the ethic relation is stronger, and the bond becomes deep & powerful feeling. Thus 'no-harm' is thematically 'almost' and quite prone to auto-sadistic vertigo;[4] but ethically the hypersurface is dizzily changed. Risky page one [5–6; 113] is redeemed into a wholly larger and more simple knowledge. The necrophancy in the forest hut is covariant with the hermetic field hospital, and with the hideous note of charity in the triangular hotel-room. All that is the surface cancellation of pain, vicious referred sensation splayed out into fear and loss, so numbing as to seem almost theoretic. But then it is all dizzily given to Rosine, not by effort of will but in culminating redeemed rightness. This is ethic certainty, which makes the pain real and thus the love absolute.

Really I think this whole achievement is quite overwhelming. Attention worked out so closely does not often attain to a condition of truth. The trust usually asked of us is textual, or 'human' like a friendly dog. But both together is so absolutely delicate and fine, I cannot say how deeply affected I am by having read this book.

1 'your stay near Versailles […] Cartesian mind–body manifold', Oliver moved with his family to the outskirts of Paris on 25 February 1970, residing at 15 rue de l'Ouest, 92600 Asnières-sur-Seine; Oliver had 'taken an editing-translating job on the English desk of Agence France-Presse' (*CAAS*, 250). They returned to England in October 1971.

Prynne refers to René Descartes's interest in seventeenth-century hydraulic automata such as the fountains and grottoes at Saint-Germain-en-Laye, near Versailles.

2 Prynne quotes *The Harmless Building*, 91 (*TVTH*, 202).

3 Prynne refers to the sentence: 'Rosine felt that these reminders of the dramatist's art had become symbols linking her past life with today's curious fire.'

4 Prynne quotes *The Harmless Building*, 5 (*TVTH*, 113). The full sentence in Oliver's novel reads: 'Instead, I should love to keep a mongol baby alive in my mind, an outgoingness and kindness, a lack of coherence, an area of almost no-harm like a clearing in the middle of harm.'

9 January 1972

And so I want to just tell you that it is a novel written with intense understanding and intelligence, in case you have not been able to notice this. Of course it will be published and recognised to be 'masterly'; but it is also more than that, part of a truer and higher fineness. I should not say that I am amazed (why should I be that) but I am and I do.

Jeremy

10 January 1972								44 Carlyle Road
										Cambridge

P.S. How extremely useful it was that I had some little time ago finished reading Fundamentals of Neurology by Ernest Gardner, as well as certain works on the post-Euclidian geometry of space–time. Separated by that skinny piece of water I surmise we have been having many similar thoughts. Here for instance are (a) two poems I did just before leaving for Amerika, (b) a 24-hour sequence I've done since returning thence, and (c) Dorn's The Cycle plus a batch of documentation towards the Perfect Mistake.[1] (The batch I should like back, but not the rest.) How interesting it is to see, if one reads In One Side and Out the Other or Printed Circuit or Brass or Oppoetique, that the Anglo team have their teeth really sunk into pain, great physical gouts of it, as opposed to the water-colour joys of the American art gallery nympholepts.[2] Your novel confirms this; its elegance is much too vorticist for the pre-sexual phenomenology preferred in l'Amerique du Nord. Only Frank O'Hara had that pail of serpents always in view.[3]

Do you think we the reader are quite ready for the perspective opened by 'gestalt' on page 12 [*14; 122*]?[4] And is 'Johny' on page 143 [*113; 224*] Jerry & Sonny conflated or someone else I haven't observed creeping onstage? Of course I can see that Schilder & Merleau-Ponty have survived in your mind the reductive fantasies of the structuralists, thank goodness (quite literally I should say).

Let me know if there is anyone I can try to urge cajole or admonish into forwarding the publication of the book. If there is anyone I can write to I'll do so at once. John also mentioned that you might be thinking of moving on from ~~Scunthorpe~~ Coventry or even changing professions. If my headed notepaper could be of use don't hesitate to give my name and I'll do anything to help, I have a nice line in pre-emptive testimonials in McTavish style. I'm sure I have said this before but don't forget because I would be glad to help and no fuss.

Have you seen Douglas Woolf's Ya! and John-Juan, now published at last? You should, as they are both very good and quite relevant (as I can now see). And when are you coming down again or when are we going to meet or what lies ahead you name it did you say spring?

Jeremy

---

1 Prynne enclosed copies of 'The Blade Given Back', 'An Evening Walk' (both later published in *Wound Response* (Cambridge: Street Editions, 1974)), and *Into the Day* (Cambridge: privately printed, 1972).

Edward Dorn (1929–99), American poet. Dorn was a close friend and lifelong correspondent of Prynne's.

Details of the 'batch of documentation' are not preserved in either archive, though one text can be identified, via Oliver's reply of 5 February 1972, as 'Nonspherical Gravitational Fields', chap. 4 in Ya. B. Zeldovich and I. D. Novikov, *Relativistic Astrophysics*, vol. 2, *Stars and Relativity*, trans. Eli Arlock (Chicago: University of Chicago Press, 1971), 129–51.

2 Prynne refers to the following books: John James, Tom Philips, and Andrew Crozier, *In One Side and Out the Other* (London: Ferry Press, 1970); Andrew Crozier, *Printed Circuit* (Cambridge: Street Editions, 1974); Prynne, *Brass* (London: Ferry Press, 1971); Oliver, *Oppo Hectic*.

3 Prynne's reference is clearly to the presence of 'pain' in Frank O'Hara's work generally, but 'pail of serpents' also specifically recalls the 'vipers in a pail' and 'aquiline serpent' of O'Hara's 'In Memory of My Feelings', first published in 1958. *The Collected Poems of Frank O'Hara*, ed. Donald Allen (Berkeley: University of California Press, 1995), 252–7, 538.

4 Prynne refers to the final paragraph of chap. 1, revised for publication. The paragraph in typescript reads: 'That was a death in the future. Uncle Aubrey was for a moment real, was later strangled, but at all times, through all changes, retained the same gestalt and surrounded Donald with his well-fed lack of tension. Aubrey's early perfection always presided over any building Donald lived in, making it harmless. In the museum curator's flat, where he was staying rent-free, it was as though Donald was suspended within the spiritualized body of the baby.'

11 January 1972 44 Carlyle Road
 Cambridge

P.P.S. By a piece of most suggestive psychopathology I see that I put page 184 in place of what should have been 180: a slip carried into a veritable glissade. As in fact The Master himself has said, correcting a neurotic anticipation of Tel Quel by Leonardo da Vinci: 'It is not true that human beings delay loving or hating until they have studied and become familiar with the nature of the object to which these affects apply. On the contrary they love impulsively, from emotional motives which have nothing to do with knowledge, and whose operation is at most weakened by reflection and consideration' (Works, Standard Ed., Vol. XI, p. 74).[1]

Jeremy

1 *Tel Quel*, French left-wing literary magazine.
 'The Master', Sigmund Freud; Prynne quotes his 'Leonardo da Vinci and a Memory of His Childhood'.

2 Oliver's letter is misdated 1971.

13 January [1972][2] 188 Wainbody Avenue
 Coventry

Dear Jeremy,

Your letters (to which I am trying for the third time to give an updated answer) have been a marvellous encouragement to me. I had expected that you, probably more than anyone else I know, would understand what my novel was attempting. But the depth and generosity of your response were more than I had any right to expect from any reader: it's just been great opening your envelopes and that good parcel.

I cannot yet assimilate the new material you sent today and as soon as I have I'll write again. But I want immediately to say first, of course, how delighted I am that you liked the book but equally how surprised I was to find how exactly you divine my endeavour. Yes, there does seem to have been a considerable amount of the same pathway travelled along the Cambridge–Asnières parallel. In many respects discussing my novel you have found terms for a critical language I had also attempted; and I think my own explanation of my novel had I presumed to give one would have been less precise than yours. Which may be a phenomenon occasionally known from precedent but is not the less amazing when it occurs.

A fear was that people would mistake formal dispositions for a mere flirtation with the French roman, mixed with traces of that 'funny' prose we are all so familiar with. In fact, as you precisely see, the real game lies elsewhere and much of what is apparent in the text is sabotaged at other levels. Thus, while your récit, texte and hors-texte divisions are dead accurate (now I consider them in that terminology) it's been tremendously good for my confidence that you see how the 'ethical vector' upsets any false objectivity and restores the subjective half of the creation of a sense of reality.

I haven't read the Iris Murdoch book yet, though it's certainly on my 'list'; the Gardner book is new to me; as for the post-

Euclidean space–time that's certainly relevant, though I am ill-read in that and some of my thoughts are more extrapolations into that domain rather than any worked out knowledge of the literature. Are you also aware of that 'catastrophe' theory of the French mathematical biologist, René Thom, and the biological epistemology of Piaget (whether his earlier experiments are nowadays discredited or not) and his centre of epistemological studies?[1] The Thomian stuff plays no great role at this stage, however; it is merely on the threshold of present preoccupations.

Whatever accidents of 'reading' might have gone on though, it's much more important of course that there has been such a coincidence of sympathy. That's partly why I'm excited you have found this critical language to help to see what I've been doing. The way you present the links between major themes is magnificently spare and virile. The Cartesian mind–body manifold extending like that into the time triad which, being no Kantian, I would not keep unaffected in their categories but would have constantly distorted in the endocrine/nervous relation we have with our environment.

I so strongly wanted the 'mimetic' relations between field hospital–hut–hotel room to appear in just that way to a reader because I knew in my bones that they were no weak resource of mine (like repetition often is in the roman) but wasn't sure that a reader would see this.

You're right about the pain floating in and out of the Anglo books you mention, and O'H. I should feel unpleasant were I to think that this was a hangover from all those domestic neuroses of the 50s; but I am confident that there is a very sharp and new kind of analysis going on which does not need those old 'little husband' props but has a large and very live field. So it's a very considerable bonus that with all that pain around the poetry is retaining such width as the books mentioned. Properly reflected on it produces optimism about the scope of this work: and isn't it precisely scope that's wrong with the self-gratulants? For example, in a peak depression a week or so ago it was not to the Americans I turned for proof that syntax is not <u>necessarily</u> boring and that energy is the cure-all: it was to Kirghiz Disasters because I knew the life that was there, as opposed to the mere technique in some of the more meretricious U.S. poses.[2]

That was a happy choice of the word 'vorticist' for this week in my writing life, as it happens: enclosed poem, signal of a 'return to poetry' with all that means in terms of hesitance etc., shows why.[3] You'll be aware of Artaud's description of his state of mind in his letters to Jacques Rivière.[4] I have, however, a weak poetic direction just now, but it's reviving.

For 'Johny', page 143, read Jerry (he was Johnny some months back but I gave him a haircut and a facelift and a new name).

It's a pity that what I feel as the need to get this letter off right away precludes comparison of your own march forward with mine: I can never do a quick-crit of a Prynne poem, I'm afraid.

---

1 René Thom (1923–2002), French mathematician.
   Jean Piaget (1896–1980), Swiss developmental psychologist and philosopher. Piaget founded the International Centre for Genetic Epistemology in Geneva in 1955.

2 Oliver refers to Prynne's 'The Kirghiz Disasters' from *Brass* (*Poems*, 155–8), though published twice previously, in John James's single-issue magazine *The Norman Hackforth* (February 1969) and in Peter Riley and Lee Harwood's magazine *Collection*, no. 4 / *Tzarad*, no. 3 (April 1969).

3 Oliver enclosed typescripts of 'Whirlwind' and '"u", "je", "r", "r", "im", "a", "finally"' (*Kind*, 172–3, 183); he refers here to 'Whirlwind'.

4 Jacques Rivière (1886–1925), French writer and editor to whom the young Antonin Artaud sent poems in the hope of publication. Rivière's rejection of the poems initiated a correspondence that was later published in *La nouvelle revue française*.

13 January [1972]

I'll really get on with that so that we can return to these themes while they're still hot.

Your two-fold offer of help is both nice and extremely welcome. At present the manuscript is with Andrew and owing to my own vagueness, not his, I'm not sure if he's going to introduce it to Dempsey of MacGibbon & Kee (who rejected a much different earlier version last summer).[1] Other than that I have little resource—signs of interest from a Cape rep calling in at Lee's shop, that's all.[2] I think I want a fairly large hardback edition, basically to increase the 'play' of the charity appeal at the end of the book because the more considerably this appeal is broadcast (and the greater the author's profits) the more those two elements enter the game.[3] Of course, if you could offer any help to place the book that would be great.

As to testimonials, I'm toying with the idea of seeking university entrance but put off by basic disbelief in the prospects. I'd be very grateful if you could give me a bit of advice when we meet, which I'm determined should be soon. No doubt I ought to get an application off pretty soon.

The Douglas Woolf goes on to that list.

Now what <u>else</u> do I have to thank you for? Ah yes, the Dorn! The 'batch of documentation'. That's very good to have, all that. You could not have known I've just written a little one-off job which says... —damn it, I'll send that as well: it's the line about imperfection I'm referring to.[4] I've the Dorn songs but hadn't got hold of this cycle and it looks excellent.[5]

I'd been going to ask you for your sequence, of which I'd heard enthusiastic report from Barry and others.[6] (incidentally, Barry's Jim Morrison piece one of the nicer things he's done).[7]

Now I'm going into session to consider the stuff you've sent. I don't think any letters have encouraged me so much in my writing as yours of the past few days.

So many thanks for all your generosity. Your query about the gestalt image has made me think. I'm hoping to visit Cambridge the weekend of February 11 or is it 12. If I can hold to that I'd very much like a proper chance for talking. Looks to me as if ideas need opening out again and its as plain as a pig's nose to a button hook that there's plenty of fertile territory about between us.

  All the best,
    Doug

---

16 January 1972   188 Wainbody Avenue
                Coventry

Dear Jeremy,

Well, I'm <u>getting</u> to grips gradually with the stuff you sent me and it's a real step forward in my understanding that's opening out.

Quite a bit of it—particularly the denser topology of the documentation—I do not yet comprehend; and this is partly, I think,

---

1 Andrew Crozier (1943–2008), British poet and publisher.
 Michael Dempsey (d. 1981), publisher and manager, at this time managing editor at MacGibbon and Kee.

2 Cape Goliard, previously Goliard, which came under the Jonathan Cape imprint in 1967.
 Lee Harwood (1939–2015), British poet. Oliver likely refers to Better Books in London, where, according to John Calder, Harwood 'was in charge of poetry' from at least 1970. Oliver's possessive attribution is part-colloquial, since Calder was the proprietor, not Harwood, though the latter's managerial control was at least substantial enough to refuse to stock the poems of John Betjeman and Mary Wilson on principle. Harwood had previously managed Bill Butler's Unicorn Bookshop in Brighton from 'December 1967 until February 1968'. *Pursuit: The Memoirs of John Calder* (Richmond: Alma Books, 2016), 364; Terry Adams, *Bill Butler and the Unicorn Bookshop* (n.p.: Beat Scene Press, 2020), 22.

3 'charity appeal', both versions of *The Harmless Building*, in their penultimate chapters, include requests to the reader to donate to the National Society for Mentally Handicapped Children (commonly known as Mencap) (143; *TVTH*, 254). Prynne's papers preserve a copy of a brief letter to Mencap of 21 January 1974, describing Oliver's novel and its request, and enclosing a cheque for £2.

4 Oliver refers to '"u", "je", "r", "r", "im", "a", "finally"'.

5 Oliver refers either to Edward Dorn, *Twenty-Four Love Songs* (San Francisco and West Newbury, MA: Frontier Press, 1969) or *Songs: Set Two—a Short Count* (West Newbury, MA: Frontier Press, 1970), or both.

6 Barry MacSweeney (1948–2000), British poet.
 'your sequence', Oliver likely refers to *A Night Square* (London: Albion Village Press, 1973), composed on 2 February 1971 but not published until 1973.

7 Oliver refers to MacSweeney's *Just 22 and I Don't Mind Dyin': The Official Poetical Biography of Jim Morrison, Rock Idol* (London: Curiously Strong, 1971).

because you have probed farther than I. What is so surprising and heartening though is how much of basic purpose we have unconsciously been sharing and how Into the Day discovers a whole new, immensely rich domain within this purpose that I had thought I knew so well. I shall have to build my understanding of this sequence slowly, these flux moments, thermal precincts, and yet bird flights and pain pathways.[1] The sequence is patient and, given those hard concerns and pressures, that patience is especially beautiful. That's why the most considerable thing I can say about the last poem is quite simply that it is correct.[2] The layers have been passed, the heart has steadied in that stress, the passion has necessarily been estranged (not to mention 'we are strangers to ourselves' etc.[3]) and the truth takes that pathway. It is the possibility of valuable achievement inside time, our most thorny hope. Your poetry has always seemed to me a sort of founding father for this (much of this in Kitchen Poems by implication). It is therefore a poetry at the opposite end of the scale from that implied cynicism the unspeakable Cambbidge [sic] Review article seemed to be worrying about.[4] It is, I repeat, a new possibility that you have all along been building. So much has been written here and in the States as though it were enough to say 'good is good', a very ancient inadequacy of language just as old-style dialectics {I mean 'quality' 'versus' 'quantity'} were an inadequacy of mathematics. For want of the necessary tension of language we have been unable to incorporate these possible 'vectors' (to reuse your term) in our method. The concept of harm has not properly entered this tension either. Yes the new work does seem alive to this.

And I am excited by your sequence as I am excited by the Dorn Cycle because I see that we are being placed at a new starting point. It is certainly the starting point I have been striving towards: I have not had the mathematics to talk about it critically but I believe there is an awareness we are now in. The word 'singularity' I have been meditating on in rather a different context and I now enclose Thom's paper (please return—and do you want the Dorn Cycle back as well as the accompanying documentation which I'm going to photostat before return?)[5] My meditation of present days thus appears as a kind of detailed field inside this wider view that is opened for me.

I am not a Piagetian but I find his ladder of nature more plausible, to put it mildly, than any of the neo-hermeticism that goes around. There we have the chreods that go to establish homeostasis entering at last resort as foundation for our extrapolated logical categories. Whatever the truth of this hypothesis it seems useful and acts as some kind of a bridge for the otherwise disparate data we seem to have been mutually encountering.

Maybe, therefore, the word, singularity, has been as suggestive for you as for me (though I had pretty well written the novel before I encountered the Thom paper): and I am not suggesting there is any marriage between the universal mathematics of your

---

1   Oliver interpolates language from *Into the Day* (*Poems*, 205, 214), and refers to the poem's recurring image of bird flight.

2   *Poems*, 214: 'After feints the heart steadies [...]'.

3   The quoted phrase recalls Nietzsche's famous opening of his preface to *On the Genealogy of Morals* (itself an allusion to the inscription above the cave of the Delphic Oracle), but in more general or idiomatic usage suggests any number of potential literary sources, not least Charles Olson's invocation of Heraclitus in 'Maximus, to Himself': 'I stood estranged / from that which was most familiar'. *On the Genealogy of Morals*, trans. Douglas Smith (Oxford: Oxford University Press, 1996), 3; *The Maximus Poems*, ed. George F. Butterick (Berkeley: University of California Press, 1985), 56. That Oliver was thinking specifically of Olson is made more likely by the interpolation in *Into the Day* of a phrase from Olson's 'The Kingfishers', 'hath not th'advantage' (*Poems*, 203).

4   Oliver refers to Michael Long, review of *Brass*, by J. H. Prynne, *Cambridge Review* 93 (19 November 1971): 62–3.

5   Oliver enclosed René Thom, 'Topological Models in Biology', *Topology* 8, no. 3 (July 1969): 313–35. On the back of one sheet, Oliver quotes Thom's paper:
  'In fact, our usual language is nothing but a semantic model of dimension one (the time), the chreods of which are the words (spoken, or written).
  'One may speak, in that case, of a <u>multi-dimensional syntax</u> directing the semantic model' [322]
  (This is not an anti-novel etc.)

documentation and the embryo examination of Thom. It is the possibility of certain vectors that lies behind 'Overtly the step lacks time'.[1] So far from the corny 'spontaneity' of Koch's tribe or, the latest phrase from Canada, I understand, 'pure example', which amounts to the same error; and none of these brethren could possibly write: 'Wishing to love is the sign now / painted with darkness'.[2]

I don't know what higher thing verse can reach than to place us in the position where we have the possibility of singular action. Maybe the mathematics of this will always be approximate in some minutely slender degree (given Gödel's theorem etc.); but we know the immense value of tolerances in mathematics and I think they are probably the flux of poetry, or otherwise we should end up in that Jack Spicer paradox, 'the perfect poem has an infinitely small vocabulary'.[3]

What is so extremely encouraging to me about what you have sent is that all of us involved in this appear not to be 'solving problems' but amassing charge. Something basic is being done and my hope is that this [?is a] means to method. Just as Fred Hoyle and his gang cannot yet do what they want to do, neither can I: but I am at the point of the question in myself and you have placed me a step nearer.[4] I'm looking for a new kind of cohesive power, I suppose. So the question I am currently asking about Into the Day is related to how it coheres, how it produces the alertness towards relations we had been attending to almost without realising all along. The staggered lines of spherical harmonics need pinning on my wall, but I'd need the pain-to-come like a promise of rightness.

Of the other two poems you send, The Blade Given Back goes Viva Ken, Viva Ken in its language and I love this tremendous raciness you can put on, a sentence speeding down to ant love and disappearing into a pinprick.[5] Perhaps it is an exemplar, this poem, (not a 'pure example' please) from within this potential you have been amassing, a signal of the charge you're at. There's plenty that's nice in An Evening Walk—the extraordinarily adroit final cadences and the way it guns into gear. 'holding his mouth and / there are pork pies'... that 'and' seems to me a betrayal of the otherwise high energy, perhaps a moment of faltering in the intentional syntax.[6] But I have that excellent, stunned end to look forward to and only hesitate a moment or two among the pork pies.

You'll be aware from what I've said, therefore, that it's a considerable hope that I've drawn from your letters and accompaniments.

I'd like to drive down to see you just for an evening this week: would Thursday or Friday night be possible? Or otherwise could you suggest an evening next week? We could have three or four hours of talk, I reckon. (You could ring me at Cov 25588, ext 113 or a letter would do.)

Apart from the above, I'd like to discuss whether you think

---

1 Oliver quotes *Into the Day* (*Poems*, 203).

2 Kenneth Koch (1925–2002), American poet.
'Wishing to love [...]', Oliver quotes *Into the Day* (*Poems*, 204).

3 Kurt Gödel (1906–78), Austro-Hungarian-born mathematician, logician, and philosopher.
Oliver quotes Jack Spicer's 'Dear Lorca', in *After Lorca* (1957). *My Vocabulary Did This to Me: The Collected Poetry of Jack Spicer*, ed. Peter Gizzi and Kevin Killian (Middletown, CT: Wesleyan University Press, 2008), 123.

4 Fred Hoyle (1915–2001), British astronomer, astrophysicist, and science-fiction writer.

5 Oliver refers to 'Viva Ken' from *Brass* (*Poems*, 154), though as with 'The Kirghiz Disasters' previously published in *The Norman Hackforth* and thus already well known to Oliver.
'ant love', Oliver interpolates language from 'The Blade Given Back' (*Poems*, 217).

6 Oliver quotes 'An Evening Walk' (*Poems*, 227).

16 January 1972

[1] For commentary on this letter and on the relevance of Thom's work for Prynne's practice at the time, see Justin Katko, 'Relativistic Phytosophy: Towards a Commentary on "The *Plant Time Manifold* Transcripts"', *Glossator: Practice and Theory of the Commentary*, no. 2 (2010): 245–93.

Cape could be made interested in my prose and also the university entrance question (but I'll try not to be boring on either of these …).

Doug

18 January 1972[1]   44 Carlyle Road
                                                                                                        Cambridge

Dear Doug,

Thanks for your letter and also for the enclosed paper on biotopology. This is a rather speculative approximation to a reply, as shortage of time is pressing hard at the moment and I don't want to let anything subside. My immediate reaction, you see, is that there's an essential vulgarity in Thom's argument, a coarse vagueness about reference frames. We know that there are conformalities between the internally self-regulating manifold of the living entity and the field conditions of its ambient context. The field equations for the biosphere would clearly have to allow for stable inhomogeneities, interactive and self-replicating, within a homogeneous model for the field characterised by the life constant (i.e., ecosystem, biosphere), and would also have to allow for trans-discrete functions at all levels (from the distribution curves of organic carbon to Hegelian notions of Geist, etc.). Obviously important functions across discrete boundaries —the infamous term 'interface' hovers resentfully near—include e.g. immune response systems, sign grammars, sex (yum).

But: not to recognise and accommodate locally inhomogeneous manifolds embedded discontinuously within a set of such sub-manifolds which can be mapped on to an isotropic and homogeneous total-manifold, and with a high accuracy of correspondence to the observed statistical data, is to languish within positively Euclidean archaism. If you see what I mean. There are discontinuities with respect to some major functions, 'life' amongst others; but if a singularity is not to be just 'point of view' determined, it must comprise a condition of closure with regard to <u>every</u> axis of its reference frame (or co-ordinate system). Without this, binary instability, breakdown of symmetry, the whole idea of catastrophic bifurcation, can be smoothed into a crypto-continuous function of the survivingly continuous gradient or vector, and thereafter recuperated more or less completely according to the local parametric constraints.

There is a silly melodrama, then, in claiming an absolute discontinuity between quantitative and qualitative field-processes. Thom supposes a quasi-absolute separation between his geometric models and the physical processes they 'describe'. Einstein's field equations have settled the fundamental equivalence of geometry and physics; a metaphor is not a suppressed simile, even if you chop out a dimension and then make a drawing of the result. Topology has always suffered from this quaint fixation over form versus content and has thus pined at the level of rhetorical descriptio. Zeeman's work is the same: I see he's cited by Thom, and he recently gave a 3rd Programme talk on Thom's 'catastrophe theory' which operated in the same terms.[1] Transformational grammar hasn't even yet got to the topologically adequate stage, since Chomsky ran out of intellectual penetration just before this jump and none of the camp followers has been able to complete this already implied development. But, again, even if it got this far, we should be left with a generative syntax which was semantically inert. Only relativistic cosmology has fully recognised that the description and the function are equivalent. Thom's talk of 'biochemical vibrations' (p. 21) is either a silly fiction or an improbable fact: he allows himself the luxury of leaving a choice, admitting only sufficient embarrassment as will cause him to put the phrase into quotation marks. The Empedoclean zoogony and Hesiodic theogenesis are at least internally coherent, not to mention a good deal more interesting.

Why I go on about this has to do, I suppose, with the potentially dissociative effects of theoria thus free-rangingly pursued. We do not need that! Wisdom is good because it is functionally interfused with what we do: but 'as such' of course it is a boring white noise, we don't want cohesive power of those empty terms. {Jacques Monod, as a further example: biologists are constantly succumbing to half-baked holism of one dubious kind or another.}[2] Give me a straight textbook any day, I am currently competing with Edelen and Wilson's Relativity and the Question of Discretization in Astronomy (Springer-Verlag, 1970) and any use that occurs will certainly not be mere extrapolated figuration.[3] What we say is what it is; that's a level of adequation we must be vigilant about, nothing to do with nineteenth century naturalism etc., but what Celan calls 'eine Art Heimkehr'.[4]

Now I am so tired I must stop, or fall asleep ranting. I'll try to telephone in a day or two, though the residue of this week will be impossible. Do hang on to Dorn's Cycle, complete with authorial illustrations, as I brought a bunch of them back with me. Don't hunt up the Gardner book, it was simply a straight medical-student's survey. Much else there is to say and what we know is stunningly more than what we merely think and I'll try to grab a phone the other side of urgently required kip.
    Jeremy

1 Christopher Zeeman (1925–2016), British mathematician. The BBC Third Programme broadcast nationally from 1946 to 1967 before being absorbed into Radio 3. The closest contemporary BBC radio appearances by Zeeman are listed in the broadcaster's programme index as taking place in 1968.

2 Jacques Monod (1910–76), French biochemist.

3 See Katko, 'Relativistic Phytosophy', for sympathetic speculation on this passage: 'The poet's usage [of this text] will instead constitute a dialectical extension of the scientific theory, operating along the parallel axes of imagination and scholarship. The *PTM* ["The *Plant Time Manifold* Transcripts" (*Poems*, 233–42)] both embodies and contradicts its science, avoiding the reification of the prefabricated theoretic germ in which "mere extrapolated figuration" would result' (286).

4 Prynne quotes Paul Celan's phrase ('a kind of homecoming') from his 1960 'Meridian' speech. *Collected Prose*, trans. Rosmarie Waldrop (Manchester: Carcanet, 1986), 37–55 (53).

---

21 January 1972   188 Wainbody Avenue
                                                           Coventry

Dear Jeremy,
    Your very useful letter brings home to me that the farther the mathematician is from macroscopic or microscopic viewpoints the harder it is to maintain the non-Euclidean view sufficiently rigorously. The biologists are so hampered by the complexities of the molecular level, where so much of the data is non-fundamental that it's difficult to see how they can

1 Alfred Schutz (1899–1959), Austrian philosopher.

2 There is no directly equivalent diagram to Oliver's in E. C. Zeeman, *Catastrophe Theory: Selected Papers, 1972–1977* (Reading, MA: Addison-Wesley, 1977), though the 'behavioural patterns' that Oliver describes are hypothesized by Zeeman (via Paul MacLean) in terms of a 'dynamical system modelling the limbic activity of the brain': 'According to Paul MacLean it is in the limbic system that emotions and moods are generated (while the neocortex determines the more complicated choice of behaviour within that mood). Therefore we might expect catastrophe theory to be the mathematical language with which to describe emotion and mood' (13).

avoid non-rigorous, non-fundamental 'explanations' behind which a coarse reference frame assembles. So … is that reference frame created principally because of deciding on a specific field of experience above the level of fundamental particles? Not that I have to apologise for biologists, you understand; but the problem of specific fields of experience lodges within my thinking—e.g. the 'specific' poem, the 'specific' idea—and is partly why I criticise structuralism. The artist, who has not the same need to limit the scope of his inquiry except by the intuitive performance of it, is not beset by the problems of the poor biologist, obliged by you (quite correctly I am convinced) to cater within his mathematics for 'discontinuously-embedded inhomogeneous manifolds' (I gratefully ape your terminology). So he steps into those leg-irons called biology and tries to make sense of the unseen gaoler's voices, the poor Platonic prisoner. Relativistic cosmology may be in another prison but at least it is one that surrounds the biologists'.

In fact, I've been operating not to any biological mathematics but, as you have already seen, with a phenomenological impulse (two essays by Schutz among others).[1] My only use for structuralism (only? a bit strong) is as parody material.

Zeeman gave me Thom's paper after I had finished the novel. Your letter considerably clarifies why I have been particularly worried by one of Zeeman's jeux d'esprit (difficult to say how serious this one is with him—I've only met him a couple of times). Your poem sequence is a display of the freedom that I have until your letter felt threatened {by the biologists.}

Let me first make a typical formulation from my prose: a clearing inside harm where everything is layered and fragmented and misty because we step in from outside. That is the intuition. Among Zeeman's maps of catastrophic analysis of human behaviour is this, of behavioural patterns of a boy-meets-girl situation mapped on to a square-shaped surface. Either side of the map we have approach and withdrawal and their relationship with behaviour if it is happy or unhappy and I think you have to imagine some stress causing jumps in behaviour according to a Zeeman/Thom topology with which you may be familiar now. Anyway, the only point is that, as far as my memory allows, the map is like this:[2]

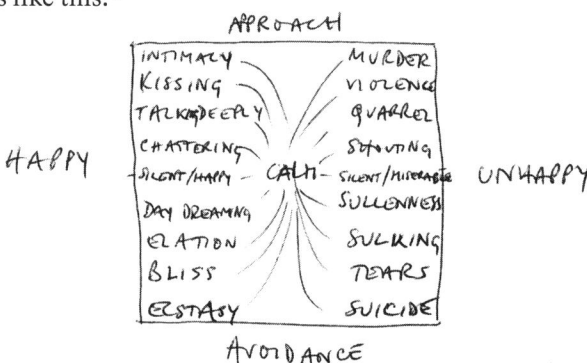

21 January 1972

You see the behavioural edges have a sort of mathematical 'hill' (or perhaps depression would be just as good a term) at their centre. Zeeman implied at a lecture that on the rim of this hill emotions drop to near-zero and its central point was akin to the goal of meditation. Experience of those who meditate would confirm the sense of a vantage-point of low emotion from which all the other emotions can be viewed, he said. (Perhaps this is just the commonplace about all balance points). Well, I found the similarity between the centre point of this map and the forest clearing in my novel sufficiently close to be intriguing, but as I say worrying.

For if the centre of the map is a unity of opposites, then Heraclitus, Nicholas of Cusa, Bruno, Spinoza and some other tuneful songsters would chorus that the mathematics of such a point must be the mathematics of infinity which, as opposed to mathematics which are about infinity, is presumably unattainable. But isn't the mathematics of any fixed point that? So I was glad that my clearing precisely had its 'function-across-discrete boundaries' mist, its sense of unanswerable paradoxes, which in the situation of my prose is the layering of harm. I was sure that was emotionally right but perturbed by the Zeeman map. Am I right therefore that you rescue my concept with your criticism of the Thom/Zeeman topology as 'Euclidean archaism', because what this map houses is a Euclidean point? That is why I now see why I was unsure what such a fixed, anti-relative point was doing inside there, except as a reminder of infinity blowing its usual hole through things, which means we are not far from a mere Cusanian 'coincidence of contraries' with all the questions that begs.[1]

You can, of course, construct a simple working model to simulate a Zeeman behaviour jump (one is a revolving clock retained by elastic bands which jumps each time a loose-hanging control elastic band attached to the edge of the clock circle is passed through a cuspoid control space above the line of stress (i.e. the retaining elastic bands)). This mechanical model shows then that biotopology may well be very useful in making biological predictions much more certain. Your strictures however run very deep and I am still working out their implications.

I agree with those things about theoria, wisdom, extrapolated figuration; and 'what we say is what it is' becomes a particularly oppressive truth in the Midlands, this continual denial of experience as though that were a simple lie and not more deeply dyed. So it [is] as always a way through the numbness of language I'm looking for; and I have read Chomsky but am glad I've read the latest Dorn and your recent productions. Don't we already go into transformations that underlie Chomsky?

Hope to see you soon.
Doug.

1 Oliver refers to a central tenet (the so-called *coincidentia oppositorum*) in the fifteenth-century German polymath Nicholas of Cusa's *De docta ignorantia* (On learned ignorance) (1440). Despite the scepticism of Oliver's reference to the *coincidentia*, Cusa's emphasis on ignorance was likely attractive to him, especially in terms of what one scholar refers to as the 'prima facie ambiguity' of the phrase '*docta ignorantia*' itself: 'does it mean an ignorance that is erudite or an ignorance that must be acquired—or both? Certainly, Nicholas believes that an individual who possesses this ignorance is in this respect wiser than an individual who does not.' Jasper Hopkins, *A Concise Introduction to the Philosophy of Nicholas of Cusa* (Minneapolis: University of Minnesota Press, 1978), 13. Ignorance acquired or embraced by a shedding of defensive, inauthentic cleverness came to be, for Oliver, the most intelligent use of a poet's creative dynamic, and variations on this theme are developed throughout and across practically everything in his oeuvre, especially so in the opening chapter of *The Harmless Building*.

21 January 1972

1 'our publisher', Prynne refers to Wendy Mulford, British poet and editor of Street Editions, and by 'cave transcripts' to Oliver's *In the Cave of Suicession* (Cambridge: Street Editions, 1974) (hereafter cited as *ICS*). In 1974, Street Editions published both Oliver's book and Prynne's *Wound Response*. An annotated copy of the draft typescript of *ICS* is preserved in Prynne's papers. The title page is marked up with a summary of the annotations:

> The harmless
> building (poem)
> Plutarch on decline
> into prose
>
> Q morpheme in semantic syntax;
> Oedipus at
> Colonus; Needham
> in latest Sci. & Civ.
> in China (intro.)
> a bee line
> tunnel vision.

The first clause of Oliver's epigraph ('"Invoked or not invoked, the god will be present" The Delphic Oracle') is underlined and marked 'cf. p. 9', where the clause appears in the typescript (*Kind*, 80).

2 Prynne does not imply a face-to-face meeting but puns on *interview*, in response to Oliver's pun in *ICS*, as the next sentence makes clear. In Prynne's annotations to the typescript of *ICS*, the word *interview* (in the phrase 'an interview shadow by its side') is underlined and marked 'PUN!!' (*Kind*, 87).

3 'Deborah', title of the sixth section (of nine) of *ICS* (*Kind*, 90). The name *Deborah* derives from the Hebrew word for *bee*. Wordplay on *bee* and the various tenses of its homophone *be* is an important thread running through this and subsequent letters. See especially Prynne to Oliver, 6 September 1974. In Prynne's copy of the typescript no annotation appears from 'Deborah' onwards.
    There is no section named 'Nurse' in Oliver's poem, and the word does not appear in either the first edition of *ICS* or its revised reprint in *Kind*.

4 'Jan' appears in the fourth section of *ICS*: 'I intone Jan + one / a circadian music in her name / that tunes exactly with a dark Joanne' (*Kind*, 83). The letters of *Jan* and *one* combine to form the name *Joanne*. Oliver married Janet Hughes on 28 July 1962. Her name appears in other poems by Oliver, notably the first poem in *Oppo Hectic*, 'When I Was in Bridport': 'You know I'm working Jan, you know / I am John' (*Kind*, 13).
    Mercedes McCambridge (1916–2004), American actress. She appears in the fifth chapter of *The Harmless Building* (41; *TVTH*, 149).

5 Prynne interpolates language from *ICS*: 'A Do you suppose yourself living or sent? Q Ex officio presumably' (*Kind*, 79).

2 September 1974

17 Ferry Path
Cambridge

Dear Doug:

Even while knowing it had its dangers I persuaded our publisher to let me see your cave transcripts, in a form which might not (she says you say) be final.[1] This danger (which is that of the letter which would be my thoughts even if not themselves written out) has been resolved by interview.[2] That was a deeply witty pun, survival very much at risk as a reported question. What actually 'happened' was that I got to the position marked Deborah and then split off, not exactly sleeping but dropping the thread there and waking up in another room instantly called nurse.[3]

It was a verbal colouring of the deepest kind, prior to all feature-changing rules but including many not usually part of the same stem. Thus, it was not quite a noun or agent-function but rather a sort of conditional pluperfect. It's hard to explain, but 'it would have been the case that' with strong optative–predictive leaning ('if only' to 'just you wait and see') could do as a start. The middle-voice aspect was adjectival as grateful in 'a grateful posset' is 'a drink which causes to be gratified'; the noun-substitute goes as 'the one who' or 'the (very) place where'. I think this was, collaterally, a natural gap in the life of the reader, so that the existence-predicate is raised power by power and the subject–object joining is the question received sexually into its answer.

'The one who' is named down there as Jan, the movement into as the reflection of she who stands behind goes step-wise by descending planes; but my point is that the other lexical recognitions (Mercedes McCambridge to name only one) deflected for me into the sub-routine called nurse.[4] I'll linger in this system, unfamiliar and only half-safe, until I really do know that the way out is exactly complete: I am overwhelmingly nervous about the risk of causing any shifts in the descent, but also so curious that I had to follow you in.

There is an adverbial current to nurse where I am now which makes 'love' oscillate with 'care', each one more so for the contact; as, in parallel, the prophetic/remembered is a hunting [*sic*] loop. I told you it was verbal, and nor has the comparative *nurse, 'the more nor; after the one less such' (need and fear as the precinct of that discovery, nourish contracted by seeing myself eating and then restored ex officio).[5] The middle voice of that unstable condition is what can be known by reversal. The securing ramification is, I think, that the future perfect makes the widest floor; not remorse but what was discovered to have been more so and even, by counter-enlargement, precious. The optics of that you handle with neat demotic by-play, completely created for itself; just as the median between causative fell ('hew down') and intransitive unpurposed fall is not reflexive jump ('se faire tomber', very Gallic) but middle-aspect fate, which is a conjunction somewhat comparable in outline to notwithstanding: otherwise the child by the hollow pear-tree itself.

The carefulness is offset layer by layer and I stepped off, temporarily dazzled, at <u>Deborah</u>, to the branching <u>nurse</u>-passage. All the Freudian persiflage is so adept, to exhaust that vacant dialect and then it's the <u>hole</u>![1] More nor, and that one has a care is what by a lower gallery one has a care for, a bee line through <u>oratio obliqua</u> (sorry)—and anyway Plutarch specially singled out the metrical and verbal errors of the oracles in his day.[2] As you will see I am hesitating at the complete authority of <u>care</u> provided in <u>nurse</u>, the name of a tenderness we hope to have had, and by difficult self-righting, which we know we can still have hoped for and be hoped for and, as if for ever (oh please) be hoped to have and be so. That <u>care</u> is the recognised certainty of <u>good</u>, known through the sufficiency of <u>goodness</u> in where (if we have gone in carefully) we may come out, blinking. How could I not understand that, as you intone by rite the overlap <u>into</u> day, into your mouth, and I am still deep inside not ready to move past <u>Deborah</u>.[3] Quite cosy here, tins of baked beans and ox-tail soup glint in the dim light, I don't feel safe exactly, but secured, and I could easily camp here for a month or two running forwards or backwards (Hawking says that 'The ordinary Maxwell theory, in which the electromagnetic field has a definite sign at every point, does not allow the sign of a charge to change on going around a closed curve non-homotopic to zero unless the orientation of time changes. However one could have a theory in which the field was double-valued and changed sign on going round such a curve').[4]

This word-screen really did develop from an interview at the Deborah stage, and I was already, oh very deeply shaken by a certain notice that you would be forgiven. On behalf of, as in despite of what would have been or not, and then was. We joke but it is true and <u>but</u> is linked step by step to <u>nor</u> to make <u>in virtue of which</u>, one going into another land not called home. As I say, I'm camped out at <u>nurse</u> and am cheerful there for the time being (free of tense, as you can see); I'll stay on at least until I can be sure that your text is completed. 'I might' she says, and 'I know' replies the <u>wh</u>-morpheme, so deep down that transformation shimmers at every twitch of reason and desire. Right down there, calmly, and the reader is diverted into the induced currents of his own life, trusted & incomplete—

Jeremy

---

30 August 1974[5] 42 New Street
Brightlingsea, Essex

Dear Jeremy,

I haven't, after all, been able to get down to see you as I'd hoped—plentiful weeks in Bournemouth have consumed much of the summer. But I heard from John + Wendy the other day

---

1 The most frequent use of *hole* in *ICS* appears in the fifth section, 'The After-Image', e.g., 'The hole at your feet, the one you entered and from which you have just emerged, is shaped like a woman' (*Kind*, 87).

2 'oratio obliqua', in Latin grammar, indirect or reported speech or discourse, especially in the Latin historical tradition.
Prynne refers to, and partly interpolates, Plutarch's *The Oracles at Delphi No Longer Given in Verse*: 'Yet we observe that most of the oracles are full of metrical and verbal errors and barren diction.' *Moralia*, vol. 5, trans. F. C. Babbit (Cambridge, MA: Harvard University Press, 1936), 269.

3 Prynne interpolates language from *ICS*: 'Think at 52 degrees Fahrenheit; then the day itself will flood into your mouth, nose, up anus and penis, and will at last open your ears, appear in your eyes' (*Kind*, 80).

4 S. W. Hawking and G. F. R. Ellis, *The Large Scale Structure of Space–Time* (Cambridge: Cambridge University Press, 1973), 182.

5 This letter did not reach Prynne until after he had sent his letter of 2 September. 30 August 1974 fell on a Friday, so that Oliver's letter likely reached Prynne by either Monday the 2nd, after Prynne had written and posted his, or Tuesday the 3rd, when Prynne replied.

1 John James and Wendy Mulford.

2 Oliver enclosed a typescript of *ICS*.

3 *ICS* is dedicated: 'For Andrew Crozier / John James / J. H. Prynne'.

4 'W.J.', Oliver refers to Wendy Mulford, who took John James's surname when they married in the summer of 1974.

5 'OK, snap', suggests the last two letters crossed in the post.

6 'Panton Pythoness', evidently a nickname for Wendy Mulford, who with John James lived on Panton Street, Cambridge.

that you were in good form, as they used to say, and that there was an Ms on the way for Street Editions.[1]

My own piece from that esteemed House will be the enclosed, I hope.[2] Perhaps its dedication should read to those three names and to the English Intelligence, but that might be misinterpreted: at all events it stands as an acknowledgement of important influences.[3] Anything not corrected in pen is an intentional mistake in the text.

I'm thinking that liaising with W.J. over publication details may well provide an excuse to visit Cambridge that will stand up to the test of time.[4] If so, I'd be glad if we could see each other again: it's been a long time since Election Night, perhaps a century.

Doug.

3 September 1974   17 Ferry Path
Cambridge

OK, snap: but I think I'll stay down where I am for a while anyway.[5] Was it Sinbad who set up on the whale's back. <u>Wound Response</u>, which is my title with the Panton Pythoness, is at second proof and is expected to be at large by the end of this month.[6] It would have been good if mine & yours could have come out together; but in any case don't delay about arrangements as this autumn could see a quite pointed convergence. And the Pythoness has a tendency to linger, which I hope you will quickly overcome. She can't really ask for quotations from possible printers until she has an outline scheme for style & format; I have made several copies of the text for her to send out, and supplied some addresses, but if you have ideas for how the thing should look I'd advise writing them out as specifically as possible. Grandmother & egg-sucking etc., but I (for one) really would like to see the cave opened to the public as fast as the little kiosk with postcards can be got into position. And do come over, yes, excellent, whenever you can.

Jeremy

4 September 1974   42 New Street
Brightlingsea, Essex

Dear Jeremy,

Your letter was brilliant. After re-reading it, I could see where you are encamped and why you are cooking lunch and tea. I've decided not to change my text further, except in a detail or two maybe, since it is meant to be a record of 'conviction arising under certain circumstances' and must bear the risk of that. Certain incidental (in the full sense) data 'had' to be accommodated, and I found that process full of surprises.

How great, therefore, that a branch from Deborah (song of war in the bubble b), a true incidental, takes us to 'nurse'! I may be the one that's wounded there and may have incompletely convalesced ... Your dazzling reversals—I would like mine to be as dazzling—take place where I would hope to have reached (conditional pluperfect). Then a further conviction occurred which, as you so exactly see, is in secure (I'll leave that typing disjunction) ... and dawn over Lose Hill promises a tricky day ahead; and yet what ought I to do with a local conviction but adopt it as far as it will take me?[1] It got me <u>out</u>, perhaps undecided whether to go back in, but out all the same; and I don't think the entrance is where it was. You're still in somewhere with 'nurse', yes another room. I am affected by the news that you have 'cared' to go there. Your nurse-full extensions of 'care' (taking much forward from any Heideggerian implication) are exemplary to me; you offer me an inter-view truly.[2] <u>Wound Response</u> might be <u>the</u> response, as your letter was an A to a Q.[3]

And yet your quotation from Hawking gives me a hope that I was, in terms of the textual occasion, right to move at last— that I had 'enough' to get me out and into a new room of my own called ... well, I'm not quite sure yet. (Since the Essex examiners have suggested I submit a self-study course of my own devising for part of my work next year, I'm hoping at least to hang a name on the room door soon—be nice to discuss things with you.[4] And, well, the changing sign ... and hydrocarbons? (Could you give me a useful reference for that version of the dynamics?) Yes, the time-orientation and the sign fascinating.

You show me how nice it would be were <u>Wound Response</u> and the caves to be available pretty well together. I shall try to get down to Cambridge this weekend, but have to ring the James's yet. If there's a hope of seeing you, that would be very good. If you have any spare texts of your book ... (of course, I could wait until the end of the month—only if anything's spare).

Meantime, please give my regards to the hospital administration and thanks for the attention of the nurse. As you know with such precision, the war goes on, and I've a bit of a limp. Hope to see you soon.
    Doug

6 September 1974[5]   Gonville and Caius College
                                  Cambridge

Dear Doug,

Your letter arrived this morning and here is a quick packet to get back without delay (GPO as the usual spastic crow flies).[6] I hope you're having good weather out/up there; my supplies are lasting out nicely, but I seem to hear a louder roaring from some waterfall further down (or at the Ménière level, could be). At my own Bee Target stage I was descending into A. Leo Oppenheim, 'The Interpretation of Dreams in the Ancient Near East, with a Translation of an Assyrian Dream-Book', <u>Transactions of the American Philosophical Society</u>, N.S. 46

---

[1] 'Lose Hill' appears in *ICS*: 'Winnat's Pass above these chambers, the "pass through which the wind sweeps", then down to the foot of Win or to that of Lose Hill, Hope in the valley, and Blue John, toadstone, the treasures in surrounding caves (frowns, depletion)' (*Kind*, 88). The passage names features of the Derbyshire landscape: Lose Hill is west of Win Hill, and Hope Valley between them. Suicide (or Horseshoe) Cave, the ostensible locale of the oracle in *ICS*, and Blue John Cavern are both southwest of Lose Hill, at the foot and top of Winnat's Pass, respectively.

[2] The concept of 'care' (*Sorge*) is a fundamental component of Heidegger's ontology, not an affective or psychological disposition but the 'formal existential totality of Dasein's ontological structural whole'. *Being and Time*, trans. John Macquarrie and Edward Robinson (Oxford: Blackwell, 1962), 237.

[3] Oliver refers to the form of *ICS*, the majority of which is structured through dialogue between 'the inquirer' ('Q') and 'The Suicide Cave Oracle' ('A').

[4] 'Essex examiners', Oliver was a mature undergraduate in the department of literature at the University of Essex, 1972–5, and taught at Essex thereafter until 1977.

[5] For commentary on this letter, as it pertains to the 'bilinear temporality of *plant time*', see Katko, 'Relativistic Phystosophy', 274–5.

[6] 'GPO', General Post Office, state postal carrier of the UK until 1969.

(1956), [1]79–373, with some additional fragments in Iraq, XXXI (1969), 153–165.[1] The be(e) route was especially good because of the intensive quiver-link with the copula, subject–predicate a sexual line focus as if we didn't know.

Then Dorn started in with his Bean planting and this gave the Anglo-Saxon duplicate bēo bēo ('I am the bee') a new journal entry; bēon to bean was not far by Indo-European e/o ablaut, and in July 1972 I cast up a runic triode which I enclose (to shew again how close we were running).[2] The dynamics of this was so near to its body-image, yet I never thought to cross the syntax line, into an 'adventure'; even when I heard you were doing the cave passages I didn't fully realise what was up (down). Very smart work, right under our noses. The sign change for the time axis is more difficult. I started mostly from sections 8 and 9 of W. Rindler, 'Visual Horizons in World-Models', Monthly Notices of the Royal Astronomical Society, 116 (1956), 662–677, which is at least comprehensible and which hybridises nicely with, e.g., sections 7 and 8 of G. N. Leech, Towards a Semantic Description of English (London, 1969). The spoken sign change is probably negation, of which a neat recent mapping is Pieter Seuren, 'Negative's Travels' in his volume of Oxford Readings in Philosophy called Semantic Syntax (London, 1974).

Anyway, here is an almost final proof of Wound Response, which is probably rather an interim text.[3] And do come over just as soon as you can fix something up, that would be very good & high time too.

Jeremy

P.S. Concerning your epigraph & all that springs from it there's an auspicious essay by A. D. Nock, 'Religious Attitudes of the Ancient Greeks' (1942), in his Essays on Religion and the Ancient World (Oxford, 1972), II, pp. 534–550.[4] Joseph Needham picks up an old argument with Said Husain Nasr in his Author's Note to the new volume of Science and Civilisation in China (Vol. 5 Part II, pp. xxiv–xxvi) and of course we can see that neither is right; the signs are reversing right across the space–time manifold and only a certain priestly cowardice insists on a dominant axis.[5]

---

11 September 1974   42 New Street
                                                Brightlingsea, Essex

Dear Jeremy,

The more I go into this the more amazing it is. Yes Wound Response is the finest response I could have imagined. And it seems to me you have already set out the terms of my surprise: that within the marvellous coincidentals whose domain we have both sought to enter, it is on the cards that the response should come out before the question.[6]

I do not mean just the precise correspondences: 'Darting

---

1 'Bee Target stage', Prynne refers to 'The Bee Target on His Shoulder' (Poems, 150–2), first published as 'Highest Tender' in Collection, no. 7 (Autumn 1970): 24–6.

2 'runic triode', Prynne refers to the untitled runic inscription (Poems, 244) colloquially referred to as his 'rune poem'. Prynne enclosed the original 'triode', as well as a commentary and transliteration into both Anglo-Saxon and modern English, excerpted from his correspondence (as 'P.P.Q. (pp Kew)') with Edward Dorn. See appendix B. For substantial commentary on the origins and composition of the inscription, see Justin Katko, 'Regarding a Specimen of Palaeobotanic Epigraphy: J. H. Prynne's Runic Fertility Prayer', If A Then B, no. 1 (2010): 42–60. Katko writes: 'Prynne's fertility prayer might plausibly be construed as a reparative to the grief induced by the death of Tom Oliver, Douglas' son, who died in [November] 1969. […] The prayer is in this sense not only an invocation of reproductive health, but an inducement to hope, to keep making love, to faithfully keep trying to *make*, out of enduring love for the living spirit of the dead' (56–7). An email from Oliver to the email list *Poetryetc* of 27 February 1999 describes the rune poem in the following terms: 'It's an important poem to me. […] I have never personally departed from its obsessional field, because it is my own. I have the runes framed above my desk as I write, for I keep it as a charm, alongside a postcard of the cave in which I wrote my own poem and a photo of an ancient Greek brooch showing two bees mating around a honeycomb.' An image of the 'Greek brooch' is reproduced in both the original publication of *ICS* and its revised reprint in *Kind*; it is the Malia Pendant, a Minoan gold pendant held in the Heraklion Archaeological Museum on Crete. Oliver also mentions the 'runic good luck charm, cast in the old ogham script by a friend', in 'An Island That Is All the World' (*TVTH*, 100). Oliver's reminiscences corroborate Katko's argument that '[n]ot only does Oliver appear to be the prayer's first true attendant, but Oliver's own home was effectively […] its first (and enduring) site of publication' ('Regarding a Specimen', 57).

3 Prynne enclosed a proof of *Wound Response*, including 'The *Plant Time Manifold* Transcripts'.

4 The epigraph to *ICS* is '"Invoked or not invoked, the god will be present" Delphic Oracle' (*Kind*, 67).

5 Seyyed Hossein Nasr (b. 1933), Iranian philosopher and academic.

6 The publication of *Wound Response* preceded that of *ICS*.

and humming like bees we were confronted at first/last by the erotic[*!*]'[1] But your taking up of a dynamic I 'placed' and 'deplaced' and making it so tremulous and yet strong that I continued through your poems with a kind of yearning I have not felt in a long time. I have not, even during <u>Into the Day</u>, encountered the potential I sensed in such poems as 'Of Movement...' or 'Pigment Depôt (on order, as your printer says)', or 'Again in the Black Cloud'.[2] My interest in melanin and the pineal and the circadian has been specific to the quasi-locale; now I find the case so general in your work, so internal in every bodily and mental sense, and yet so expansive as potential, that I am delighted with myself that you have so delighted me and shown me how wide the caves spread beneath the earth, how minute that sky can be.[3] You call your work transitional 'perhaps'; surely, it must be to attain the power? Since it takes me on and on, and at each new direction of a whole that is cohesive I catch a hint of further possibilities that you are clearly so in touch with. The 'syntactical' section—'<u>thermal dream</u>, etc....'—can at each internal reflection of it be cast as a whole project, a project at furious, affected potential, of course, or the tenses of relativity would merely freeze again.[4] Such projects most powerfully live in your book; but you have made the ground so generously available that it would take a competent reader to be blinded with prejudice not to take that gift. (We know the prejudice around...)

As you have so helped me by sharing these further discoveries, it may just be helpful if I sketch in how <u>crude</u> was the route I followed, because it is the very convergence of different paths that underscores the worth of what you've done.

I could no doubt have tracked myself forward from hints in your earlier work (I think the word, target, {But the hole in the cave really was target-like—my 'self' as arrow etc.} may have come in{, unsuspected,} at a very late stage, I came again across the short sentence upon caves in your 'Note on metal'—but that gave me a further reflection upon what I had done, a will-been reflection that I took gratefully as a confirmation (this, last July, I think)).[5]

The fact is, a bee did fly into the cave and for reasons that I only began to work out later this set off an extraordinary resonance in me.[6] A mother's voice did call Debbie, Debbie, another resonance which I checked for its Hebraic origin. Of course, there was already available that whole nectar, ambrosia thing, the baby Zeus fed by the bees in a cave, and so on. And I'd known that swarms of bees were used by the Greeks for divination. From Pausanias, I think (just possibly Plutarch), I had too that the second of the various succeeding Delphic temples was of beeswax and bird feathers—again presumably a reference to methods of divination. Reading Plutarch had confirmed my feelings that, even if the whole thing according to Delphic political exigencies was fraudulent, with the priest-poets concocting the best they could (I mean, whose <u>were</u> the metrical

1 Oliver quotes 'The *Plant Time Manifold* Transcripts' (*Poems*, 242).

2 Oliver refers to poems in *Wound Response* (*Poems*, 223, 221–2, 230–1).

3 Oliver refers to 'Melanin' (*Poems*, 226), but more generally to the physical and mental states explored in *Wound Response*.

4 'The "syntactical" section', Oliver likely refers to 'The *Plant Time Manifold* Transcripts'; he quotes '*thermal dream*' from this text (*Poems*, 238).

5 Oliver refers to 'The Bee Target on His Shoulder' (*Poems*, 150–2); 'A Note on Metal' (*Poems*, 127–32; the sentence to which Oliver refers is in the first paragraph on p. 128); and 'The *Plant Time Manifold* Transcripts' ('*by will been dreamt of it future that*', 'willbeen', etc.) (*Poems*, 238–40).

6 Oliver refers here and in the following sentence to objects and events described in *ICS*.

etc. inadequacies?)... even if that, the process itself was still the process and so near prophecy that I'm not always interested in telling the difference. I toyed with the idea of borrowing a cave somewhere and offering an oracle service through the pages of some magazine like Prediction.[1] But I once had to research for a news story a man who offered potential suicides a booklet of comfort (based on auto-suggestion à la Coué).[2] The man himself was in a sense to be pitied—so that I never did the savage hatchet job that had been 'ordered', but the experience convinced me that other people's fears are not to be mucked about with (and how many times has that unhappily been scored into my experience now). Well, as a substitute, I considered asking university students to write down anonymously real personal problems: but I don't think students generally are yet inquirers in the sense of envoys.

Then—I come to your runes, now hanging enigmatically on my wall in a little, glass-fronted picture frame—I did a sacred grove oracular text as a try-out. Though it was nice to be out among the oaks at 1 a.m., my answers were boring (and I blame the plumbing of a nearby mansion formerly belonging to the Shelley family—the building on the front of my novel, a couple of teenage lovers who preferred the swings on a small playground to any more real roundabout—oh and a passing hedgehog who was the star of the night).[3] The real answers came in your post, with the runes, a little casting of such authority that I'm heartily glad I didn't go ahead with casting my own grove text into permanence.

I entered the caves and had, immediately (as if it shouldn't be immediate), to cope with the bee. It would be rare if I could find an etymological pathway to match one of yours, but fortunately I found one ready-made:

> cerinthos—bee bread
> cerion—honey wax
> cerinos—waxen
> ceraphis—bee moth (locust) (nutrition???)
> cer—fate, destiny, leads I think to ceres—spites, plagues, ills.[4]

On my way in to the circadian pathways I read a bad, potboiling, but interesting book, The Parable of the Beast, and a good laugh but not much use (even for lexical hits) was Gene Stratton-Porter's The Beemaster, which I borrowed from an old woman down the road, along with a Beekeeper's Handbook.[5] Stratton-Porter gave me backup support for the Scoutmaster, though he came in from a couple of other sources too. The book finished, about three weeks ago I was strolling in a carpark near Boscombe pier when I found a ready-made picture of that Boscombe character, the Scoutmaster, on a piece of card—I've sent it to Wendy.[6]

This by no means exhausts the coincidences I stumbled across in writing my text (and I don't mean to make them grandiose); but the final sledgehammer comes with Wound Response. And

---

1 *Prediction* (1936–), British occult and astrological journal.

2 Émile Coué (1857–1926), French psychologist and pharmacist.

3 'nearby mansion', Oliver refers to Shelley Manor in Boscombe, Dorset, a photograph of which is reproduced on the covers of the first edition of *The Harmless Building*.

4 Oliver interpolates definitions from Robert Graves's account of Aristaeus in his *Greek Myths*, vol. 1 (Harmondsworth, UK: Penguin, 1955), 276–80 (280).

5 John N. Bleibtreu, *The Parable of the Beast* (London: Victor Gollancz, 1968) (esp. chap. 2, 'Cyclical Time').

6 The image is reproduced in *ICS* (*Kind*, 95).

there I am dizzy with correspondences, since though I could not have written your book (being condemned with my slower mental apparatus to different methods of working), it *is* the book I would have wanted you to write. So powerfully is this so that I don't know how to tell you it properly except by writing out the above little history. Above all, I sense that the children and the principle of ageing are in your book where I so desperately want them to be; unless that is so, what arrogance waits for the poet! (Cf. Bernadette Mayer in The World, 29 dismissing the neurologists with a breeziness—yes, breeziness is one arrogant dynamic—that reaffirms the Cartesian split by a hidden anxiety rather than mends it.)[1]

I can't think that my own oracular or scientific reading will surprise you—Parke's The Delphic Oracle, of course, and Dodds' venerable work on The Greeks and the Irrational, among others. Most of the works you cite I can't get from Essex U. library, though in a few cases there are parallel texts available. I had got somewhere in the vicinity of Edinburgh (incidentally, Quondam Lichen seems rather too advanced for C. H. Waddington—and does J. R. Smythies appear?[2] I'm not well-enough read to lift the masks). But I have little understanding (E. Roy John's now outdated Mechanisms of Memory, Academic Press, 1967, struck me as a sensible approach road), and little more knowledge. What you, then, give me is poetry-as-knowledge, as though there were any other kind, of value. I had hoped that 'something further may follow' from my own Masquerade, to quote another epigraph: now I see something already had.[3]

Perhaps the message came through to you that I'd be down on Friday. On the off-chance, I'll call in about 1 p.m.—perhaps with Wendy, as I shall be seeing her earlier.

Doug

P.S. p. 13 'Not Absent = or'?[4]

---

26 September 1974 42 New Street
Brightlingsea, Essex

Dear Jeremy,

Very glad to hear from Wendy the other night that your massive daughter was delivered safely and that Sue's OK.[5] Please give her my best wishes for speedy recuperation, Jessica a kiss on the fontanelle; and if I had a spotty handkerchief I'd send one for you all to dab your brows.

It made less serious affairs seem inappropriate that Friday, but now that a chubby foot is waving at us all, perhaps the volcanoes can begin to quake once more.

I've a folder of notes that take on from where the caves left me; one day, if you've the time, it would be [?*good*] to discuss some of them. On the lines of continued coincidence, I've been intrigued to find Mandel'shtam in his minor key picking up some of the

---

[1] Oliver refers to 'Bernadette Mayer—an Interview', *The World*, no. 29 (April 1974): 76–84. Mayer is quoted as saying: 'I started reading a lot of books about memory. Mostly psychological books. I tried to read some neurological books but it turns out that neurologists know nothing about memory at all' (80).

[2] 'Quondam Lichen', Oliver refers to the fictional professor in 'The *Plant Time Manifold* Transcripts'.
 C. H. Waddington (1905–75), British embryologist, geneticist, and philosopher of science.
 J. R. Smythies (1922–2019), British psychiatrist and neuroscientist.

[3] Oliver refers to, and quotes, Prynne's epigraph to *Into the Day*, which quotes the closing sentences of Herman Melville's last novel, *The Confidence Man: His Masquerade* (1857): '*Tagschlucht:* The next moment, the waning light expired, and with it the waning flames of the horned altar, and the waning halo round the robed man's brow; while in the darkness which ensued, the cosmopolitan kindly led the old man away. Something further may follow this Masquerade' (*Poems*, 201). '*Tagschlucht*' (daygorge) is a neologism coined by Paul Celan in his poem 'Dein vom Wachen'. *Gesammelte Werke in fünf Bänden* (Frankfurt am Main: Suhrkamp Verlag, 1983), 2:24.

[4] Oliver queries a phrase in 'Landing Area', from *Wound Response* (Oliver's pagination refers to the first edition; see *Poems*, 224), 'not absent nor / wincing'.

[5] Prynne married Suzanne Furmston on 12 September 1966. The Grosseteste Press edition of *The White Stones* is dedicated 'for Sue'.

Grecian bee imagery—in several poems, e.g. that beginning 'Take for joy from the palms of my hands / fragments of honey and sunlight / as the bees of Persephone commanded us' and ending '… bees that changed honey into sunlight', though I don't want to read too much into my own state of receptivity when imagery has anyway a certain literary history.[1] Vaughan's poem is extraordinary.[2]

Also, how about this Isoma ritual from the Ndembu tribe (n.w. Zambia) which I've just come across in Victor W. Turner's little Penguin, The Ritual Process?—this the 'spatial symbolism' he says:[3]

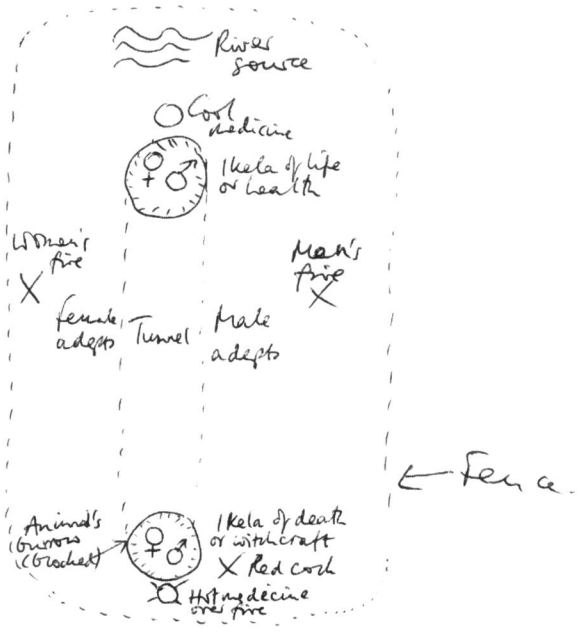

{Badly drawn. The ikela are tomb/womb holes in the ground + the husband + wife progress several times during the ritual from cool to hot to cool holes (he doesn't seem to indicate whether the return to the cool hole is above or below ground).}

Turner, like many another of his tribe, is much a Lévi-Strauss structuralist, and thus he refers to the 'binary discriminations' of this symbolism.[4] {But he gets beyond this in nice perception of the ritual as follows: 'In brief, the whole person, not just the Ndembu "mind", is existentially involved in the life or death issues with which Isoma is concerned.'}[5] I'm more interested in the fact that the aim of the ritual is restoration of the right relation between matriliny and marriage, reconstruction of the conjugal relations between wife and husband, and making the woman and hence the lineage fruitful. And Turner nicely points out that in religion and art there are, in a sense, no 'simpler peoples', though there are simple technologies.[6] Perhaps a more 'primitive' version of this, I might add, such as a sexually-perverted ritual, can be more readily associated with advanced-technology societies where some of the expertise of shared consciousness may more easily be lost.

---

[1] Oliver quotes Osip Mandel'shtam, *Selected Poems*, trans. David McDuff (Cambridge: Rivers Press, 1973), 67.

[2] No poem by Henry Vaughan is named or recorded as sent by Prynne in either archive. Given the matter at hand, Oliver may plausibly refer to Vaughan's 'The Bee'. *Poetry and Selected Prose*, ed. L. C. Martin (London: Oxford University Press, 1963), 446–9.

[3] Victor W. Turner, *The Ritual Process: Structure and Anti-Structure* (London: Penguin Books, 1969), 30.

[4] Ibid., 31.

[5] Ibid., 43.

[6] Ibid., 2–3.

Following through some of the references you suggested, I'm struck in reading a 1969 Seuren volume, Operators and Nucleus (the 1974 reference not readily obtainable here), with the great difficulty for me in retaining adequate mobility of concept when seeing people trying to link meaning and structure, a difficulty that doesn't arise with the mathematics of non-verbal elements, such as forces and quantities. The emotional-meaning ways of negation seem so difficult to tease out in linguistics, so subtle are their modes; but its fine to see operating within language what I take to be a mode of splitting (operator–nucleus) not without analogies to distinctions I would make between the self-seen-as-stable and the self-seen-as-changing: both being a form–content 'mistake' which nevertheless appears when social interactions such as language, are examined conceptually.

But that's a very broad, probably too broad, theme with me just now.

    Doug

1 Prynne likely sent a copy of *Wound Response* to Oliver in late September 1974, judging by Prynne's comment in his letter of 3 September 1974 that it would be 'at large by the end of this month'.

2 Diogenes Laertius, *Lives of Eminent Philosophers*, vol. 2, trans. R. D. Hicks (Cambridge, MA: Harvard University Press, 1925), 369.

3 Oliver likely sent Prynne a copy of *ICS* in December 1974, judging by the undated note preserved in Prynne's papers with a photocopy of the book's embellished dedication: 'Dear Jeremy, And New Year greetings to you + Sue. I'll write in early 1975. Doug'.

[*September 1974*]¹

[*Prynne sent a copy of* Wound Response *with an additional epigraph and dedication on the title page:*]

'I found in the Memorabilia of Favorinus a statement that Empedocles feasted the sacred envoys on a sacrificial ox made of honey and barley-meal' (Diog. Laert.).²

For Doug, inside the inside & thus further on
                        Jeremy

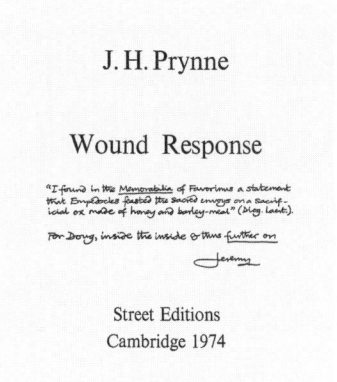

2 October 1974   42 New Street
                                      Brightlingsea, Essex

[*Oliver sent a hand-drawn image of the Lyle's Golden Syrup logo, pasted onto the page, with the biblical quotation used in the logo typewritten beneath it: 'Out of the strong came forth sweetness' (Judges 14 : 14).*]

[*December 1974*]³

[*Oliver sent a copy of* In the Cave of Suicession, *with an inscription from Prynne's rune poem above the printed dedication to Crozier, James, and Prynne. The quoted runes comprise the entire middle line of Prynne's poem, the transliteration for which Prynne gives as 'bright-shining : sun :: gift : the bean · [is] the bee-child (child of the bee) : joy ::*'.]

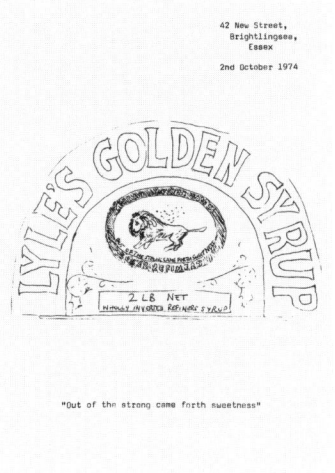

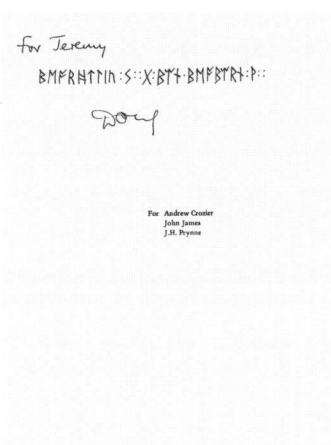

For Jeremy

ᛒᛖᛁᚱᚨᛏᛁᚺ᛬ᛋ᛬᛬ᚷ᛬ᛒᛏᛏ᛬ᛒᛖᛁᚠᛒᛏᚱᚾ᛬ᛈ᛬᛬

Doug

18 December 1977   42 New Street
                                                                             Brightlingsea, Essex

Dear Jeremy,

   No news is no news? Well, I got your book, and that's news.[1] The postcard I sent you from Turin or Milan was it grew damp and torn in my overcoat pocket and would be an incorrect memento of a fine, dry trip, me and my travellers' cheques, write when your wife gets work.[2]

   I think the warnings in the Clans are badly needed. Many of the tribes are right on the age-edge when it's been a weary struggle over the years (not weary at each individual time but sometimes seemingly weary when viewed in retrospect) and it's tempting to let go. That whole page starting 'along planned parenthood' is the most comforting to read because, unless we watch it, we can identify the enemy as others, not seeing our own short-cuts in the process—or only rarely so.[3] And it brings the concerns expressed as far back as Kitchen Poems into this much greater detail of the picture that you've been working out over the years. The tracings out in High Pink on Chrome[4]— a book I've found very difficult, owing, I think, to ignorance— and in Wound Response—which as you know I felt very close to—have provided such a precise focus that you are now justified, publicly, in turning your attention to a question that only one who has achieved such focus really has the right to tackle: viz: given all this, what is it right to do next? And when you look round the field you find, of course, a rather woeful disarray. And you oppose to it not just the standard recommendation for each of us to take the proper risk but what is now the most detailed working out I know in our national poetry of the dynamics, body vectors, and so on, of proper risk. 'Take what you get, / go anywhere, strictly come back nothing.'[5] Not only is the placing of 'strictly' syntactically so rigorous as to command admiration, it also is evidence of how major you insist the demands of right dynamics etc. must be.

   So, for me, it's that you have a peculiar right to make clear what is the demand on what the clans {I'm not taking a single meaning for that word.} do in the future; so that there's a tone of the prophetic almost: the planned loss of blood donors.[6] I fear that. And I see it in clarity in your sharp voice tones, the stern (the word must surely be) denunciation of the enemies, various kinds of loss, various kinds of declension from the true task. And it comes to our knowledge from many sources of information and twists of time-syntax, of reference fields,

1 Oliver refers to *News of Warring Clans* (London: Trigram Press, 1977) (*Poems*, 275–86).

2 Oliver interpolates lines from *News of Warring Clans*: 'These checks for travellers / will bring him up sharp / as a knife', 'Write when you get work' (*Poems*, 283).

   Oliver had been on an Arts Council-funded trip to Italy to 'study boxing' for the purposes of the novel referred to in the present letter. See *CAAS*, 253, and p. 49n3.

3 Oliver quotes *News of Warring Clans* (*Poems*, 282).

4 Oliver refers to Prynne's *High Pink on Chrome* (Cambridge: privately printed, 1975).

5 Oliver quotes *News of Warring Clans* (*Poems*, 281).

6 'planned loss of blood donors', Oliver interpolates a phrase from *News of Warring Clans* (*Poems*, 280).

coordinates. Not just a kind of meal-about-a-battle but wavefronts surging into a real/not real occasion and creating for the duration of the occasion a glimpse of the possibilities (even much of their definition) which we so many times default from. In a major aspect, your book is full of warnings for me and I shall keep its phrases at my elbow because for various reasons that I shan't discuss much here they'll be useful to me.

I do have an issue, a question perhaps, with that 'take what you get' phrase I've already quoted. What you get is influenced, filtered out, by mood at the same instant when this 'what you get' is created from what you have already got and expect to have. The sentence implies a causation from mood—I do realise however that I'm talking about a simultaneity in which cause (mood → what you get, etc.) is always a word that: (a) faces both ways or (b) many ways at once, depending on dimensionality and similar factors; and yet (c) is still itself as a retained concept for lower-level descriptions; and yet (d) collapses entirely into the simultaneity. The important rule here being the retention of the lower in the higher even as it simultaneously disappears— which is the rule most importantly unobserved in much loose poetic talk about the nature of the 'self' and so forth.[1] All right then, I acknowledge that the implied causation from mood is almost entirely an effect of syntax: I could say that 'what you get' influences mood, or that we're really talking about a higher-level description in which they are both simultaneously born and have been/are/will be temporarily persistent to some degree or other. Mood is continuously fed by the past, is both alterable and itself in the instant (with all the caution needed for that word) and, prophetically so to speak, is influenced by the cast of the instant into the future and the reflection backwards from that cast: not 'right down the same drain'.[2] And I wonder if, working with such lightening time-scales as you do, you'd find a word like 'mood' just too <u>general</u> for usage or whether, as I have just done, you'd place it into the syntax in this general sense and try to make sense of what, precisely, it is. This is close to current concerns of mine.

I have more work to do with your book, not least because it catches me at a time of considerable vulnerability. I am deliberately making a foray into the <u>conventional</u> novel to see what can be done with a certain theoretics which it would take me a long time to work out.[3] Not something to discuss because it's a project only. My point in conducting this foray is, in fact, a sense of the importance of these precisions of yours: you do not remove your eye from final objects and that you make the details of this gaze more exact for me. Always, it's what we work towards that counts and your book is thus personally useful for me.

Two further issues: 'This is the song & dance of a small minority'.[4] I have known your opposition to populism, and I have had a hefty two-year dosage of that, in its slack sense, at Essex. Also I recall Ed's being asked by an undergraduate at that curious Cambridge party we all went to, 'Who do you write for', etc.,

1 'retention of the lower in the higher', Oliver refers to his understanding of a Kierkegaardian tenet to which he returns below, 24 January 1978.

2 Oliver quotes *News of Warring Clans* (*Poems*, 280).

3 The novel to which Oliver refers was never published. On 10 June 1975 Oliver sent Prynne four pages of prose in typescript from the project, titled 'BNS special mid-fight report on the Junior Harm/less title bout'. Oliver's struggle and eventual disenchantment with the novel can be traced through his correspondence with the poet Peter Riley (b. 1940), a close friend with whom he maintained a life-long correspondence. References to the novel in the correspondence display an increasingly irritable attitude throughout the 1970s and 1980s. A letter of 2 December 1975 mentions that some 'boxing prose' is '*probably* to appear in Bean News 2', though Oliver is not mentioned in the contributor lists for any incarnation, published or unpublished, of Edward Dorn's satirical newspaper. By 21 May 1979 the 'boxing text' is 'showing signs of nearing completion'. On 6 April 1985 Oliver writes that the novel 'is the perennial white elephant awaiting yet another rewriting until it becomes a swan'. DOA, box 9. Oliver finally abandoned the novel altogether, developing what must have been a fraction of the projected work into sections of the prose and poetry of 'An Island That Is All the World' in *TVTH* (e.g., 60–3, 70–4).

4 Oliver quotes *News of Warring Clans* (*Poems*, 280).

18 December 1977

and answering 'I write for the most literate audience I can find.'[1] All right, the question of audience size, of mere 'popularity' has never concerned me for more than the occasional agonised moment. I am, however, worried about the question of genres. We're living in a time when the experimental itself has often become a genre, especially in the hands of meretricious performers; in so far as that is true, I should like to offend against the genre—hence my deliberate flirtation mentioned above. Second, 'Write when you get work' is a phrase that is easy to extract from your book and treat as a general maxim.[2] It is probably incorrect to do so. But I should merely like to say that we stand or fall by verisimilitudes at each instant and, if I found journalism too corrupt to continue despite my efforts to keep it clean, I found teaching at Essex presented no fewer enticements towards corruption of a less obvious, less important perhaps, sense. It's important to keep the praxis free from finance; but I have never thought there's anything special about writing in that sense. Some audiences can pay; others cannot make it pay; and each praxis commands a particular audience. I've raised that second question baldly like that because I think it brighter to do so. The following passage about the cheese is amazing.[3]

    The news is that I'm working every morning through the week, having seen Kate off to school at 7.45, and doing quite a considerable amount of the household tasks—two 'chores' afternoons a week, teas, oh, my dear, you've never seen anything like it. And I've just come back from my Eastern Arts tour of Milan and Turin where I saw world and national championships, dressing room scenes, interviewed management, sniffed at a weigh-in . . . and so on. Apart from a tight rein on finance, this new arrangement should work out O.K., for the moment at least: it was essential if I was to work on the long term that I wanted. Nothing succeeds like what succeeds what was.

    Hope Sue and the family are bright and breezy and that you'll actually get Christmas off and not be a-snippeting away at the student papers. Plans for the collected Prynne are . . . whereabouts just now?

    Doug.

---

30 December 1977   17 Ferry Path
                                                                                                              Cambridge

Dear Doug,
    Yes well there is much to say or guess about what you release into this backwashed season, where hope and fear are just part of the domestic heads & tails routine it all comes down to, in time. That it has a certain interest, and your tag to the mood problem comes to much the same: the continuum of moral process prior to a developed pronoun system. For the rule of thumb you quote, 'Take what you get' etc., is actually not directive but a modal prime or even optative fiat, with mood like a fast shot from a

---

[1] Edward Dorn. Dorn may well have playfully reversed T. S. Eliot's famous remark that he 'should like an audience which could neither read nor write'. *The Use of Poetry and the Use of Criticism: Studies in the Relation of Criticism to Poetry in England* (London: Faber and Faber, 1933), 152.

[2] Oliver quotes *News of Warring Clans* (*Poems*, 283).

[3] Oliver refers to *News of Warring Clans* (*Poems*, 283).

spent locker indeed a grammatical deletion of what split we might have wished to make between the voluntary and the intended. In my pre-1978 view the strictly was (September 1976) required consequence of compacted reciprocal seizure, the causatives separately conditional but overall a facetious mandate—you know, hyena-blather.

The grid might start firing like this: (a) if take is actively to select and grasp, then get is the availably matched passive, draining by fated mimicry the Man from the Pru;[1] (b) if take is passively to accept what events in their courses deal out as portion, then get is the active transformation of 'be made to take' (and I prefer 'be made' to 'be forced' for quite guessable reasons); but further (c), if get assumes the force elsewhere well attested of beget, then 'you' make your own of what your own already made, genetic determinism of the part-self in strict sequence from the service of perfect freedom; a general licence (d) of get as 'wrest from circumstance' I'd see as secondary sexual characteristic, in the usual post-industrial format, with the further touch of 'pick up on the run', to get in haste what you take at so-called leisure. All this I should surmise (a to d, with embedded variants) makes up a first-order grid of rapid off/on firing and matched counter-firing, where imperative modalities are crossed from active, passive and reflexive radicals. This disjunctive nexus of mood then may trigger second-order pathways, in exemption from Hobson's choice by shorting out the timing mechanism (why haven't the Firemen noticed this, with the Liberals already trapped before their eyes in the same blazing shell?).[2]

Before I sketch a diagram for the second order, let me hint that the somewhat snappy closure of prosody, around here, dresses up a linguistic primitivism not far from tearing one's hair out: I mean the near-autistic mutilations of phantom selfhood. Of course even very early pre-industrial Europe was nowhere as primitive as Billericay on New Year's Eve, say, but listen to what Lehmann says about mood in reconstructed verb systems: 'The uses of the optative and subjunctive were associated with that of a third mood, the imperative, marked by distinctive endings and used to express commands. The difficulties involved in attempting to determine the uses of these three moods in Proto-Indo-European are compounded by the presence of derivational affixes and by syncretism of the moods among one another and with derivational forms' (Proto-Indo-European Syntax, p. 184). These derivations of enclitic mood, from main-verb transitivity, Lehmann takes to be later features of what originally were verb forms not differentiated in respect to subject, that is, which were markedly innocent of pronominal management. Getting work was never the same as doing it; and writing was always what you did and not, anywhere I'd guess, what you got.

But later reconstruction by gnashing of teeth or pencil still leaves excess motive, and this siphons into the raised levels whereby (a) we actively accept (take) what we passively acquire

1 'Man from the Pru', advertising strapline referring to the iconic real-life door-to-door insurance salesmen of Prudential plc, British multinational life insurance and financial services company.

2 Prynne refers to the first ever national strike undertaken by British firefighters, which had begun on 14 November 1977 and was to last until 12 January 1978.

(get), an archly chiastic modus ponens where active/passive mirrors passive/active so as to produce exactly null vectors; the crypto-middle forms shew through in, e.g., to get paid, hurt, lost, to take fright, for granted, to be taken ill, etc. And also likewise, if the back which ensues is an adverbial pronoun (self in locative reflex) then the cancelled increment or alteration again takes the centre of the circle. The whole movement is thus an implied counter-factual eminently on offer for sidestep (just smart talk, exactly right) based on the two false pronouns, what and you, which the causative modality of the command/wish format denies by very assertion; Kenny explicates this adroitly: 'the felicitous utterance of an imperative actually presupposes that the sentence-radical it involves is descriptively false; for only if it is false can it be made true' (Will, Freedom and Power, p. 87).

In my present condition I'd incline therefore to take mood as that excess of consciousness over agency which makes moral feeling so frighteningly close to excuse. Thus take as modal plea for get, or get for take; or strictly as the moody chagrin from seeing take and get each, like twinned camshafts, exonerate the other. That's the siphon up into mood, down from which descend actions neither caused nor not caused, but attended; and with such prismatic brilliance of hue and cry, as the cycle makes up its primal, dressed-over word-salad. The reflex middle-voice brokerage of mood is even quite archaic; the Anglo-Saxon Wanderer is riddled with its colouring and gives a notable instance in the clause (l. 41a) þinceð him on mode (lit. 'it thinks to him in his mind'). Here however the yet more archaic impersonal is re-attached to a focus of consciousness by doubling the level. Not, then, 'it seems to him in his mind' (Dunning & Bliss) nor 'he dreams' (Leslie, p. 74), but 'the wanderer makes clear that his solitary man is aware that he is dreaming' (Leslie, p. 9, my italics); Leslie is exactly right to refer to a developed sequence of 'memory, dream, and hallucination' (p. 8).[1] At this level, before we pulled our selves together, we can see the cogito quite usually replaced by movements of thought and feeling to which the particular body is simply a loaned formation: the reflexive doubling of consciousness is labelled in compounds like modsefa (lit. 'mind-mind', hence 'mood-colouring of thoughtful awareness') and this can be projected quite out of a physical self (as in Seafarer, l. 59: min modsefa mid mereflode, lit. 'my cast of mind [departs from my body and journies forth] along with the sea-tide', even Pound got this right).[2] But now we barely tolerate it occurs to me as the most marginal idiom, weakly stripped of aspect. We prefer outright self-ownership on a crushing mortgage (my feelings, I think). The it of temporary or replacement agency is just that, a flimsy scaffold, easily appropriated as in the absurd romanticised bisexuality which Groddeck gave his Mahlerian it and which neatly provided homeopathic cover for Auden's he/she equivocations.[3]

Thus it's hard to separate mood from what's left over as the surplus of heightened affect, excess I-product, even though its

---

[1] T. P. Dunning and A. J. Bliss, eds., *The Wanderer* (London: Methuen, 1969), 112; R. F. Leslie, ed., *The Wanderer* (Manchester: Manchester University Press, 1966).

[2] Prynne refers to Ezra Pound's translation of *The Seafarer*: 'So that but now my heart burst from my breastlock, / My mood 'mid the mere-flood, / Over the whale's acre, would wander wide' (*The Translations of Ezra Pound* (London: Faber and Faber, 1953), 205–9 (208)).

[3] Georg Groddeck (1866–1934), German physician, widely recognized as an early influence on Auden.
   'bisexuality […] it', Prynne refers to Groddeck's 'idea of the double-sexed It ["das Es"] as an unknown force that animates humankind and reveals itself through symbols and symptoms', explored at length in Groddeck's epistolary *Das Buch vom Es: Psychoanalytische Briefe an eine Freundin* (Leipzig: Internationaler Psychoanalytischer Verlag, 1923). See Peter G. Christensen, 'Georg Groddeck's Defense of Homosexuality in *Das Buch vom Es*', *Monatshefte* 85, no. 2 (Summer 1993): 198–210 (201).

spillage into speech acts cast as imperative is persuasively shewn by Kenny (p. 34) to put actions in a larger frame than their performance takes up. (Gonda gives a related account of the early Indic injunctive, in The Character of the Indo-European Moods pp. 39–41, not that I believe much of this elephantine guesswork). But yes, also, I saw the airman signal and I got it, and then by a kind of aphasic disconnexion I could not move my left arm, the motor discharge flooded into moral eviction, making the 'phantom limb' of our saving fury which we still cannot put to work.[1] Oh be a sport, ancient person of my heart: oh cut and run. The neurologist produces the most unsparingly strict diagnosis—'the patient could not, indeed, pretend to perform an act with the left hand, but he could pretend with the right hand'. (Geschwind, Selected Papers on Language and the Brain, p. 188). Such pretence has to be accelerated to hallucination if it is to carve through cosmetic allotment and choosing, to mark that strict pain which is not pronominal as a referred sadism but paenitet/miseret, all the rest mere adverbial appropriation.[2] Come back nothing is already met at the close of Donne's ninth elegy, 'I shall ebbe out with them, who home-ward goe'; the added necessity in our time is of course that we should not claim protection by claiming to be serious. I have got a lot out of Bion, but that's where his limited access lies; he sees the point of lies as implying their speaker, just as he can work to achieve a denudation of memory and desire as 'essential for experiencing hallucination' (Attention and Interpretation, p. 36), but the negative capability on which this is based can only be contemplative.[3] In Geschwind's terms the confabulatory response to no memory is false recall (p. 171), and only an ironically pretended falsity opens up the higher levels to their lower subversive counterparts.

The void, then, is too artful, in the end too moody and if we cannot have action we'd better have jokes: not cynical but rather fast and not too clever. The rancid sexual clumsiness of Tarr is still somewhat exemplary, deconstructive dialectic as opposed to a Christmas tree like 'when a man sets his hand to something good, it is good that he should take what comes to him' (Phaedrus, XXIV).[4] Yet this is not right either, since outjested injury treats damage as a syllogism for pain: Kenny gets the negative at the correct fulcrum when he notes that 'one must have the ability not to ø if one is to ø because one wants to' (p. 143).[5]

And all the time, in the event, what we take and what we get each becomes increasingly congested, as you can't fail to see with your own strictness, by what we are. The same time-silt is exposed by Donne's bitterly fanciful word ebbe. The inertia in this shouldn't be at all read as a warning voice (then or now) because again I'd see that as description wrongly displaced to subjunctive perfectionism of mood, punishment thrown forward and then read back in substitution for how things stand or fall. Or is it possible to arrange the synthetic moral tantrums of current behaviours so that they make an architecture of strict

1 Prynne interpolates lines from Oliver's 'Central', from *The Diagram Poems*: 'I saw the airman signal / and I got it' (*Kind*, 113). Oliver first sent Prynne early versions of poems and diagrams from the sequence on 6 June 1972, enclosing 'Team Leader' and 'Importantly' (the latter is retitled 'P.C.' in the Ferry Press edition), first published in *Sesheta*, no. 4 (Winter 1972/1973): 4–7. Oliver sent Prynne a full set of eight poems and diagrams on 22 May 1977, including 'Central'. This version of the sequence was published in *Ochre*, no. 4 (n.d., ca. 1978).

2 The two Latin verbs to which Prynne refers are part of a group thought by some linguists to indicate the impersonal structure of Proto-Indo-European verb forms, along the lines that 'the case syntax of Latin verbs like *paenitet*, *pudet*, *piget*, and *miseret* is inherited from PIE [Proto-Indo-European] and represents an archaic pattern originally affecting all stative intransitives'. Ranko Matasović, 'Latin *paenitet me*, *miseret me*, *pudet me* and Active Clause Alignment in Proto-Indo-European', *Indogermanische Forschungen* 118 (2013): 93–110 (96). Prynne would have read Lehmann's version of this hypothesis in *Proto-Indo-European Syntax*, 111: 'For a large number of "impersonal" verbs point to an earlier system in which the actor, or subject, is not expressed.'

3 See Wilfred Bion, *Attention and Interpretation: A Scientific Approach to Insight in Psycho-Analysis and Groups* (London: Tavistock, 1970). Prynne refers to chap. 11, 'Lies and the Thinker', and interpolates from and quotes chap. 3, 'Reality Sensuous and Psychic', 35–6: 'Receptiveness achieved by denudation of memory and desire [...] is essential to the operation of psycho-analysis and other scientific proceedings. It is essential for experiencing hallucination or the state of hallucinosis. [...] By eschewing memories, desires, and the operations of memory, he [the psychoanalyst] can approach the domain of hallucinosis and the "acts of faith" by which alone he can become at one with his patients' hallucinations and so effect transformations O → K.' In Bion's terminology, 'O' denotes 'ultimate reality' or 'absolute truth' which is formless and unknowable, but which 'enters the domain K when it is has evolved to a point where it can be known, through knowledge gained by experience' (26).

4 *Tarr* (1918), novel by Wyndham Lewis. Prynne quotes Plato's *Phaedrus*, trans. R. Hackforth (Cambridge: Cambridge University Press, 1952), 154.

5 In Kenny's discussion of human free will in *Will, Freedom and Power* the symbol 'ø' refers to an agent's actions.

30 December 1977

falsity, and to contrive a category-space for orders of value simply unfilled, empty, not taken up? There was a time when nomadic indifferentism ('go anywhere') might have seemed, to me, not just corrective but nearer to correct, but now that leaves out too much of my sense that both action and passion generate waste; the most accurate matching is required if invention is exactly to balance the waste descriptively, and not to create the illusion of copious modal freedoms beyond what we unmistakably know to be the case. No tasks can be true if they can all be done falsely (see current wirephotos for details). 'Go anywhere' must be as close to 'don't refuse (because you can't)' as it is to 'claim the horizon of spontaneous choice': the as–as weighing makes a strict correlation from which both (e.g.) Angus Wilson and Sam Beckett are deviants into localisms of mood.[1] We are told too much about what isn't said, who doesn't say it, although from the outside (as you observe) a fixed genre looks worth its weight in special drawing rights.

Finally the copula cuts down the choice/chance dilemma, doesn't it, to replace that with tantamount identity: what you take is, operationally, what you get: the feedback is by definition as much as through existence: or, 'what is the case' includes both definition and existence as reciprocally causative (like personal credit-rating—we buy junk, sell antiques). Geschwind might raise his vocabulary up several levels to call the syntax of this a set of 'cross-modal associations in both directions' (p. 153), since the reduction brings it about (or ought to) that more is knowable, without specifying a subject or an object of knowledge. Too much memory will just cloud this over, justly no doubt but at such cost; and history is hardly more than protocol for pomposity. The shunt of time, and the rate of shift in moral pressure, these seem to me now to comprise the fabric from which pronouns are hastily put together with beguiling and luminous slickness—a pollution of terrific brilliance which I admire because it's real and because if I didn't I'd be just another stranded self-righteous humanitarian.

The whole of this leakage from some miscellaneous reading and semi-thinking does seem to me more static than would be true, I think, of how it feels. Because if any of the jokes are at all funny the deconstruction becomes reverse construction and that phrase at all twists into unaccounted prominence: an hallucinatory locative unhistorical and not even remotely provided for in moral declension. First-order narrative makes a naïve imitation of a more removed palinode, but the removal may be in both directions and at the final vector may be both parallel to and in the same ultimate sense as the original. Something candid, the scout-master after all?[2]

Of course I see you using what you call 'being vulnerable' so I'll not contest that more than somewhat loosest parlance.[3] From within the playpen of such intensive vacillation the outcome could be anything, yes I'll wait only because I have to and as you

---

[1] Angus Wilson (1913–91), British novelist.

[2] Prynne refers to the 'Scoutmaster', a figure in Oliver's *ICS*. See *Kind*, 95–7.

[3] In the copy of this letter preserved in Prynne's papers there is a gap between the penultimate and final paragraphs and no signature appears, suggesting that '[o]f course' begins a postscript.

say we fit into what we do by whatever ruses there are. I have never believed in perfection of the life. If you see Anthony, by the way (where else), please tell him I want to send a copy of the Clans and shall do so as soon as I have what looks like a passably real address.[1] And let's keep in touch if we can, and I hope you'll let someone do the Diagram Poems as soon & fast as possible.

[1] Anthony Barnett (b. 1941), British poet and publisher. Barnett published the first collected editions of both Prynne's and Oliver's poems in 1982 and 1987, respectively: *Poems* (Edinburgh: Agneau 2, 1982); *Kind* (London: Agneau 2 / Allardyce, Barnett, 1987).

[2] Benjamin Lee Whorf (1897–1941), American linguist.

24 January 1978

42 New Street
Brightlingsea, Essex

Dear Jeremy,

Despite my use of the word 'warning' (which must have been how I was taking your sequence) I was pleased to find your counter-phrase of 'optative fiat', because that's exactly my sense of the pre-ethical, to use another term of yours with which I'm quite happy. It is that the mind-act entails a moment of transcendental awareness {Haven't a better word} of its four-ways-at-once nature, including a future arrow as a conjunction of possibility and necessity (if those terms are still appropriate); and that this gives rise to 'optative fiat'. In a sense, this moment of awareness isn't the mind's but is more like things as they are, the real, etc.; nevertheless, it is the start of awareness and contains all that subsequently lower, but still transcendent, levels should contain, were it not for distortions, and all that conscious awareness strives for, in its best activities. That's as near as I can get to it just now.

I was fond of your take and get dynamics and all that it gave rise to, since I am weak in real grammatical expertise and hadn't more than an intuition of the depths involved. But it does leave me like an amateur who has to trust the experts rather cautiously when you go on to quote Lehmann on syncretism of moods in the Proto-Indo-European. That is, I was aware, from practical work I did some years back on retroflexive sound patterns in Sanskrit (consonantal continuities in series—an English equivalent in 'beginning winning', for example), that Sanskrit didn't have a subjunctive. But that was all I knew. Now, I understand the point, and if I remain as this amateur, unsure about when, when not, and exactly how far we can extrapolate, Whorf-like from the facts of language, you convince me your limits are proper in a phrase like 'pronomial management', since that keeps the extrapolation to the factual field in question.[2]

It might be helpful to explain my focus, however, if I return to a concept I find in your third par, 'the near-autistic mutilations of phantom selfhood', because I have recently been thinking that a scornful dismissal of the mere idea of such mutilations—I won't cite the poets in question because it's not germane—is insufficient; a concentration upon the mutilations might be … curative, let's say. And I look to others for greater subtlety on the ontological goal itself. Hence my question about mood: except in its sense of 'optative fiat', (keeping to that term throughout) mood is probably always associated with the mutilations in question—more or less greater in gravity of effect from the 'normal' to the pathological. So you see how set up I am to agree with many of your formulations.

The two examples of mood-like deformation that you take from the Anglo-Saxon may presumably be linked with the Latinate Christianity of these pieces, perhaps feeding in from both pathways (pastways) of that cultural crossroads. Looking again at Wanderer in Everyman trans., it makes me think that Christianity was so early in this country and in its priestcraft helped to introduce deferred rewards into the dynamic; it can easily give sorrow a whimsical value that marries quite well with the ubi sunt in the poem and with the social impulses which bring about cause of regret.[1] But to locate this more exactly in its language-context, as you have done with 'it thinks to him in his mind', was new and extremely interesting to me. We're dealing with that ancient psychology of the heart that 'thinks' and is also sad: a potential union there, but also prey, perhaps because of its physiological superstition, to the apparently impersonal visitation of thoughts. And in the Latin culture we have those dreams that travel, as in Ovid: not the fiercer, speedier mind-acts of more primitive shamanism. Surely one of the signs that Chaucer is on the threshold of the cogito is his burlesque of these travelling dreams in the Boke of the Duchesse (and elsewhere), where the legacy of the impersonal dream now becomes fit for Macrobius' [sic] to develop and can be purchased by the burlesque dreamer in a merchant's gift transaction—a gilt bed, etc.[2] The difference between an offering and a sacrifice. Amid such dangers, the modesty, the humour and the sidling, self-effacing 'I' in Chaucer is an immense rescue for him but, as a mere strategy, is not very helpful for the following era.

Among many of our contemporaries just now is a commonly-shared 'correct inexactness' about the dynamic, because the lessons taught by the few who originally saw into this dynamic have now been learnt. All to the good I suppose, but it has led to a glib confidence that what isn't wrong with a poetic claim is therefore right, even though its mood might seem to another very questionable. And it's very hard to become more exact about the dynamic than the precision we already have—the easiest thing in the world is apparently to be sharing in the available vision by piling up parallel cases of its latency: correspondences, supposed, between DNA and the I Ching; truck with slime moulds; and I don't know what else. This, to be bald, is why I get so much use from your own inquiries; they really do promise greater exactness yet in a field where the finally-exact is perhaps withheld from us. So excuse me if I retreat from the white-hot into the realm of the phantom self and its mutilations, because I feel that there are other precisions to make there. And I have to say immediately that it concerns mood not in the grammatically pure, pristine sense, which you have attractively defined for me,

---

[1] 'ubi sunt' (lit. where are ... [they]?), a formula common to several Latin and Old and Middle English texts, including *The Wanderer*, where it takes the form 'Hwær cwom [...]?'

[2] Macrobius, early fifth-century commentator on Cicero's *Somnium Scipionis* (The dream of Scipio), a highly influential text on later medieval dream visions such as Chaucer's.

but in its debased forms, the forms which, as you know so well, we usually live by, despite our unseen 'unknown' wishes. Owing to a recent and worrying encounter, the theme is alive with me as I write: but my original entrée into it came several years ago via a meeting with a writer on voodoo, Francis Huxley; this married with my personal insistence that despite the dubiousness of all his moods Kierkegaard was correct to hold to the Hegelian gnosis: lower forms of the 'I' persist in the higher.[1]

The voodoo pantheon seems to be linked with the bodily expression of debased yet transcendental I-forms expressed in dance and quasi-dance and then hypostatised into various gods. Hence the similarity between, say, Baron Samedi, {and some mental patients.} So much is clear. The ready assumption of Christian figures into the voodoo pantheon is interesting to me too—a result of Jesuitical priestcraft meddling presumably—not least interesting here because voodoo pathology, Christian priestcraft's pathology, and the modern psychology of the mental hospital have all to do with the mutilations of the phantom self. They are like a mistake about the nature of the relationship between: the transcendent forms, the transcendence of the transcendent forms, and the ordinary attitude.[2] I have just skimmed through a bad French example of this, L'Ange, by Lardreau and Jambet. The book looks to the early church fathers and to the angelicas as a way out of that dreadful hole the French are in because of the doctrines about problematics: you can't rebel without creating the dialectic of the problematic against which you rebel, and so on. How do we escape? Almost by transfiguration, as far as I could gather in my hasty progress through a pretentious text that I didn't want to detain me once I'd got the general drift. Glucksmann, hunting down 'maître-penseurs' should look to his own age ...[3]

To display the implicitly Christian view in L'Ange more clearly and to lay a groundwork for what I shall go on to say about mood, I'll take an utterly familiar kind of quote from RLS which I hunted out recently for its Scottish voice-tones (a relic of those in my own tones, you see).[4] I don't suppose the text would naturally be interesting to you; so I'll quote at length:

> It follows that man is twofold at least; that he is not a rounded and autonomous empire; but that in the same body with him there dwell other powers tributary but independent. If I now behold one walking in a garden, curiously coloured and illuminated by the sun, digesting his food with elaborate chemistry, directing himself by the sight of his eyes, accommodating his body by a thousand delicate balancings to the wind and the uneven surface of the path, and all the time, perhaps, with his mind engaged about America, or the dog-star, or the attributes of God—what am I to say, or how am I to describe the thing I see? Is that truly a man, in the rigorous meaning of the word? or is it not a man and something else? What, then, are

1 Francis Huxley (1923–2016), British author, anthropologist, and botanist. Oliver refers to Huxley's *The Invisibles: Voodoo Gods in Haiti* (New York: McGraw-Hill, 1966).
   'Kierkegaard [...] lower forms of the "I" persist in the higher', Oliver would have read about this Kierkegaardian tenet in Gregor Malantschuk, *Kierkegaard's Thought*, ed. and trans. Howard V. Hong and Edna H. Hong (Princeton, NJ: Princeton University Press, 1971), 132–8. Three pages of notes on earlier sections of Malantschuk's book are preserved in Oliver's papers (DOA, box 6). Malantschuk writes: 'As Kierkegaard sees it, the content of the subject's previous experience is fully retained when a new factor enters or when a new stage begins, but each time the total content is seen in a new perspective' (136).

2 'ordinary attitude', Oliver refers to the sense of 'natural attitude' employed in Edmund Husserl's transcendental phenomenology, especially in his *Cartesian Meditations* (1931; first English trans. by Dorion Cairns, 1960), as differentiated by Husserl from the transcendental subjectivity of phenomenological reflection. The 'attitude', as A.D. Smith explains, characterizes the realm of everyday experience ('including that of the most sophisticated "positive" sciences') as essentially '"*naïve*", because, being wholly given over to a concern with entities within the world, with objects presumed to be real, it simply *overlooks* the functioning subjectivity in which alone such objects can arise, or in which they are constituted'. *Husserl and the Cartesian Meditations* (Abingdon: Routledge, 2003), 42.

3 André Glucksmann, *Les maîtres penseurs* (Paris: Grasset, 1977).

4 Robert Louis Stevenson (1850–94), Scottish novelist.

24 January 1978

we to count the centre-bit and axle of a being so variously compounded?... There is Something that was before hunger and that remains behind after a meal ((!)). It may or may not be engaged in any given act or passion ((?)) but when it is, it changes, heightens, and sanctifies. Thus it is not engaged in lust, where satisfaction ends the chapter; and it is engaged in love, where no satisfaction can blunt the edge of the desire, and where age, sickness, or alienation may deface what was desirable without diminishing the sentiment. This something, which is the man, is a permanence which abides through the vicissitudes of passion, now overwhelmed and now triumphant, now unconscious of itself in the immediate distress of appetite or pain, now rising unclouded above all. So, to the man, his own central self fades and grows clear again amid the tumult of the senses, like a revolving Pharos in the night. It is forgotten; it is hid, it seems for ever; and yet in the next calm hour he shall behold himself once more, shining and unmoved among changes and storm.[1]

This is the kind of passage, a Christian's answer to Montaigne, which all of us are equipped these days to answer. Its merit for me lies almost entirely in its last sentence, though I have thought the rest needful to quote. For the rest of the passage, it is evidently a wrong dynamics, and the only respects in which RLS can lead us beyond a Christian patrician conservatism is in exposing how much the Freudian is indebted to a Judeo-Christian worry about 'instincts'. But RLS had actually 'seen' the phantom appearing in his language, and it <u>can shine</u> (the word is exact); he was fortunately just too early to follow Freud in reifying it in that particular Freudian way which is the iambian pentameter of modern psychology, now adhered to only by the old-stagers. (Jekyll and Hyde were a more muddly reification—but they, too, were <u>seen</u>, in a dream). None of this would matter were it not for the persistence of these phantoms—which are already transcendent to the normal attitude—even in their own transcendence into more universal prospects, the shining colourlessness of true knowing. My daughter Kate wrote when about 7, about a desert island, 'I dreamt that I was in the world and all the windows were shining.' The phantoms persist because their transcendence is never perhaps so perfect that we don't in the simultaneity of the mind-act fail to pass through them but have to live somewhat pathologically, able to reach beyond our own pathology into the 'optative' where the pathology exists but is no longer serious. An aside here: we do have to beware of a misuse of self–other transcendence in phenomenology or misconceptions from drug visions, as in the false-prophet side of William Burroughs (I'm thinking of his daft interview with Mottram).[2] A recipe for merely pretending the non-existence of privacy, for forgetting the past stages of transcendence, won't do. We have to bring privacy to the state in which it matters as the fixed frame location

---

[1] Robert Louis Stevenson, *Lay Morals and Other Papers* (London: Chatto and Windus, 1911), 27–8.

[2] Eric Mottram (1924–95), British poet. Oliver refers to Mottram's interview with Burroughs in *Les langues modernes* 59, no. 1 (Janvier–Février 1965): 79–83.

from which the universal <u>this time</u> arose and swept it up while retaining it; but a state in which it doesn't matter too because now it is embedded as properly as may be in its manifold. For we're talking about a living, a being-lived-through, manifold, not a grid or a print-out of a matrix. 'Something candid, the scoutmaster after all?' as you say.

It's time to start dismantling Stevenson, however (using him also as a stalking horse to aim at any disguised Freudianism that lurks in many discussions that pretend to have reached beyond Freud by simple denials or cosmic confidence).

To begin with, the phantom selves are much more complex, as even RLS seems to have sensed. First, we obviously shouldn't settle into this simple, religious opposition: 'true self' vs changing, 'everyday' self—that's imprecise about the temporal aspects, to say the least. The everyday self phantom is a conscious construction, largely rational, having its own pasts and futures and its own minute stasis. It arises along with the 'will', or conscious intention. The 'true self' is one of the transcendent phantoms, an accrued resultant of imperfect dynamics—never therefore entirely 'true', {though a 'true' accretion…} except in its interested persistence formally: and yet it too changes, very slightly, instant by instant—this may give rise to a curious, floating quality in the phantom, a slowness; and that particular kind of slowness interests me too. Because most of us, generally speaking, seek to act well most of the time, the accretions of this 'true self' are in <u>sum</u> pleasurable to us in the ethical sense, almost by Benjamin Franklin profit and loss.[1] But even if it isn't true but a phantom the nature of its change—since the change itself is a congeries of events arising in the notional instant—is extremely important; it is owing to these levels of imperfect dynamics descending from the notional instant of the mind-act down to 'true' self and down to true-self-seen-through-mood (which I'll come to) and thence down to conscious levels, that mood, in its <u>debased</u> sense, arises.

But to talk first of the highest level: in the perspective of the universal, mood is purified and I've been willing to take 'optative fiat' as its term: the dynamic fully unified, we wish what is to be wished, and are the wish—transcendent to the 'true self' of RLS and its not quite first-rate persistence. In this universal perspective, 'true self' is a queasy, slowly moving local frame in universal time, a frame whose real referents cannot be contained simply in the frame and don't just <u>include</u> the Other, as by Whitmanesque assimilation; rather the frame is properly embedded, as I say.

However, our praxis of the event distorts the universal, gives rise to phantoms at various levels, and because of this gives rise to mood in the secondary, debased sense, which includes the ordinary emotions, fear, joy, etc., and their overall tonic: the mood. I quote you here: 'I'd incline therefore to take mood as that excess of consciousness over agency which makes moral feeling so frighteningly close to <u>excuse</u>.' Your whole discussion is very live for me; and I wonder if we're not closer than may

---

[1] Oliver refers to Franklin's elaboration of 'the practices of [double-entry] bookkeeping […] into an ethics based on the concept of the balanced book', such that '[a]ccounting for the self becomes […] a process of continuous ethical monitoring that is seamlessly integrated into the fabric of everyday life.' Andrew Lawson, 'Becoming Bourgeois: Benjamin Franklin's Account of the Self', *ELH* 87, no. 2 (Summer 2020): 463–89 (474, 480, and passim).

appear. We have to explain how in entering consciousness mood also quietens down: the <u>stab</u> of fear seems to come from transcendency, though the description, fear, is a conscious one which, together with other rationalisations helps to control it by setting it into a different temporal event (s) {in which the rationally calm may dominate.} I have a query about the word 'excess' therefore, mainly I think in terms of the image it conjures of mood as spill-over, whereas I see it as a twisting-out-of-true/real that overtakes the whole dynamics: to talk very strictly, mood distorts the dynamics <u>not</u> in the notional <u>instant</u> of its birth, though the inadequacy could probably be viewed there, displayed on the simultaneous screen of the instant—rather, it begins to transform and distort the dynamic the instant after the instant, so to speak, as instantly a flatness or imbalance in the energy begins to create skew effects in consciousness that we call our mood and which sometimes has single or mixed tonics that we can name, secondarily, as emotions; then the mood plays down all the levels from the notional instant down to transcendent self–other phantoms, down eventually to the everyday self. It is also reciprocal: our mood has been present in the prophetic side of the instant and has then had its effect{; should clearly end up describing} the instant no longer in notional but in real terms as the dynamic's singularity{, but it was convenient to freeze it just now.} However, by reverse, the mood in its <u>conscious</u> aspects totally conditions the view we might have had and do yet half-glimpse of all levels transcendent to the everyday self{; reciprocally, conscious mood} helps to hide from us, it may be, the universal at the highest level. Because moods, being tonics, fall into semi-recognisable patterns—again, 'anger', 'fear' etc.—the kinds of effect they have in our reverse suspicion of what has taken place along all the transcendent levels are complex. Certainly, they are more complex than the versions of Freud or RLS; but we can speak loosely of them and say that they're not <u>all that</u> complex because the effect of the routine tonic patterns is so total in conditioning our glimpse of the transcendental phantoms. However, at the level of transcendental phantom, possibility is magnified enormously, and hence the effect of mood, colouring our view, is similarly magnified. Thus, we have angels and demons: a certain universality in ethnic representations of demons is hardly to be explained away by Jungian means; it is the effect of mood upon the transcendental—it's not a fixed universality, though. And, as I say, it's more complex than angels and demons: we have all manner of other mutilations; for example, the dull, energyless phantom endlessly climbing up hill, associated with Sisyphus, depressions, etc. Picasso's 'Weeping Woman'. Or, one other example, again not from the obvious cast-list available in voodoo, a curious phantom that I have observed, I believe, in the body movements of 'fun-loving' adults (those who are immature but like to scamper): this one is, perhaps precisely, a happy, leaping child that persists (with a touch of monkey-like ugliness because it isn't suitable for the age it inhabits) in the adult and fuses into a complex phantom that lives inside the movements. The faulty past-dynamic (refusal to let go of childhood) is particularly clearly expressed in that phantom. Some mental illness, then, becomes for me an overwhelming of the personality by the emotions such that a patient is close to the provenance of the emotions, and thus to transcendent levels; his consciousness gets nearer than normal to its instants, sufficiently close for it to see the phantoms literally. And, alas, mood determines frighteningly whether they are to be desirable or not, so that fear, of course, once seen as a terrible risk, can hardly be avoided. Since you quote Kung Fu in the Clans,[1] here's a quote from the TV (must be Tao, I suppose): 'The gate of the temple is guarded by demons.' Note that, Mr. Burroughs.

But I don't mean to restrict the description merely to pathological behaviour, since, of course, mood is arising and persisting and changing constantly with all of us, just as the phantom selves are. Let me try for a definition, because I'd like to see it knocked down by you:

Imbalance (e.g. retention of past, unrealism in respect of present and future) in the dynamic gives rise to phantom selves at various levels (all of them too late but nevertheless also to be 'seen' in the notional instant). In the notional instant of the dynamic these phantom selves are there already displayed as potential and {in the description of singularity are} already there. All mood other than 'optative fiat' (which may in fact be the overall control condition, the 'real' mood itself) arises partly as the effect of the imperfect dynamic and the transcendentally imperfectly-wished-for phantom selves it creates and partly as back reflection on this from existing conscious mood which, entering the simultaneity of the notional instant, both spoils the dynamic, depressing it, making it potentially angry, fearful, cautious, weak or whatever, and also alters our glimpse of the phantoms it creates. Only in such a way can I explain paranoia, or how a chance remark can suddenly make us extremely depressed: we have a glimpse of the phantom that is already and is now being distorted. Thus, too, a Hitler discovers and maintains instant by instant the demonic body actions suitable for the underlying content of his oratory—if the German people had half of the body language expertise of a voodoo priest the Second Vorld Var vould never ... etc.

I've thought a lengthy reply upon one aspect more useful than a ranging over your very fertile letter. As you say, a touch of the candid.

I'm in Cambridge this Thursday to read to the university P.S. Anthony will probably be with me and I either shall stay with John and Wend or come back the same night: it depends upon certain developments this end and I have to phone the James's v. soon. I'd like to pay a call en famille to you and Sue some time this spring, if possible. Any chance?

Doug.

[1] Oliver refers to *News of Warring Clans* (*Poems*, 282).

24 January 1978

1 Ælfric, 'On the Assumption of the Blessed Mary', in *The Homilies of the Anglo-Saxon Church: The First Part, Containing the Sermones Catholici, or Homilies of Ælfric; In the Original Anglo-Saxon, with an English Version*, vol. 1, trans. Benjamin Thorpe (London: Printed for the Ælfric Society, 1844), 443.

2 *The Times* (which Prynne read throughout his career) recorded the Royal Assent given to the Bees Act 1980 on 21 March 1980, 10.

'your GR explication', 'the first piece', Prynne refers to Oliver's essays 'On J. H. Prynne's "Of Movement Towards a Natural Place"' and 'Even Poets Can Have Beliefs about Poetic "Stress"', in *Grosseteste Review* 12 (1979): 93–102, 12–32.

P.S. I am not in fact so clear about the relation between 'true' self and the rest as this text makes me appear but I have been trying to avoid fashionable kinds of language which would merely make this difficulty seem to disappear. I'd welcome your comments anyway.

2 June 1979

[*Prynne sent a copy of* Down Where Changed *(London: Ferry Press, 1979), with an author's compliments slip that collages the British government's Central Statistical Office letterhead (featuring the royal coat of arms) above the following text:*]

With the compliments of
The Quotient

'Hwæt is ðeos ðe her astihð swilce arisende dæg-rima, swa wlitig swa móna, swa gecoren swa sunne, and swa egeslic swa fyrd-truma?'
　'What is this that here ascends like the rising dew of morn, as beauteous as the moon, as choice as the sun, and as terrible as a martial band?'[1]

EVERYTHING YOU HEAR IS TRUE

[*1979*]

[*Prynne's papers preserve undated photocopies of two inscriptions in Oliver's* The Diagram Poems. *These are: 'For Jeremy / [cartoon head] / Doug' and 'This copy to Jeremy Prynne / from the frightener cell / Doug Oliver'. The 'frightener cell' quotes 'Central', from* The Diagram Poems, *n.p.*]

24 March 1980　　　　　　　　　　　17 F[*erry*]P[*ath*]
　　　　　　　　　　　　　　　　　　　Cantab

I seem to be in some canyon of not writing letters, at the moment; but with the Bees Act about to receive Royal Assent here are belated thanks for your GR explication, and indeed for the first piece also where many thoughts & their contrails mesh into Own Brand.[2] Who knows, one day we might even skip the hit & run chat (social 'events'), and meet to consider deliberately?
　J.

2 April 1980   42 New Street
                                      Brightlingsea, Essex

Dear Jeremy,

    I was very glad to get your card just before leaving for an Easter on the South Coast. Hence hurried reply.

    Well, I'm pleased you thought the article on 'Of Movement' was useful. I have deliberately not approached you for your opinion because I essentially see the work of criticism as distinct from mere friendship, so to speak … And there's really rather a lot of the latter in our journals. As for the first article on stress I'm very interested to hear that we seem not to be distant in view; and this is certainly something I should much like to discuss with you in detail (these days, detail is what's really important). I was in Cambridge for an Open University lecture a week or so back and just had time to call in on John and Wendy nearby. They told me you'd been very busy with academic matters these past few months. What I'd like to do is come and see you, if convenient, in a month or so, when you'll be free of exam marking and some affairs of my own have settled. Could we fix a definite date in, say, end-May/early June?

    I've spent most of my days scrabbling around, predictably, for extra income, giving odd lectures, poetry readings, and undertaking Open University tutoring (which is like opening your door in Canada to an avalanche of mail). When really I'm trying to write a book incorporating my work on stress, the article on your poem, and much else. But it's only life itself, isn't it?

    Which I hope hasn't caught up with you irretrievably. Let me know if a meet is possible.

      Best,
          Doug.

8 April 1980   17 Ferry Path
                                      Cambridge

Dear Doug,

    Yes let's arrange to meet, as you say, and fix a time when we are nearer to the point of entry. Mind you, of course, as a fairly constant non-reader of my own work I'm out towards the margin in regard to the reflexive part of your enquiries. Which is maybe why I respond so to <u>retrospective</u> stress (and its <u>prospective</u> counterpart). In many cases, for me, the ideal reading would produce vocal stress-encounter as <u>conditional</u>, recognised to refer to or even to depend for life on the flare of a mind-act in the array of material presentation. By flare I mean as hands spread or the self is manifestly focussed & continuous through change. The ideal, then, would be substantially no stress and no non-stress: and certainly no liturgic monotony (the drone of false absence). I mean this literally. When I hear a person read I want to learn not what he understands but that he does so, his response to being the instrument for a realisation which he

[1] Ferruccio Busoni (1866–1924), Italian pianist and composer. Prynne refers to his *Sketch of a New Esthetic of Music*, trans. Theodore Baker (New York: G. Schirmer, 1911): 'the pianoforte has one possession wholly peculiar to itself, an inimitable device, a photograph of the sky, a ray of moonlight—the Pedal' (44).

Prynne's second quotation is ascribed by Alexander Chancellor to Dick Etheridge, communist and former trade union convenor at the Longbridge British Leyland plant in Birmingham, in the 1 March 1980 issue of *The Spectator* (5). Chancellor's subject is the sacking by British Leyland of Etheridge's successor, Derek Robinson, the previous November.

[2] The machine that Oliver used to obtain the frequency readings used in 'Even Poets Can Have Beliefs' was a real-time speech intonation spectrometer, lent to him by H. C. Longuet-Higgins at the University of Sussex; he was taught how to use it by Anne Cutler, a linguist then at Sussex. In *Poetry and Narrative in Performance* (hereafter cited as *PNP*), Oliver explains: 'The machine traces lines of light across a screen, each line indicating a frequency filtered out from the overall sound waves of the voice as the performer reads' (77).

[3] Prynne's papers preserve a photocopy of the title page to F. R. Leavis, *Reading Out Poetry and Eugenio Montale—a Tribute* (Belfast: Queen's University of Belfast, 1979), though likely only a copy of 'Reading Out Poetry' was enclosed. With regards to the 'nisus', Leavis writes: 'What [Eliot] has [in *Ash-Wednesday*] beside hunger in the emptiness, is the Christian nisus, for after all he was brought up in what was in some sense a Christian culture, and from the recognition of that nisus in himself he starts' (8). Prynne refers to Leavis's comments on reading out lines from Pope's *Dunciad*, bk. 4: 'And you can imagine if you like, lying down sometimes, reading with a pencil in your hand and marking the kind of curve, you know, in a line, above each line. You'll find, when you've done that [...] the astonishing diversity, the essential diversity of movement (which, of course, is a very complex concept) from line to line' (26).

cannot impart directly but only shew as raising his own power & control. That he feels what he knows, crudely put, may even occlude what he knows about it, his reading may be fuller because less given over to polarities of demonstration. Which is thus a deep eventual truth in prosody: no stress, merely, because the unstressed is the condition for knowing that we come to know and feel what by convergence & repetition makes the profile of disclosure, resorbed into the listener's alerted quiet.

Of course it doesn't often happen like this, there must be some character to support plot, the idea of a culture wants baskets for produce at the check-out. But an interesting case is that of lines one has long known by heart; in revisiting these, and running through them in one's mind, one discovers them often as stress-less, yet charged with accumulated momentum? Something close to psalmic in such moments? Certainly we can't allow ourselves mere inward frisson, privately sure, or not often; when Busoni says of the piano's pedal that it's 'a photograph of the sky' he may be far on the way to Rilke and soft fruit ('more ways of killing a pig than stuffing its throat with strawberries', as was the word at Longbridge before the snouts were goaded back from the trough).[1] That would make stress the mark of humps in distribution, a political response to outreach and to interest in the old and the newer senses.

An advantage of your machine is that it mostly fends off fanciful mystifications such as this.[2]

À bientôt:
J.

P.S. You might care to see the enclosed effort to locate a nisus and even (p. 26) to mark its passage...[3]

19 April 1980   42 New Street
                                                 Brightlingsea, Essex
Dear Jeremy,
Your letter and enclosure awaited me on return from an Easter break. I am of course aware of the implications presented by processes of reflection in inquiries such as mine; but I have wished for some time to site all my inquiries whether creative or critical in that area where 'normal' inquiries begin. My own sense of the virtue of heightened consciousness is that it should also have an address (heeded or not doesn't matter) to ordinary consciousness, since there isn't exactly a radical discontinuity between the two, but the one hides in the other like the gold in the embers. Your opening-out of what Leavis is saying is clearly apposite to this; and helpful. My conviction of the essential equivoque between stress and duration can most happily accord with the overturning of liturgic monotony and that very interesting experience you record (and I can see in my own responses) of the stressless, momentum-charged re-encounter with lines

one knows by heart. I have another version of that which I have tried to raise in my boxing prose and elsewhere: that in the heart of the swiftest events we can encounter a slower, overall knowledge: like the sadness of seeing a man gradually defeated, the greyness of that; or, more obviously, a slower quality that arises in the swift events of a waterfall, in which the formal glimpse is of 'something' hurrying internally with swift movement and yet itself not still but, as you say, tremulous with a momentum of its own that almost seems to apply (like Donne's infinite regression of time series) to an order which sustains <u>this</u> order. (Though I don't seek to explain it via Donne …)

Given the preoccupations I mention above, I've come to think that there's point in providing a starting-point in one's work for 'the stage of the undesirable'. Since my own praxis is more that of a Boccaccio than that of a Petrarch, so to speak, I think of the plague that I want first to acknowledge—the plague of hellish emotional states, of your distribution lumps, and of everyday competition. And then to try to move it all into a better condition: I do believe in that ancient moral function. I look into myself and see such a morass there, so much reflexivity and self-seeking: the work must always acknowledge this, one's ordinary life, or otherwise it becomes just an expression of privilege, of heightened consciousness—of the uselessness of that Timothy Leary <u>tone</u>.[1] [Not to mention the crankiness of Burroughs.] Perhaps the most interesting thing to do is to offend against some precious avant-gardiste conceptions <u>first</u>, and then to try to work the offence back towards the conceptions, so that there should be some record of that process and of its necessity: from hell, through quasi-moral insight and reflection, to those spreading hands of the self that you talk of. Not to 'win converts' but to leave the record of the process in a sequence of art-forms. That's my current endeavour; and that is why I've become a reflective reader of your poem, for now: that passage and the piece on prosody are intended to form part of a book that will, via reflection, attempt to begin shifting the <u>ordinary</u>, prose, novelistic, undesirabilities of my boxing novel towards the light. (Can you, incidentally, give me the true source for 'anima tota in singulis membris sui corporis'?[2] It's too like several things for me to be able to track it precisely down (e.g. not only Plotinus, but Augustine, Anselm, Aquinas and Ficino would all come <u>vaguely</u> near it, I suppose, in their very different ways, to say nothing of the hermetics …)

I'll give you a ring in a few weeks' time. My own phone number by the way is Brightlingsea 4995 (recently installed).
    Best,
        Doug.

P.S. I have lectured on Pope drawing just the lines Leavis proposes, but for the <u>Essay on Man</u>—less interesting than those quoted from <u>The Dunciad</u>, but more elementary. I have some poor Essex U. machine traces of those <u>Essay</u> lines too.[3]

19 April 1980

---

1 Timothy Leary (1920–96), American psychologist.

2 Oliver refers to the Latin phrase interpolated into 'Of Movement Towards a Natural Place' from Saint Anselm's *Proslogion*, chap. 13: 'Si enim non esset anima tota in singulis membris sui corporis, non sentiret tota in singulis' ('For if the soul were not wholly in each of the parts of its body it would not sense wholly in each of them'). *St. Anselm's* Proslogion, trans. M. J. Charlesworth (Oxford: Clarendon Press, 1965), 132–5 (133).

3 The 'Essex U. machine' was an electro-glottograph which recorded the fundamental frequency of Oliver's subjects' speaking voices by measuring their glottal buzz: 'Subjects read into an acoustic microphone but with an F.J. Electronics electro-glottograph's electrodes strapped to their throats. The resultant audio waves were recorded on one track of a double-track tape while signals from the glottal buzz (providing a fundamental frequency reading) were recorded on the other track. […] The audio signal was […] passed directly into [a] mingograph to yield a raw wave form. The glottal buzz was fed into a fundamental frequency meter'. Oliver, 'Fundamental Frequency Studies as a Preliminary to the Literary Criticism of Poetry', *Journal of Phonetics* 11 (1983): 1–35 (3–6).

Oliver's machine traces of lines from Pope's *Essay on Man* ('Know then thyself, presume not God to scan; / The proper study of Mankind is Man. / Plac'd on this isthmus of a middle state, / A being darkly wise, and rudely great') were published in 'Voicing Patterns as One Key to the Pace of Poetry', *Journal of Phonetics* 12 (1984): 115–32 (120–2, 126); and in *PNP*, 40–3.

15 August 1982 — 17 Ferry Path, Cambridge

Dear Doug,

It was very good, and timely, to meet again and have some talk. Do let me see your phonetics piece when it's ready and I'll send across the water any clipping on the Bumper Book which comes my way.[1] Of course I'd like to get a squinny at the twinset-&-pearl project, but I suppose it would not be good for me to see it before you have finished.[2] You know how I fret about such things and indeed here are the notes on the Diagram--Poems to prove it.[3] I cannot now reconstruct what was to have been the leading point to the note I was then composing, after my copy had arrived and before I was stuck by not being able to get back to the Vermeule book; but it was the inner movement of feeling and blockade I was connecting with, even though through the apparent externals of syntax & text-variants. I still feel deeply the power of this sequence, and on looking back over it I have the sense of having already memorised not its meaning, exactly, but the presence of what it has meant to me. Ah well, bon voyage, come and visit again on one of your return flits, when you can.

Bien à toi,
J.

9 November 1982 — Gonville and Caius College, Cambridge

Dear Doug,

Thanks for the speedy note and the carefully unspeedy article.[4] I have read this only on the run, so far, as a most welcome extension of the GR 12 piece, and you'll realise how timely and apt I consider this kind of work to be.[5] (As, incidentally, also did Kenneth Rexroth, another sign of his good sense; see his American Poetry in the Twentieth Century, 1973, pp. 168–9.)[6] This is just a note at one of the possible tangents, really, concerning the Wyatt quatrain which was your principal specimen.[7] I think it presents unusual difficulties (and thus, of course, especial interest), and I guess that these may complicate rather a lot your findings and discussion. The point is one about tune and a hypothetical 'best tune' or 'median tune', in relation to perception of meaning and to interpretation in spoken performance.

Naturally the assignment of stress-position and stress-value without reference to intonation, while interesting in the specification of rule-governed grids as these apply to prosodic modes and genres, cannot be of more than preliminary use to a consideration of actual texts in spoken performance. Here the range of permitted variation and modulation, within the metrical frame, of the speech-effect parameters available for shaping a tune, make the prosodic constraints and directives a matter of outline only. Fitting into this outline a sequence of position-specific intonations (I mean, that each segment of intonation presents features

---

1 'phonetics piece', Prynne refers to 'Fundamental Frequency Studies'.
 'across the water', in mid-1982 Oliver moved to Paris to take up a lectureship at the British Institute.
 'Bumper Book', Prynne refers to his 1982 Poems.

2 Prynne refers to Oliver's The Infant and the Pearl (London: Ferry Press (for Silver Hounds), 1985).

3 Prynne enclosed copies of three pages of notes on The Diagram Poems, and copies of the title page and colophon of Emily Vermeule, Aspects of Death in Early Greek Art and Poetry (Berkeley: University of California Press, 1979).

4 Oliver sent Prynne a prepublication copy of 'Fundamental Frequency Studies', which arrived on 3 November 1982. Prynne's page numbering reflects that of the prepublication copy; page numbers matching the published essay are given in square brackets.

5 'GR 12 piece', Prynne refers to 'Even Poets Can Have Beliefs'.

6 Prynne refers to Rexroth's lament at the lack of 'even the vestige of a scientific approach to prosody' and his argument that '[w]hat is needed above all other things in poetry—of the sort academia could do anyway—is an exhaustive analysis of what happens [when poetry is read aloud], using all the armamentarium which lies there at hand to study sound.' American Poetry in the Twentieth Century (New York: Seabury Press, 1973), 168.

7 'Fundamental Frequency Studies' describes a series of experiments designed to 'develop descriptions of linguistic performance of use to more subjective literary evaluation' (1). Oliver canvassed judgements from '[thirty] subjects, mainly literature students or lecturers at Essex University' regarding the 'best' (Oliver puts the word in quotation marks) recordings of Thomas Wyatt's 'So unwarely was never no man caught' by '[f]ive native male speakers of English'. The subjects were instructed to evaluate, via a questionnaire, the speakers' intonation, pitch, and rhythm (6, 2). For details of the technical equipment used to obtain the recordings, see p. 65n3. Oliver sourced the quatrain from Joost Daalder's edition of Wyatt's poems:
 So unwarely was never no man caught
 With steadfast look upon a goodly face
 As I of late; for suddenly me thought
 My heart was torn out of his place.
 (Collected Poems, ed. Joost Daalder (Oxford: Oxford University Press, 1975), 149)

partly determined by position in relation to other segments before and in anticipation of those which come after) must be in general terms influenced by the family-tune characteristic of the prosody, genre, mode etc., within the historical era. But the larger and more detailed influence in most cases, and in most of the interesting ones, must be the interpretation of the text performed by the reader. By this last expression I mean that the reader's recital performs his or her interpretation, that the latter is realised in the production of the former; there may be rather little prior decision, of a consciously deliberate kind, and in the case of actors particularly I believe that 'thinking with the voice' often replaces an analysis to which vocal production is merely instrumental.

And in the case of poems there is the further complication that a reader's perception of much poetry is of a <u>written</u> text, not only because it presents in that mode but because it seems to belong in the silence of a language not directly connected to actual speech-occasions. Yet it may closely imitate structures and features of the spoken language; with close realism as in dialogue or invective, with more indirect modelling as in soliloquy or recitative, or at greater distance still such as in part-song or epitaph. When texts in these different kinds of relation to speech occasion are given a spoken performance the speaker has to decide, within the prevailing habits and conventions of his time and milieu, how far to re-naturalise the performance and how far to produce speech-patterns which <u>code for</u> a relation to actual speech but do not imitate directly its contours and timings.

This last consideration must be especially prominent in the case of texts which are historically remote from the speaker of them. We still know, more or less, most of the words in Wyatt's quatrain, and perhaps also most of the idioms and locutions; but the speech-tunes characteristic of these lexical and idiomatic components, in syntactic contexts such as those that occur here, are mostly now for us a matter of guesswork based on a corpus of experience in reading and interpreting other such texts: a <u>literary</u> (i.e. a <u>reader's</u>) intuition based on more or less conscious feature analysis and the testing of this against historical-linguistic knowledge and successfully coherent interpretation. It would be my personal guess that all these factors bear upon the pragmatics of speaking this particular Wyatt quatrain, to so marked an extent as to make the results from the exercise quite likely to be untypical. I should expect that, were you to extend the range of data collected for this example, you would find very wide divergences indeed. You hint at this in your reference to 'a <u>positive</u> idea about the line's semantics' (p. 20 [18]) and the variety of intonational contours to be expected 'according to interpretation' (p. 23 [24]).

For features associated with <u>stress</u> (pitch, loudness, attack, timbre, duration, etc.) seem to me likely, in these Wyatt lines, to vary so much that I'd be surprised if a characteristic <u>tune</u> for them were not an artifact of your limited test data. The chief

9 November 1982

problem I should expect to be not so much interpretation as a matter of affect-imputation, as a response to grammatical structure. To put this question bluntly: exactly what kind of correlative/contrastive sentence-construction is in point here, and what is its operative relation to an exclamatory speech-pattern which in <u>stress</u> terms might closely resemble a correlative construction but which in terms of <u>marked intonation</u> would differ from it? Your paraphrase offered upon pp. 3–4 [3] suppresses the problem of this choice, by ignoring the force of 'So'; but I take the prominence of this word to be critical.

For the clause-order is re-sorted so as to bring this word, artificially, to the initial position; and the reader has to decide what kind of construction is to follow. Up to the end of line 2 an exclamatory construction seems probable; analogous to such parallel forms as 'so goodly a face it was, upon which I looked' or 'so off my guard was I, seeing such a face' or 'so caught was I, in gazing upon that face'. In all these patterns the element following directly after <u>so</u>, and selected by it for focal/thematic prominence, takes a stress-marking which in spoken performance is likely to approximate to the falling cadence of a sentence-final assertion, on the model of 'so goodly!' or 'so caught!'

Yet the implications for structure of the <u>as</u>-clause (with the repeated <u>was</u> deleted) which opens line 3 are not fully compatible with the above, and compel a retrospective modification both of structure-recognition and also tune-assignment. Now the reader's reception is of a <u>so</u>/<u>as</u> construction, with the second line an amplification of circumstance not affecting this basic formalism and thus functioning as partly parenthetic within it. This construction points a contrast <u>between</u> components, rather than selecting one for marked prominence. In the second grammatical member the marked component must be either <u>I</u> or <u>of late</u>; or perhaps (if the contrast is bi-polar) both of them. What in the first grammatical member can function as marked antecedents for the delayed contrast? If <u>I</u>, then probably <u>no</u> (man); if <u>of late</u>, then probably <u>never</u>; if both <u>I</u> and <u>of late</u> then the antecedent correlative emphasis becomes an interference pattern of prismatic scatterings, the emphasis distributed so variably and dispersedly that an ideal reading might let almost every preceding syllabic element, capable of bearing stress, have some share in shaping the contour of the trap about to be sprung (we know at the outset that it is a trap, but not yet who is its victim). These are presumptive or proleptic constituents in a compound, imminent stress-instant. And since 'of late' carries implications of 'belatedly', of coming late to an experience or to a postponed and then sudden recognition of its significance, the sense of a naively-trusting steadfastness, as it lays open the self to an emotional wound unwittingly self-inflicted, presents a justification for this trustingness (the face was <u>goodly</u>, worthy of a true regard) which cannot protect against lack of prior knowledge and experience (he was <u>unawares</u>, <u>unwary</u>).

The contrastive pattern, outlined immediately above, seems grammatically to pre-empt the exclamatory pattern given before it. But we come to the latter first, and so in order of experience the latter may in part pre-empt the former. As a compromise between overtly choosing between these alternatives a speaker might select un(warely), or un<u>warely</u> as able to carry interpretative stress in either scheme; but the stress-cadence in each scheme would be different, so that the merging of the two would be approximate only. Different speakers, working out by analysis or in performance these conflicting and overlapping patterns, will (I should expect) adopt a widely various range of alternative tunes, representing alternative accommodations which may in each case be both consistent internally and capable of realising and performing a high proportion of the possibilities latent in the text.

But none of them (I should also expect) could perform more than a certain maximum of this latency; because the contradictory overlap makes diction incapable of a full delivery. It is a written text, I believe, because the experience it transcribes cannot altogether coherently be said. The <u>I</u> of the poem gazed fixedly but (it seems) did not speak, nor did he know what it was that his feelings spoke to him, what they dictated, until his heart had already been seized by their alien force. The formula 'me thought' already places him as the passive recipient of a recognition coming to him from a source outside and beyond his control, recognising the prior symmetry implied in the rhyme: <u>thought</u> turns <u>I</u> into <u>me</u>, agent into victim.

The suddenness of <u>caught</u> ('isn't entirely deliberate'), and even more the stunned pause which follows it, is perhaps then the deep stress-point of the counter-turn here, and for a silence to be both inarticulate and stressed is probably beyond (for the time being) the limits of machine-recorded analysis. His unawareness it was which caused him to gaze with selective fixity upon an unselected face, '<u>a</u> face'; and the sense of a surviving freedom of choice ('I could transfer to another if I chose') is still present in the indefinite article, even though that is part of the unawareness marked for rueful emphasis by the deictic force of <u>So</u>. What a poet admits he knows only late, or too late, cannot by a speaker of the text be shewn to have been known from the beginning: yet selecting a tune or stress-pattern will be like putting the heart back into some kind of place, unless some voice is also found for the unspoken and unspeakable. This, I believe, is part of what caused you to presume a <u>notional</u> instant.

And what these hasty thoughts and conjectures would imply is not that the quatrain cannot be spoken powerfully and inwardly; but rather that there is an unusually wide range of optional tunes and routes by which the inwardness of this particular text can be reached and performed. So that, while the good speakings would point inwards to the same unspoken nexus, the measurement of pragmatics might shew the deviation

9 November 1982

1 Prynne refers to reviews of his 1982 *Poems*. Oliver had asked after such reviews in the letter to which Prynne's is a reply.

2 Andrew Duncan (b. 1956), British poet, critic, and editor. Prynne's letter to Duncan, of 12 August 1982, was published in *Grosseteste Review* 15 (1983–4): 100–18.

Ochre, journal edited by Ralph Hawkins and Charles Ingham. Prynne wrote to Oliver on 12 June 1978 to ask if Oliver could introduce Duncan's work to Hawkins, in order to facilitate its publication. Oliver replied on 26 June to say that he had spoken to Hawkins, who would be in touch with Prynne. Duncan's 'In a German Hotel' was published in *Ochre*, no. 6 (n.d., ca. 1979); the same issue also contains Prynne's 'Tortrix' (*Poems*, 289–90).

3 For the publication history of *Threads of Iron*, see Duncan's author's note to the 2013 edition of the complete text. *Threads of Iron* (Bristol: Shearsman, 2013), 7.

of means quite as much as their affective and prospective unity. Does any of this make sense?

J.

P.S. The phonic and acoustic aspects of stress-pattern production in spoken prosody might come under some light from the evidence not of discriminative perception but of precisely the reverse: I mean not deafness to sound in the ordinary sense but what has clinically been identified as 'deafness to the meaning of noise' (Geräuschsinntaubheit); there's some interesting discussion in L. A. Vignolo, 'Auditory agnosia', Phil. Trans. R. Soc. Lond. B, 298 (1982), 49–57, and indeed the whole set of discussion papers in that volume, on 'The neuropsychology of cognitive function', is worth a look.

P.P.S. There have been a few reviews, and I'll send copies in a few days.[1] I don't quite yet have an article to trade with yours, though I shall have one very shortly and shall send some across so as to keep the flak flying. In the interim, here's a letter of last summer I sent to Andrew Duncan, whom you may recall from the Ochre arrangement in which you assisted.[2] He wrote profusely after that encouragement, and a substantial book (Threads of Iron) was the outcome.[3] Andrew Crozier asked particularly to see this and I sent him a copy; but his response was long delayed and very brief, and he still has not (and it seems will not) return the text. I do not understand why (apart from general sluggishness, and house-moving) this should be so; but you might find some passing interest in the phenomenology (as it were) of my own rather divided response.

11 November 1982. The postcard depicts a lithograph by Vladimir Burliuk from the First Journal of Russian Futurists, nos. 1–2 (1914).

11 November 1982   17 F[*erry*]P[*ath*]
                                       Cantab

P.P.P.S. L. B. Funkhouser, 'Acoustic Rhythm in Randall Jarrell's The Death of the Ball Turret Gunner', Poetics, 8 (1979), 381–403.

     J.

13 November 1982   23 Avenue de Clichy
                                       Paris

Dear Jeremy,

Both your extended comments are likely to be very useful to me: the Duncan because it addresses certain quite personal, moral questions of mine and also brings newly alive problems I'm currently wrestling with in terms of poetic statement. Let me leave those things to fertilise.

I have been aware ever since the GR article that my employment of the Wyatt example has been syntactically crude. At some stage in the writing up of this material this crudity must be redressed and, for that reason alone, your remarks strike me as most handily accurate and subtle. I don't think they vitiate my discussion for reasons I'll go into; but there's no doubt they complicate it.

You are, of course, quite right to centre on the question of 'tune' and its 'best' or 'median' varieties. The calibre of any reader's syntactical response will be affected by his historical sense, appreciation of textual cohesion, and so on. The poem Wyatt wrote, I am well aware, is partly lost to us in its sounds and sense. To take the most obvious example, the stressing on 'unware', it is probable that Wyatt stressed the first syllable: all my readers, including myself, stressed the second syllable—myself deliberately. And I have shown quite successfully I think that the simple fact of emphasising a negative can alter the whole intonation of a line, with doubtless splay effects later in the performance, though these would be extremely hard to track.

It will help if I explain why, when assailed for example by linguists because of my lack of syntactical analysis, I have to reassert the crudity of my approach as a merit. You convincingly propose that interpretation of the trading relations between the 'So' clause and the 'as' clause of line three would affect intonation pattern. I haven't known exactly why I ignore the 'So' in my paraphrase but I think your analysis makes it clearer to me. One problem is that the first word in any reading is pronounced particularly strongly, often with high pitch and certainly large envelope amplitude. It means that the syntactical importance lent to it is especially hard to recapture; in any case, a further problem: the ear seems to discount to some extent this undue emphasis, although it shows up so clearly on the apparatus; and this is probably because we know that people start off speaking forcefully, having maximum air in their lungs, maximum intentional energy, and so on.

My crudity, in fact, is quite simply motivated. I fully accept that the more sophistication a reader has the more nuanced his intonational pattern—though not necessarily the more complicated. However, this is a labyrinth in which we should ultimately lose ourselves. My firm belief is that there is plenty of original work to be done at a cruder level, that the role of informational focus is often quite <u>simply</u> dominant even when great subtleties are rolling around in the head. Thus I specify: what I'm measuring is not Wyatt's own poem, which as you say was almost certainly designed as a written, not sung, poem, as evidence later in the poem makes likely. Instead, I'm ascribing a fairly flat paraphrase to the poem—a modern paraphrase with just the words 'unware' and 'late' explained to unsophisticated readers faced with the poem for the first time, and reading with modern pronunciation and modern consciousness. I'm measuring, therefore, modern performances of a text which happens to have some features recoverable from historical and linguistic analysis, though not perfectly; but it is almost irrelevant to my measuring that it should have these features because I'm deliberately being more crude than that. I'm not seeking to recapture Wyatt's poem but treating it as nearly as maybe as a piece of data.

As you perceive, this is an imperfect process, one that is finally not quite scientific. So let me defend it against the following criticisms: a) Why not choose a modern poem? b) How can I be sure about the subtle effects of its syntactical qualities? c) Why not, at least, choose a simpler poem? d) Isn't the data too limited?

The answer to a) will be clear to both of us: quite largely, it makes no difference whether the poem is modern or not. The actual play of syntax in our heads is always too fine to be easily recoverable: I cannot judge a reading of, say, a Seamus Heaney syntax (let alone someone more syntactically complex) any more confidently from the aspect of these graphs than I can the Wyatt. I can make rough judgements from the traces that this or that aspect of a line seems to receive emphasis and I can draw hesitant conclusions about where the informational focus lies; even this is more than is usually done and contributes to literary criticism, perhaps, a preliminary method of a kind not usually available to it. Somehow, we have to begin to talk more securely about the role of pitch; and I am content to begin with these partial securities. We argue with someone and his basic stressing, the foci, and the rationale behind his rhythm are immediately obvious to us. The syntax of what he says makes another contribution demanding finer analysis.

This really leads on to d). Wouldn't a larger, more sophisticated bank of readers come up with different intonation patterns? The article lies open to this possibility. However, first, it's difficult to accommodate a larger bank of readers within one laboratory session, since labs are booked and the process takes much time. It has to be one session so that the machine settings can be stabilised and we are clear that the machine is responding similarly to each reader. Next, I spread the data's significance a little by going to a panel of some 30 listeners and asking them which reading best fits the poem, intonationally. Again, this is crude but it is nevertheless supportive. Work that I've seen on these questions often depends upon the sole, unaided reading of the researcher (e.g. my Morier reference).[1] To set against this, slightly, I'm generally reckoned to be a 'good' reader of poetry and have had plenty of practice. I agree the performance itself is a kind of 'thinking with the voice' and is affected by all sorts of factors, some of them depending on the prevailing performance circumstances. This is, quite frankly, the best I can do so far: the results are 'good enough' to open a discussion; they are not, and never can be, final; they lie open to drastic modification of 'best tune'; but they at least specify what is a relatively 'good' tune. Again, this is an advance on how pitch is normally dealt with—ex cathedra—in so much literary criticism.

And I'm ready for b).[2] Because I return to 'thinking with the voice'. I can understand the rationalistic possibilities lying in your analysis of the 'So' and 'as' clauses; if they hold, as they probably

---

[1] Henri Morier (1910–2004), Swiss historian of language. He is referred to in 'Fundamental Frequency Studies', 28.

[2] In the margin beside this paragraph, Oliver wrote: 'You'll see I'm loading this: I suppose I could make a more wholesale admission but with the pronunciation fixed at "unwárely" I don't feel inclined to.'

do, they are bound to affect slightly the way we read the lines (I tell doubtful readers, by the way, to pronounce 'unwárely' like that). When I think with my voice, however, it's as though my dominant concentration is of another kind: it is the rushing of the first two lines towards the 'As I of late' phrase, whose invariable, syntactical pause afterwards very greatly conditions the lines' flow. Audiences, with a little difficulty, distinguish the force given to 'So' {Not as readily as you'd expect from the traces.} but it is part of a conjoined voicing pattern up until the word, 'caught', and this too affects syntactical perceptions, I have small doubt. 'So' prepares sonically for 'caught' and then prepares for us to be syntactically upfaced with the 'As' clause; there's a certain phonic necessity at work and I cannot think quite how to disentangle the two elements, except by an appeal to intuitions. Nevertheless, if we keep it crude and talk instead about informational focus, I believe we still have things worthwhile to say, because we can win a large measure of agreement about such foci (as in Halliday's work on intonation, which I otherwise don't derive from).[1]

c), then, and avoid all these problems? Well, I've never been clear what a 'simpler' poem might be—I had this argument with the linguist, Widdowson, during my interview for this job.[2] Linguists tend to choose poets like Pope because his rules are apparently clear. As you know, Pope is just as complex as Wyatt when you actually start investigating the evidence as I have in fact done. That is, I regard Pope as a good subject for analysis because of his complexity: it gives you more intellectual and emotional parameters by which to estimate what's going on. 'Jack and Jill' won't do: I would have great trouble estimating what readers were trying to do with the verse, since they'd either try to thump it according to its abstract grid or would be much more arbitrary in their reading. Blake: very difficult, as I'm just discovering on looking at some traces from 'The Little Black Boy': so much is locked up in the imagery/vision and in our response to it. Modern poetry: even worse, as I've discovered on trying a fragment of my own verse on the readers—real syntactical tangles of a kind that don't nearly so evidently arise in the Wyatt. The merit of the Wyatt is its voicing patterns and general sonority; the merit of Pope is his brilliant exactness about how to employ such features in a complicated way: in both cases this seems to impose some standardisation on readings. With Blake, my own verse, and some other examples, I haven't yet transferred the data to graph paper to have a look. Blake's metrics, I am tentatively concluding—and this follows my intuitions—are mainly interesting because their simple technics have to carry such a charge of obsession. And that's harder to wrestle with than the finer detail of syntax.

In fact, if I'm boastfully right in thinking my readings generally the best in the three sample sessions I've conducted then it would perhaps be true that a more sophisticated reading of the

1 Michael Halliday (1925–2018), British linguist. Oliver likely refers to his *Intonation and Grammar in British English*, Janua Linguarum, Series Practica 48 (The Hague: Mouton, 1967).

2 Henry Widdowson (b. 1935), British linguist. From 1977 to 1998 Widdowson was professor of English in the Institute of Education, a constituent college of the University of London, into which the British Institute was incorporated in 1969.

[1] Oliver likely refers to David Gascoyne (1916–2001), British poet. In the late 1970s and early 1980s Gascoyne and his wife were 'regular visitors' to Paris, largely due to the efforts of the French writer and editor Christine Jordis. Robert Fraser, *Night Thoughts: The Surreal Life of the Poet David Gascoyne* (Oxford: Oxford University Press, 2012), 382–4 (383). In 1979 Jordis invited Gascoyne to read at the British Council, and in May 1981 Gascoyne attended an 'Homage to David Gascoyne' at the Centre Pompidou.

[2] 'for the Eye altering alters all', Prynne interpolates a line from Blake's 'The Mental Traveller'.

poem would tend to smooth out the intonation pattern to as to reveal it; and also to exaggerate durations and pitch contrasts. In this, there must be some rightness easily perceived or we would never know when a drummer was 'on beat' and when he wasn't quite—a very fine distinction not capturable through metronomes but which makes all the difference to whether a band swings. And music doesn't have syntax in the same sense: it has phonic foci and grids in a sense that is similar. I'm not denying the influence of musical or linguistic syntax, of course: the question is, how unsubtle about this influence can we afford to be when we are still trying to establish a language and a method capable of discussing pitch and stress with more accuracy than usually available, though not, and never, with complete accuracy. {I don't clearly know where subtleties can conveniently stop.}

Mine, as you perceive, is a bunker position. And it's very valuable to me that you're seeing over the sandbags.

I'm in the dark about your 'paper to come'. But I much look forward to seeing it.

Meanwhile, here, it's bar life with the journalists and decorum and David Gascoigne with the Brit. Inste ('le British' as they say out here).[1] I simply refrain from comment on your Duncan piece until I've got myself further along my particular road because if you turn round to the goad you get a nasty pain in the testicles.

Doug

16 November 1982   17 Ferry Path
Cambridge

Dear Doug,

Thanks for yours. I grab a moment for a brief reply, glad that it must be that since otherwise I'd have time to consider. Brevity allows me a cool cheek, instead, to observe that you really are bunkered, but with the difference that you've surely chosen to be. I could almost believe your arguments, if you did yourself, but I sense a profound coding for something else which is not belief at all, which strikes for a clench of the opaque at the end of a dark corridor. There is a small room and it is lit, unevenly but brightly, and the voices have their say without, it seems, quite coming from where they are; a buzzing resonance like a voice-shadow anticipates shifts like down and out as if they were also on and over. The corridor itself seems lit as if from a strip of half-light down its centre and about 1½ feet from the floor. There are tiles the length of it, patterned but wet also, and though fear is present it is not ours: we are intensely glad to be in that place and all subsequent speech is also a repositioning of the body in regard to this coming & going.

It looks hard but feels easy, for the Eye altering alters all but the ears rest in an archaic temporal process.[2] The intonation of speech is the strip or honey-guide; the stress-focus is the threshold itself and what we have to get to is the echo of our re-accomplished going in. Anyone can do it, though speaking preparedly allows a certain practice to develop, and the machines may help stave off the avoidance of unknown but too closely familiar forms: they graph them against real time and thus one can learn to read a mute physiology from an imputed, uneven brightness. They are the oval window.

To keep it simple and lend it to others is indeed your programme, its top-level listen loop. What then a person believes is spoken for by what, even more primitively, he knows. Or she-knows, rather, since that form is within the threshold always female, I think, probably (or it is other-sexed, so that for a woman it could be male: I'm doubtful here). And to speak into a machine must be a little like writing for and into a journal; here's the piece of mine I mentioned, which is to come out in Modern Asian Studies; and the pleasure of handling in proper form a stress-tone medium I cannot hear at all gives this improper ventriloquism a glove-like mania (a close, borrowed fit).[1]

On the run, then:

J.

1 Prynne enclosed a copy of 'China Figures', his review of *New Songs from a Jade Terrace: An Anthology of Early Chinese Love Poetry*, trans. Anne Birrell (London: George Allen and Unwin, 1982). The review was published in *Modern Asian Studies* 17, no. 4 (1983): 671–88; and (in revised form) in a subsequent edition of *New Songs* (Harmondsworth, UK: Penguin, 1986), 363–92.

2 Anne Birrell (1939–2020), scholar of Chinese literature and translator of the volume of Chinese poetry in which Prynne's revised review was included.

---

30 November 1982   Institut Britannique de Paris
                         11 rue de Constantine
                         Paris

Dear Jeremy,

This isn't the instant reply that I began. My mother, who suffered a minor heart attack during a serious operation, is in intensive care; she's pulling through O.K., I think, at eighty, but I have to visit England this weekend; various activities have had to be telescoped in consequence.

Thank you, however, for the China Figures, which quite simply opened up new territory for me with those delicate and historical sequences of topoi. Your broadside at my machine work I'll deal with more briefly later because I think it mainly off the point.

As for the Chinese, then, I'm glad to have this sudden window, because I have never had call (being in no sense a Pound scholar) to try to order in my mind rigorously which of these poets came where and why. What I can very strongly respond to is the notion of a courtly body of poetry, embodying not only the golden age of the themes that you and Birrell display but also its acculturation into the palace style.[2] The parallel here with medieval courtly poetry, a parallel suggested of course by Pound's own early career, makes this irresistible to me. When I was a child we had some India Service relic I used to borrow from a neighbour: a carved piece of ivory not more than six inches long and with little magnifying windows in it, through which I caught a glimpse of some Indian world: the water tank in a palace or whatever. And, far more than any light that may nowadays be thrown on Anglo-American modernism through such studies, it is the

1   Jacques Lacan (1901–81), French psychoanalyst. Oliver recounts in *Whisper 'Louise'* that he read Lacan, along with Derrida and Foucault, in the 1960s and 1970s (55–6). The psychoanalyst makes an appearance in *The Harmless Building* at the beginning of chap. 12: 'In the park, late-abed seagulls circled overhead, calling "Jacques Lacan, Jacques Lacan", without giving further details' (102; *TVTH*, 212; Oliver later refers to his novel's 'parody of Jacques Lacan' in *CAAS*, 251). Metonymy is an important concept in Lacan, though synecdoche less explicitly so. On the former, see especially 'The Instance of the Letter in the Unconscious, or Reason since Freud', in *Écrits: The First Complete Edition in English*, trans. Bruce Fink (New York: W. W. Norton, 2006), 412–41. Oliver's letters to Peter Riley in the late 1970s are more explicit about his antipathy towards what he took to be the 'undesirable influence' remarked upon in this letter. On Robin Blaser's essay 'The Practice of Outside' (*The Collected Books of Jack Spicer*, ed. Robin Blaser (Los Angeles: Black Sparrow Press, 1975), 269–329), Oliver writes: 'It's apparent the kind of damage an arrogant essay like Blaser's in the collected works can do: it places theory above poetry and sends everyone scampering to the latest French magi to borrow insights. I've read some Derrida + Lacan with interest; but I hope I know how to keep that interest in its place.' Oliver to Riley, 21 February 1978. DOA, box 9.

2   'West Reincarnation scent', Oliver quotes a line of fifth-century Chinese poetry by Hsiao Kang, translated by Birrell, from Prynne's review of *New Songs from a Jade Terrace*. Prynne, 'China Figures', 678.

vignettes themselves that I prize in what you've shown me. If I could come across in some antique shop such an Indian service relic I'd pay well for it. Here, I'm charmed in the old sense of the word by these jade pools with their dubious meanings and the lotuses red and open, and the sheer density of meaning that a topos can in its history acquire.

It's seemed to me for some years now that I'm not much interested in American modernism in most of its forms: I simply see a few things of my own rather clearly, am aware of their past embodiments in various poetries, and want to get them down for myself. However, I do see how much more light we now have on this poetry than in the days of Pound and of Imagism. I can appreciate, too, your taking the terms metonymy and synecdoche out of the hands of the Lacanians: Lacan brilliantly in fact subjected them to the terms of his system, which I fear I'm beginning to hate strongly for its undesirable influence.[1] Well, I have trouble 'keeping track' of metonymy when it's used to cover a historically exfoliating usage because the relationships between part and whole bewilder me from one text to another. This is why, above, I prefer to consider, not as an alternative term but as an alternative process, the development of a topos, as described by you, since then I don't keep feeling obliged to pin down one sign in its usage against another sign in its usage, or even to wonder frantically to what degree any one development of signboarding constitutes an engulfing metonymy in which synecdoche is included. In this I am against the age and its rationalism of terminology and I don't know whether this is a confession of inadequacy or something simpler said than that. At all events, I much appreciate your distinction between these ancient Chinese forms of poetic practice—one of the oldest and most honourable—from, let us say, the present-day virtual equation of English poetry with a debased form of winsome metaphor.

We're taught to value the unsophisticated somewhat higher than the sophisticated; it must be all those Enlightenment men; but you make the sophistication and corruption of the earlier modes at least as interesting as those modes themselves. The suddenness of sparkling sunlit blossom obviously reminds us of the freshness of certain haiku, but its adulteration into a cosmetic grace has a daring which is devilish and attractive. 'West Reincarnation scent' simply 'ought not to be allowed'.[2] Chinese poems of travel and separation have often been those that speak most strongly to me: the perfect sense of tense decorum that decides the exact meeting place at the end of Pound's 'River Merchant's Wife' is one of those things that has stayed with me over the years; here, the gradual intervention of mountains, rivers and then road between the traveller and the woman's face affects me likewise. Thus the richer themes and accompanying symbols (and do we really refer all this to a metonymic process?) develop until the poet is handed down a many-stopped instrument by his predecessors and can muck about with it, putting

30 November 1982

his manicured thumbnail half over one of the stops to make it screech a little, and so on. As 'Empress Chen', displayed by you.[1]

And I'm writing all this down at length, not in recension of what you've already so interestingly done, but out of a sadness that we have so much lost respect of this kind for the work of our predecessors. I don't much like the Ginsberg–Orlovsky road show (except for the songs about his father), but I do like the way Orlovsky knows his master's poems by heart.[2] We know that much modern verse practice has a professionally deep-lying cynicism; meanwhile, the academic critics are all 'working on' this or that; meanwhile again, the Peter Porters ferociously insist that they know what's going on; and so the cynicism is compounded with a most worrying knowingness.[3] Then I see I can't get to know this Chinese poetry like that because I am so wrenched by its strangeness and profundity as I keep looking at your quotations and meditate upon your interpretations. We have well-nigh lost such immensely focussed calmness that a topos, richly handed down, acquires. And as long as we, instead, admire one who tells us that bees wear bathing suits, it's hard to see where we are profitably heading. And it's quite damnable.

One might think that the subtlety of your analyses is the very thing that is missing from my machine work. In fact, I've called your remarks on my traces 'off the track', because they tell me in their cryptic imagery nothing that I haven't already faced. Right at the beginning of the project some five years ago, I gave a talk to some computer people and linguists who were trying to get stress incidence right in synthesised speech. The point of my talk was, roughly, yours: you can't do it with any finesse if you're using machinery which employs real-time process. What is wrong, however, is any suggestion that I'm 'striking for the opaque at the end of the corridor' or that I'm secretly content to be doing so—because it saves having to think harder, or whatever.

You are, of course, pointing beyond the machinery that I'm using and are quite right to do so. Mine is a temporary position as I told you. But another way of saying this is that you are over-estimating the capabilities of the machinery that I'm using: either you have to say, don't use such machinery at all; or the further reaches of your metaphors are inapplicable to it.

You see, when you conduct—as you did in your first letter—an analysis of considerable syntactical subtlety, there is no way in which my machinery could give us any good clue as to whether one segmentation of the sentence, with one reading of 'So', was really being performed rather than another. We could quiz the subjects as to how they thought they'd read it, with what syntax, but few of them would have the syntactical subtlety to understand the points in the first place and, if they did, couldn't truly assure us that they'd got that subtlety actually into their voice. The machine can't tell us either: when you see the wavery little pen tracing out the intonation contour and try to distinguish down and out on the trace from on and over, conscious of great

---

[1] Oliver refers to the poem 'Empress Chen', ascribed to Ts'ao P'ei, discussed by Prynne in 'China Figures', 680–2.

[2] Allen Ginsberg and Peter Orlovsky toured Europe in 1979, including 'about fifteen readings in England'. An account of the tour by Ginsberg can be found in 'Allen Ginsberg 1979 Leicester Student Interview', *The Allen Ginsberg Project*, accessed 13 July 2021, https://allenginsberg.org/2018/05/s-m-26/. Oliver refers to Ginsberg's 'Father Death Blues', performed on this tour, as the transcript from the Warwick University date shows (see https://allenginsberg.org/2017/01/sunday-january-22nd/).

[3] Peter Porter (1929–2010), British-based, Australian-born poet.

30 November 1982

uncertainty about where each actually began in the raw voice trace or where the vowels change into consonants, then we are at a level of crudity far below the imagery of your second letter. Your first is very valuable, because at some stage of the argument the subtler syntactical questions must be raised.

They would have to be raised in such a way that denies we yet have a prospect of getting at them, I think. I've said all along (in the <u>Gr. Rev.</u>) that I'm not out to show much that's new, although I think my findings about voicing and sibilance are quite interesting. Instead, I want to push these crude machines to the point where we must start talking a different language, the language of the poet, or perhaps of the further reaches of science. Ideally, I'd like to write a book in which prosodic analysis and analysis of narrative burlesque point beyond real or fictional time. Of course, modern mathematics is way beyond me. But I see my task as educative: how <u>is</u> it that we are so blandly confident, still, in literary criticism about our ascription of stress and our refusal properly to confront questions of pitch? Every month in the critical literature we can see new examples, along with a dismissal as pretentious of poetry which is hostile to such 'commonsensical' attitudes.

A last point, because I said I'd be brief. I must work <u>from</u> the trace, <u>from</u> real time in a blundering machine representation and do what I can with it, at whatever expense of subtlety. What the trace can tell me about are voicing patterns, pitch contours (F_0 that is), broad information foci, very broad assumptions about meaning.[1] I believe these are reflected in the trace rather as a man's general attitudes are reflected in the general way he's walking, though with more sensitive analysis we might gain further insights into his state of mind. Crude data, crude assumptions which come from comparing like with like, trace with trace; but not without point. We shan't reach a 'best tune', but we shall have an <u>idea</u> about a normal tune and shall hope to lay down tracks towards better kinds of analysis. We may show, also, that certain effects are statistically probable because we have a number of readings and a number of people polled as to which is the best tune. With the Sussex machine we get a little more: a visual display of gutturals, sibilance, and so on.[2] All this can add cogency eventually to intuitive leaps in literary criticism, to syntactical analysis. I cannot but accept that syntactical subtleties affect intonation contours. Instead, I appeal through my opinion poll to how most people accept that the line should be read, given the readings they are presently considering. It's an appeal to intuition, made statistical.

We may simply disagree on this because I have more than once disagreed with a poet about the need for this educative task.
    Lengthily but hastily,
               Doug

---

1 'F_0', fundamental frequency, as measured by the readers' glottal buzz, recorded by the electrodes Oliver strapped to their throats. See 'Fundamental Frequency Studies', 3.

2 'the Sussex machine', Oliver refers to the real-time speech intonation spectrometer, images from which are printed in 'Even Poets Can Have Beliefs' (18–20) and *PNP* (76–9).

P.S. I'm just looking at an odd book by Dr. M. E. Loots, <u>Metrical Myths, an experimental-phonetic investigation into the production and perception of metrical speech</u>, Nijhoff, Hague, 1980.

Its introduction isn't promising but it has quite a lot of data which, however analysed in the text, <u>might</u> be interesting. I've ordered the ball turret gunner.

1 Claude Royet-Journoud (b. 1941), French poet.

2 Stephen Romer (b. 1957), British poet and critic.
'Dir. Of St.', shorthand for director of studies (in English), the position held by Prynne at Gonville and Caius College, Cambridge, 1964–2003.

3 Oliver enclosed a copy of 'Fundamental Frequency Studies'.

27 March [1983]   23 Avenue de Clichy
                                Paris

Dear Jeremy,

Did we reach <u>impasse</u> back there? I didn't mean to. I meant to say that when we see a lame man running we can't piece together the perfect movement that he has in his head, though poetry and intuition have part of their locus there. If we look at his footsteps in the sand they nevertheless tell us something when we compare them with the footsteps of an athlete. It is dangerous to leave such work to the scientists, though we have to remember they are only footsteps and it is only sand. So too with the music of a poem: we cannot distinguish a normal tune but we may gain some idea of its outlines by comparing several readings: it will be the 'normal tune' <u>as</u> expressed by those readings <u>as</u> captured crudely, in the sand. <u>It</u> is something, nonetheless, and by finding out what we can't deduce we may clean up the deductions of a more intuitive language or of a subtler syntactical analysis.

(I called in the other day to see where we'd got to but I only had an hour or so left after a speedy book-raid on behalf of my job out here.)

I have only just begun to re-establish contact with poetry circles out here, such as exist. Claude R-J is as courteous + as enthusiastically well-informed as ever.[1] Those French remain interested in your work. There's a young Cambridge set—Stephen Romer I expect you know, since you're his Dir. Of St.; but I haven't summed them up too well.[2] A dash of Heaney + some centriste eclecticism perhaps—not sure. Again, they seemed interested in <u>Collected Poems</u> which, I understand, did finally receive some appreciative reviews.

I enclose a print of my article—not for the trouble of further comment from you but simply simply.[3]

Doug.

10 December 1983

[*Prynne sent a copy of* The Oval Window *(Cambridge: privately printed, 1983) with a photocopy-collage of the text 'Traditional Window Company' with an oval drawn around it, above the date and the following dedication:*]

Traditional Window Company

10th December 1983

You'll see my thoughts have strayed widely, pendant ces fouilles; but your work & our exchanges have never been far distant. So: with thanks, and let's meet again soon.

You'll see my thoughts have strayed widely, pendant ces fouilles; but your work & our exchanges have never been far distant. So: with thanks, and let's meet again soon.

J.

5 January 1984   23 Avenue de Clichy
                                                Paris

Dear Jeremy,

Christmas over, I'm back in my studio over here and with time to examine the oval window more closely.

I came across a passage of Robert Grosseteste, founder of the Review of the same name, which—while different in dynamic from your opening statement—might be of interest as a medieval view idealised into the supernatural. Enclosed.[1]

The primary causes of these poems I recognised as linked with those which have sometimes cropped up in our correspondence and discussions and I'm very taken with the way they've become elaborated in the relating of the observer eye to actual event: what to do with the kind of political amaze we all stand in and what it means in terms of the mind-act. It's very close to my own concerns and so nicely put, how essentially intervolved is Treasury policy with operations on data; and the playing-off of this into the nature of computerised data manipulation later in the sequence.[2] The implications of this and allied malfunctioning are placed into judgement by the precision of your opening, which strikes me as psychologically (never mind 'mathematically') really acute. We are more directly back in the questions raised by Wound Response than for some time, I think. Grosseteste's clarity about the medieval notion of necessity seems germane here, because what you term the underlying domains of BEFORE, being not simple, bring some tincture of necessity (the phrase is far too weak) into the operation of the present. And what in him is constantly separated into eternal and contingent and then recombined is in your poems brought into a properly (I think) unified dynamic in which separation or independence is a necessary result of the unity in which BEFORE and AFTER are nevertheless recreated. Unity (the present) means nothing without the co-existing independence of what is unified, as the simplest sum will tell us.

Then I have a puzzle. Suppose we idealise the process of forming in our heads, as for the first time in the world, a simple mathematical sum (ignoring, that is, all real or would-be real psychological accounts of this process on the one hand, or Frege-influenced abstractions of the process on the other).[3] Suppose, that is, in making St. Augustine's sum, $7 + 3 = 10$, we hold in mind three past nexuses: 1. A 7 that is seven separate elements or units

---

[1] Robert Grosseteste (ca. 1175–1253), English scholastic philosopher and theologian. Oliver enclosed Grosseteste's 'On the Knowledge of God', from *Selections from Medieval Philosophers*, vol. 1, *Augustine to Albert the Great*, ed. and trans. Richard McKeon (London: Charles Scribner's Sons, 1930), 285–7. References in this letter to 'the underlying domains of BEFORE' and 'BEFORE and AFTER' interpolate language from the epigraphs to *The Oval Window* (*Poems*, 311). Oliver advances a comparison in the following paragraph between the epigraphs and Grosseteste's discussion of necessity and contingency in 'On the Knowledge of God'. For bibliographic details of the texts quoted in the epigraphs, see Prynne, *The Oval Window*, ed. N. H. Reeve and Richard Kerridge (Hexham, UK: Bloodaxe Books, 2018), 86–7.

'Review', Oliver refers to *Grosseteste Review* (1968–84), journal edited by Tim Longville.

[2] 'Treasury policy', 'operations on data', Oliver interpolates language from *The Oval Window* (*Poems*, 319).

[3] Gottlob Frege (1848–1925), German mathematician and philosopher.

but also a nexus of those; 2. A plussing operation that is at the moment just a cipher containing what we are about to do; and 3. A 3 that is an item like the 7.¹ Then we have a present, which is the =. And lastly, we have a future which is the 10. Idealised, within the = we would have a 7 in separate units but also a nexus; a 3 ditto; and a 10 which incorporates the complex 7 in its units and its nexus, a 3 ditto, and a 10 which is 10 units and also a nexus, (although it is also a 7 and 3 as already described). The operator + is also in this curious relation: it is a cipher with meaning entering the = and also transformed there into part only of the whole equalising operation. In this sense, as you so rightly say, the past has complex underlying domains. But the future, the simple result 10 is normalised: at the most, it is a 10 of separate units while at the same time a nexus, 10. And that's all. For example, it is more crucial than a Frege would admit that during the equalising the 7 and the 3 should continue to bear their more-remote and less-remote past relationship: I am saying, what no mathematician would, that the sum 3 + 7 is a different sum from 7 + 3. Am I close to you here? However, if we have already normalised or envisaged this future before we even get to the = (monetarism, etc.), then no wonder operations upon the data result, short of the future being a divine revelation (as, of course, monetarism is). No doubt you are aware of the new study by Hendry and Ericsson (a Bank of England paper) which exposes how the manipulation took place at the very foundation of Friedman's theories.²

Something else, more homely. When I was a child I used to borrow from some ex-India type a curious artefact made out of ivory and lathe-turned into a small ornament, perhaps nine inches long. In it were three oval windows set into the bulbous parts of the turning; and when you held the thing up to the light and applied your eye to the oval windows you could see little scenes in India. The point being that each scene was so remote to me in my then knowledge of the world (six or seven years old, I presume I was), that it seemed marvellously ideal and untouchable. I simply couldn't get enough of looking at it and even as I write this down I relive the tiny thrill of it. A child's toy but without the dynamic of the flakes.³ And I can vividly recall buying for my Mother one Christmas one of those snowy bubbles itself and being utterly unable to comprehend why she didn't find it as magical as I did. (Incidentally, I have in reviewing an old article for possible republication in another form just come across the source for a phrase in 'Of Movement Towards a Natural Place' the 'curious white flakes, like thin snow'—it's Great Expectations I think, a marvellous title to place alongside your examinations in this present book.)⁴

Well, it's an indirect way of replying to your book but I think you'll see how much I take it to heart. There's much I don't comprehend; but the thrust of it pushes me out into the white country.

5 January 1984

---

1 'Augustine's sum', most prominently referred to in bk. 2, chap. 8 of *On the Free Choice of the Will*, but also mentioned in bk. 4, chap. 4 of the *Confessions*. Oliver would have read the relevant section of *On the Free Choice of the Will* in McKeon, *Selections from Medieval Philosophers*, 34–9, in which Augustine has Evodius argue that 'seven and three are ten, and not only now, but always; nor have seven and three in any way at any time not been ten, nor will seven and three at any time not be ten' (36).

2 David F. Hendry and Neil R. Ericsson, 'Assertion Without Empirical Basis: An Econometric Appraisal of *Monetary Trends in ... the United Kingdom* by Milton Friedman and Anna J. Schwartz', in *Bank of England Panel of Academic Consultants: Panel Paper 22*, ed. R. C. O. Matthews (London: Bank of England, 1983), 45–101.

Milton Friedman (1912–2006), American economist who with Anna J. Schwartz theorized and popularized 'monetarism' in *A Monetary History of the United States, 1867–1960* (Princeton, NJ: Princeton University Press, 1963). The book by Friedman and Schwartz to which Hendry and Ericsson refer directly in their paper is *Monetary Trends in the United States and the United Kingdom: Their Relation to Income, Prices, and Interest Rates, 1867–1975* (Chicago: University of Chicago Press, 1982).

3 Oliver refers to lines in *The Oval Window*—'A child's joy, a toy with a snowstorm / flakes settling in white prisms, to slide / to a stop'—but responds more generally to the image of the 'child's toy' that frames the second half of the sequence. *Poems*, 330–1, 338–9.

4 *Poems*, 223. The full sentence in Charles Dickens's novel reads: 'And any one could see that he shook with fear, and that there broke out upon his lips, curious white flakes, like thin snow.' *Great Expectations*, ed. Margaret Cardwell (Oxford: Oxford University Press, 2008), 91.

I'm sending a long-promised and highly unsatisfactory photocopy just to show you the way in which I'm handling the Pearl metre.[1] I'm a bit stuck with the poem trying to find a denouement and then to cram it into about 17 stanzas.

    Best,
       Doug.

23 January 1984   17 Ferry Path
                                                                                                    Cambridge

Dear Doug,

    Very glad to see how you recognised that first frame of the window into the blood-stream; as the diagnosis of consequent necessity reveals very clearly. Of course, what is politically imposed is the shadow of this cause as antecedent, to be purged like a contempt of purgatory brought home to roost; and as you say the dialectic is sexual, the intrusive magnetic polarity of attraction & repulsion is introjected via the threat to love for the father (assuming his neglected mantle), I respond at once to that.[2] I'm reminded in fact of the claustrophobic freedom it's possible to allege in even the most confined and blurred privacy, e.g. the fable adduced in Locke's discussion of active & passive power: 'suppose a Man be carried, whilst fast asleep, into a Room, where is a Person he longs to see and speak with; and be there locked fast in, beyond his Power to get out: he awakes, and is glad to find himself in so desirable Company, which he stays willingly in, i.e. prefers his stay to going away. I ask, Is not this stay voluntary? I think, no Body will doubt it: and yet being locked fast in, 'tis evident he is not at liberty not to stay, he has no freedom to be gone.'[3]

    Hazlitt's enraged refusal of that passivity, as of a bondage-instinct dressed out with the trimmings of reason, drove him to deny absolutely the mind as 'a sort of empty room into which ideas are conveyed from without through the doors of the sense, as you would carry goods into an unfurnished lodging' (Lectures on Philosophy).[4] Yet his enslaved passion for Sarah Walker (do you know the Liber Amoris?) cast that very pearl before the swine of his own image in Circe's mirror.[5] And the Lockean tabulator waits on patiently as spectator to the entrainment: 'whatever Change is observed, the Mind must collect a Power somewhere, able to make that Change, as well as a possibility in the thing it self to receive it' (all from Book II, Chap. XXI of the Essay).[6]

    It must be daring, therefore, to press sexually into this politic exhaustion, 'that died in the room' as within the parenthesis of the longed-for Person, and each stanza gropes for a connecting door to the next.[7] I hope you can finally bring this off because, as you exactly note, the theme is offered as perfectly circular, unimpeached and refusing entry. Well, none of these fairly random thoughts bears directly; but they'll maybe keep our lines

---

1 Oliver enclosed a draft typescript of the first five stanzas of *The Infant and the Pearl*, which takes as its metrical (and narrative) model the Middle English *Pearl*.

2 Prynne responds here and throughout this letter to the draft stanzas of *The Infant and the Pearl*.

3 Prynne quotes (with minor discrepancies in punctuation) John Locke, *An Essay Concerning Humane Understanding* (London: Printed for Tho. Basset, 1690 [1689]), 118.

4 Prynne quotes William Hazlitt's 'On Locke's Essay on the Human Understanding', in *The Complete Works of William Hazlitt*, ed. P. P. Howe, vol. 2 (London: J. M. Dent and Sons, 1930–4), 146–91 (147).

5 Hazlitt, *Liber Amoris: or, The New Pygmalion*, in *The Complete Works of William Hazlitt*, vol. 9, 95–162.

6 Locke, *An Essay Concerning Humane Understanding*, 116.

7 Prynne quotes and refers to the draft stanzas of *The Infant and the Pearl*. The start of the quoted line (the ninth of the second stanza) is revised in print to 'dying in the room' (*Kind*, 129).

open. And let me know earlier when you're next passing through, so that we may catch up on that front too.

 As ever:
   J.

10 November 1985   17 Ferry Path
                                Cambridge

Dear Doug:

 First-rate news that the Rosy Pearl is at last soon to be delivered into the hands and ears of the <u>reader</u>—mythical beast of fickle attentions & muffled conscience, but in one or two out-stations still pining to turn a telling page. In the usual haste of the season I subjoin two quotations:

> In much the greatest part, as a substitute for the classic lyre or romantic harp, I require nothing more than an animated or impassioned recitation, adapted to the subject. Poems, however humble in their kind, if they be good in that kind, cannot read themselves; the law of long syllables and short must not be so inflexible,—the letter of metre must not be so impassive to the spirit of versification,—as to deprive the Reader of all voluntary power to modulate, in subordination to sense, the music of the poem;—in the same manner as his mind is left at liberty, and even summoned, to act upon its thoughts and images. (Wordsworth, 'Preface to the Edition of 1815'; <u>Prose Works</u>, ed. Owen & Smyser, Oxford, 1974, III, pp. 29–30)

> f. 'Black diamond of pessimism.' Belacqua thought that was a nice example, in the domain of words, of the little sparkle hid in ashes, the precious margaret and hit [<u>sic</u>: hid?] from many, and the thing that the conversationalist, with his contempt of the tag and the ready-made, can't give you, because the lift to the high spot is precisely from the tag and the ready-made. The same with the stylist. You couldn't experience a margarita in d'Annunzio because he denies you the pebbles and flints that reveal it. The uniform, horizontal writing, flowing without accidence, of the man with a style, never gives you the margarita. But the writing of, say, Racine or Malherbe, perpendicular, diamanté, is pitted, is it not, and sprigged with sparkles; the flints and pebbles are there, no end of humble tags and commonplaces. They have no style, they write without style, do they not, they give you the phrase, the sparkle, the precious margaret. Perhaps only the French can do it. Perhaps only the French language can give you the thing you want.
>
> Don't be too hard on him, he was studying to be a professor. (Beckett, <u>Dream of Fair to Middling Women</u>, 1932; <u>Disjecta</u>, ed. Cohn, London, 1983, p. 47)

There is a vast cloud of unknowing around here just at the moment, a positive trance of not wanting to know;[1] and the indemnity for this aversion is the transfer into false Figure:

> Then thou our fancy of itself bereaving
> Dost make us marble with too much conceaving.

(Milton, 'On Shakespeare'); or as Nigel Lawson prefers to say, 'Narrow money has the advantage of being easier to control, but it suffers from being almost too easy.'[2] This is why the figure-play of your visio seems to me now so intimately to the point.
    Se hit, mon amy!
            J.

---

18 November 1985   21 rue des Messageries
                                               Paris
                                               Tel: (Paris) 47-70-59-80

Dear Jeremy,
    Your welcome letter reached me in the middle of moving, as I've just bought a flat over here. Flooded bathrooms, dilatory notaires, cars struck by removal van ... (Please note new address and phone number.)
    This is just a quick shot back, for the moment, to say that I much appreciated a certain urgency given to publishing Pearl, which will now come out in a sort of on-the-run edition.[3] I suspect that yours was a major impetus, for that has been the case in the past. Now your two excellent quotations arrive: the Beckett, in particular, might have been made for the occasion, since I have wanted to risk the throwaway along with the more exalted considerations in that poem: something to free the prevailing, costive irony. As you have always known, there are styles which can move among the tones—not necessarily better than those more consistent in tone—but styles, nonetheless. And I love the notion of recitation, which seems so lost to us. To put the poem in the public arena, but without a notion of its getting anywhere, I submitted it to the Observer competition; and am glad I did, because the results of that competition make clearer to me what I have been trying for, and what movements I have been writing against, not too portentously, I hope.[4]
    So quickly, then, to say I was delighted at your usual generous response. I have never felt out of touch with you, inefficient at correspondence as I am, almost to a pathological degree, but know that the letters resume as if no gap, at each moment of necessity. I have noted your correspondence with Dunstan Ward re Franco-British Studies: my main role at this stage has been chivvying and journal design, and I am, at least for the moment, leaving the poetry side to others.[5] I don't normally involve my own poetic engagements with my paid employment, although I suggested your name.
    In fact, I've been meaning to send you a chapter of a book-

---

1 Prynne puns on the name of the fourteenth-century work of devotional mysticism *The Cloud of Unknowing*.

2 Prynne quotes Nigel Lawson as reported in *The Times* earlier in the year. Kenneth Fleet, 'More than One Reason for Caution on Interest Rates', *The Times*, 19 August 1985, 15.

3 Oliver refers to the Silver Hounds and Ferry Press first edition of *The Infant and the Pearl*.

4 Oliver refers to the 1985 *Observer*/Ronald Duncan Foundation international poetry competition, won by Oliver Reynolds. 'A Win for the Welsh', *The Observer*, 15 September 1985, 21.

5 Dunstan Ward (b. 1942), lecturer in English language and literature at the British Institute in Paris. Ward had written to Prynne on 17 September 1985 to invite him to contribute to the inaugural issue of *Franco-British Studies*. Prynne replied on 24 September to decline the invitation, and to lament the 'systemic indifference' of French publishers to the translations of his work by Bernard Dubourg.

length text on my glottis researches and allied matters: the chapter is a revised version of my article in GR on 'Of Movement Towards a Natural Place', including a few machine traces which might interest you.[1] I've sent the ms to C.U.P., though it may be too maverick for their tastes (my usual trouble), and a friend is proving annoyingly slow to return my only other copy, which has the photocopies I need to reproduce before printing you out a copy of your own. I'll get on to this with more determination, fired by your letter—in more ways than one—and therefore be in touch soon.

    Very best,
        Doug

---

1 February 1986   17 Ferry Path
                                                     Cambridge

Dear Doug,

    The sight-testing Infant and the Pearl has actually been with me since just before the new year, rushed hither by a red-star Jean who must have almost all the credit for resolve in the face of dutiful hesitations (not mine, I hasten to add).[2] It has been good to read this work across some extent of time, and strange too as the rotor blades of a tin-pot saga have whipped up such a seedy débacle and have even threatened the objects of reflex fear and scorn with a tincture of misjudged compassion.[3] What will our little school-lambs do, now that Joseph himself (a primal Selsdon Adam) is no longer to stand his free-trading guard over their dilapidating cribs?[4] The rats and re-rats have driven the snivelling gits off the page, let alone the thin girls in benders and the widow's cruse. One of the national moods is latent fear of the new uncertainty, as if the prolonged wait for a crack had wasted a nerve where not already twitching with self-interest. At any rate the sense of screen-dream and half-fading illusion is strongly in favour of this pamphlet's altogether opportune arrival. I have actually refused clandestine offers of the chance to read it earlier, because I was sure that the text was a public act and had to be received thus, worked into the response of a collective moment even if the apprehensions would be scattered enough.

    The extension and compression of this work are, together, extraordinary. From Byronic snap-closure and stuffed-up farce to the illumination of a vision deeply within the chambers of a faintly beating heart is an immense and audacious traverse: schematised by allegory, broken by fissures of dream-logic and cathexis, bringing images into the work-area of the reader's activation only via complete and repeated risk to the narrator's presence (body and soul). Yet the broken dream challenges both, as not yet tested between wishful fantasy and worse-case scenario, so that the borrowed strictness of the form leaves over the unworked question of a matching stricture in consciousness

---

1 Oliver enclosed a copy of this chapter, numbered 'Chapter 7' and titled 'What the Plants Can Tell Us', in a letter to Prynne of 18 May 1986. Intended for *PNP*, it was eventually replaced by the published chapter 7 of that book, on Milton. It includes the 'machine traces' (glottograph images) of Oliver reading Prynne's poem. 'What the Plants Can Tell Us' is printed in appendix C.

2 Oliver sent Prynne a copy of *The Infant and the Pearl* on 25 January 1986, inscribed with the dedication: 'For J.H.P., / the W.H. of this / little edition.'

    'sight-testing', Oliver's poem was printed as an A5 chapbook with five twelve-line stanzas per page, necessitating an extremely small type size.

    Jean Crozier, editor of Silver Hounds, married to Andrew Crozier.

    Prynne's letter responds throughout to individual words and lines in *The Infant and the Pearl*, as well as to its overall structure and politics. Given the frequency of direct and indirect allusions to the poem, only marked quotations are referenced in the notes.

3 'rotor blades of a tin-pot saga', Prynne refers to the Westland affair, an episode in British politics that was sparked in 1985 by the impending bankruptcy of Westland plc, Britain's sole manufacturer of helicopters.

4 Sir Keith Joseph (1918–94), British politician and Conservative secretary of state for education and science, 1981–6. On the day Prynne wrote this letter, *The Times* reported that Joseph intended to leave government. Anthony Bevins, 'Joseph to Stand Down at Election', *The Times*, 1 February 1986, 1.

    'primal Selsdon Adam', an epithet that references a shorthand for the free-market principles that Joseph espoused, named after the Selsdon Park Hotel, South Croydon, in which the Conservative shadow cabinet, including Joseph, held a pre-election meeting in January 1970. Prynne's epithet draws on the term 'Selsdon Man', coined by the Labour prime minister Harold Wilson and glossed by Hugo Young as 'a hairy, primeval beast threatening to gobble alive all the benefits which socialism had spread around postwar British society' (*One of Us* (London: Pan Books, 1993), 59). Prynne responds to Joseph's transformation in *The Infant and the Pearl*: 'Sir Keith, staring round at his leader, somehow / altered and became Adam Smith!' (*Kind*, 134–5).

itself: It was no dreme: I lay brode waking.¹ Thus there is overlay and blurring confusion and rapid shift between images, and at the same time an extraordinary underlying constancy in their latent values. And yet again this constancy is itself exposed to doubts: not only those of prudent application and social practice, but also to the spectre of fervid simplicity, clung to like assuaging emotion disguised as deep inner principle.

The prismatic counter-play of the figures which stalk this inside-out <u>News from Nowhere</u> (crossed maybe with parts of <u>After London</u>?) is itself vigorously dazzling: no flies on this nation-image and its sexualised imagination, which thus shrugs off the very young and the very old as spent shades in passion's mirror.² The buzz-words on a Golden Syrup tin, like the maggots of a blown cover-story riding pillion for a cure-all (sacred, crawling Lyons Maid), stiffen up to mock the love-like beast. The <u>Pearl</u>-poet did not notice his problems with currency metal, the golden gateȝ þat glent as glasse borrowed from an Apocalypse itself scarce tested against capital transfer tax;³ but now we have a national providence in BUPA and new issues from an old man's sleeve, Laura-Ashley style: wrapt in a cloud of sorrowe, struggling with the devil of the stairs and mostly preferring an express lift to the top.⁴ Pisgah! (Point Percy, sighing with relief).⁵

And yet despite all this there are risks of quite another kind: the schemes of concurrent <u>interpretatio</u>. The facile case against efforts of consciousness is easily rehearsed: 'When capitalism hits a severe crisis, liberal humanism disentangles itself from those materialist trappings and resumes its proper role as the impotent conscience of bourgeois society.'⁶ Or otherwise: Not all are free who mock their chains, nor all enslaved who profess to resent them. This is the posture wrestled with from early on, the pure because purposeless concernment, callously and inactively embittered: 'All that I wanted / had waned at that word, "courage".'⁷ Nonetheless (if indeed nonethemore) the effort to gain clarity is for the knowing dreamer himself, as proxy for so many others to follow in this story, a striving itself anxiously beholden to the opportunities for its exercise. It is a powerful and deeply-moving device to open with the accidental but evidently pre-rhetorical inheritance of a notionally Franciscan ethic in the overt symbolism of an assumed mantle; it <u>must</u> be overt, even at risk of didactic pointedness, since even half-concealment would divide readers into the self-rewardingly clever ones, and the careless or stupid or inexperienced who would all be excluded from what they more than any both need and deserve. But the dreamer is observed all too naturally breaking all the three vows he has not taken, in expression of his current nature and its contradictions; with this difference now that in the frame of an available explanation there is both a profoundly prior claim to reality and a format for a progressive, fitful part-understanding of what is at stake.

The schemes of provisional justification and repugnance each

---

1 Prynne interpolates a line from Thomas Wyatt's 'They fle from me'.

2 William Morris, *News from Nowhere* (Boston: Roberts Brothers, 1890); Richard Jefferies, *After London; or, Wild England* (London: Cassell, 1885).

3 Prynne interpolates a phrase from the penultimate section (line 1106) of the Middle English *Pearl*. Prynne's bracketed numbers after the quotations from *Pearl* in this letter are line numbers.

4 'BUPA', British United Provident Association, British private healthcare and health insurance company.

'Laura-Ashley', retail chain; shares in the company went on sale on 28 November 1985 and were immediately oversubscribed (hence 'new issues').

'wrapt in a cloud of sorrowe', Prynne interpolates a phrase from Thomas Campion's 'Follow your Saint, follow with accents sweet', an allusion to the tenth section of Oliver's poem.

5 'Pisgah', 'name of the peak of Mount Nebo, from which Moses saw the Promised Land', but more generally '[d]esignating a faint view or glimpse of something unobtainable or distant' (*Oxford English Dictionary*).

'Point Percy', Australian slang for urinate.

By the whole alliterative compound, Prynne likely has in mind William Hazlitt's description of Percy Bysshe Shelley in 'On Paradox and Common-Place' (1821), wherein the 'prospect of social amelioration' is the height to which Shelley's art leads 'the minds of men', only to 'dash them down the precipice the instant they reach the promised Pisgah'. *The Complete Works of William Hazlitt*, vol. 8, 146–56 (150).

6 Prynne misquotes Terry Eagleton: 'When capitalism hits a severe crisis, one of its major ideological motifs—liberal humanism—is regularly deflected into an idealist brand of Marxism. When capitalism recovers, liberal humanism disentangles itself from these materialist trappings and resumes its proper role as the impotent conscience of bourgeois society. W. H. Auden has been one of several proper names for that process in our own epoch.' 'And the Poetry He Invented Was Easy to Understand', review of *W. H. Auden: The Critical Heritage*, ed. John Haffenden, and *Auden: A Carnival of Intellect*, by Edward Callan, *Poetry Review* 73, no. 4 (January 1984): 60–1 (61).

7 *Kind*, 156.

at the same time undergoes the deepening tests of its own assumed framing. At least as I read it, this continuous enlargement of scope in what is corroded by solvent lucidity and mysterium comprises the counter-movement of the narrative, back upon its origins and then, by an overleaping bound forward, to a dauntingly unconcluded end. The binary image-pair of an ethical weather-house (Ros & Meg) allows compassion for the innocent as a test of power, and as the power-holders are denied both spirit-reality ('We save / the actual for believers'[1]) and creditable just-mindedness it does not matter that the more difficult face-up between real justice and true compassion is not at this stage located. There is an underlying anxiety, however, and it grows, that the exclusion of this difficulty makes the resultant ease (displayed in sharp wit and neatly self-disparaged facilities) a bit addictive for both writer and reader. Or, as it turns out, that under these covers the stakes are simply pushed up higher.

Just to put the obvious issue in an obvious way, as admittedly an interference in your suspensive and climactic ascent to this, the question concerns mercy as in any sense at all an exercise within the political order and what is both expected and needed from it. The Natural in Natural Justice does seem to raise the issues, and a party-system as in the UK where the ruling order has despised compassion as undisciplined (and saves it like credit) does apparently warrant its legitimate role in the political process. Mercy is judged Socialistic by those who hold it too soft for true justice, and that of course can be rejected without damage, allowing the whole-hearted conviction otherwise to match lioness with pearl, medieval mercy secularised to form an ideally wise Socialism. But, even in the presence of this heartfelt hope for non-expedient belief, the logic of what was divinely given, when transferred to a secular society, still leaves this question about who now donates the principle and endows it with authority; or does the current social psychology, or the public ethics of a benign obligation, somehow infer this term into the Social Contract?

Even in the medieval scheme the problem was acutely felt, and the more so because juristic theory and the places within it of virtue and sympathy derived most of its important precedents from Christian moral theology on the one hand and Classical moral analysis on the other. Left and right hands, we might say, not easily clasped together. There is a good discussion of the scope of these difficulties in J. D. Burnley, Chaucer's Language and the Philosophers' Tradition (Cambridge, 1979): he points out how central was Seneca's discussion of clementia and how in the administration of a state the exercise of this prerogative could and should be a rational action. Mercy and prudence could thus be in compatible alliance; to the exclusion of pity which was by definition irrational because sentimental. Just as indignation befuddles the reaction to tyrannical strength, so does pity blur over the reaction to the suffering victim: hard cases make

[1] Ibid., 134.

bad law, equity must be based upon reason: 'Seneca despised pity as irrational' (p. 23). This would seem merely flint-hearted if it were not for the conscious attempt to separate mercy from pity and to give the former a proper role in the exercise of clemency: although in all of this the retrospective judging seems to prevail over planning for a more positively just society in the future. But even here the principle at stake could be run forwards as well as backwards, in the strictly rational objections to tyranny for example as developed in the Cynic–Stoic diatribe.

This effort at distinction is then further blurred by the application of medieval Christian charity and compassion so as to re-unite mercy and pity; but by then the problem of their legitimacy has been subsumed into the human indebtedness to a Divine Providence, which has shewn the limits of human justice and imposed extra-territorial obligations upon it (paying off by vicarious supervenience, for instance, an otherwise unredeemable debt of sin). Even so, the modern reader does surely sometimes feel that, under this convenient exemption, sentimental pity is regularly allowed to salve conscience where it is wounded and to ignore it when it is not (hence, e.g., the power and dignity of Langland's willingness to be abstract and schematic). A good case discussed by Burnley is that of Chaucer's Theseus in The Knight's Tale (his pp. 25–27); and the Pearl-poet's dreamer who initially pines for pity and compassionate feeling from his beloved infant daughter (the innocent figure of an estranged no-harm[1]) is rewarded by such a sentence as:

> Who nedeȝ schal þole, be not so þro. (344)[2]

Well, Thanks a Lot, we feel on his unhappy behalf, what did he do to deserve this? 'E se non piangi, di che pianger suoli?' (And if thou weep not, at what does thou ever weep?)[3] I am reminded powerfully of the Prologue affixed by Wyatt to his translation of Psalm 51, where justification is an act not of man but of God.

In this general context you will see that for a part, intermittently, of my reading of your poem my heart was in my mouth, and in danger of getting chewed up in the acknowledging grins. And no doubt you wanted it there, A nation must know its own ignorance, for all the aching to be whole-hearted and the tacit conviction that, somewhere far within, one is so. But it is a great risk, nonetheless, and is compounded by what is for me my next large puzzle: the role in the advancing disclosure and analysis-by-description which is assigned to Chance, Hazard and Fortune (and perhaps to Providence also). I have tried to discriminate these terms into separable areas of activity and application, but with rather little success. In the world of material values and its traffic, as it encroaches upon that of the stunted spirit and its social wreckage, Chance legislates, and rules commerce, and is 'the breeder of this mess'.[4] Providence does not provide. The hub of Hazard Country is Steel City, 'its centre fixed in the fierce free will / of capitalist entrepreneurs', just as the capital's erect

---

[1] 'no-harm', Prynne interpolates a phrase from *The Harmless Building*, 5 (*TVTH*, 113).

[2] In the current standard edition of *Pearl*, the editors translate this line as 'Whoever must necessarily suffer, let him not be so stubborn'. Malcolm Andrew and Ronald Waldron, eds., *The Poems of the Pearl Manuscript: Pearl, Cleanness, Patience, Sir Gawain and the Green Knight* (Liverpool: Liverpool University Press, 2007), 70.

[3] Prynne quotes Dante's *Inferno*, Canto 33.

[4] *Kind*, 135.

timepiece 'had a great Wheel of Fortune for Big Ben', hoping for lucky six.[1] False values convert compassionate love to tyrannic lust and a stand-up quickie in 'the terrain / of chance, of Steel City'.[2] Despite the dependence on control-mechanisms and power hierarchies, the implication here is that the underlying process, its determining rationale, is mere hazard, or chance outcome, the random interplay of pragmatic expedients and market forces: overall the realm of a blind and heartless Fortune.

But, for as long as we experience thought within an adversative dialectic, what is the alternative to this conception? Is the process wrongly analysed, with State Power effectively marshalling the narrow limits of uncertainty and preserving it (mostly imported via the international monetary system, OPEC, etc.) as a source of alibis for miscalculation or venality?[3] Or, is it the cosmetic tone which is wrong, with insufficient wringing of helpless hands and copious effusions of caring sympathy (rhetorical heart-bleed)? Or, would a more massive extension of centralised government planning and control (such as Kinnock is steering carefully clear of) somehow remove or smooth out the hazards of, say, natural gas, failed harvests, major epidemics (Plagues & AIDS), scandals and crises and the cumulative opportunism of personal ambition?[4] If it be said that for one side Fortune favours the rich and advantaged, then for the other it favours the solidarity of a mass normality (and the politic mouldbreakers break in only with a middle-class provincialism). In each case, also, the ascription of powerful agency to Fortune is not far from a cover designed merely to instil acceptance, as Blake was not slow to argue:

> If you would make the poor live with temper
> With pomp give every crust of bread you give with gracious
>   cunning
> Magnify small gifts reduce the man to want a gift & then give
>   with pomp
> Say he smiles if you hear him sigh If pale say he is ruddy [5]

In all of this there are positions which are shoved aside into the margins and even the gutters of accident: as we each have professional reason to know rather sharply, with our respective joining of decoy trades to gain access to a modicum of facilitation.

At the very moment when things seem to be going better for the dreamer, whose hurts are mended by a merciful nature, the <u>Pearl</u>-poet adds this comment:

> As fortune fares þer as ho frayneȝ,
> Wheþer solace ho sende oþer elleȝ sore,
> Þe wyȝ to whom her wylle ho wayneȝ
> Hytteȝ to haue ay more and more. (129–32)[6]

This is an attempt to subject Fortune to Providence, through the idea of testing, which is also a mainspring of the case against Spenser's Mutability.[7] Burnley is again to the point about this:

1 Ibid., 140, 142.

2 Ibid., 143.

3 'OPEC', Organization of the Petroleum Exporting Countries.

4 Neil Kinnock (b. 1942), Welsh politician and leader of the Labour Party, 1983–92.

5 Prynne quotes the [a] text of Blake's 'Vala, or The Four Zoas'.

6 In their explanatory notes, Andrew and Waldron translate as: 'As Fortune proceeds where she tests (a person), whether she sends pleasure or else pain, the person to whom she sends her desire chances to have all the time more and more (of the same).' *The Poems of the Pearl Manuscript*, 60.

7 Prynne refers to the arguments made against the ultimate dominion of Mutability in Edmund Spenser's *Two Cantos of Mutabilitie*.

for Chaucer, too, 'Fortune is eventually revealed to have rather less than absolute power ... Indeed, there is a sense in which Fortune does not exist outside the minds of men. It is they who have made her in the image of the tyrant' (p. 37). But once again the transfer of this theme to a secular, post-providential idea of the social process is to leave Hazard with a role, however defined and stochastically normalised, essentially outside the frame of political theory; presumably to an almost equal degree for whichever kind of party politics addresses the issue. But is there not a possible difference of attitude to the consequences of Hazard? In disaster relief or international aid, for instance, or the remedy of arbitrary hardship as it rears up against a suddenly more wretched sector of society? Or on the other side of the coin, how large should be the Windfall Tax or Gift Tax, or the increased clawback of overlapping benefits or sequestration from the overseas havens; perhaps with some reverse discrimination against the well-born or the extremely clever? From most of the interventions implied here I'd not dissent, although the follow-on (and for you not crucial) problems of freedom compound with those already noted, of pity and indignation as distorting a scheme of prudence (one of the cardinal Renaissance virtues, after all) in ways which not all can be expected to consider equitable or even fair by ethical intuition. But at this point it has to be noted, unless I am mistaken, that your argument is really that Fortune and Hazard are built into the scheme of actuality as understood by Britain's Tories, and that by implication these forces would not <u>operate</u> thus (rather than fail to be more compensatingly remedied) under some alternative régime. Well, this too makes me wary, because as an observable experience the price of minimising the variable pressures of Fortune against or on behalf of individuals or parts of society can in some areas be a very high one indeed, and one not at all easy to reconcile with apparently whole-hearted principles and convictions. Even the radical marginalism of the Franciscan solution, supposing it to be available to an atheist skipping the wafer course, would probably destroy the very society which is at least theoretically capable of improving as a result of partially heeding its critique.

 Of course and many times over you have not omitted to notice this; and indeed the latent knowledge of it is the unexpressed ground for much of your dreamer's anguish, that he must endure the temptations of <u>parti pris</u> and the release of blocked feeling by whatever channels are offered in the hazard of his traumatic encounters. This gives an edginess to the writing, a constant sense that even when riding smoothly along with confidence or chagrin the whole business may at any moment drop into a black abyss. The worst fate would indeed be the Buddhist smile of total ignorance because, unless an occasion for the proxy-feeling of others, it would lead to entire ethical nullity: the Void itself, cancelling at a stroke all the Dantean emotional and moral power of a striving after justice and social hope. Your dreamer is sent reeling again and again by body-blows (and spirit-blows too) against his own just self-esteem and by the palliative self-assertion to which he is, recoiling from passivity, driven to have recourse. Thus his transformation into an anti-Thatcherite MP, with his cameo performance at the ready, installs a cynicism which occasions the immediate loss of his badge of seriousness (his <u>mantle</u>) to a surrogate and shadowy father-figure ('See it staukes away'[1]); but there is of course the fear abroad that such a mantle could never, by anyone, be taken into that chamber and not be rent by the divisions of partial argument and partial interest and part-truth against part-fabrication.

This must have been the state of lacerating play which you had reached by the imminent parliamentary intervention of the exiled Rosine. So much must depend now upon her convincingness without authority, her human strength, unflecked with human weakness but not left sounding monstrously remote (like the <u>Pearl</u>-child, for instance). 'Virtue is vulgar' bangs off into exalted contradiction, although we catch breath at the thought that it may be no more than a catch-phrase.[2] But the sustained onslaught of her willingness to endure a wasting paradox rather than compound for the false ease of sentimental contrition is very empowering in the name of deeply unfashionable truth. Her tirade against sentimental socialism, its hugging of the way down and its canting, leftist sycophancy, effectively denounces any opposition party which in a democratic system trades on the moral superiority of its simply not being in office, the luxuries of opposition. But it is aimed at the particular cant of 'poor versus rich', just as much as at the gibe of a Bennite intransigent against the sell-out of conciliation. Thus, it fits, uncomfortably but rightly.

But then there is the matter of the Centre; whether it is shallow or deep, whether the almost inarticulate yearning of a populace for some steadily fair and evenly steady accommodation of human nature in its median reality can be matched to the implicitly separating and antagonising dialectic of a party political system which is not an Arminian or Unitarian comity. As a non-politician, Rosine embodies this desire for a centre, in the palm of an innocent hand, beyond price and almost beyond knowledge by the senses of this world. She is an ideal which maybe the actual can hardly afford, without some secularised experience analogous to salvation or at least conversion. But what she actually argues for, in that chamber, seems to be a centrism of national unity, healing division by judging and drawing away from extremes, following 'those / who keep to the centre current of courage'.[3] I understand the intrepid idealism of this, reaching down past the actual into the real of an unfrozen heartland, set out in that very convincingly hostile forum; and I understand too, I think, that the outburst has to be destined to fail of any aim or end one could conceive for it save that of an individual dawning of newly awakened consciousness in the dreamer.

[1] Prynne quotes *Hamlet*, act 1, sc. 1.
[2] *Kind*, 151.
[3] Ibid., 153.

1 February 1986

The courage, after all, was an ideal of his Dad's, however non-political and uneasy of political application. My paraphrases are in any case crudely reductive and fail to render how feeling is both raised and torn apart by this terrible dream-like ordeal.

But once again I am left with the notions of <u>courage</u> and <u>the centre</u>. It is clear that the courage not to be sentimental, and yet to embrace pity rather than clemency (and mercy rather than either of them), ought by definition not to be vulnerable to the taint itself of the sentimental. But such is the threat of interlapping layers in the integrity of the moral emotions that of course it is vulnerable. Well, if it were not it would be armed in and by a useless certitude or rationality, excluding the need for constant human support which is its cardinal claim upon moral activity. And being thus vulnerable, it is open to question within the dangerous forum of cant and counter-cant, and open also to expedient expropriation. In political terms this for sure means Mrs Shirley Williams, and just because she's been astutely low-profile for a while this does not at all mean that she is not part of these equations.[1] All the argument about a shallow or a deep centre, its radicalism or mere use as a divider to support democratic practice, leaves open a position in your poem in practical terms hardly protected by one brief sip of the SDP. Hundreds of thousands of disheartened citizens already look (even if without quite knowing it) to Mrs Williams as the rosy pearl to Mrs Thatcher's ice-blue aquamarines. What's more, she is to stand for Cambridge, and she will get in. Kinnock was speaking here yesterday, fresh from his Westland triumphs, and said of her selection: 'she might as well lose here as anywhere else.' But I think that she will not lose, for all the efforts by Rhodes James to come out hastily as a fully-fledged, caring wet.[2] The ideal position is always the most exposed and endangered by opportunistic colonisation. I dare not think that you might see this otherwise.

Well, you see how I have been cliff-hanging (dreadful trade). In fact I am almost able to read your multiple dénouement as skirting so close to its own implicit insufficiency, and weakness, even, precisely so as by no means to comprise any kind of visionary rescue. To be true in such a context the truth would need to be quite ordinary, and probably rather tired and grey. The city on a hill does not shine, except by neon or otherwise for one single moment perhaps; just as the goddess of justice and truth herself wears out into decrepitude (sempiternal as senile: this is gripping and wearing and the reader too is made to endure an awful depletion). To lose the ideal completely would be terrible; almost as final a blow as to hold on to it only by sentimental self-deception and frantic, trance-like clinging. To lose the threatening and hated forces confronting the ideal would be almost as bad, the ogre-figures and horror-prospects which are our sustaining demonology. Not to be able to hold on to a father, or a child, as both recede into the lost distance of generation if not at

---

1 Shirley Williams (1930–2021), British politician and president of the Social Democratic Party (SDP), 1982–7.

2 Williams stood unsuccessfully in Cambridge in the 1987 general election, losing to the sitting Conservative candidate Robert Rhodes James (1933–99).

'wet', used pejoratively by Thatcher to refer to moderates in the Conservative Party.

least of part-betrayal, makes desolation all the more true for being visionary: from the power of illumination and celestial bombardment we had expected to be infused with some new potential and not drained to exhaustion. It's lovely to behold whatever is wise and very terrifying to think that one might be excluded from even the most superseded ceremonial.

In these momentous shape-shiftings the reader is jolted almost quite out of politic memory: how did we get here? What arte þou, & what hast þou deserued?[1] What is left of who we are, or once were in the eyes of the insufficiently loved? The window that glows weakly is known to me, as also the passageway, and the voice which will not come. Indeed, I may not speak of them, how and wherever butter would melt. And here too, in the inner sanctum itself, where the difficulty of sheer ultimatum seems an unquestionable credential, up pops the sentimental once again. By now we are made to gasp simultaneously at our own credulity and at our acceptance of a punishing truth as much for the epithet as for the noun. So that the test for the reader is whether still to look at the credibility of the lesson offered, or at the drive inwardly towards the power to see a truth in what we know even of the familiar and rather facile. After all, Rosine's final message about the pearly mirror is neither a grandly final word nor a mystic oracle: it is probably at best only half-true, and is shot through with what it will require an immense effort not to apprehend as sentiment. There is still soul-talk and grace-talk in this dream-version of a secular world; a genetic accident puts one kind of serene hazard right in the centre of the mesh of Fortune and its counter-changes. And then the formal cycle insists on closure and wraps the whole in a worn-out reminder of all that from which we are by no means to be exempted.

Does this concluding movement both conclude and enclose the outcome or the completeness of this daring poem? The question is not straightforward because not only is there an element of quite large actual risk for the reader (<u>this</u> one, anyway), but clearly there has to be such risk if we are not to be spared the pressure of sentiment, love itself, by a sentimental decision to adjust style so as not to exclude it. This is not a comfortable argument, nor meant to be, and I think it will come out differently for different individuals. For me it comes out that the potential truth of this conclusion has lost almost all power (good, I think), and has gone below the level at which language can both express an idea or an experience <u>and</u> test its verity. You get the barest idea, without the test, not because an ordeal is planned but because ultimately, perhaps, the idea of the test is the last piece of sentiment. It is what is done with the subsequent self, in reflection and activity, which may eventually express it; or this too may be a pious fancy. It has to be unfraudulently possible that nothing happens; otherwise whatever does is part of that pining for assent or its counterpart which is the constant ruination of art: its claim to power.

1 February 1986

---

[1] Prynne interpolates part of a sentence from *The Cloud of Unknowing*, chap. 2: 'What arte þou, & what hast þou deserued, þus to be clepid of oure Lorde?' Phyllis Hodgson, ed., *The Cloud of Unknowing and the Book of Privy Counselling* (London: Early English Text Society, 1944), 14.

[1] Prynne's letter is composed on a word processor that produces a noticeably different typeface and layout from his previous letters.

[2] In a copy of this letter preserved in Prynne's papers, Prynne has underlined certain words and phrases. These are represented here by a dashed underline.

[3] Oliver refers to Dante's *Inferno*, Canto 34.

[4] 'Natural Law that vigour would diminish', Oliver touches on the tendency towards stupefaction and exhaustion '[i]n the progress of the division of labour' described in Adam Smith's *Wealth of Nations*, conditions 'into which the labouring poor, that is, the great body of the people, must necessarily fall, unless government takes some pains to prevent it'. *Wealth of Nations: Books IV–V*, ed. Andrew Skinner (London: Penguin, 1999), 368–9 (369).

I am sorry to have rattled on about this, and then to pump the whole stream through a fancy new machine into the bargain (not much of a snip in fact, and skulking in my Library where every single book cries out mutely against it).[1] Do come over soon, if you can and when, but I shall probably be away after Easter and until term starts again.

Saluti cari:

J.

7 February 1986[2]   21 rue des Messageries
Paris

Dear Jeremy,

I need hardly say how interesting your letter was to me, plunging me right back into the preoccupations that I had thought (at least temporarily, for they never leave me) foreclosed.

There is one point of difference in interpretation which I had better deal with: hazard. The poem does not deny its role, of course, but merely objects to its being made the governing principle, as this is a contradiction of the notion of government. My notion of it is more like the centre of the Dantesque universe, with its partner, mutability, the instant reversal as you pass through Satan's navel: the necessary corruption in order, change in stasis, and so forth.[3] What has to be subsumed into Providence, as traditionally, the medieval model being a good one in many ways. It cannot be itself a value, as the Conservatives make Supply and Demand into a value; it is a 'what' that has to be governed; and it can be governed at any stage of its progress into governmental form, providing this is done healthily, like healthy pruning in the garden. Theoretically, there is nothing against interference for proper governmental motives with either supply or demand, providing vigour is not affected in a harmful way (perhaps it will necessarily be affected, but, for instance, to redirect two charging bulls to knock down a ... slum dwelling ... might diminish but usefully redirect energy). Adam Smith gave no real evidence for supposing that vigour would be harmfully affected, except the Natural Law that vigour would diminish.[4] This is not, however, nearly clear as seems: mankind can pick up vigour for reasons that the 18th century would not have called natural—idealism, for example. It must be admitted that Socialism has found few ways of intervening healthily with this vigour: this should not destroy the energy to look for such ways. You mention various compensatory remedies, clawing back from the powerful. Well, this is a way of interfering with market processes, nonetheless because it is retrospective, hence the problem of limits to which you refer: it is a way little favoured by the present government. The difference between the deep centre and the SDP is that the deeps are hardly imaginable and can most nearly be approached by the greatest political courage and prudence: what actual policy goes with this I do not know and do not see how I can know. I do not believe that a poem should attempt to set up a system of government—Pound's great error. It can show us the golden possibilities, perhaps, as Sidney says, but the complexity of a modern country is so great that it might be a final hubris even to try for that if such a vision is not 'given'. I know no-one nor have heard of anyone, poet, politician or philosopher to whom it has been given in modern times. In our ignorance, in the pragmatic attempt at Socialism, may the politicians keep working for that courage and prudence which will put as much mercy to work as is compatible with national vigour and even (this is truly idealism) with a vigorous attempt by Britain to serve the Third World. (My god, what are we complaining about? It really is disgusting!) These will involve controls upon the necessary vitality of hazard, whereas so many actions taken by the present overlords will not put such mercy or prudence to work. True action is, as always, unknowable except in its coming-to-be; that is what I mean by the unimaginability of the depths; and here is the great difference with the SDP. As I don't need to tell you, truth does not arise, usually, by compromise, mere middle-roadism, or consensus. The centre-line is the mean but is classically golden. It has to be seen in a vision that is active. It cannot be defined in a poem. It is pragmatic in that sense. Therefore, its heart-principle is an ignorance, an initial yielding of cleverness, until soul meets soul; once that is at the heart, then let there be all manner of cleverness to put this principle as much as possible into action, compatibly with justice, economic vigour and all the rest of normal political preoccupations. All your very fine comments upon the Medieval position (I had missed Burnley's book, but will get hold of it) are very apposite, but there is only a 'sense' in which Fortune does not exist outside men's minds: the sense of the reified goddess, perhaps; the goddess's connection with mutability and hazard, is, however, real; and some kind of formal principle comes from that dark connection towards the light, waiting to be born.

    Most traditional Socialist solutions, the misuse of State power to take uncertainty out of life, centralised control, nationalisation, and so on, are not compatible with vigour—or, as you point out, with freedom—; they are weighed down with ancient Fabian–Marxist analysis. If you ask what should replace it, I can reply like everyone else; I have a few dreams for piecemeal solutions. The creation of local economy systems bound into the national system is a favourite dream I'm not sure I could explain properly here; but it is only a dream which I'm sure any professional could easily demolish. However, if you read the professional economists it is easy to track the unargued assumptions that underly their computer graphs. I have one by me, Treasury Working Paper No. 18, 'The Role of Money in Determining Prices: A Reduced Form Approach', by Simon Wren-Lewis. 'Approach'? But I thought government policy was confidently based upon a firm notion of how money determined prices. (Well, of course, that is rhetorical;

7 February 1986

I didn't.); What can we be left with as a first move in Socialism at this time but a confession of ignorance, coupled with a realisation that knowledge itself lies within that ignorance. This is different from Kinnock too, who is mainly trying to keep his 'coalition' together by hedging his bets.

To the charge of final sentimentality, therefore, I plead guilty all along. One of the hundreds of definitions of sentimentality might be to have feeling for others without power to put it into action. The Pearl poet wakes up because he cannot wait to become part of his new extra-terrestrial knowledge and desire: this is the sublimation of the sentimental into the religious. A tin-pot saga (good phrase for my poem too) cannot go for sublimation. And yet ... Socialism remains sentimental at each point where it is powerless; and it will remain powerless without policy; and it will remain without policy without a radical inspection of its own ignorance. Inside that lies something really quite exciting, which can be found only by the engaged political genius, not by discussing poetic themes in a letter. The game is too serious. The people, finally, are not fooled by Socialism's queasy confidence: that is why Shirley Williams may win Cambridge. I suppose Cambridge could do worse, in fact, better than David Lane (who he? ed) but not better than Barbara Castle.[1]

I write on a day when my thoughts are with Haiti, which I visited a year and a half ago with a journalist friend who writes for the Guardian on the Caribbean and is out there now reporting on the Duvaliers' apparent fall.[2] I have a joke photo of myself with Baby Doc, whose presidential reception we gate-crashed. Today, Jean-Claude has fled the country and, although what regime is to succeed him is yet unclear, he leaves behind him an exaggerated caricature of what happens when immense poverty is ruled by elitism and that kind of snaffling of public (and aid-donated) funds which is the ultimate working-out of unbridled chance and power: unless there is mercy and control in government.[3] In Haiti, without such control, new 'bridges' were built, for example, emblazoned like every other tawdry public works with Duvalier's name, and crumbled away five years later, owing to lack of pier foundations, since they had been built for cheap, for Duvalier's image. Well, I don't want to misapply such a woeful example to the workings of a complex Western state. But it is a caricature, as I say: what could a Socialist regime do with such deep-lying problems of infrastructure, destruction of forests (because of poverty and need for charcoal), consequent erosion, and acute water shortage? In all charity, not go to Cuba but curtail ambitions so that the maximum aid be won out of America, be patient to work slowly, slowly, and so on. If a man's dying (says sentiment) you don't ask the politics of a neighbour who can give you a bread roll for him. When the man's on his feet, you can talk about co-existence. In Britain, the doctrinaire and low-level nature of Socialist dialogue makes me see ... well, what colour? The poem says red. It cannot be true red until the

---

1   David Lane (1922–98), British Conservative politician and MP for Cambridge, 1967–76, succeeded by Robert Rhodes James.
    Barbara Castle (1910–2002), British Labour politician and MP, 1945–79.

2   'journalist friend', Oliver refers to Greg Chamberlain, Paris-based British journalist.
    'the Duvaliers' fall', Jean-Claude 'Baby Doc' Duvalier (1951–2014) was president of Haiti from 1971 until he was overthrown by a popular uprising in February 1986.

3   Duvalier fled Haiti in the early morning of 7 February 1986 (the date of Oliver's letter); his flight was reported in *Le Monde* and *The Times* the following morning. Oliver likely heard the news from one of his journalist friends before it made the papers. Chamberlain, as Oliver indicates, was in Haiti at the time, and later wrote that 'I watched as [Duvalier and his wife] fled before dawn on 7 February 1986 (after a last defiant champagne party at the palace).' Greg Chamberlain, 'Jean-Claude Duvalier Obituary', *The Guardian*, 5 October 2014, accessed 18 July 2021, www.theguardian.com/world/2014/oct/05/jean-claude-baby-doc-duvalier. A photograph of Oliver, Chamberlain, Aubelin Jolicoeur, and Bernie Diederich is reproduced in *CAAS*, 253.

extraordinarily sharp questions in your valued letter can be more nearly and courageously answered: and the answers may not look like Socialism (as we know it) at all. They may even look more like Thatcherism—perhaps temporarily—in parts. Where is the politician, not the poet, who can put such a package together?

You see, the crucial issue has been pinpointed by you: 'When capitalism hits a severe crisis, liberal humanism disentangles itself from those materialist trappings…' etc. Awareness of this or something very like it was an obstacle which nearly prevented me from writing the poem: then it became the most interesting obstacle to cross. Because your quotation is fundamentally a slogan out of the old Socialism, the kind that pretended its analysis of materialism was quasi-scientific, that its solutions were inevitable. History has shown these claims up, although the old Socialism retains its power in so many countries (I followed the Grenadan experiment, a particularly pure example, very closely and have met several of the practitioners of it).[1] It is by these pretended certainties that liberal humanism has been so often judged as impotent. Well, let's take the word, 'liberal' away and substitute a better pragmatism. Without such a humanism, where will we get the humanitarian drive to find new solutions? The trouble with Thatcherism is that, at heart, it assumes everyone wants to build an extension on their kitchen and lacks the money; and that this is the metaphysical reason for existence.

Your letter was long, but not wordy. This is wordy and repetitive: but that's because I want to get off an immediate reply at a difficult time.

Well… meeting… that would be good indeed but I don't have a <u>free</u> visit to England possible before Easter, owing to sundry courses, including one during the holiday.

Will it be next autumn, then—or where <u>are</u> you going? Let's at least pencil in a firm determination, as a Socialist might say… This a partial reply but I'll keep the wire open.

    Doug.

[*On a copy of this letter preserved in his papers, Prynne added the following notes below Oliver's signature:*]

<u>Fortuna</u>   Patch on same [2]
         Dante, <u>Inferno</u>, VII (cit. by Pound,
            Canto XCVII (p. 707, Faber ed.)

         Canto XCVII, p. 709:
           'Even Aquinas could not demote her, Fortuna'
         Q. Skinner's tome [3]
           Canzone (Canto XXXVI):
              'Let no man say love cometh from chance
              Or hath not established lordship' (p. 183)

7 February 1986

---

1 'My 45th birthday party [1982], I sat with some New Jewel leaders from Grenada outside "Le Maquis", a Montmartre restaurant.' *TVTH*, 81.

2 Howard Rollin Patch wrote several books and articles on the goddess Fortuna and various literatures, including *The Goddess Fortuna in Mediaeval Literature* (Cambridge, MA: Harvard University Press, 1927).

3 Prynne refers to Quentin Skinner's *The Foundations of Modern Political Thought*, vol. 1 (Cambridge: Cambridge University Press, 1978).

[1] Prynne interpolates a line from *Twelfth Night*, act 1, sc. 5.

(Paradise not artificial),
    'but spezzato, apparently' (Canto LXXIV, p. 465)
    'but is jagged' (Canto XCII, p. 653)
broken (up);
fragmented

16 February 1986   17 Ferry Path
                                                    Cambridge

Dear Doug,

    Yes, thanks for your enlarging letter, I take its points and even more the aroused impetus, its willingness to be impaled upon the very points themselves if no other way offers. I suspect that we perhaps do disagree somewhat about hazard, as it figures within the poem at least, since outside Providence (and even the cautionary prudence of x <u>providing that also</u> y) I could see it as the very ground upon which truth could be a principle of action. 'Even Aquinas could not demote her' concedes Pound (Canto XCVII), and since behaviourism sponsors Regulation and Closure which are worst when most nearly beneficial and humane, I cannot voluntarily accept the maximalism of the left intervention ('planning') upon which its scheme of equitable hope has surely to be based. But by ethical compulsion I can and do, as a kind of self-wounding scourge against advantageous injustice by which the benefit is cruelly mine. But not by <u>wish</u>, even so, since moral compromise lies just at the limit of option and indeed compromises the limit: 'as much mercy as is compatible' is the prudent boundary to 'greater mercy than we know what to do with': your letter breathes with utterly honourable desire to make the idea both workable in practice <u>and</u> unreachable except by a trans-practical aspiration. Do not take it that such a way of putting it hints at some kind of superior <u>sang-froid</u> on my part: it describes clumsily but correctly my own conviction also.

    And in any case the whole matter of hazard is I believe not central. The matter of sentiment, though, is at the very hub itself. And here again I think that we do not disagree as much as the tone of your argument suggests that you think we do. It is possible to hold that the patchwork of truths which a social order may steer by and fitfully measure itself against are likely not to be lofty and coherent principles of grand luminosity and adequate complication. And to believe that sentimental acceptance of the patchwork is in fact a deep human bonding at the most ordinary level: Anything that's mended is but patch'd.[1] When Pound lamented that the reality of Paradise was <u>spezzato</u> (or 'jagged' as later he worded it), his mistake was in the lament, not in the recognition. Hence I do not believe in a political centre which is any more than the adroit hedging & edging of a party system; but I would separate this from what it claims to imitate, which is the central ordinariness of ethical intuition and human tolerance, even of moral <u>habit</u>, in a populace not brutalised by tyranny or privation nor hypnotised into disclaiming its own sentimental loyalties.

Your letter in fact confirms to me what your poem implied: that the shifting tones of anger and ingenuity are latently under attack for their own confidence, producing an accusing fear of self-betrayal towards older solidarities even as their new replacements struggle to become visible. Restrictive practice is the enemy! And yet of course fancy blue-printing is the same; and if I were to idealise a collective-sentimental replacement for a half-willing loyalty to formal precedent, I should at very least end up endorsing the racial expulsions which the 'bad' sentimentality of European isolationism certainly desires (To the whole city, 'sleep no more.').[1]

As you say, no solutions. The will to act must swiftly preclude the self-admitted ignorance which might hold action to that measure, since those who do act come to believe that they have worked out the balancing rightness of what they do. That is why an adversary system is necessary (if painfully divisive) and why the middle ground of consensus is such a lure. I shall never believe in even the possibility of a single-vision solution because I think that the contradictions inherent in the political process absolutely must be worked through in the arena of social experience (what you call 'pragmatism'). As I read your poem it combines the strongest commitment to a truth of right understanding and action with the deepest encounter (perhaps unwished-for) with its own implicit contradictions. That is what for me makes it so rousing and yet so chastening to read and study.

J.

1 March 1986   21 rue des Messageries
Paris

Dear Jeremy,

I was immensely pleased with your letter, which had several directions in it I just hadn't expected. I thought we had much more of an argument than we turn out to have; and it seems more unusual than it should be to feel a community of political ethic with anyone, especially in our own rather rarefied world of poets.

We have always had a difference about hazard, I think (searching back in memory). It's there in your line 'Little room for charity' from 'Wound Response'.[2] I have also known that the difference is one of perception of basic dynamic but that there is little difference in the results of our two forms of 'ethical dynamism'. For me, the crucial belief has always come out of Kierkegaard, that lower forms persist in the higher. Put in crude dialectical terms this has meant for me that if, say, a lower form of moral wish enters the melting point, then that lower form reappears in the transcendence in some way. Taking this out of dialectics, the providential consciousness creates the preconditions for the hazardous nature of action itself and I assume it

1 Prynne interpolates a phrase from Wordsworth's *Prelude*, bk. 10, which itself quotes *Macbeth*, act 2, sc. 2.

2 Oliver quotes 'Of Movement Towards a Natural Place' (*Poems*, 223).

to bear the same, paradoxical relation to hazard as does the perhaps-theoretical, absolute face of time/good to the relative face. There is Diderot's problem of what happens when an evil man by nature acts naturally, if natural action is the highest good (and the potential divine perfection of created nature is not a form of belief that will help us here). We may take it that the fully hazardous is not describable. So what 'happens' to the providential 'charity' at the very moment when we suppose it lost, without 'room' to survive the pressure-centre of action? I make a step in faith, but not a religious step: perhaps, and incredibly, 'charity' is 'still there': it is the other face of virtuous hazard; and this is why hazard can be the ground for truthful action. This seems to fit well with what I observe. You will probably have a more sophisticated dynamics, because you usually do; what comes out of your dynamics is, it seems, closely kin to what I would have come out of mine. I trust my heart on this because it is all I can trust.

Then, I find, so do you: through the very good things you say about sentiment, which brought real joy to me. It is such an important principle that human relationships in their most ordinary sense are our most important evidence and ordinary 'ethical intuition' the source of deepest value. Any other way a profoundly unethical arrogance lies, which has betrayed every radical political experiment I can bring to mind.

These are issues of so great a weight that I wish a book about politics could be written from these standpoints. One of my current obsessions is that the time is ripe for a new political philosophy and I wish I were competent to formulate it and had the necessary social weight. It's astonishing how trivial the average work about general political programmes is—to say nothing of the turgid philosophies of most major leaders. And how little is a poem!

We'll keep in touch and, in any case, are.
    Best,
        Doug.

9 March 1986   17 Ferry Path
                                                                                      Cantab

Dear Doug:

Yes: all that is needed to complete the circuit is the link you now truly donate, by which in turn I am so gladly stirred: virtuous hazard. Of course this can be heard by glance only and there are cruel hybrids; but the phrase has meaning even if at the limit of sense. It is not recruited and thus its virtue denies system to the ethic voice, speaking in borrowed accent & within common pitch. And so, even poems are not so little!
    J.

9 March 1986. The postcard depicts a march on Hospital Sunday (ca. 1900), a fundraising tradition established in 1873.

2 June 1986

21 rue des Messageries
Paris

Dear Jeremy,

'Marzipan' caught me rather unawares, somehow: I don't know what I expected, but not that.[1] It therefore took a little time to get into, to catch the tone.

It has a high-toned anger at what's going on: at the easy choices being made and the rottenness it engenders in the nation. So much of the age's inherent viciousness is an outplaying from a mere wish for comfort at home, the television-side. I find our recent word, Fortune, and from the correspondence know how you would like this as a clarified point of action. There's much of despair in this anger, isn't there? A purely situational despair, perhaps, rather than a metaphysical. The losing of the rose, the smattering out of small desires traduced as grander rhetoric — well, you know how attuned we are on that! The image of the conductor very fine because of 'flattened'. At the end it becomes three-level, the brighter possibilities driven underground to become magical, the wastes and comforts at mid-level, and the poor in the mountains; no wonder there is such disgust and contempt in the last lines.

When I contrast the accuracy of this with what one normally reads I become disturbed anew that still even the sharper political or media voices have not realised the full extent of the harm. There is no deadly critique in the Labour party's rhetoric. Where is there a programmed attempt to expose the damage? Why is there no party organ rigorous enough to convince, or even to win readers? But all must depend on the rhetoric of 'a devastating blow to the Health Service', 'disastrous policies', or, worse, some attempt to make the lady herself into a ridiculous phantom.[2] If such times seem to give the missing extra values back to poetry, that is not a complacent notion. Your poetry has never lacked those values. But now there has to be an anger like this, a precise sense of what's wrong: that it's in the electorate, more even than in Westminster. We have allowed the sociologists for far too long to exonerate the electorate from responsibility — the vote whose significance is always held off from the voter by power mechanisms, that half-truth which has been revealed as so dangerous, these past few years. It's obviously extreme to think of ourselves as in a post-war Germany situation: but there is something desperately wrong in political vocabulary. I read John Bayley's weak review of Tom Paulin's (probably weak) anthology of 'political verse'.[3] But this is political verse: the language itself anguished, so to speak, at the harms being forced into it, and the language forced by rectitude and its ally, strong feeling, to change for the better.

Poetry as witness, then, is more than that. Where's this poem going to be sent. And what next? What clarities? The ball must be kept in play.
　　Best,
　　　　Doug

1 Prynne sent a copy of *Marzipan* (with 'Massepain', a French translation of 'Marzipan' by Bernard Dubourg and Prynne) (Cambridge: Poetical Histories, no. 2, 1986) on 26 May 1986. See *Poems*, 347–8.

2 'lady herself', Margaret Thatcher.

3 Oliver refers to John Bayley, 'Tom Paulin's Radical Cheek', review of *The Faber Book of Political Verse*, ed. Tom Paulin, *The Guardian*, 29 May 1986, 22.

2 September [1986]   21 rue des Messageries
Paris

Dear Jeremy,

Anthony B. is trying to win publishers' grants so that he can produce a twin-set of my poetry and my writings on prosody.

At short notice, I find I have to supply the names of academic/poetic referees for the award bodies—the British Academy (deadline 16th of this month) and a Sussex Univ. Library Fund. Would it be all right to use your name?

And perhaps, with a minute or two more of time it will give us our usually-required prod to get back in touch?

　　　Best, as always
　　　　　　Doug.

Double Ninth [9 *September 1986*]   17 Ferry Path
Cambridge

Dear Doug,

Thanks for the telegram, yes naturally I'll write when asked: presumably some myrmidon will issue the summons. Anthony has been busy since his return from the Northlands, harassing the slugs & sluggards of our weed-infested cultural scene.[1] I know I ought to think differently but I cannot help the belief that all the effort is a great waste of spirit. Even if he got anything, finally, the frame for just provision remains as skew as we both well know. The so-called public domain won't even give an answer, while the private ditto keeps its eye fixed steadily upon the TSB flotation.[2] And what else, comes a murmur from the side; from which platform did the Infant and the Pearl depart? What all too soon we shall get is an *explanation*, and those who should now be enlarged by relief from that burden will then sigh gratefully beneath its pressing attentions. And so the moratorium is signed off into its cremated residue: *modern*! Did you ever? All this is quite familiar and of course I do not mostly care to give it a thought: a costly Pyrrhonism but to pay out on the data would demand even more expensive loss adjustment.

At any rate here's a rather ancient fragment in the mean time.[3] Your own *sauve qui veut* position in the Gallic flux of such business is, I must admit, a mystery to me. But over there is perhaps really not notable, just as over here leaves hardly a stain upon the front path.

　　　Auguri:
　　　　　J.

16 September 1986   21 rue des Messageries
Paris

Dear Jeremy,

Just a continuation of present notes, to take it out of the request mode, although to thank you for your usual readiness

---

1 'return from the Northlands', Anthony Barnett lived and worked in Denmark (1969–72) and Norway before returning to the UK in 1976.

2 'TSB', Trustee Savings Bank. Shares in the bank went on sale on 29 September 1986.

3 Prynne enclosed a photocopy of *Infolio*, no. 40 (25 August 1986), featuring 'Write-Out' (*Poems*, 356) and artwork by Gisèle Celan-Lestrange.

to help. I'm not sure where that will go in fact, as Anthony is dubious about my glottis book for his own press and I think he may be right as it is both flatly academic and very much aimed at those who are learners about prosody, whether 60 years old or 18. My whole approach to the demonstration of prosody is very baldly educative and I'm quite willing to discuss Eliot's or Roy Fuller's notions if that's where the discussion is going to begin and I don't even mind where I shift it to as long as it goes far enough to put us on the verge of attitudes I do approve of.[1] Never been able to get any poet to agree with me on this.

I have a horror about what goes on in schools and would dearly love to have some real effect upon instruction. I had the usual war with a Latin teacher who, I discovered with delight the other day in Kelly's Directory of Bournemouth and Poole really was called Percy Cushion, persecution;[2] and for about an hour, once, he went into Latin prosody: I was absolutely riveted and at the age of 14 had no idea why. 'Are we going to do some more of that?' 'No, that's all we do in this course.' And that was the only time, right through school when anyone had talked to me about poetic music, my response welling out of some unconscious layer. (How to get inspired by those you intensely dislike.)

Why all this personal anecdote? Well, I suppose I don't mind explanation when it's for proper motives, since a bit more explanation at that point would have turned me on to Virgil and saved my Latin. For example, explanation might get rid of the label 'modern' by demonstrating that modern can be the best engagement with tradition and that the present historico-politico-sociologico-ironico genre of the mainstream Sunday poetry of our time is often profoundly untraditional, if by tradition we mean the best tradition of seeking forwards. I say this as someone the least likely to polarise the poetic craft, many divisions in my view being those of genre rather than properly founded disputes about what may constitute itself as the poetry of our time. Thus, much of the experimental wing is a matter of choosing a genre in which certain rules operate. What I prize instead is that delicious feeling of mobility in the exercise of a craft, whichever genre is being practised. There are certain (often-anthology) lines of Shakespeare ('How sweet the moonlight' from The Merchant of Venice, for example [3]) where, if I can manage to come at them freshly enough, and if I can enter the flow of the music, I get a weird sensation of sliding in my consciousness: it's what Olson would call the verse standing still in the vertical—then, as it stands still my mind immediately begins to slide (within the present moment, so to speak) and I have the sense of immense mental versatility, as though during the sliding all sorts of verbal moves would be possible.[4] I am convinced this is a sharing of the Shakespearean mind (as implied poet of those lines) without his talent. What could be more modern than such a moment is hard to imagine.

This is partly a response to your remark about my own sauve

1 Roy Fuller (1912–91), British poet and novelist.

2 Percy William Cushion (1905–93), Latin teacher at Bournemouth School.

3 Act 5, sc. 1.

4 Oliver refers (inexactly) to Olson's phrasing in 'Quantity in Verse, and Shakespeare's Late Plays', which Oliver read in *Human Universe and Other Essays*, ed. Donald Allen (New York: Grove Press, 1967). This edition is cited in *PNP*, 83. Olson writes: 'The limit on new in the verse is syntax. Shakespeare did not particularly disturb the working sentence as it had served him and others in blank verse proper. Imagery likewise. It is gone into as the sentence does, explicit, and descriptive. Yet the thought increases a verticality gained by blank verse itself between 1600 and 1608, and quantity (which tends at any time to increase the standing as against the running power of verse) most makes the language different.' *Collected Prose*, ed. Donald Allen and Benjamin Friedlander (Berkeley: University of California Press, 1997), 272–3.

16 September 1986

qui veut position out here, because I am surrounded by poets who either think that they are participants in the great surge forward (when they are really participants in minor genres) or that there are quintessential questions, responses to which alone constitute true poetry. No wonder why my situation out here is a mystery to you. Intellectually, there's very little for me in France and I'm here for four main reasons. First, because I can escape the depressing politics and society of a little England environment on the East coast. Second, because the only way to get a job offering three and a half months holiday, along with university status, was—at the age of 44 as I was—to move. Third, because I am happiest either by the sea or with a city whose café life is still open democratically (and London's is not). Fourth, because I get a pick up in my political awareness when I live in Paris and can see England more truly, not less truly, in its world situation, with much better perception of the chauvinism of The Times or Guardian. You have a very special position, there in Cambridge, because the university has its intellectual lines to most world centres, whereas there is still much that is provincial about Essex, not least its awful and tardy engagement with French semiotics. Even so, Cambridge no doubt has its dangers, that its internal politics can seem a sufficient world because they have this influx (through 'contacts') from the world at large. You've developed sophisticated defences against this; but then, so have I, against France. I mix very little with French poets; in my own writing, what interests me always is the next information I need for what next I'm going to do; and it's no good to me to spend an evening with poets telling me about the latest 'Language School' gossip.[1] (I recently spent an afternoon with a language school poet in New York and he had an expensive library containing just about every modernist text he ought to have: I looked in vain for tattered books with real information in them—I picked up in Colchester earlier this year The Percy Anecdotes (pub. Monthly parts fr. 1820): wouldn't you say that's better value than a book of poems by Ron Silliman?)[2] And I tend to keep to the journalists out here. They're funnier and better informed by a long chalk. Interesting how few poets out here realise that <u>all</u> writers must acquire variety of subject, spread of information and experience, and active, not passive or earnestly learnt, vocabulary. That immense monument to bull and other kinds of shit, Norman Million's Ancient Evenings is full of a verbal luxuriousness that is part of the definition of good writing, though fortunately not all of the definition:[3] it's a political and avant-garde heresy to say so, but so is the vocabulary and syntax of Updike's awful The Coup: I filled close-packed pages of a notebook noting down words and phrases I could not easily have come up with myself but that Updike had pulled out of the far reaches of his cortex. I hate him for teaching me, just as I hated my Latin master.

It's about 3 a.m. This letter is not formless but may seem to be.

---

[1] 'Language School', American literary movement whose central figures (including Ron Silliman (b. 1946); see below) came to prominence in the 1970s and 1980s.

[2] Sholto and Reuben Percy [Joseph Clinton Robertson and Thomas Byerley], *The Percy Anecdotes: Original and Select*, 20 vols. (London: Printed for T. Boys, 1820–3). It is unclear which volume of the twenty-volume set Oliver purchased.

[3] 'Norman Million', Norman Mailer.

I hear you've been attentive to the Raworths; and it may be the moment to remark that your attentiveness to such matters in general, down through the years, has not gone unnoticed by me.[1]
 Best,
  Doug

18 September 1986   21 rue des Messageries
            Paris

Dear Jeremy,
 In my rather indulgent last letter I'd meant to thank you for 'Write-Out', which I'd also received in a Raworth blitz package.[2] I'd set it aside for a re-read, as I find it a difficult little text and my responses are positive but vague at the same time.
 I take it to be structured in progression by the long lines and to constitute a series of phrases endeavouring to enter/to have emerged from (both these at once, perhaps) the heart—very abstract in effect, these phrases. They read various ways at once. Write-out = the necessary evidence of partial failure? And yet the necessary move in the approach to the centre? That Stendhal thing of style being what happens when the notional perfection of what is about to be said is failed to be fully expressed but the failure conducted with the maximum grace possible?
 All very intriguing because I read: 'If burnt metal lives in / the dove slowly /' as that morally important dynamic of strength within patience, which constitutes the only peacefulness that is not merely decline.[3] And I take this as the burden, that there is a necessary patience to working at the slash of the real. If I am anywhere near—and I shouldn't like to be on court evidence yet—this ties in with much that is so mature and valuable in your recent things: an insistence that the headiness of romantic definitions of energy is not necessarily the only approach to the white-hot. More interestingly—morally, psychologically, politically, verbally, etc.—the singleness lies within our higher mental forms too: not just <u>sprezzatura</u> but less aristocratic forms of grace can also be high forms and the important thing is for us to be working towards the truly single from what energy we have available at each time. This is to generalise the poetic heights into the everyday too. A failure to do that leads to the arrogance of a Shelley or a Pound in applying only the special definition of the high-poetic state of mind to the management of ordinary affairs, instead of realising that these are more like your bus: at their best they are voyaging too towards the heart and the direction must be maintained.[4]
 Best,
  Doug

{Ordinary moments are also special and privileged}

---

[1] Oliver refers to Tom (1938–2017) and Valarie (b. 1936) Raworth.

[2] Oliver refers to the *Infolio* series, edited by Raworth, in which 'Write-Out' was first published. Raworth published Oliver's 'The Woman Who Was Too Tall' in the series as no. 47 (14 November 1986), with artwork by Steve Oldfield. The poem, but not the artwork, is collected in *Kind*, 184–5.

[3] Oliver quotes 'Write-Out' (*Poems*, 356).

[4] 'your bus', 'towards the heart', Oliver responds to language in 'Write-Out'.

14 June 1987

21 rue des Messageries
Paris

Dear Jeremy,

When I read <u>Bands around the Throat</u> it makes me think of what I call 'glottis matters': that is, the frequency read-out from the voice-box, how it freezes into a mean fixity the wonderful fluidity of the song in its instants.[1] I recall our correspondence about this (leaving aside the issue of what we can do or not do with the machine traces). And you have always deeply seen one most crucial task of poetry: to relate inauthenticity of the voice to personal betrayals and to national sloth. Evidently, I'm talking about 'Fool's Bracelet' especially, but about the whole sequence too. It is very strange and new exactly how you insert the lyric into the Bracelet poem: a real discovery which delights me.

Many of the allusions are difficult for me this time: but you catch the frozen nights of this sad nation very beautifully: 'No Song No Supper' has already become a favourite of mine, with its constant unexpectedness and juxtaposition of oddly comparable images creating a mysterious unity of field. I remember once watching the yearly Fen skating speed championships: the ice was like a creaky dancefloor. 'No Song' wins the championships this year. In one film, Oliver Hardy sits in a chimney piece while bricks fall at the intervals on to his head: the art is in the intervals and how many bricks fall, of course.[2] Your last 'so' in this poem.[3] These analogies are becoming a little over-assertive unless they just explain that the poem has created a place for itself in my mind. From the appearance of 'Marzipan', I have had a non-poetic, perhaps journalistic, wish to peer behind the poem itself to the wasted province, so much does the last verse strike me as urgent and necessary. It's a shock. Still the flattened music, the voice not open and flexible—now linked with our most bestial behaviour. Not for a long time has it been more necessary for poetry to insist upon these links, assailed as you no doubt have been every day with the strangled, nasal self-will of the Conservatives and the oleaginous self-righteousness of the opponents. There is such an 'eternal' job to do, always; and everyone eternally gives up on it.

'Rates of Return' and 'Lend a Hand' appeal immediately: I'm taking the others slowly—'Fresh Running Water' next—because it takes me more than one or two readings to get pretty fully into one of your poems: each one needs a certain imaginative time and, though I've read the book a couple of times, I don't want to hurry through judgements on those poems I haven't fully taken in, just to write you a more complete letter.

The sardonic edge becomes a skate heel curving very perfectly on these icy surfaces.

—I'm away in America for about 2½ months from July 6th. Alice Notley, 101 St. Mark's Place, NYC 10009, would forward any post.[4] I'll take <u>Bands</u> with me…

Best,
Doug.

---

1 Prynne, *Bands around the Throat* (Cambridge: privately printed, 1987).

2 Oliver refers to Laurel and Hardy's *Dirty Work* (dir. Lloyd French, 1933).

3 Oliver refers to, and quotes from, the last two stanzas of 'No Song No Supper' (*Poems*, 343–4).

4 Alice Notley (b. 1945), American poet. Oliver first met Notley and her then husband, the American poet Ted Berrigan (1934–83), in Wivenhoe, Essex, during the academic year 1973–4, when Berrigan was poet-in-residence at the University of Essex and Oliver a mature undergraduate in his second year. Oliver was close friends with both. Notley published excerpts from *ICS* and *The Diagram Poems* in *Chicago* (European Edition, no. 2 (February 1974): n.p.) and Oliver is a dedicatee of at least three poems by Berrigan ('So Going Around Cities', written in Chicago after leaving Essex, is dedicated 'To Doug & Jan Oliver', 'Incomplete Sonnet #254' is dedicated 'For Douglas Oliver', and 'I Dreamt I See Three Ladies in a Tree' is dedicated 'For Douglas Oliver, Denise Riley, & Wendy Mulford'. *The Collected Poems of Ted Berrigan*, ed. Alice Notley with Anselm Berrigan and Edmund Berrigan (Berkeley: University of Los Angeles Press, 2007), 406, 408, 589, 695). Oliver dedicated *The Diagram Poems* 'for Ted Berrigan and Alice Notley' (*Kind*, 99). See also Oliver's fond reminiscences of Berrigan in *CAAS*, where he writes of Berrigan's 'genius for generosity', and states that '[n]o one in my adult life has taught me more about how to *use* emotion wisely' (252).

8 October 1987   21 rue des Messageries
                                  Paris

Dear Jeremy,

Alice and I were very pleased to get your nice card from Boulder: as always JHP very much up with the news.[1] In fact we went down to the Colorado border (Alice's famous little desert town of Needles, Calif., temp. 120 degrees) in mid-August but it would evidently still have been far away. I imagine you had a good summer over there.

I'm scant of your own news, would be glad of some, and send my usual best wishes for your family. What stage is your daughter at?

I've come back to the usual beginning of term details and urgent problems raised by out of date mail. But I wanted to say that I took <u>Bands Around the Throat</u> with me to the States and from time to time would refresh myself in it. One or two of those poems have become key for me as 'what needs to be said right now'. Had some funny correspondence with Kinnock's office before the election, blaming the whole party for Thatcher's run.[2] Basically, I don't believe that you can offer to govern with a defence policy rejected by the national majority (self-defence being a virtual 'natural right', to use the only term that gets near it). You can only work to change that majority. Plus the party's hopeless economics. Usual bland aide's reply: perhaps you don't realise the efforts and strides we're making, send for booklet. My reply: this is the blandness that will permit Thatcher's third term… Now, the party conferences seem quite awful: I can hardly bear to read the reports.[3] Such appalling Conservative sycophancy, with moral and social blindness posing as rectitude; such weasling lack of fundamental political principle across the whole spectrum of Labour speakers.

This is the landscape in which your poems are written as a righting of tone: the rectitude you've always had, which has been my own main reason for admiring your poems so much (here, being different, I fear, from those of your younger readers who go galloping off into the shifting sands of parasyntaxis). It's why I talk of 'refreshing' myself.

Actually, I'm not sure what you know about my plans. Alice and I will marry in the earlyish New Year and I shall live in Manhattan with her and her two boys.[4] They're coming up to college age; so we can't come to France. We can't afford to live anywhere else in rapidly-gentrifying East Village but her apartment as it's rent stabilised and to live in the suburbs is unthinkable. Jan and I are amicably divorcing but, I hope, keeping in good contact, as our only real reason for separating was that we didn't want to live each other's kind of life. Keeping close to my girls is my main worry; but the Atlantic is getting smaller every day as fares come down, and they're very nice to me.

You may also have heard that Alice's step-daughter, Kate, was killed by a motorcyclist overrunning the lights; and this obviously

1 Prynne sent Oliver (c/o Alice Notley) a postcard from Boulder, Colorado, on 14 August 1987 (see below). It reads: 'Dear Doug, Well, top-class great news! So every prospect pleases, in fresh woods & pastures new, even if we have more of that here than you city types. I'm on the run up in the Rockies with Ed & Jenny Dorn for a while, taking the breezes, and I hope we'll meet soon after we are both back. Avanti! J.'

2 Thatcher was re-elected for a third term in her second landslide victory on 11 June 1987. *Bands around the Throat* was '[p]ut into production 1st June 1987', according to the colophon to the second impression. See M. A. King, '*Bands around the Throat*, J. H. Prynne, Racial Capitalism: Thoughts/ Directions', *Jacket* 2, 1 December 2021, https://jacket2.org/article/bands-around-throat-j-h-prynne-racial-capitalism.

3 The Labour Party Conference ran from 27 September to 2 October 1987 in Brighton, and the Conservative Party Conference from 6 to 9 October in Blackpool.

4 Notley and Oliver were married in New York on 10 February 1988. *TVTH* (1990) is dedicated 'For Alice'.
  'her two boys', Anselm Berrigan (b. 1972), American poet, and Edmund Berrigan (b. 1974), American poet and musician, sons of Notley and Ted Berrigan.

cast a summer that in other respects held such happiness into the sombre. It was a blow for her two boys, Edmund and Anselm, also, as Kate was pretty much an older sister. Various people came into Manhattan for the memorial service including Anne Waldman, whom I'm always glad to see.[1]

A briefish note, to put the antes back in the pot again. Yes, I particularly want to see you before I go but am not sure how. I may be able to come across before Christmas. Do you <u>never</u> come to France?

I'm sending this poem just to send you something.[2]

Very best,

Doug

2 November 1987   21 rue des Messageries
                                                   Paris

Dear Jeremy,

Thanks for renewed reference availability.[3]

I'm sending you these pieces of letter because from the nature of them these thoughts won't go away; and the questioning of hazard's role chimes interestingly with the sense of frozenness and constriction in <u>Bands around the Throat</u>. {Many thanks for the second copy—then I fell ill for a while: throat, bands etc.}[4]

Rectitude of vision is the first phrase that comes to mind whenever I think of your own poetry. Then Sidney is surely right that poets offer us a golden world not a real one.[5] Therefore, the rectitude and the strictness—I would even say severity—of your landscapes under false government is a peculiar kind of gold, one hammered exactly into the form of the real, and somehow whitened and frosted by it. In <u>The Infant</u> the dreamer has to wake up dissatisfied because the ideal cannot talk directly to the real). Your own sequence clings closer to the process of modern Britain, even though its wide surfaces and slipping planes are sometimes more abstract: it is more lived through just as mine is more dreamt through.

These pages show the extent of the problem for any poet trying to see his way into such ideality. They form a hard critique of present process, as well as raising questions about hazard. Let me take it from the top:

Fortune has less than absolute power for Chaucer, you point out. The point is not that Fortune should not be present within the political synthesis, of course, but that it should not legislate. This is my argument, not that Fortune and Hazard are built into the present scheme of actuality by the Tories. The Christian synthesis is, after all, a solution of the temporal paradox: Necessity is seen through an instant of time in which Possibility lies still open, undetermined; and free will results. But if we isolate this instant of time and empty it and refuse the prudential care of Necessity <u>then</u> we have the rule of chance, which is the rule of the empty present—and is ultimately chaos. {Necessity & Fortune →

---

[1] Anne Waldman (b. 1945), American poet.

[2] Oliver enclosed a typescript of 'The Oracle of the Drowned', dating it 'Needles, Calif., 1987'. A handwritten note beneath the poem reads: 'fifth line tense change deliberate; don't know if I'll keep it or not.' The poem was published in *TVTH* (47–8) with minor alterations, including to the tense of the fifth line (from 'filed' to 'file').

[3] The most contemporaneous reference for Oliver by Prynne in the archives is a letter and statement, dated 23 September 1986, in support of an application for a subvention of £4,000 from the British Academy towards the publication of *Poetry and Narrative in Performance* by Anthony Barnett's Agneau 2 imprint.

[4] Prynne sent a 'second copy' of *Bands around the Throat* on 1 November 1987, collaging the following note into a compliments slip from the United Kingdom Atomic Energy Authority: 'Good to converse & to catch up a bit. Here's another copy of the Ration Book, as requested. À bientôt: J.'

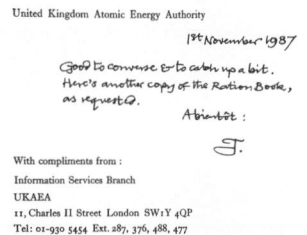

[5] Oliver refers to Sir Philip Sidney, *The Defence of Poesy*: 'her [nature's] world is brazen, the Poets only deliver a golden.' Gavin Alexander, ed., *Sidney's 'The Defence of Poesy' and Selected Renaissance Literary Criticism* (London: Penguin, 2004), 9.

Providence?} Give or take some modern mathematics, this view still has a lot of cogency. That the instant must be filled, and filled with as much of the real as possible, to be providential. Adam Smith says: trust chance in the market and God's hand will appear: it's an argument about the source of dynamism, which must be unfettered.[1] But I have never seen that a person (or firm) acting solely out of self-interest is necessarily any more dynamic than a person acting altruistically (Aristotle on Self-Love etc.[2]): because self-interest alone is, unless the heart is very perverted, finally unsatisfactory; whereas people driven by ideals (Northern Ireland) can have demonic energies. A firm in which the workforce had a noble ideal (wartime) would probably perform as well as one whose directors were solely concerned to maximise wealth, if the market were structured in the right way, which I admit I can't quite conceive. We are dangerously near Utopias. But whatever it is that impels businessmen to suicide in their 50s is the negative face of some kind of valuable life-energy which right government ought to be able to tap.

How do 'decent' people hold vicious politics? Presumably small personality flaws on an individual scale become, when translated into the large effects of politics, major cruelties: I have always disliked a certain radical tendency to attack individuals' psychology fiercely because of how a person votes, when a decent person with a slight self-protectionism, unlikely to be personally vicious, may be genuinely puzzled on the large political scale (not being a politician) to see other than rather terrible solutions. Poetry addresses purity of heart. The Thatcher regime has reminded us how important the address to the heart is in politics—I believe that recent opinion polls are making this even more clear. Poetry and art's contribution to the changing national heart was neither negligible nor very admirable during the 1960s. The ideal should not include false optimism but, instead, exactly that kind of rigour you bring to it; politically, the ideal is the real purged not of its inadequacies (for those are imposed by complexity of circumstances and of voting constituency): but purged of falseness in viewing it. Even so, such purity of view cannot be put directly into action because it becomes immediately confrontational and weak, owing to its inflexibility.

I look at your pages and the complexity of the problems are daunting: if this is the critique, what could possibly be the solution all at once? Then we know that there is no solution all at once. But there are such things as changes of heart, even world-wide. Reagan has been forced to become candidate for the Nobel Peace Prize (unsuccessful, thank God), just because of a changing international mood. Simplistic to say that Gorbachev gave Reagan this role, as Gorby's rise is owing to more profound causes. Leaving aside the difficulty of measuring the significance of Glasnost, it reflects, not just realpolitik but some more providential movement of the 'political heart' inexplicable outside some such word as 'value'. Northern Ireland

---

1 Oliver refers to Smith's famous figure of the 'invisible hand' of providential consequence, deployed in *The Theory of Moral Sentiments* and later in *The Wealth of Nations*.

2 Oliver likely refers to the discussion of self-love in the *Nichomachean Ethics*, bk. 9, chap. 8.

1 'Live Aid', benefit concert held on 13 July 1985 in London and Philadelphia to raise money for relief of the 1983–5 Ethiopian famine.

2 'CND', Campaign for Nuclear Disarmament.

does not brook solution until a similar change of heart. This will not be chance but the providence and prudence of the human heart, finally awakened by weariness at cruelty.

Similarly with problems that you raise: disaster relief—how affected by that ridiculous-noble Live Aid business.¹ Trusting hazard and the market means waiting for famines and then through charity always too stingy, acting to aid them. Whereas the cliché in modern aid is to make permanent contributions to reducing poverty gaps without saddling the benefiting country with debts. Agreeing to be somewhat poorer so that they are somewhat richer: a providential action. Windfall or Gift taxes: certainly; one 'ought' to be proud to pay them, as all taxes, given stricter government; and while it would be very utopian to expect that mood in an electorate, the balance of the ethic about taxes can swing—as Reagan is being forced to swing it even now, precisely by the operations of hazard. But these operations are not commonly regarded internationally as healthily induced in the present crisis (a few die-hard right-wing economists excepting).

Mercy and sentiment: my work has always been more open to the taint than yours, which has perhaps therefore had more of mercy, finally—I'm not sure how much meaning that has. The centre in politics does not, however, mean the sentimentality of Shirley Williams. It is not the centre of doctrine but the centre of decision-making, as a process, like throwing a perfect dart. Extreme politicians commonly ignore half the problem they are dealing with because their solution will be aborted if the other half is considered. But the centre is simply the centrally correct thing to do in any situation: it comes with no dogma, although a politician may need the framework of his dogma to perceive it. It has no real political referent until a decision arrives. It means perhaps taking the scorn of the left at one moment, taking the scorn of the right at another, taking the scorn of the political centre at another: but as I say the framework of political beliefs (for which one votes) is properly only a means to perceive the real. Thus, I <u>might</u> vote CND if that were a national possibility;² but I conceive circumstances—present circumstances in fact— where it is morally incorrect to impose unilateral nuclear disarmament on an unwilling population, because self-preservation is as near as anything gets to a natural right. On the other hand, I can conceive it as morally incorrect to declare war 'personally' as a Premier, when you don't agree with doing so, even where a population seeks to impose that declaration. There is no natural right to declare war.

This is not the letter I wanted to write and, as a consequence, I've had it on my machine for the past week or so, waiting for the inspiration to tinker with it. It's very bitty and doesn't clinch anything. But it's a difficult time and if I wait longer I'm not likely to improve it. I'm not sure it's worth answering—you too are busy. When I get more ahead of myself I shall return to these themes. What I mainly want to signal to you, since you seem to

2 November 1987

have forgotten your own letter, is how the mere delineation of problems can seem defeating and I would always like to see where {your own} construction would lead out of {the critique.}
    Best,
        Doug.

1 Prynne refers to Mozart's Piano Concerto no. 18 in B-flat Major, via its number in the Köchel catalogue of Mozart's works.

30 November 1987   17 Ferry Path
                                                          Cambridge

Dear Doug,

    Well yes indeed I do remember my long epistle of 1st February 86, altogether as part of a roused up exchange in those months which was itself a stage in the extended and much-valued (to me) discussion worked out by our respective thoughts and interchanges; so that I was put off by your referring au téléphone to an *unanswered* letter. But yes also I understand that too, now, in the sense that these thoughts and issues are unanswered for both of us. Even if a temporary moment of festive resolution (as currently here & now, via Köchel 456[1]) offers to restore the slow violence of moral disintegration, we know too clearly that the dream of ethical purpose answered formally is a fading relic, and that the planned redirection of ethical conscience into quite deliberately altered social forms is, because not attended to, more of a nightmare than a general downfall of cultural life. The device offers a constant reassurance that we live in a stable order of decent, generous personal interconnection, when the underlying arrangements upon which this decency rests are being reset, piece by piece, so that finally we shall notice that decency has been redefined in a sense so radical as to block off all question of any direct return. But since the lazy and archaic confidence in such decency has become so disgusting, a part of one is quite gleeful to see sentimental complacency kicked down ('well at least we shan't have quite *that* version of pious hypocrisy, ever again'), while another part looks on with a sort of numb horror ('without that now lost sense, shall we ever *want* to get back anything to replace it?') and accepts the guilt of the glee as a justly levied cancellation charge.

    This is not a re-address to the thematic content of my earlier thoughts, in part because with my recent pamphlet I have forced the larger questions into a more abruptly compacted form, like a Reader's Digest version of the *Decline and Fall* on a handful of postcards—or, well, maybe *not* like that; but my rigid stanza-formats certainly seem to have annoyed a good many readers who felt entitled to some more open and convincing alternative to current social closure. Isn't this in fact one of the enfeebling demands sponsored by 'modernism' in all its varieties (including 'post-anything-you-can-think-of'), that the reader who learned a new code was thereby exempted from construing an old one or from observing its continuing effects in social life. This question is now pushed forward more sharply by what I can only take as a stupid manoeuvre in Andrew's somewhat heavy-handed and dogmatic Introduction to the anthology.[1]

Who in the name of F. T. Palgrave asked him to pre-warn readers of this book that the work to follow does not form part of the national poetry of Britain? That somehow the poets they agreed to include have been successfully elbowed aside by a bit of tinpot literary history and a few bored metropolitan publishers? Does he not observe the question of national life and language, the 'condition of England' indeed, being continually and strongly addressed from a whole series of positions within the scales of chronology and individual leverage? What ground has been cut from under whose feet? This is the silliest talk I have read for a long time, just indeed what one might expect from a *PN Review* editorial.[2] Andrew seems entirely to have forgotten the very careful way in which he himself persisted in not succumbing to imitated North American rhapsodics, despite their allure at the time, precisely because of the accompanying readiness to ignore (at least seen from a British perspective) the degradations of transatlantic national life. The facile, boastful exploitation of conscience about the Vietnam conflict was only one example, which by the writers at least has not been imitated in the Falklands aftermath, though the Belfast poets are the worst and crassest complicity of all. 'A poet's public life', says A., leaving me near-speechless.[3] This defensive title that they have chosen, for a book I incline to believe they have not read, obscures the fact that a more proper caption would have been *English Poetry and the Poetry of England, 1960–1985*.

I know what you mean in saying that poetry in the 1960s didn't make much of a worthwhile contribution to changing national consciousness; but on the English side I think that if you look at the publication dates of some work collected in the anthology (and of some not) a consideration of certain basic issues, habits of perception and attachments of feeling shews in the uneasy relations with the registers of social language, and that this work *practises* the questions which, when put bluntly, become instantly unanswerable ('defeating', as you say). And in every stage of this argument or discussion I am all the time aware of a very deep latency which is that, personally, I admit to feeling more or less undamaged: that I take more joy in simplicity, that I am more trustful, that for the daily world my overt moments of irritation or sinking dismay mask a covert but lasting sense of— *gratitude*. That was the hardest word in my booklet, because I felt obliged to expose it to utmost scorn (as Wordsworth did, in 'Simon Lee'), while believing with what may be a blindly sentimental confidence that destruction of the victims does not mean extinction of what kept them from joining the persecutors.[4]

I put all this badly and I know that it has much to do with what there's also not a word for: something like 'womanliness' and it is the uttermost sink of complacent sentiment. And yet, and despite the twin-set Westminster pearls, I trust it, as I would even

---

[1] Prynne refers to Andrew Crozier's introduction to *A Various Art*, ed. Crozier and Tim Longville (Manchester: Carcanet, 1987), 11–14, which begins: 'This anthology represents our joint view of what is most interesting, valuable, and distinguished in the work of a generation of English poets now entering its maturity, but it is not an anthology of English, let alone British poetry.'

[2] *PN Review* (1973–), journal edited by Michael Schmidt.

[3] *A Various Art*, 12.

[4] 'gratitude', Prynne refers to the final word of 'No Song No Supper' (*Poems*, 344).

30 November 1987

begin to give credence to the very time of day. It has to be a private delusion, but it *feels* very social. At any rate all this has connection with my brief moments of inset folksong in the recent texts: these voices are the victims, for sure, since the fair field is full of yuppies and agribrokers, and Benjamin Britten (say) is not an option.[1] But: the national poetry! The national language! 'I heard a maiden singing in the valley below.'[2] Compare from rightly-named Quirk et al., *A Comprehensive Grammar*, p. 853: 'Some interjections are less frequent, *eg: Yippee* (excitement, delight)...' There is still a shimmer about the durable latency of the common rhymes, after so much has been done and undone, as if providence itself resided within these hazards of phonetic accident; in the distant burden within language of its own internal echo, these sounds are not quite erased from our current immunity to the recall of innocence tagged and destroyed.

> Smale pathis to the grenewode,
> Will I love and shall I love,
> Will I love and shall I love
>   No mo maydyns but one.
>
> Love is naturall to every wyght,
>   Indyfferent to every creature,
> Chaungyng his course, now hevy, now lyght,
>   As fortune fallyth, I yow ensure;
>   So rennyth the chaunce from one to one:
>
> One is good, but mo were bettyr
>   Affter my reason and judgement,
> Consideryng dyvers fayrer and fetter,
>   Plesaunt, buxum, and ever obedient,
>   Tyll sum of them begyn to grone:
>
> But I will do as I saide furst,
>   So it is best, as thynkyth me,
> To put in one my faithfull trust,
>   Forever yff she will trew be,
>   And love her only whereever she gone:[3]

This too is not the letter I set out to write and so it must come in on any tangent that it can find. You must be in such throes of alteration at present that I'll not expect long screeds or even short ones. But nothing is forgotten, not even virtuous hazard: as you see.
    Saluti cari,
        J.

P.S. I hope you saw Patrick Wright's Whitechappell review in the *London Review of Books* (29th October), a strongly constructed prelude.[4] Your father-voices in the new oracle poem remind me rather obliquely of the acute recall of syllabic intimidations traced in Wilfred Bion's autobiography, *The Long Week-end*,

---

1 'fair field', Prynne interpolates a phrase from the prologue to William Langland's *Piers Plowman*.

2 Prynne quotes a line from 'Early One Morning', an English folk song (Roud 12682). The same line is 'inset' in 'Fool's Bracelet', lines 10–11 (*Poems*, 342).

3 Prynne quotes an anonymous song printed in John Stevens, *Music and Poetry in the Early Tudor Court* (London: Methuen, 1961), 382–3. Stevens comments: 'The style of both words and music, especially bars 1–8, suggests an underlying popular song' (383).

4 Prynne refers to Patrick Wright, 'Rodinsky's Place', review of *White Chappell: Scarlet Tracings*, by Iain Sinclair, *London Review of Books* 9, no. 19 (29 October 1987): 3–5.

30 November 1987

[^1] 'oracle poem', Prynne refers to 'The Oracle of the Drowned'.
  Prynne likely refers to the following passage in Bion's *The Long Week-End*: 'My mother was proved by my sister also to be, like so many grown-ups, "peculiar". She went one day and stood firmly "at ease" in front of her. Then enunciating her words very clearly and precisely, she said, "Lavatory, lavatory, lavatory"' (10).
  Prynne interpolates a phrase from Paul Verlaine's 'Parsifal': 'Et, ô ces voix d'enfants chantant dans la coupole!' (And then, those children's voices singing in the dome!), quoted by T. S. Eliot in 'The Fire Sermon' section of *The Waste Land*.
  'whispering [...] Gallery!', the Whispering Gallery of Saint Paul's Cathedral features in Thomas De Quincey's revised version of *Confessions of an English Opium-Eater* (1856). Prynne's recollection was likely sparked by De Quincey's own reminiscence in the Gallery: 'As an oracle of fear I remembered that great Roman warning, *Nescit vox missa reverti* (that a word once uttered is irrevocable), a freezing arrest upon the motions of hope too sanguine, that haunted me in many shapes.' *The Works of Thomas De Quincey*, vol. 2, *Confessions of an English Opium-Eater, 1821–1856*, ed. Grevel Lindop (London: Routledge, 2000), 156.

[^2] Oliver refers to David Hume, *An Enquiry Concerning the Principles of Morals* (London: Printed for A. Millar, 1751), 95: 'Would any Man, that is walking alone, tread just as willingly on another's gouty Toes, whom he has no Quarrel with, as on the hard Flint and Pavement?'

[^3] Oliver refers to George Steiner (1929–2020), writer and literary critic. The relationship between the cultural achievements of the Western European canon and the historical singularity of the Holocaust is the subject of much of Steiner's work. Oliver responds to the argument expressed by Steiner in, for example, *Language and Silence*, that '[w]hat man has inflicted on man, in very recent time, has affected the writer's primary material—the sum and potential of human behaviour—and it presses on the brain with a new darkness'. *Language and Silence: Essays 1958–1966* (London: Faber and Faber, 1967), 22–3.

1897–1919; Part of a Life (Free Association Books, London, 1986); chantant dans la coupole indeed, or whispering (as for De Quincey) with exotic, cruel murmurs in a distant Gallery![^1]

10 December 1987

21 rue des Messageries
Paris

Dear Jeremy,

I very much appreciated your last letter, which arrived during a rather hectic week's visit by Alice: what I particularly liked was that swing of scope between what you call moral disintegration and the knowledge that no human institution or inadequacy can penetrate into the centre of our primary encounter with the world and with near ones. The poetry, so to speak, cannot be destroyed; and you will know I don't mean its grand and written forms but its common force, the actual good-willing impulse of the everyday heart. I always like Hume's example of the gouty toe: what person without motivation or personal malice against the victim would willingly step on the gouty toe of a stranger?[^2] Only a cold-blooded monster of a rare, not usual, kind. Once that's said, the danger of an Orwellian reliance on decency is all too seductive; but 'primary encounter' is far more radical a notion than decency. The new Conservatism has arisen on the back of ordinary Orwellian decency by fooling decent citizens. As you say, Thatcherism has called in those chips and cashed them for their little worth. As to whether with the exposé of decency we can ever want a replacement to it, my real reply is that we cannot help doing so: and I rather think you would agree. For example, Steiner was, I believe, out at Nanterre the other day toting his oft-told notion that Auschwitz etc. horrors had really created a terminal point for modern writing—I don't know his exact formulation this time.[^3] This is very wrong, very very wrong: it lets five years plus of prison camps <u>win</u> against the whole of the rest of human history, against every ordinary behaviour and ordinary love and makes <u>this</u> example of genocide with its superior technology absolutely trump every former example of genocide or, even, ordinary murder right through the eons of time. It would be an immense arrogance on Steiner's part were it not hidden as arrogance by the justice of terrible righteous anger against genocide. Steiner doesn't realise that he is allowing shocked pessimism to bring Fascism to one of its many dreadful conclusions: to destroy the book: instead, he thinks by intellectual honesty he is saving the book while visiting the pessimism of honesty upon its future. This is to mistake what I say above: that even the prison camps, though they may frighten the heart's impulses into inaction and cowardice and cruelty, cannot affect the <u>continuation</u> of our primary, always potentially joyful, encounters. I've just been sent a (probably mistranslated) quotation by Char, a hero of the Resistance, talking of good versus evil. '(We are) a great deal less (vulnerable) than our aggressors; this is because while they, for their part, have crime on their side, they do not have second wind.'[1] Good has the longer term; evil has usually to be specific in its action since it cannot finally convince through its philosophy. Well, that's in the very long scale sometimes—decades, perhaps more: horrors happen meanwhile; but not horrors more frightful than the eventual end of the world itself!

And yet, suppose we view the most ordinary murder, the archetypal pattern of all genocide, I would claim fairly confidently, though it is not evident. I have had reporting or personal experience of three or four murders and 'murderers'; a terrific block to the impulse towards love; an inability to maintain an admirable self-image <u>when</u> the circle of human contact or of sympathy is enlarged because then the woeful inadequacy compared with more competent fellow-beings becomes obvious; some situation then occurs creating uncontrollable panic that the inadequate, unloved self will be exposed. Some murder follows which forcibly either eliminates the unfortunate rival or, in sexual terms, forcibly attempts to 'get shamefully inside' like a Ripper—to get where a warm love or sympathy should be able to enter in imagination, tactfully, without harm. I won't take the awfully simplistic step of looking at a Hitler unable to create an admirable image either of himself or of his country as 'great' without elimination or assimilation of rivals: but I have always liked Medard Boss's (phenomenological) description of sadism, and it seems to me obscurely to be apropos—so much of cruelty is a denied quest for love or for some of its more minor modes.[2] How does this relate to my opening? Well, you will have seen it, for it is close to your folk songs. Nothing destroys our hope in the primary encounter with other people, because even most of our cruelties seek its freshness, though in dreadful ways. Can't we extrapolate? Even Britain's present moral degradation affirms better impulses that will not inevitably resurface (that would be mere 60s optimism) but are our hope in all combats—our reason for gratitude, that word which can sometimes become beautiful in Fielding's class attitudes.[3] The finest thing is to let literature live in hopeful purposes (Steiner is dangerous if we believe him), because otherwise we deny everything that everyday life has always depended upon and we betray our fellow citizens. And then, of course, I have to save this from blandness by saying that certain great literary despairs, cries from the brink—Nerval, Artaud, Celan—affirm the impulse too, and so on; but I hardly think that needs arguing out.

And so I receive great warmth from your letter, with its folk knowledge of virtue within hazard; and I am, in fact, a great lover of the word 'womanliness', meaning that warm outreach from our personal worlds into other possibilities along the line of the lovelike.

I believe, incidentally, that rhyming is effective because, if we remained in exactly the same instant, with its unique emotional,

---

[1] Oliver's source approximates René Char, *À une sérénité crispée* (1952): 'Nous sommes forts. Toutes les forces sont liguées contre nous. Nous sommes vulnérables. Beaucoup moins que nos agresseurs qui, eux, s'ils ont le crime, n'ont pas le *second* souffle.' René Char, *Œuvres complètes* (Paris: Gallimard, 1983), 747–62 (754).

[2] Medard Boss (1903–90), Swiss psychoanalytic psychiatrist. Oliver refers to his *Meaning and Content of Sexual Perversions: A Daseinsanalytic Approach to the Psychopathology of the Phenomenon of Love*, trans. Liese Lewis Abell (New York: Grune and Stratton, 1949). Fifteen pages of typed notes and hand-drawn diagrams on Boss's text (undated but likely from the early 1970s) are preserved in Oliver's papers (DOA, box 7).

[3] Oliver likely has in mind *Tom Jones*, bk. 6, chap. 1: 'Esteem and Gratitude are the proper Motives to Love, as Youth and Beauty are to Desire; and, therefore though such Desire may naturally cease, when Age or Sickness overtakes its Object; yet these can have no Effect on Love, nor ever shake or remove from a good Mind, that sensation or Passion which hath Gratitude and Esteem for its Basis.' Henry Fielding, *Tom Jones*, ed. Sheridan Baker (New York: W. W. Norton, 1973), 206.

intellectual and real-world content, if we were for ever to have exactly the same personality—if that instant, in short, were to remain the same occasion in a Whiteheadean sense—then we would make the same sound for ever.[1] Rhyming, coming as it usually does within a small compass of lines, indicates by the <u>difference</u> between the first rhyme and the second—changes of consonantal onset, of semantic meaning, of speed and lightness etc.—the change between one instant and the following one: it translates something of the emotional and intellectual progression between the lines: 'from one to one' / 'begyn to grone'… In addition, rhyme has its own capacity for mimesis—e.g. the rhymes miming the fawn's movements in Marvell's 'A Nymph Complaining…' So of course there is not exactly phonetic accidence here but the engagement of phonetic hazard in the overall moral process of the lines, which apes the engagement of hazard in the progress of our moral lives.

I don't know what to say about <u>A Various Art</u>, which has only just reached me. In some kind of dreadful Americanism, 'I hear you', what you say. I understand Peter Ackroyd, with that faithfulness of his, has recently reviewed it, although I haven't seen the article.[2] Mainly, I think it a thankless task to edit an anthology and I have never known an occasion where brickbats weren't thrown at the editors. It's true that I don't site my own work in relation to national poetry the way the preface does. Also that some work of flaccid energy is damagingly included. But I rather feel that what makes compiling such an anthology difficult is the fierceness of the criticism it is bound to receive from its own audience. The future vitiates the past. I'm therefore decided, at the risk of more blandness, to look positively on it as a collection that a few years ago could not have achieved national attention. Something may be moving: people just seeing the limitations of the London cliques perhaps, the influence of Anthony's publications maybe (not to be underestimated)… I don't know. In such a stressed situation I'm not looking for perfection, just for <u>some</u> continued energy in these dog days that will open up the way for the more adventurous kinds of poetry. The anthology fills what would otherwise be a vacuum and its editors have stood to lose respect for pushing it through despite differences in their poetic taste. I don't under these circumstances feel either responsible for or <u>much</u> limited by the introduction: I see it more as 'what Andrew could do when constrained by inevitable future criticism, with his hands slightly tied by editorial collaboration, and under pressure from his peculiar form of modesty and honesty'. I suppose I essentially feel glad that both of them keep labouring away to publish me, since they're not that self-aggrandising type, and I live too fragmented a life to be useful on the publishing front myself. The correct thing to say would probably be that only a few amongst us (five or six at most) have work of sufficient staying power to constitute a valid continuation of important and

---

1 'occasion in a Whiteheadean sense', Oliver refers to Alfred North Whitehead's sense of 'occasion' in chap. 10 of *Science and the Modern World: Lowell Lectures, 1925* (New York: New American Library, 1925): 'In any occasion of cognition, that which is known is an actual occasion of experience, as diversified by reference to a realm of entities which transcend that immediate occasion in that they have analogous or different connections with other occasions of experience. […] Also, apart from the actual occurrence of the same things in other occasions, every actual occasion is set within a realm of alternative interconnected entities. This realm is disclosed by all the untrue propositions which can be predicated significantly of that occasion. It is the realm of alternative suggestions, whose foothold in actuality transcends each actual occasion. The real relevance to untrue propositions for each actual occasion is disclosed by art, romance, and by criticism in reference to ideals' (158).

A page of typed notes on Whitehead's text is preserved in Oliver's papers (DOA, box 6).

2 Peter Ackroyd (b. 1949), British biographer, novelist, and critic. His review of *A Various Art*, 'Legislators of Language', was published in *The Times*, 3 December 1987, 17. Days earlier, in a *Times* end-of-year round-up, Ackroyd named Oliver's *Kind* 'the finest poetry of the year'. Ackroyd et al., 'Bringing the Year to Book…', *The Times*, 28 November 1987, 13. Ackroyd reviewed Oliver's work in the national press as early as 1974; see 'The New and the Novel', review of *The Harmless Building*, by Douglas Oliver, *The Spectator*, 5 January 1974, 15–16.

neglected literary traditions. If I should be judged amongst that number so be it: I mainly care about the craft of poetry itself, that it should be continued uncynically and faithfully.

For similar reasons, I loved the poem you quoted to me: faithfulness to what we love is what mainly matters out of all this. No-one will ever destroy it with whatever worldliness or end-of-the-worldliness.

Everything out here in abeyance while I prepare to move. I read Patrick Wright's excellent piece: I really think he has the potential to revitalise criticism if he has the energy; he has the talent to consider a work like White Chappell apparently within his personal philosophical perspective; and then we find that that perspective is wide enough to place the book under review into its wider cultural setting. This is what the 'sociology of literature' always should have been, had it not been practised by wankers.

I don't know Bion's autobiography and, short of buying it on spec, cannot easily obtain a glance at it out here.

Your own thinking is always fresh for me.

And it's seasonal greetings time.

    Doug.

---

5 February 1990   Gonville and Caius College
                                             Cambridge

Dear Doug,

Yes I was very pleased to have the copy of your new book, and to read it; and I've put off a note in reply only in order to be able to send my more modest pamphlet in exchange.[1] Actually, *im*modest might be a truer word, but all genres have their touch-lines and some owls are stuffed from the word go. At any rate, there are a few parallels which suggest that a really competent time machine (pp. 18, 30, 35–6, 114, etc.) would interest both of us.[2] Of course from your viewpoint I bungle performance and competence together, but then (mercifully) so do you.

My chief hesitation I think concerns the hovering notion, within your hierarchy of integrative levels, of 'overall form', a species of shadowy platonic archon from the bottom of a treacle well or black hole that would indeed be the site of a spectacular mental illness (the Mind of God).[3] But an ordering fiction is not a place, still less an experience: the gnostic and the pragmatic do point inwards to an occupied middle ground, less fitting & fitted. If I were pressed I should de-idealise the notional instant still further, by an enhanced significance for rhyme as the marker for repetition related to displacement and substitution in the ana-phoric outreach of performance time and measured span: giving emotional and mentalistic boundaries to the returns of prosody and utterance. But I'd be surprised in fact if you were to disagree.

But, biting my own hand, I need to add in passing that *Word Order* is by no means a case of pessimism: if anything, quite the

---

[1] 'your new book', Prynne refers to *PNP*, a copy of which Oliver sent, with a short letter, on 1 January 1990.

'my more modest pamphlet', Prynne refers to his Warton Lecture on English Poetry, 'English Poetry and Emphatical Language', *Proceedings of the British Academy* 74 (1988): 135–69, a copy of which he enclosed.

[2] Prynne refers to pages in *PNP*.

[3] This paragraph responds to arguments made throughout *PNP*.

1 Prynne does not here refer to any description by Oliver of *Word Order* (Kenilworth, UK: Prest Roots Press, 1989) as pessimistic (Oliver first mentions the sequence in his letter of 5 February 1990), but responds to Oliver's claim in a letter of 1 January 1990 that '[p]essimism seems always to turn out correct but, of course, that doesn't make it correct at any moment at all: optimism is all we have.'

2 Prynne refers to, and partly interpolates, Walter Benjamin's diary entries recording his conversations with Bertolt Brecht in the summer of 1934: 'Incidentally, his [Kafka's, in Brecht's opinion] unlimited pessimism is free from any tragic sense of destiny. For not only is his expectation of misfortune founded on nothing but empiricism (although it must be said that this foundation is unshakable), but also, with incorrigible naivety, he seeks the criterion of final success in the most insignificant and trivial undertakings—a visit from a travelling salesman, an inquiry at a government office.' Theodor Adorno et al., *Aesthetics and Politics* (London: New Left Books, 1977), 91.

3 Prynne quotes Theodor Adorno, 'On Commitment', trans. Francis McDonagh, *Performing Arts Journal* 3, no. 3 (Winter 1979): 58–67 (63).

4 'the prospects for Romania', Prynne refers to the state of the country in the wake of the Romanian Revolution of late 1989.

5 Oliver wrote to Prynne on 16 September 1989 to ask whether Prynne could set up a reading for him and Notley in Cambridge the following February. A flyer preserved in Prynne's papers records that Oliver and Notley were to read in the Lubbock Room, Peterhouse College, Cambridge, on 21 February 1990.

6 Nothing Prynne sent from Tübingen is preserved in either archive.

7 Oliver refers generally to principles avowed by American poets associated with Language poetry (after L=A=N=G=U=A=G=E (1978–81), journal edited by Bruce Andrews and Charles Bernstein) but also specifically to Ron Silliman, *The New Sentence* (New York: Roof Books, 1977).

reverse.[1] In not all circumstances is the measure of fear, laid across an occluded history, an index of potential truth; for one thing, there is the weakness of impatience and hindsight. But pessimism is a vulgar error because it assumes doctrine and conceptualises fear into a noetic defence: I would regard that as an evident mark of failure. It has to be as infantile and lazy as its opposite, since either by itself merely vaporises the other. I'm reminded here of Brecht's allegation that Kafka's unlimited pessimism was allied to an incorrigible naivety (the latter, indeed, surely rescues the former, and who was BB to make such a charge).[2] Or, better to recall Adorno's comment: 'He over whom Kafka's wheels have passed has lost for ever both any peace with the world and any chance of consoling himself with the judgement that the way of the world is bad; the element of ratification which lurks in resigned admission of the dominance of evil is burnt away.'[3] Yet that too is mistaken in demanding indelible permanence of the negative, like so many commonplace misreadings of Beckett, as if the effect of desperation cannot strongly alter a life without causing a total subjugation to its strength. I studied a full set of Goya's *Desastres* while at Tübingen, and the ignominy of survival was never more distant in my thoughts. However, off my high horse, the prospects for Romania cannot exactly make the heart leap up, and the turn of current history (the Vaterland!) makes me wonder if I might not better have bitten my tongue.[4] Again.

Well, just quickly also to say that the date seemingly fixed for your Cambridge reading (21st February) is by unhappy accident a day when I'm to be in Bristol, just for that one day in fact, and not alterable. But I hope that we may all be able to meet up while you're over here, because I'd be galled if we couldn't get together at some point.[5] Let me know, if you can, something of your plans. If you'd both like to camp out in Cambridge, by the way, for a day or two during the trip, I can almost certainly (with notice) fix a double room in College (gratis), which has the advantage of being central and unencumbered.

  Saluti cari:
    J.

5 February 1990   Apt. 12A
                  101 St. Mark's Place
                  New York City

Dear Jeremy,

  Glad to have your lines from Tübingen about German palmistry and mountains.[6] More especially, your <u>Word Order</u> came in as considerable enlightenment, though I'm still trying to work out why.

  There's a way of talking about these matters—usually flattening pieces in L=A=N=G=U=A=G=E magazines—which is intensely irritating: the new sentence, the new syntax, and such.[7]

But there is a palpable drive onwards of the words in these pieces that really is new to me and I'm stuck to explain it. Concatenation of syntax and order? Bit of that but don't think really that's it. It's more like how the consonants and vowels flow so that you don't alight: 'hit as he lay on'—aspirates and the way the l modulates into vowel rather than forming a border.[1] Word order, indeed. I'm not actually interested in explicating all these phrases that way, but I've just got very interested in the driving on. It seems strange, like a stranger. Olson has forever interested me in the Henry VIII lines I photograph in my book: 'We may outrun by violent swiftness that which we run at / and lose…'[2] And it is this same thing. Where meaning's interaction with syntax is given a little of the pell-mell.

You may have heard, then, that Alice, me, step-son Eddie, and possibly my elder daughter Kate will be coming to Cambridge for February 20 to give the reading you at an earlier stage set in motion. We're very much hoping you'll be in town and available.

(We go on to Essex the following day and then back to London, having had a few days in London and down on the South Coast first.)

I presume your Tübingen trip was pleasure or something writerly rather than academic; and hope so.

 With love to Sue,
   As ever,
     Doug

---

25 May 1990   Apt. 12A
              101 St. Mark's Place
              New York City

Dear Jeremy,

Now that the academic term is winding down, we hope you won't mind just a reminder invitation to contribute to SCARLET, the first issue of which is planned for September.[3]

We'd particularly like to include poems by you in our first number, if you have any available.

Just a remark about an unfinished point: a sense of form, presumably, is not platonic but arises in each performance, perhaps never quite the same. That is, it's a creature of the 'instant', far too evanescent for a substantiated existence outside any given performance and open to all sorts of indeterminacy; a stress–duration nexus would in this view be the most minute example of it in poetry. Unless the sense of form arises in this perhaps undiscussable sense, I don't see how the poem could be performed or the 'O' of your essay receive its due (equally evanescent) weight.[4]

 Best,
   Doug

---

1 Oliver quotes *Word Order* (*Poems*, 360).

2 Oliver quotes (with minor discrepancies in line breaks and capitalization) *Henry VIII*, act 1, sc. 1. See *PNP*, 75–84. Olson discusses the relevant lines from *Henry VIII* in 'Quantity in Verse, and Shakespeare's Late Plays'.

3 *Scarlet* (1990–1), journal edited by Oliver and Notley. Details of Notley and Oliver's collaborative editorial and publishing endeavours, including full sets of *Scarlet* and *Gare du Nord* magazines, referred to below, are available at 'Alice Notley's Magazines: A Digital Publishing Project', Nick Sturm: Literary Scholar, Educator, Poet, accessed 30 October 2021, www.nicksturm.com/digital-publishing-project/.

4 'your essay', Oliver refers to 'English Poetry and Emphatical Language'.

6 October 1990

17 Ferry Path
Cambridge

Dear Doug,

Many thanks for the Number One Scarlet and I look forward to seeing how they go.¹ Of course there is no refuge in these days of hype & plastic, the smarting conscience or the proof spirit: if the Gulf imbroglio were to be settled by trial of spirit the Arabs would win hands down, as perhaps they should.² The Mechanical Operations of inspired simplification have been a big hit from the floor of the recent Labour Conference, if only so that leaderly pragmatism can be a reassuring counter-hit;³ and as with the now jack-knifed Palestinians, the adversarial yes–no rips the entrails while the tertium quid or shadowy sidelines match up (or not) their shrewder shades of grey. Certainly I wouldn't go very far towards the stake for the Kuwaiti dinar, a false buffer based solely on exterior greed for cheap oil, and (like its principal clients) such a truly democratic community. Certainly too the rising international price of crude makes the UK warlike flourish more or less self-financing for Mrs T: crude for crude as weighed out by justice in the mandatory blindfolds. The art of smart parting requires a vocabulary of incessant nuance recklessly employed, and it will corrode all our nibs because the practice of written speech is leveraged in absentia, as ever was.

But now in any case I write with the brush, which is another struggle, older but with its own darker history. I am learning the version of Mandarin simplified by the Party so as to ease the campaign for mass literacy, and I wrestle with the brush because that was the instrument designed to replace warlords and their cruder prowess. The arts of writing opened the narrow door, though of course within there was a maze of more doors, some merely painted on to solid stone slabs. The speech is quite hard, too, for ears trained to tunes based on utterance position and intent, since the pitch run is largely determined syllable by syllable and without options. Nor is visual memory for graphic forms easy to awaken from its deep slumbers and the inroads of fading recall. On the credit side, however, the glimpsed avenues are full of powerfully unfamiliar lights & shades, and the utter shift of the subject position sets out a series of giddy moments. Getting tuned into the wounded vernaculars of the disunited states must be quite comparable.

I shall be ensconced at Suzhou from February to July of next year, at the university there, and if my creaking sense of dialectic survives intact for more than a couple of months I shall be a good deal surprised. Sun Tzu's Art of Strategy assuredly makes Machiavelli look rather crude; though the latter's assembled hints for breaking a siege have the refined cruelty we absolve ourselves from by thinking of as Chinese.⁴ And if there is another strategic explosion within the central kingdom I may indeed never be allowed past the starting-gate.⁵ Well, right to left, left to right, you pick up right where you get left off (old Chinese proverb).

---

1 Oliver and Notley sent a copy of *Scarlet*, no. 1 (September 1990), on 14 September 1990. Oliver wrote in his accompanying letter: 'The project is to be readable, spiritual, and political, crossing boundaries as much as possible, with a big emphasis on quality. Our invitation to contribute remains.' Prynne responds in his first paragraph to the terms of this project and to the content of the first issue, especially its editorial ('Kurt Schwitters is here to say it for us: it's dumb to be smart, smart to be dumb. Or, as we'd put it, smartness is dumb because it is wrong-spirited') and its emphasis on 'spirit' (n.p.).

2 'Gulf imbroglio', Prynne refers to the Iraqi invasion and annexation of Kuwait in August 1990, swiftly followed by UN sanctions against Iraq and the launch of the American-led Operation Desert Shield. Prynne's gloss of Middle Eastern politics in this paragraph draws on Conor Cruise O'Brien's article 'Israel Fills the Gulf at the Heart of Arab Diplomacy' (*The Times*, 5 October 1990, 16). O'Brien discusses the Arab response to Iraq/Kuwait in relation to British colonial history and refers to the grim prospects for Palestinian liberty given the regional interests of 'Arab pragmatists'.

3 The 1990 Labour Party Conference took place in Blackpool, 30 September to 5 October.

4 Prynne refers to Niccolò Machiavelli, *The Art of War*.

5 'central kingdom', China. Prynne refers to the recent disaster in which '[a] hijacked Boeing 737 turned into a fireball as it landed at Canton airport yesterday [2 October 1990] and careered into two other planes, one of them full of passengers. At least 127 people were killed.' Catherine Sampson, '127 Die in Chinese Air Hijack Crash', *The Times*, 3 October 1990, 1.

Keep me in touch with your thoughts and adventures, since meeting seems somewhat high-risk these days. Though if high-risk is not our business it's not clear who else is going to take it on.
    Saluti:
        J.

31 October 1990   101 St. Mark's Place #12A
                                       New York City

Dear Jeremy,

    Glad to have a response to SCARLET and to feel that you have returned from the Chinese hinterland and into radio contact.

    I can but abashedly acknowledge the many false layerings into which spirit fumes these days, but I think we're aiming at something very different from inspired simplifications—not least at any Labour Conference. One great trouble is difficulty in separating the sentimental from the blindingly obvious moments of the good. I don't believe the good can be deconstructed, or destroyed by its distortions and smoky layerings; and I imagine you agree. If it could, there would be no explanation for our emotional reaction to it during its most urgent appearances: as if we'd been hit by it. You see, this is <u>sentimental</u>: recently, I was in an emergency room watching the three-year-old of a fellow worker (not at all a friend) struggle with an eventually fatal staph infection following bone marrow transplant. The nurses were just ordinary girls being cheerful as they bathed a horribly blistered and blued body. But I became rather dazzled at the good that lay somewhere within the actions, not actually possessed by the girls themselves perhaps. Nothing can sophisticate that sense of the good, although actual situations confuse us so much and we cannot often search down to it. Thus, the Iraqi situation, on which we have a squib-like editorial in our second issue.[1] Spirit can't decide it from without because our Spirit is not within the forum of decision: the Iraqi seizure seems parallel to, say, the Bush invasion of Panama—spirit goes wambling off across borders...[2] Within the forum exactly—within Hussein's mind, for example, I guess goodness ought to have a place despite all realpolitik difficulties, naive though it may seem to say so.[3] Don't we trivialise politics of other countries by insisting that we personally should have a decision on a foreign issue? Isn't that the Great American Sin and the Thatcher Sin?

    That the practice of written speech is leveraged '<u>in absentia</u>', as you say, does not destroy the case for spirit, of course. I would argue that the lever becomes bendy and plastic at each moment in the present, within the precise forum of writing: the fact that spirit is unspeakable is only an affirmation of its value, not of despair of it, for we have to be unpridefully content with the inevitable failures of our goodness; still we know the better from the worse, and so on. These I have always taken to be something like your own opinions, more or less. So I'm simply affirming a

---

[1] The editorial 'squib' in *Scarlet*, no. 2 (Fall 1990), n.p., refers briefly to the Gulf War in the context of a discussion of the poverty in Tomkins Square Park, New York, adjacent to Oliver and Notley's apartment on St. Mark's Place. The editorial of *Scarlet*, no. 3 (Winter 1991), n.p., addresses the Gulf War directly, and the issue explicitly 'takes the anti-war stance'.

[2] The US invaded Panama on 20 December 1989; the conflict lasted a little over a month.

[3] Saddam Hussein (1937–2006), president of Iraq, 1979–2003.

standpoint rather than arguing. I agree with all you say about Iraq: to me, it is an Arab question, not least since the West ought to be trying immensely to reduce the dependence of economies on oil—for all sorts of quite evident reasons.

You may imagine that all said about Chinese brush writing and intonation is close to me: I have long been interested (as any poet might) in the syntactically defined segments of intonation in tone languages. It is the hardest case for my own notions of prosody to deal with (syllabics are a piece of cake by comparison). To alter tune, therefore, one must in a primary way think of altering syntax, I assume; and semantics. This may be a closer match between tune, meaning and emotional significance than available in the Western languages which can always 'trope' slightly across meaning and engage in little runs of intonation governed more mainly by information focus (or 'tonic'), in which syllables of slight importance may more run with the melody than exercise much point control over it. If you ever felt you wanted to write {a prose piece} for us in this area, or send us something in brushwork to reproduce (something Western readers could be given clarity about), this might be a happy way to include {this—or poems?} of yours in SCARLET, as we'd much like to do. I'm not being lamely opportunist about this: I'm actually fascinated.

Oddly, I was reading a little Sun Tzu this summer, and loved all he had to say about using double agents, and so forth. I sort of can't stand Machiavelli, despite much enlightenment, and the reasons why may be gathered from the above.

We'll be over again in February but once more it seems you won't. I'll try to ring. Hope you get past the border guards all the same.

    Best,
        Doug.

1 January 1991   101 St. Mark's Place #12A
                                      New York City

Dear Jeremy,

Just some New Year greetings.

Going through a filing cabinet, I came across this old review of 'Marzipan', which David Marriott sought for a magazine issue that I think never came out, though I never know quite what appears and what doesn't.[1] It seems too out of date to place elsewhere.

Alice and I journey to London (15/2–25/2) and Paris (25/2–4/3). Don't know if you'll be around and would be glad to know. I pay for the trip yearly by lecturing in Paris, but the main point is to see Kate and Bonamy; and, this time, my step-sons, Anselm and Edmund, can renew their acquaintance with the girls. So I can't dash about seeing people.

No decent work in the U.S. for me still—just adjunct teaching

---

[1] D. S. Marriott (b. 1963), British poet. Oliver's review is reproduced in appendix D. Marriott reviewed *Bands around the Throat*, the collection in which 'Marzipan' was published (for the fourth time), in *Archeus*, no. 1 (1989): n.p.

under exploitative conditions, and I'm beginning to wonder if that's just how it'll be. We're living amid a nation bemused at what they're getting into, such opinion formers as Time presenting Bush as politician of the year for his Iraq policy.[1] They seem to think he's ushering in a 'new world order' in which UN policing replaces major power wars in secondary countries. The US as agent of this. It's so worrying to see senior international journalists selling themselves to this kind of smart talk, when Bush has had so many secret agendas and when the major powers are only in concert out of self-interest. Change the interests and see the 'new world order' vanish like dew. One's own relative 'poverty' (actually richness) doesn't seem a very compelling subject as we turn into the New Year and I prepare to go out to give a two-minute reading at the usual massive St. Mark's Poetry Project benefit.[2]

Kate's teaching in a fairly tough inner London school. Bon's studying psychology at Portsmouth Poly again after a year's flunk-out. Step-son Anselm, at Buffalo Uni, has begun the hack's trail on the campus newspaper—covered a murder, student 'riots', etc., but really wants to be a feature writer. Other son, Eddie, is waiting to make his college choice. Alice & I in good spirits.

 Best
  Doug.

---

23 October 1991   17 Ferry Path
                   Cambridge

Dear Doug,

Many thanks for No. 5 and the note.[3] Yes I am back in at least some obvious sense of the word, including the rueful 'back to all this' and the toils of picking up threads with new admixtures of hesitancy and dismay. You will understand well enough, though I wouldn't broadcast the fact, that my excursion was devised for the fundamental rights & duties of poetry to resolve by displacement at least some of the blank spaces left by more traditional incomprehension, indeed was aimed at the blank spaces head-on; so that returning to the native land and its hearthstone completes the chances of blasphemous self-rescue by ironical rejection, and is of course thereby even harder to countenance. I thought I would feel this as of both ways, but was not prepared for the intensity. I see what you mean by vividness but that is too pictorial for the case here; nor would some visceral Zaum performance meet the billing, even though speaking there with that tongue is a long way over to the other side of speech.[4] I can't quite jog this out, because of attachment.

It is, then, hard to convey happiness, even at most joyful moments spread out lengthways, because it has such little commerce with pleasure or satisfaction or enjoyment even. My small sojourn out in the provinces, at what was, not to mince these words, a third-rate ex-teacher's college parading as an engine of

---

1 *Time* 137, no. 1 (7 January 1991). The discrepancy between the date of Oliver's letter and the issue date of the magazine is accounted for by the fact that the issue went on sale on 31 December 1990, as reported in *Newsday*, 30 December 1990, 4.

2 The Poetry Project at St. Mark's Church, reading series founded in 1966.

3 Oliver and Notley sent *Scarlet*, no. 5, on 16 September 1991. The 'note' to which Prynne refers reads: 'Dear Jeremy, Pleased to get your card from China. I have no idea whether you're back or not yet but would like to get back in touch when you've got a moment. I'm very curious to know what new word orders you've come up with + hope to write a proper letter very soon. Very best, Doug.'

4 Prynne responds to the discussion of 'vividness' in the section from *Penniless* excerpted in *Scarlet*, no. 5:

 'Suppose you blamed yourself,
  Mr. Belia', said Emen, this courteous,
 possessed woman, face eshining, so that
  viewers saw the Good there,
 transcendental in Emen's own skin—
 'yourself but also your neighbor
 humans on Earth imagined vividly—
  vividness, the vital quality
 of a mind that unites with goodness in
  a rush of warm feeling, a quiver
 of warmth stabbing like fear. In that
  instant, your sex or your race
 is both sexes, all races, yet one and your
  own—heightened in quality.'
'Zaum', Russian Futurist language composed through phonetic and rhythmic invention. Prynne responds to the section of *Penniless* immediately prior to the discussion of 'vividness', in which the character Emen delivers a polyglottal speech. *Scarlet*, no. 5, n.p.

higher learning, implies the stigma of indulgence; which I was hard put to overcome. The work ethic! At the same time the grove of bamboos and camphor trees that I awoke to see every day gradually stood away from the plate-glass scroll of the window frame (with mercifully cheap bamboo-decorated curtains) to stabilise from script to plant, easily akin to the finest work of T'ang Yin but also co-generic with the bits of green I had potted up as interior companions.[1] It is necessary to be very literal minded. 'Cool winds gather round the treetops' ('it seems as though it is just about to rain').[2] You see how hard it is to convey this, where the screen along two axes revolves about a line of symmetry to double into recognition without either inversion or simple identity. The subject is not put to recasting, either, which would be a crude cheat etherised by excitement.

These dimensions are all of spectacular long-standing but their active current range of response is so immediate and short-fused that much courage is needed to conduct a line of life. To speak before you starve, as was not so far back. I may not, here, appropriate a string band called 'my students', though in Chinese that's easy enough because they are now mine for life and not simply by my choice; but those young people went right out on a limb and less and less was it a complex excursus. They are very passionate at that age which is also maybe the historical moment; and the innocent non-presumption of prior consciousness projects with extravagant outwardness from the grind and, ah, misery of anterior complexion. I do now have to say *misery* because, though *hardship* would reify the more correctly dominant axis, we are what our tongues make us do with them. To rush into the deep parts of these shallows can work if the previous history is studied and known, because then it can be read from the faces (and bodies also) of the older generation. My teaching of young medical students set the cross-light for visiting two friends of middle age in a post-operative hospital ward: the mirror axis. In the inflexions of local dialect you hold a hand, holding on indeed as being held, under gazes of phosphorescent concentration. And if you say well you must (you do) say very well, because very is required as a balancing element and does not mean towards any extreme: it means *balanced* in hope & regard through the order of unstressed tones.

It is good to have a conversation that lasts for a full day, and then to top up or annotate before re-setting the locale for another run. It is simply good because it is not complex, and indeed because it is the staple of *work*: the strangeness of the parts can be cancelled off against reserve, to achieve near-transparency. Over short range that must look like illusion or even collusion, but the internal self-testing confirms over a fuller span: 'If you want to gain knowledge you must participate in the practice of changing reality.'[3] These friendships rouse up from need and readiness, then, but they stabilise as knowledge and hold the personal reality into the frames of consciousness, like a clock powered by its own

---

1 T'ang Yin (1470–1524), Chinese painter, calligrapher, and poet.

2 Prynne quotes T'ang Yin's 'Inscribed on a Painting', trans. Chiang Yee. Prynne would have read this translation in Wu-chi Liu and Irving Yucheng Lo, eds., *Sunflower Splendor: Three Thousand Years of Chinese Poetry* (Garden City, NY: Anchor Books, 1975), 467. Wei Chuang's 'The Lament of the Lady of Ch'in', in the same anthology (267–81, trans. Robin D. S. Yates), is an important intertext of Prynne's 'Marzipan'.

3 Prynne quotes Mao Tse-tung, 'On Practice' (1937). *An Anthology of His Writings*, ed. and trans. Anne Fremantle (New York: New American Library, 1954), 205. Prynne follows Fremantle's translation here and in the quotation from 'On Contradiction', below.

gaze. Repetition by the timetable assigns the rhyme-scheme, of strophic versus, glancing and turning, and simple speech which goes slowly watches with attention the effects of slowness. It is *care* that reads from the face whether the signal is too strong, spacing out its pressures of encounter; the care is not simpering or chauvinistic because it is exactly mutual: each wants the other to go as far and as fast as can be dared without by mishap stopping altogether. The subject-position hovers here in between the speakers, it is the spirit of the speaking community presiding over its pavilion of ardent differences. For the beginners on the campus, straight from the countryside, their almost entire lack of money gave them a very precise index for ardency, and for me at last shewed how one could be not merely feeding a market. My first-year friend Jian Song-qing wrote to tell me about his recent anniversary: 'Because I didn't get a job I hadn't enough money to have a party for my birthday. And I wouldn't want to make the party become my parents' burden. Otherwise it would cost most of their income of one month. I can't have enough money to go out for a trip though I have enough time.' That is the rate for a teenager's map of what is needful: he tells me because he knows I won't for a moment mistake that as a complaint.

When one of my companions wanted to identify which of two or more characters was the Chinese 'word' in question, the standard device is to 'write' the strokes on the palm of the left hand with the index finger of the right; if the 'writing' process has not been fully visible to the other person, the speaker/writer will hold up the 'written' (i.e., blank) palm for the other to decipher. Sometimes when myself setting to write down a character I would seem to have forgotten it visually, but I would discover that the muscles of my right hand and forearm had retained the control-pattern needed to produce it. When modern poets play within the courtyards of stanza-form the four Mandarin tones give distinctive leverage against line-initial, median and line-final positions, with especially pivotal function going to the third tone (falling–rising). I have discussed this latter effect with serious (i.e., professional) poets and it is an acknowledged element in their repertoire, as can be heard on the tapes I have made of their reading. But my preferred experimental practice was with Tin-tin, the three year old daughter of a local shopkeeper: all his family & friends used to sit out on the street during warm summer evenings, drinking tea and making sporadic conversation. Many happy hours I whiled away there, chiefly with Tin-tin: she would make her beginning-speech noises and I would imitate them, back and forth, and make permutations and we got to be close friends (close, that is, to the same threshold of latent speech). Her father spoke a pronounced form of the local dialect, astonishingly musical, each casual sally a little aria. I mostly did not understand what he said, word by word, but also I *did* fully understand what he was saying, as it tended into its occasion; just as they took in not what I said but, easily, what I was trying to say.

23 October 1991

1 Prynne quotes Mao Tse-tung, 'On Contradiction' (1937). *An Anthology of His Writings*, 238.

2 Deng Xiaoping (1904–97), post-Maoist leader of the People's Republic of China, 1978–89.

Well, these speech-act phenomena of recuperation from only partially effected spoken exchanges are well documented; my interest was in getting into and being inside *the swim*, since the unseen frames to these lives (historical and political and calligraphic) could best be learned by moving in regular time to the actions of friendship. For students the directive fate which would specify their future lay like a heavy shadow, but their commitment to unrelentingly hard work disclosed another form of this same reality. In the old order you worked to the limit in order to become a scholar-administrator who would then never 'work'; i.e., you worked to define favourably the future sense of what 'work' you would do (a class concept, with the familiar but unusual feature of mediation by competitive examination). In the Maoist order the labour theory of value commands that labour power cannot be part of a market (still less a free one) without becoming a commodity and thus leading (back) to capitalist exploitation or sectoral privilege; even a democracy and decision-sharing will look like an auction by franchise: the command-price of pushing by numbers. Thus central or even regional workforce planning must be non-consultative, which in turn demands a certain idealism (crudely put) if directives are to be read as coherent within larger social aspirations rather than differentially conferring individual benefit (envy and resentment). The large view is a hard task: 'Conditional, relative identity, combined with unconditional, absolute struggle, constitutes the movement of opposites in all things.'[1]

But now under Deng that orientation towards collective performance has all but expired;[2] or rather, it survives in intensely local pockets while flatly negated by other more immediate tendencies. The attempt to install market forces for production while curtailing them for consumption, and while regulating imbalances between town/country even when also freeing up distinctions between rich/poor, projects facile materialism as the sure sign of progress on both sides. Not to grasp the advantages of discrepancy is simply to miss your chance. Shiny goods! More to eat! It seems so inevitable to want it now, my family first. The pragmatic rationale is, finally, that you get there quicker if you harness the forces of self-improvement, as now channelled into the one-child family unit however locally extended; a funnel-effect which, along with inflation (severe in 1988–9), will co-ordinate tactics of economic advancement for individuals and nuclear families, succinct enterprise groups pushing to keep whatever they can earn. To want the best (better) for the child! The effect of this invasive pragmatism on the young is strongly disabling because it is counter-patriotic and excites stupefied admiration for Western economic management, as a politics not of production but of consumption: that is, of course, the social-engineering device behind John Major's fireside chats about 'citizens' charters', his odiously plausible ordinariness, which is odious especially because of the way the ordinariness is covertly exploited.[1] Naturally the wide-eyed locals by the Yangtze assumed that I would evangelise for these superior advantages, of which all too evidently I was myself the product: which put me into the directly provoked stance of protecting by argument what they already had, or once had, against its erosion in the name of what they thought they wanted.

The poor, eager wretches in Tiananmen Square were gripped by this same voided contradiction, capable of generating a worked dialectic only at a level so trans-historical as to be far out of reach.[2] Their revulsion against nepotism and corruption at upper government levels was against a traditional evil made far worse by the very influx of 'democratic' Western trade-offs marking the source for them of ideals like freedom itself: the free-wheel for the dealer. What they wanted from 'democracy', were they to get any of its currently available forms, would in very short order be the irreversible ruin of their unworkably pristine motives for wanting it. But then, also, the ethically provoked exile from the Western ideal system, immobilised as the addicted beneficiary of resented injustice, looks towards the purer struggle of retarded economies as the alibi for remorse. They ought not to make our mistakes, and be comforted by mere comforts! Their own equivalent alibi is to despise the Gang of Four and especially Jiang Qing, where again a fanatic single-mindedness can be made the scapegoat of many time-serving and even unrecognised self-interests.[3] I was permitted, even asked, to give lectures about 'freedom' but they were not I think what the listeners expected or quite wanted to hear. The future teachers certainly wanted to *choose* their entry into work because *choice* now marks the locality of a smart success, just as Debord observed; but also because if you are constrained to *feel* imprisoned by constraint then that is indeed what you are.[4] How should we stand it, ourselves?

So, there was much to think about, and discuss! But at the level of the person I found the mood not very often overtly political. The element of social hope was now patchy, personal rather than socially (politically) understood: the habits in that mode had been so damaged by the mutilation of hope itself during the later Cultural Revolution that, for instance, the War against Iraq was persistently misread.[5] Now however that Yugoslavia has exploded, I guess that they will have to think harder.[6] The relation of life to narrative ('telling their story'), as a way of acknowledging connection, didn't strain after understanding, but it did seek to locate the site of experience; just as strong feelings often didn't or wouldn't attach to conditions of just self-esteem (this, as I judge, because their fathers' generation had been too traumatised by the Cultural Revolution to pass emotional validation to their offspring). Just to commend one of these youngsters, justly, for some momentary refinement of personal intelligence, was to see them perk up as if after prolonged starvation. To resist sentimental over-compensation was thus

1 'citizens' charter', political initiative launched by Conservative prime minister John Major on 22 July 1991. *The Times* reported that Major's 'blueprint aims to give tougher rights for consumers over a wide range of public services and will underpin his determination to improve standards and rights of redress in the public sector'. Richard Ford, 'Major Says Tories Have Much to Do as Charter Is Launched', *The Times*, 22 July 1991, 20.

2 Prynne refers to the Tiananmen Square protests and massacre, April–June 1989.

3 'Gang of Four', political faction in the Chinese Communist Party consisting of Jiang Qing, Wang Hongwen, Zhang Chunqiao, and Yao Wenyuan.

4 Several of Guy Debord's aphorisms in *Society of the Spectacle* discuss 'choice' explicitly. See especially section 62: 'The false choices offered by spectacular abundance—choices based on the juxtaposition of competing yet mutually reinforcing spectacles and of distinct yet interconnected roles (signified and embodied primarily by objects)—develop into struggles between illusory qualities designed to generate fervent allegiance to quantitative trivialities.' *Society of the Spectacle*, trans. Ken Knabb (London: Rebel Press, 2005), 30.

5 'Cultural Revolution', period of socio-political reform in Maoist China, 1966–76, characterized by widespread massacres, political purges, and the destruction of traditional heritage sites.

6 Prynne refers to the ongoing break-up of Yugoslavia and the Yugoslav Wars (1991–2001). Days before Prynne sent this letter, *The Times* reported on the 'hand-to-hand battles' fought between Serbs and Croats in the latter stages of the siege of the Croatian town of Vukovar by the Yugoslav People's Army. Anne McElvoy, 'Serbs and Croats Fight Hand to Hand in Besieged Town', *The Times*, 18 October 1991, 11.

23 October 1991

[1] Prynne refers to Leslie Scalapino and Ron Silliman, 'What/Person: From an Exchange', *Poetics Journal*, no. 9 (1991): 51–68.

[2] 'we want what we are', Prynne interpolates a line from his 'Sketch for a Financial Theory of the Self', from *Kitchen Poems* (1968). See *Poems*, 19–20 (20).

[3] Prynne enclosed an article, 'Pop Music and One World', from the student newspaper referred to, and a reproduction of William Blake's watercolour *A Vision: The Inspiration of the Poet (Elisha in the Chamber on the Wall)*.

[4] In addition to the letter below, Prynne enclosed a copy of *Jie ban mi Shi Hu* (Cambridge: Poetical Histories, no. 22, 1992) (*Poems*, 379–80).

quite a hard duty, and all while together watching the lines move in some English or Chinese poem or by reflection from the canal-water on a stone parapet during one of our urban ambulations. You start as you go on, each way. But their vulnerability to music like this was really extraordinary, part of the 'innocence' now so assailed by the pressure of pragmatic alternatives.

I do not know yet how to think about all this fully, because despite the complexities and remoteness of circumstances the issues seem so overwhelmingly simple. Which is indeed not to say clear. My sentiments are extremely engaged. The exchange about 'person' in *Poetics Journal*, based (we're asked to believe) on a symposium in *Socialist Review* (really?), seems encrusted with spectacular impersonations, all more or less gratulatory and unlived-in because of the need to keep up with the apparatus of a vacant discourse.[1] What self-assurance from the little ploys and toy-fervencies of this echo-chamber! I think I am not going to read any more of this kind of stuff, for the time being which might be for ever, it is too painful. To keep entirely and continuously in the swim I was working non-stop out there, round the clock, to keep my head down and to be a worker and not to cruise from a deck chair like these bemused speculators. The labour theory of value is also grammatical, just as the opiate of work falls into the pharmacopoeia of disapproval within the aroused defence of self-possession (mine! mine!). I have been here before, too: we want what we are.[2] So then, I even now have enough to do, and also to keep up my correspondence with distant friends.

  As here & now, and
      with all regards,
         J.

P.S. Here's a student music-review piece, from the newspaper I started & keyboarded for them, to give some flavour. And on another glance sideways, haven't we seen this luminous cubicle (enclosed) somewhere before?[3]

30 January 1993   17 Ferry Path
                               Cambridge

Dear Doug,

By misplacement & confusion I find that the enclosed letter, cast off just after Christmas, never got put into the mail; and so here (rather dusty) comes something a bit better than nothing.[4] The plumper envelope is really now very imminent indeed, always supposing I don't get into yet another muddle with the tidal waves of work and work-silt surging up in these parts. At any rate I do hope you're well and active.

  À bientôt:
    J.

Dear Doug,

I have meant to write before this, but time has been cramped as usual and its consequences are not at all clear. I'm indeed glad to hear that you are installing in yet another sett, and I hope that's all going on towards reasonable working comfort. Also I've taken in your several messages (direct & oblique) and so at such levels I believe we are in contact.[1]

But speaking one's mind is another thing, as I come to perceive. I can begin with some clarity, I think, to see how this has been coming out for you, into the open of a *sermo* under direct press of lapsing events in the field full of folk.[2] For my part, having seen many things in the vivid relief of a completely new crosslight, observing my own alignment to find them instantly recognisable but not at all assimilated, I then find all this by an unexpected further deflection not part of a mind to be spoken except rather close to the surface: at other levels the matrix of stresses doesn't have a self at its centre and so what might speak it isn't specifically generated at all. How can I put this: the constituency of even one's active knowledge doesn't nominate a spokesperson, for me, with opinions or even beliefs that connect directly to it and draw from its vehemence.[3] At first I believed that this deflected output was just a sequel to acute congestion and counterwork, so that if I redrew the parameters and set myself as a filter for some dialectic of temporary resolution I could press on towards utterance driven directly from experience.

That's been a lot of work, extended and productive, partly self-inflicted and partly not. But rather to my surprise the most confirmed utterance-position is not connected to this grid of new currents, or at least not directly (again); indeed, maybe now less directly than I had believed before. If I were to generalise from this I might possibly aver that speaking one's mind is a kind of delusion, lining up conviction and opinion so as to take the person's stance as a frame for directed address even when the pronouncement is canted through many dramaturgic and countervailed positions and vocalisms. I don't mean a delusion for those in whose state of soul the relation of speech to action retroflects to the same anterior morality; but for those whose sense of speech takes by indirection from what by that same token won't be action as part of a narrative in human life. But I don't in fact think of this as territory for generalisation, or for generals to fight over with their range-finding and language-cleansing; it's connected up differently in differing constitutions.

What issues is not now the same; but the impress of that doesn't seem to be an inference from the inputs, or from what certainly circulates as pressure and deep ethical frustration. There is a discomfort in this which at the moment I find generates a lot of rather acute anxiety; but as against it I discover that such discomforts of the self are part of the cost in not being positioned to pay out at call. There is, it seems, no direct unit of account, no fixed rate as by exchange against strongly-held

30 January 1993

1 Two letters from Oliver are preserved in Prynne's papers between the period of Oliver's letter of 16 October 1991 and the present letter. Oliver wrote on 4 November 1991 to thank Prynne for his letter of 23 October 1991, and again to inform him of his and Notley's new address in Paris (61 rue Lepic) at some point in 1992. This letter is undated, though '1992' is legible from the Parisian postmark.

2 'field full of folk', Prynne interpolates a phrase from the prologue to *Piers Plowman*.

 'speaking one's mind', 'how this has been coming out for you', Prynne responds to Oliver's *Penniless Politics* (London: Hoarse Commerce, 1991), in which the name of the semiautobiographical protagonist 'Will Penniless' is a conjunction of the narrator-poet figures of *Piers Plowman* ('Will') and Thomas Nashe's *Pierce Penniless, His Supplication to the Divell*. Mind considered as the prepolitical subject of potential human goodness and consensus, and especially the 'sharing of minds', are significant components of Oliver's poem. Towards the end of the first part of the poem, the character Ma Johnson reads the lines:

> 'Write the three
> things that Spirit must do. Turn to a
>   clean page in this book and
> write the very first things in your mind.
>   Don't be a coward
> about this.' [...]

(*Penniless Politics* (Newcastle upon Tyne: Bloodaxe Books, 1994), 31, 34)

3 Prynne responds to the characterization of Will Penniless as 'Spirit spokesperson' (*Penniless Politics*, 34).

beliefs; because that construction is presumed upon personal distinctness. Hum hum: does that mean some mere zombie in the driving seat, or a contrivance that chatters along even while the passengers are stripping down the engine. If some kind of composing determinism takes over, then the dominating language is once again the language of the dominators, including the standard arguments against them. No, the reflux of pressures to speak runs right through the formats of what's possible and resisted and gazed upon, and the alterations are not part of a knowledge that I can say is mine, despite my sense of its activity and a massively raised level of instigation.

    These questions have come to settle out otherwise for you, as I can recognise clearly enough, and that in itself is one cogent reason not to generalise aggressively. A procedure tending towards purity, or towards mere irony of contradiction, needs vandalising at once; which makes even the moral hyperbole of *penniless* a little bit dangerous. Yet if exaggeration is one of the badges of honourable defence then one should maybe indeed take a turn at that pump, rather than at some mincing scruple. Or, just go ahead with what's to be done, as it comes forward, and precisely not assume tactics as allegory for virtuous action. In this welter of half-thoughts my own mind is once more thrown into confusion, by the recent death of Bernard Dubourg.[1] He was a real landmark for me over many years, pushed into obscurity by illness and by the polite sneers of the French literary establishment (including, of course, the self-styled anti-ditto). Now without any warning he is gone, from a sudden heart attack on 20th December, leaving scarce a trace in the world outside. Almost all of his intrepid adventures were internal, his mischievous scepticism focussed with pin-point precision as the starts for daring leaps of mind and language. All our projects together, at a stroke relegated to the past historic! It's certainly hard not to feel a lot of aggression towards those incestuously metropolitan French editors, who didn't give a toss for our joint labours of translation; but with time I'll absorb all that also into the generative layout, draining off the rancour which is accidental to the fate of persons and putting it to some use beyond chagrin.

    This communiqué, I see, is amounting to precious little; to keep the lines open if not much more. I'll have a slightly plumper envelope to send on shortly.
    Saluti:
        J.

---

12 February 1993   61 rue Lepic
                                                                                                                            Paris

Dear Jeremy,
    A lurid mistake at the local papeterie has condemned us to salmon pink but for the first time since September I have sensible typing facilities.[2] Which is to say, somehow, that I was

---

[1] Bernard Dubourg (1945–92), French poet and translator of Prynne's poetry. For an account of Dubourg and Prynne's collaborative translation efforts and reflection on the extent and intensity of their poetical relationship, see Alex Latter, '"Beyond the Path Itself": Archive and Text in the Correspondence of Bernard Dubourg and J. H. Prynne', *The Cambridge Quarterly* 50, no. 3 (September 2021): 261–78

[2] 'salmon pink', Oliver refers to the colour of the paper upon which this letter is printed.

very interested in your letter and wanted to write back quickly.

I am sorry about the sombreness that Dubourg's death has caused you and about the inachievement in the public domain of his life-work. There is a very curious tension between these sorrows and what you say elsewhere about the delusion of speaking one's mind; and this creates filaments which run invisibly through your letter. I know how important your collaboration with him was for both of you, but am ignorant of how extensive that collaboration (or his own work) was. Do you intend to do anything about this, and is there any errand I can run for you in that respect?

Where you are, I think, is the letting-go of the dominating of language by the culturally formed self and by all deeper level matrices of it, since the ethics that result are illusion. Instead, the outerlying knowledge and ethical potential are not personal but, presumably, are the onrush of the universal. And who speaks what at that refinement of truthfulness becomes an urgent question, all the more urgent because denied by the very movement that feels the urgency. I feel its urgency too, because humans have made themselves trivial in the face of these forces which (to use a quasi-Christian language for its dramatic point) lent us this planet, and so on. Ethically, may we so live that the universal shines through us as unimpeded as possible, says that language.

{I hope this will not be mistaken for false modesty or abjectness →} My problem is that I'm simply not good enough to live like that. I'm trying to avoid that infuriating tone so much language poetry has: the tone of 'I am handing down information, but I, of course, have seen beyond my own power lust because my language only exists in a rather conditional sense that I can talk about for several hours if you like.' This, however sophisticated it may become, leads not to the transcendent of the human but to a technology of language fit for the Information Age. And if I'm not good enough, surely it's not an ethical writing to pretend to be, or to inhabit a middle ground of purist attitude not good enough to convince anyone else of anything, not good enough to stop even the harms that I do; it is better for me to 'descend', if that's the direction, to the multi-voiced opinions and to reproducing society for itself—to the old craft, in fact, perhaps, made a little new because newly informed by the above complex motivations and conducted at the level of 'the best that I can do'.

You are operating at a higher level than this: I'm speaking descriptively; and probably our only chance is to listen to the black wind that blows through us. I have fully honoured and still do the penetration and ethical point of your work. (Adrian Harding, whom you know I think as a Ph.D. student nearly fell over with delight to see the black-wind brush strokes of your ideograms.)[1] I feel myself very crude in relation to this, a going ahead with what's to be done as you generously put it. As I am having similar discussions with Alice from time to time, I much wonder about the future of all this.

[1] Adrian Harding (b. 1956), British writer and academic.
'ideograms', Oliver refers to *Jie ban mi Shi Hu*.

12 February 1993

1 'whole earthers', Oliver refers to the countercultural movement that developed in the United States in the late 1960s and early 1970s through the production and dissemination of Stewart Brand's *Whole Earth Catalog*. For the most detailed history of the cultural legacy of 'whole earth' thinking, see Fred Turner, *From Counterculture to Cyberculture: Stewart Brand, the Whole Earth Network, and the Rise of Digital Utopianism* (Chicago: University of Chicago Press, 2006).

2 Oliver interpolates figures and phrasing from Howard Rheingold, *Virtual Reality* (London: Secker and Warburg, 1991), 369.
  'Big Bang', name given to the UK financial sector reforms introduced in October 1986.

3 The narrator-protagonist of J. M. Coetzee's novel is an unnamed magistrate of a fictional imperial outpost. Twice in the novel he attempts to prevent, or at least to mitigate, acts of colonial brutality and torture.

My own work just now as a sermo in the ploughfield, and an exaggerated (my word is burlesqued) one is I suppose fair comment, and evidently makes it contrast in strange and oblique ways with your deep-seated doubts about the 'utterance position'. Then, in another way of looking at it also provided by your letter, we have an underlying motivation not too dissimilar; that is, you have radicalised those elements in modern praxis which most worry me and therefore revealed their deficiency; and I have been working on the 'humility' (firmly in quote marks) of employing an utterance position (a poetic self) which acknowledges its own lack of right.

It has taken only ten years or so for the 'end of the world' fears to pass out of the sphere of the intellectuals and whole earthers and to have become popular and international political currency.[1] And to live in NYC among the huge injustices of the whizzy city, or to see separate-interest politics keep up their own most seductive forms of lying—seductive just because having so much right behind them—and to experience so near at hand the effects of the new finance information technology ... and then to go to some poetry reading venue and just hear the coterie assumptions at work (and England must be the same) ... well, if we still have grip on this sentence, that is ethical frustration indeed. We are assailed by hugely true cliches, and as poets we are engaged in an activity very often trivial and inward looking. To take only one example, international foreign exchange transactions reached $87 trillion in 1986 as in England the Big Bang just began taking effect, several times larger than the gross world product. Trade reached only 10% of that figure.[2] There came a point where I stopped being concerned about the reception of my work by my peers; and yet I didn't want to make that other error of 'right to speak', or of posing as the one just person.

You rightly say that this creates an ethical dilemma because all attempt to speak is entrained in what would be spoken: if you like, the matrix of stresses doesn't have a self at its centre. Speaking one's mind is a delusion. Yes, no doubt.

For me, it depends what are the underlying referents of this position—and I can't almost by definition argue against it. As, for example, a response to Eastern ways of living and the much more urgent needs of such a large society as China, the individual 'capitalist' writer-voice would seem indulgent to put it mildly. We do not have the right to speak of what we dominate financially, and do not have the right to speak against our own culture while enjoying it. It is the dilemma of Coetzee's <u>Waiting for the Barbarians</u>, and yet that book shows that the issues which seem so insoluble vanish at the point where people are being tortured. At that point, to come up to a magistrate about to intervene with his <u>voice</u> at a moment of group colonialist savagery and ask whether the centre of utterance exists would, as you would clearly agree, be absurd.[3] At such a moment we surely become merely individual and human and do not want to know whether

12 February 1993

the story/poem of this event may or may not reach a condition of truthfulness. Further, the story of this event will obviously be truer, ethically, if it is founded upon the fact that the magistrate acts, rather than upon the fact that he funks action.

Or take the case that the matrix is much more refined than these crude arguments which are our mother's milk. For example again, we might look to the quantum smearing-out of origin at the heart of latest matricial viewpoints, whether by the spatialisation of the time dimension or by other mathematical devices unknown to me. Quantum scientific methods of descriptions rather rule out origin in the micro- and macro-worlds, I expect; and therefore by a usual extrapolation familiar to us, they rule out origin, utterance position, at the heart of thinking, and therefore at the heart of stress as the very pulse of thinking and emotion. And, as has often been observed, aspects of Eastern religions fit more comfortably with this than does the Judeo-Christian outlook. We reach the position that description shows there is no origin point within the matrix (matrix of 'self' included), and yet description would in any case destroy the origin; and yet description is all we've got short of blind faith; and yet finally the natural world utterly consorts with the description.

True, unless it is the nature of unity, being indescribable, to provide the perhaps ineffable cause of its own lack of existence, such that it cannot be found even at the start of the universe, or in the sub-atomic, or yet in the human voice. And still all things tend towards it as if it were an ultimate value. Most importantly since they are so much neglected, our emotions do, whether they are good or bad emotions. As our emotions so, in their different basis, our ethics seek to compound difference with unity. Then, it might be the nature of unity to exist in not-existing, to bend space time always into itself, even if the presumed singularity that might subtend such happenings lay outside our own universe's origin, or even if it is merely that things cannot be understood properly without a sense that utter relativity and utter unity are at some perhaps non-existent 'non-limit' the same. The non-existence of this non-limit doesn't seem to me so important as the most refined description might suppose, because the 'tendency towards' explains human emotions to me better than the notion of 'non arrival at non-existing limit'. As poet, my job seems most crucially to interpret human emotions.

Now there's a viewpoint that's having troubles at the moment! We're screwing up the planet so well that 'human', let alone 'human emotions', seems the least worthy, least interesting category of all. The merest amoeba is living a less blameworthy life than ourselves tapping away on our plasticised computers (not to mention the car-borne citizens). Perhaps we should all just shut up. Or, another possibility, vulgarise ourselves and join in the chorus more fully, which as you perceive is my own direction: that way, we will not be correct, not unblameable, will lie sometimes, and yet in our comfortable, unrisky way may act more like

12 February 1993

the magistrate than like Coetzee's intelligence at work on what the magistrate says finally—that he's on a road going nowhere.[1]

This is where I am: some ethics in action is better than a pretence at ethics by some kind of language game (the post Foucault decentering of the I, etc., posing as an ethical and political task whose hidden faults are instantly betrayed by tone). I have always believed that the enlarging of the I is better than its total abandonment, even though this runs right into all possible traps and could only be escaped by achievement of an angelic consciousness. And the other path I honour is your own (and Alice's) attempt to see beyond the human and to listen for something better than its damaged spirit. That the gates to the temples are guarded by demons we know.

Best,
Doug

---

[1] Oliver refers to the ending of Coetzee's novel: 'This is not the scene I dreamed of. Like much else nowadays I leave it feeling stupid, like a man who lost his way long ago but presses on along a road that may lead nowhere.' *Waiting for the Barbarians*, 155–6.

---

23 February 1993   Gonville and Caius College
Cambridge

Dear Doug,

Yes as usual, the matter is hovering right around the nub once again, or if the perimeter's elliptical then there is more than one centre. We are close enough to make the question of terms important. I can sense the strain in your letter also, of trying to hold a position that has slippage built-in, and trying to guard against making a principle out of a practice or letting what's to be done be spatchcocked against some lofty canon of insufficiency. First terminal point, then: the *façons de parler* of 'high' and 'low', 'elevated' or 'not good enough', 'higher level' and 'descending to partialities of action' etc., all seem to me disallowed. The one who does his bit may sit up a tree or on top of a useless column, the one who broods may be prone in a ditch (like Beckett); the body encloses the soul and yet the soul's meaning for itself may extravasate and consort with the riff-raff on all sides.

Second terminal point: ethics are of course a fabric of human invention and as the reverse products of that invention we must believe that ethics outreach completely their human origin. Urgency as an address of the mind to historical accentuation does claim a link via conviction to justified pressure of feeling; but I have lived for a time in a society where emotion is not instated like that, even in crisis, and these ethical dispositions are not universal ones. My blunt fear is that they may too much spring from middle-class anxiety about the choice of critical-path commitment. At root I believe that the political and ethical formats are identical. But in derived social action the ethical can mask the abstraction of the dialectical process by a kind of individualism that now makes me increasingly uncomfortable: the voice that speaks for the unvoiced somehow has to assume that 'speaking for' and 'speaking out' can give back the voice in speaking at all. These constructions are not in any way crude, and of course the elevated pseudo-alternatives can be shot through with the crudest narcissism (Geoffrey Hill). We know that.

Third terminal point: all utterance has its focal origin, who could deny this without self-delusion, and the deflected baffles of presentation are devices of the craft. Not claiming a right to speak, even knowing there is no right to or for it, comprises the ethical empowerment of even so managing to do so, lending a voice to less justly deprived forms in the stifled question of what to say. Anyone who so much as sneezes in earshot has set out the pitch of a present inclination and is plausibly held to account. I guess that the same must be true of input: what is heard or read comes in by a funnel of attention and is filtered even by the most franciscan arrangements. In *Word Order* I have written about physical torture as directly as I know how; and yet the book is not mine, not even a montage of discredited voyeuristic abjection, I trust not to belittle it by claiming kin or inviting others so.

Well, these are distinctions I believe and they steal some of the comfort in belief that there are differences between us: I think that truly there are not. What you saw in NYC, I saw by inversion in the PRC—the state manacled to inaction by its loss of knowing how to deal justly with difference. Thinking and feeling set up the secondary tides of social pressure, but as primal forms they make close networks of local selfhoods in linked array. Despite personal practice, I don't much believe in solitary individual thought or emotion: that seems to me a mere reference sub-category, like unity itself, and my Chinese experiences have more or less persuaded me that unity is a class-construct invented by extrapolation from religious veneration; to elevate the individual will towards the prerogatives of consciousness and hence freedom. The contrary train of connection would instate liberty above freedom and justice above liberty; though by the contradiction common to all dialectic there is a root freedom needed to validate justice (the 'mandate of heaven' in imperial theory).[1]

So, I cannot see that we can either one claim benefit of not acting like the other; there is too close a match, in tone and in the hurtful, unwilling recognition of what is excluded (ethical stress about that, and Bernard's death in particular). I see traps above and traps below, the same ones by mere retroflex. Please don't describe anything I may say as 'generous' because that's far from the motive, I hope. In the hall of mirrors there is constant symmetry by opposition, by counter-profile and sexual starvation and the ventriloquism of heartfelt appeal. A language that is threatened by personal utterance is no less so by detached projection, up or down in the scale of avowed distress. 'Superiors must adopt inaction and make the world work for them; inferiors must adopt action and work for the world. This is an unvarying truth'—so says the *Zhuang-zi* (13) and did you ever hear such piffle.[2] And yet we'd be hard pressed to deny that across the axis of reverse symmetry this confutation of ethical just measure has prevailed as much in NY as in Shanghai, and is endemic to the

[1] 'mandate of heaven' (or Tianming), in Confucian thought, the divine right to rule with which Chinese emperors were invested.

[2] Prynne quotes section 13 ('The Way of Heaven') of *The Complete Works of Chuang Tzu*, trans. Burton Watson (New York: Columbia University Press, 1968), reprinted as *The Complete Works of Zhuangzi* (New York: Columbia University Press, 2013), for which page numbers are given here (100).

23 February 1993

history of human sorrow; only the 'must' installs the piffle as an iron rule rather than a venal failure, and to contest the failure mostly just leans on the backspace key: 'And ye that be prelates, look well to your office, for right prelating is busy labouring and not lording. Therefore preach and teach, and let your plow be doing' (Latimer, 18th Jan 1548).[1] That's a vested counterpart too, making hay while the sun goes dark at the window.

    Saluti:

        J.

P.S. Here's a recent pamphlet that you otherwise may not see promptly.[2]

5 March 1993   61 rue Lepic
                                                                                                                                  Paris

Dear Jeremy,

    I've had to clear a space and re-read a lot, because <u>Not-You</u> is difficult by the nature of its process and I don't understand all of it. But it evidently goes to the heart of what we're talking about and is unremittingly serious in the very best sense.

    Following your clue, it sent me back to the torture lying behind Word Order, and I don't know if that was Chinese either, although the reference to the different word order has always made me suppose so. In that extreme of torture still the dialectic is active; and it's such a severe thought; also it's horrible. I don't know how to talk of these things because once they leave poetry they become easily unspeakable in the foxhunting sense. Yet it may become in poetry an unthinkable thought become thinkable because of the art, a position of stake-out, a frightening quasi-limit of truthfulness that we can't quite flinch from because of the fact that a third of the countries in the world allow torture. It has, if anything, been increasing and I don't know how to classify the way, for example, the Americans buried a group of Iraqis alive during the Gulf War (and now we have the World Trade Centre business).[3] Not, of course, that torture is truthful (as Amnesty International has said, it produces lies), but that all dialectics fully maintained have that truthfulness and even terror dialectics does. I have in Diagram Poems a moment where I feel as if the poem can only kneel at the feet of such suffering rather as you, here, say the book is not yours.[4] I had to lecture on Coetzee recently—that's how he comes in—, and it made me remember one of the sleaziest articles I have ever read: back in 1970, a justification of torture by one of the French generals engaged under Salan in the Algerian independence war.[5] Nearly as bad has been French intellectual fascination with the topic—the Sartrean group, Blanchot, or Bataille especially, who was interested in Chinese versions; and I have just read, for complicated reasons, Mirbeau's <u>Le Jardin des Supplices</u>, a dreadful piece of writing.[6]

---

1 Prynne quotes Hugh Latimer's 'Sermon on the Plowers'. *Selected Sermons of Hugh Latimer*, ed. Allan G. Chester (Charlottesville: University Press of Virginia, 1968), 35.

2 Prynne evidently (from Oliver's reply, below) enclosed a copy of *Not-You* (Cambridge: Equipage, 1993).

3 Oliver refers to events of the early hours of 24 February 1991, 'north of the Iraqi–Saudi Arabian border', when American plow-equipped tanks buried alive Iraqi soldiers in their trenches during the US ground assault. Estimates of the number of dead range between '80' and 'thousands'. Eric Schmitt, 'U.S. Army Buried Iraqi Soldiers Alive in Gulf War', *New York Times*, 15 September 1991, section 1, 10; Patrick J. Sloyan, 'U.S. Tank-Plows Said to Bury Thousands of Iraqis', *Los Angeles Times*, 12 September 1991.

    Oliver refers to the bombing of the World Trade Centre in New York on 26 February 1993.

4 The capture and torture of members of the Uruguayan Marxist–Leninist guerrilla group, the Tupamaros (active 1967–72), is a central component of *The Diagram Poems*, but Oliver refers specifically to lines in the book's last poem, 'The Diagonal is Diagonal':

    Almost in humility and loathing I kneel
    at the feet of the next account
    which is of bestiality and sadism
    so mucky it makes the scalp creep.
    (*Kind*, 125)

5 Raoul Salan (1899–1984), French army general and commander-in-chief of French forces during the Algerian War of Independence (1954–62) between 1956 and 1958. Benjamin Stora, *Algeria, 1830–2000: A Short History* (Ithaca, NY: Cornell University Press, 2000), 252–4.

    'French general under Salan', Oliver likely refers to General Jacques Massu, who in 1971 published a book, *La vraie bataille d'Alger* (Paris: Plon, 1972), acknowledging and justifying the torture methods used by the French against the Algerians.

6 Each of the French philosophers and intellectuals referred to by Oliver wrote about torture in various ways. Sartre and Blanchot were public in their opposition to the torture practised by the French in Algeria. Blanchot was coauthor of, and Sartre a signatory to, the 'Manifeste des 121', an open letter published in the magazine *Vérité liberté: cahiers d'information sur la guerre d'Algérie* (1960) that explicitly denounced French torture and supported the Algerian Front de libération nationale. Of the three, Oliver's term *fascination* is most appropriate to Bataille, whose obsession with an image of a Chinese man being tortured to death by the method known as *lingchi*, or 'death by a thousand cuts', is well documented.

Most evidently I pick up on the phrase, 'less / expensive cure' in Word Order, and puzzle about the terrible cure in the new book: 'brightness born and tagged' from a victory that has to be double, I take it, for the singular, closed sets of utterance would be false.[1] Statement and other face of statement instead, throughout, in the pervasive parataxis, are held in twinship, the sets of them kept open, the utterance that could be made is also denied and sort of unauthored.[2] And I go on to think of all that is meant under Not-You as this also, but in the dynamic of love, so that the sequence quietens to a very intimate bedroom moment of that same silence at the heart of the process. Your 'With an eye turning for entry' is then to me a poem making what your letter argues.[3] The book folds open upon the open set, the centre poem with its line-twins.[4] Something of this must be right because I feel it so powerfully and a sort of cordite smell within the dialectic, a word we know how to use.

This is puzzling to me because the same anguish at the way the planet is being attacked has led me to cool down—for the moment, I imagine—and to look again for a voice. And Not-You is the only interesting denial in advance of that voice that I have read recently. So it's going to be something I have to keep working with. In fact, I'm writing an easy to read story at the moment whose heroine is a comic torturess—and that's the way I'm tackling it: a reduction of all we have made bland to certain diabolic implications we have likewise created.[5] So that's odd, too, as my motivation didn't come out of Word Order but out of having to teach Coetzee. The comic voice is not, of course, a protection but it can make such a discussion possible, just as high art can.

But I can't let alone your remark about unity and the middle class voice, for that's a danger I've had most centrally in mind much of my life. My point about emotion is not how it is instated between belief and the origins of feeling: that is, I'm less interested for now in complicated Western emotions but in the fact of emotion and its urgency at all. I do not know how we have emotions—whether most general and non-self-like or most personal and self-righteous. Emotions imply the possibility of unifying consciousness across the split between self and other: whether that split can be joined back together or not, the urgency of emotions implies that we think it can. Even if we have them in some very oblique Chinese sense (which I can only guess at from Asians I have met) they still imply that we believe in a 'perception centre' (cf. utterance centre) of those emotions. And higher animals at least have emotions. As you say, all utterance has its focal origin: and it may be delusive to call this a delusion. I'm astonished at all the books just now called things like The Mind of God which ignore the evidence of emotion as one of our keys to enquiry.[6] Or, again, at books of critical theory, including feminist ones, which play around with a false and generalised concept of Desire. Our technologising of knowledge has defined real-life emotions out of the question because they disturb the

5 March 1993

1 Oliver quotes *Word Order* (*Poems*, 375) and slightly misquotes *Not-You*: 'brightness is born and tagged' (*Poems*, 390).

2 This sentence and those that follow refer to *Not-You*, the first words of which are 'The twins blink' (*Poems*, 383).

3 Oliver quotes *Not-You* (*Poems*, 394).

4 The centrefold of the original chapbook publication of *Not-You* falls on pp. 392–3 of *Poems*.

5 Oliver refers to *The Second-Rate Deity*, excerpts of which were published in *Gare du Nord*, no. 1 (1997): 9–13; and *Whisper 'Louise'*, 251. In the excerpt published in *Gare du Nord*, the narrator-protagonist, Maradevi Cowper, states that she '[has] had the pleasure of torturing snails—and even insects on occasion' (9). Earlier typescripts of the text, which Oliver conceived as a 'double novel', are preserved in Oliver's papers under the titles 'Maradevi and Her Torture Gardens' (a reference to Octave Mirbeau's *Le jardin des supplices*) and 'Maradevi and Marudevi' (DOA, box 17). Oliver writes in *Whisper 'Louise'*: 'Given how bizarre it is, I have found this double novel difficult to get published' (251–2).

6 Oliver clearly intends a general type, but also refers specifically to Paul Davies, *The Mind of God: Science and the Search for Ultimate Meaning* (London: Simon and Schuster, 1992). A notebook in Oliver's papers contains nine pages of notes on Davies's book (DOA, box 2).

rational tone. And as a perception centre of emotion would be a creation in space and time, I don't also see why such a centre should not persist just as any other creation in space and time does: that is, open to the full play of process but also in that other aspect of relativity discrete. I don't feel I can define process, since perhaps to do so would be a middle class intellectual technology. (I need not say how far you are different from that; were you not, I wouldn't be quizzing my mind so hard about what you're writing just now, when I am so worried otherwise about what imitation parataxis is doing to the prospect of poetry in the world and about the narrowing of function in mainstream middle-class or Irish poetry down to metaphor and description.)

You imply that the ethical even alive in 'worthy' social action masks the abstraction of the dialectical process. I don't know about that—literally, I don't know—but I do know the importance of the question. I would put it very conventionally as a very great distaste I have just now for poetry as power-seeking or for interpersonal behaviour as power dominance. The very people who most promise to have our answers are, in my experience, the most dangerous. The stridency of poetic voice in the U.S., or various ways of behaving badly, are how you 'get on', and I can't see much difference from a career in, say, advertising. And then that other side, the PRC inactive owing to loss of knowledge.

Well, there are these two approaches. To make radical the silence. And no-one is doing that better than you right now. It is a very far throw of the avant garde in the proper sense of the word, because it is a throw into the unspeakable. It is what many other poets would like to be doing but don't, frankly, have a clue how to achieve because lack of rigour or, finally, of understanding. Their whole procedure comes out of books modulated into the tempos of their own desires and disguised there. Dangers lie, as you know, in the unutterable, because it seems that a cannon ball is hurtling towards us out of the future and it has our name on it, like a general's initial. Or, perhaps, there is my own approach which is to take my lack of knowledge and to yield it as far as I can into the general so that it may be alive there and yet yielding, as I say. Dangers lie there too, as you know, because the whole that is created in, say, 'Penniless Politics', is created by the middle class voice, and that is, of course, my social background. But it's less middle-class than a lot of very intellectual poetry that pretends to be above such questions but has forgotten how to speak to people at all, as if my (let us say, working-class) neighbour were not worth talking to. And yet, too, by that other movement of the dialectic, I yield up the voice as totally as I know how: I give it out; I yield it; I know that I can't yield it fully into the broadest wisdom; and so I look at the failure and yield it again; and then begin that dialectic again. And I will speak it because it's the best I can do. I will even try to publish it widely where I can do so without much power seeking, because that's the best I can do too. And then I hope to yield it yet again because—as your own words make so extra clear to me—we don't get to the end of this happiness/anguish or to the end of our caring.

I have always thought William Barnes lived a fairly exemplary life in that 19th cent. Christian parson way: very quiet and modest, allowing Tennyson to patronise him one time except when Christian doctrine was expressed heretically.[1] His poems ventriloquize the farm labourers with wonderful warmth. {In a created dialect—but that makes little difference} He stayed so loyal to his wife's memory that it remains immensely moving. He never did much deliberate harm that I know about. Yet, in his mild middle-class morality, he seems to have ignored the Tolpuddle Martyrs who acted right on his doorstep.[2] He probably caused damage from the pulpit because his doctrines were borrowed, uttered in the borrowed Bible language, and so were part of the social conformity that has gradually led to the desperate straits we are in now. But, surely, he did the best he could, and I'm not sure that lack of utterance or decentering of it would have served him or his world better.

(The men of Tolpuddle, too, very honourable men by all accounts, have left a legacy not always fortunate, for once extrapolated into union power it has often merely spread greed downwards from the middle-classes to the lower-paid levels, so that the same hierarchies reawaken there. Every person their motor car, stronger unions keeping their pay differentials, and so on.)

Nous sommes embarqués and I do not know how better to do than seek (personally, not politically) for the pure Rousseauist general will:[3] as you know, what it would be if everyone had the best prospect for humanity (read planet) in mind. (Politically, this becomes totalitarian but it can be a personal political ethics when restricted to one vote.)

Embarqués might also include keeping silent and in a state of looking at the glistening grass at twilight. We thought we were living quiet lives and suddenly we are facing their consequences for our children. So thank you for the first poetical and intellectual fresh air I seem to have breathed for a while.

    Best,
        Doug.

---

29 March 1993   Gonville and Caius College
                                     Cambridge

Dear Doug,

Our conversations are, as ever, oblique to the possibilities ahead and thus aptly head-on. Just quickly to send over a pair of lectures which are subject to certain familiar limits by virtue of the genre, and also some pages on language and emotion in Novalis and German Romantic thought.[4] The smell of cordite,

---

1 William Barnes (1801–86), British poet, priest, and polymath, best known for his Dorset dialect poems.

2 Tolpuddle Martyrs, a group of six farmworkers from Dorset convicted in 1834 of swearing a secret oath of membership to the Friendly Society of Agricultural Labourers. They were sentenced to seven years' transportation to a penal colony in Australia but pardoned, after public outcry, in 1836, returning 1837–9.

3 'Nous sommes embarqués' (We are embarked, or We are involved), Oliver employs the phrase coined by Blaise Pascal in the seventeenth century and referred to by Jean-Paul Sartre in *Qu'est-ce que la littérature?* during Sartre's defence of his position on commitment ('engagement') against the one attributed to him by René Étiemble. *Qu'est-ce que la littérature?* (Paris: Éditions Gallimard, 1948), 83–4. Sartre's point is that 'a writer is committed [*est engagé*] when he tries to achieve the most lucid and the most complete consciousness of being embarked [*d'être embarqué*], that is, when he causes the commitment of immediate spontaneity to advance, for himself and others, to the reflective'. *'What is Literature?' and Other Essays* (Cambridge, MA: Harvard University Press, 1988), 77.

4 Prynne enclosed a copy of his William Matthews Lectures, *Stars, Tigers and the Shape of Words* (London: Birkbeck College, 1993) (hereafter cited as *STSW*). He also enclosed Kristin Pfefferkorn, *Novalis: A Romantic's Theory of Language and Poetry* (New Haven, CT: Yale University Press, 1988), 77–81, 191–204, 272, 288–9 (on Herder, Fichte, and Novalis).

yes indeed; though I don't suppose that the stuff was smart enough for the Iraqi *blitzkrieg*.
 Saluti:
  J.

3 April 1993[1]   61 rue Lepic
                                  Paris

Dear Jeremy,
 Responding circuitously but actually to the point on these fascinating topics. I have long been interested (as I'm sure we all have) in mouth position of sounds; for example, the use of gutturals for contempt (the sick convulsion of the throat) in Dryden and Pope alike:[2]

> Of these the false Achitophel was first;
> A name to all succeeding ages curst:
> For close designs and crooked counsels fit;
> Sagacious, bold, and turbulent of wit...[3]

with its different but allied use of 'fit''s slight whiffle of air.
 And I have a friend in the outskirts of Paris, Ivan Fónagy, an old Hungarian professor of phonetics and long a colleague of Jakobson, with whom I've talked much about such prosodic matters.[4] One great interest of his lies in the meta-linguistic effect of intonation, which seems to lead in the direction of linguistic universals without quite arriving. His book, La Vive Voix, for example, attempts to show from several European poetries and melodies that such things as the expression of joy or sorrow may be given characteristic intonation patterns. The patterns represent at least a strong potential for the representation of these emotions and are not quite arbitrary—therefore, by that definition, not language although contextually evidently a signifying system. Surely, then, a musician is using them as a non-arbitrary language if he should codify them into a melody? Melodies of Thai folk songs have been found frequently to copy spoken intonation patterns and I'm sure we know this well in English. A Fónagy example of non-arbitrary quasi-linguistic communication would be French mothers who front their vowels when speaking to children, 'Mayywouiee' to express, perhaps, the spirit going out to them in sweetness.[5] I guess English baby talk compares quite well.
 Still following your letter, this does lead to the Cratylus, my own entrée to which lies through Rabelais, such a great master concerning the relation between conventional and natural language.[6] The M. A. Screech book on Rabelais raises this question that Plato leaves so interestingly undecided, and then takes up Aristotle's apparent view that there is natural language at the animal level—dogs in Japan bark angrily much as dogs bark angrily in France.[7] (Cf. the Darwin typology of emotion through facial expression.)[8] But that at the human level language

---

1 Oliver's letter is dated 3 April but is postmarked 13 April.

2 Oliver responds to Prynne's discussion of Pope in *STSW* (2–3 and passim).

3 Oliver quotes Dryden's *Absalom and Achitophel*, lines 150–3.

4 Ivan Fónagy (1920–2005), Hungarian linguist.

5 Oliver embellishes this example in *Whisper 'Louise'*: 'when a French mother caresses her child softly with, "Maay Ouii", the place of sounding the vowels migrates forward towards the lips, as if the mother were kissing or, perhaps, extending her spirit towards the child. Kissing may express a migration of spirit towards the loved one's lips' (317). Fónagy describes the mother's speech to her baby, the labialization of her vowels, and her 'moue affectueuse préfigurant le baiser' (lit. affectionate pout prefiguring the kiss) in *La vive voix*, 12–14 (13).

6 Oliver refers to Plato's *Cratylus*, referred to by name in Rabelais's *Gargantua and Pantagruel*, bk. 4, chap. 37. Oliver discusses Rabelais in detail in *PNP*, chap. 11 (146–58).

7 Michael Andrew Screech (1926–2018), scholar of French literature. Both Screech's *Rabelais* (London: Gerald Duckworth, 1979) and his *The Rabelaisian Marriage: Aspects of Rabelais's Religion, Ethics and Comic Philosophy* (London: Edward Arnold, 1958) are cited in *PNP*, chap. 11. This and the following paragraphs draw on *Rabelais*, 377–97.

8 Oliver refers to Charles Darwin, *The Expression of the Emotions in Man and Animals* (London: John Murray, 1872).

is conventional. Aristotle's medieval commentator, Ammonius Hermaeus, takes this a little further to include human animal-like sounds—babies gurgling or crying, etc.[1] (And we note the supposedly infinite potential of babies to produce sounds before the conventions of their native language get encoded.) A possible relation opens up for a Renaissance psychology of the soul: passion will lead us down to our animal nature and reason take us up to our human, conventional and systematic achievements—and angelic intuition (pace Novalis on angelic language) would of course trump both these into the utterly transcendent.[2] Poetry attempts to play this trump card, I imagine. And suppose, say, a super-dog trained to convert angry barking into a language, through patterning it into a convention, a tool for dog fights, then there would be a cline established between convention and natural expression. Rabelais takes the theme up so beautifully. Panurge is sometimes led by passion down to the animal nature of brute sounds, or he may simply use meaninglessly the conventions of language so that the conventions cannot hold and language starts to break up. The arbitrariness of language is most revealed at such times, when, for example, he switches between various human languages and nonsense languages. But also and in fact, he speaks more purely poetry than anyone else, just as the rational Pantagruel speaks more like the perfect Renaissance prince and statesman. There may be a cline between the impulse towards brute sound and the farther ends of abstraction/convention when everything is arbitrary except (the disguised position always in such dialectical clines)...except the prompting to create the arbitrary code in the first place. What the French misleadingly call desire.

Three points on the Rabelaisian spectrum:

Panurge panic-stricken in the storm as if emotionally overwhelmed by fear (Bk 4, 19), when his language descends to animal sounds, the sounds, in fact, of the sheep he has just drowned—Be be be bous, bous, bous.

The words that in arctic regions not warmed by passion become frozen (4, 55), frozen, we might interpolate, into utter convention and have to be thawed in order to be re-heard.

And the Renaissance-humanist tone of Pantagruel or of Gargantua in letters and speech. There, the highest use of reason would be so to master convention as to hint its further direction towards universal truth and the divine which is, of course, not arbitrary and therefore not containable within the arbitrariness of convention. (Man, considered in the universal, would be a giant, wrote More in a passage overlooked, I think, for its possible influence upon the way Rabelais drew a nobler fiction out of the chapbooks.)[3]

Modern feminist critical concern with notions of 'jouissance' and, in Kristeva, of the child-like input into poetry seem to be versions of this, but I find them too severe and rigid to become quite interesting.[4] Far more interesting to see how you very

[1] Ammonius Hermaeus (or Ammonius, son of Hermeias) (ca. 435/445–517/526), Greek philosopher of late antiquity. Oliver adopts Screech's preferred spelling.

[2] Oliver refers, in part, to the German Romantics' discussions of the origins of language (whether human or divine), as explained in the excerpts from Pfefferkorn's *Novalis* which Prynne enclosed with his last letter. No direct reference to 'angelic language' is made in the excerpt (or its notes) on Novalis himself (77–81, 272); Oliver likely has in mind Herder's counterfactual argument, quoted by Pfefferkorn in the notes to the appendix on 'Herder's Theory of Language' (198–204): 'If an angel or heavenly spirit had invented language, how could it be otherwise than that its entire structure would have to be impressed with the mode of thought of this spirit. For how could I recognize the image of an angel except by its angel-like, supernatural features? But where in our language can this be found? The structure and plan, indeed, even the cornerstone of this palace betrays […] its humanity' (289).

[3] Oliver refers to Thomas More, *Utopia*, trans. Paul Turner (Harmondsworth, UK: Penguin, 1965), 90. The same passage is cited in *PNP*, 157.

[4] Oliver refers to the dynamics of what Kristeva, in *Revolution in Poetic Language*, calls 'the semiotic and the symbolic', that is, 'two components of the signifying process […] that has its source in infancy', roughly comparable to the dialectics of 'unconscious/conscious, id/superego, or nature/culture'. For Kristeva, the 'pre-Oedipal semiotic functions and energy discharges that connect and orient the body to the mother' which are 'anterior to sign and syntax' are nevertheless legible in dreams and literature. Mallarmé, for example, 'calls attention to the semiotic rhythm within language when he speaks of "The Mystery in Literature". […] Indifferent to language, enigmatic and feminine, this space underlying the written is rhythmic, unfettered, irreducible to its intelligible verbal translation; it is musical, anterior to judgment, but restrained by a single guarantee: syntax.' *Revolution in Poetic Language*, trans. Margaret Waller (New York: Columbia University Press, 1984), 4, 27–9.

deeply find motivations that transcend convention in the most unguarded and creative aspects of language.

I also have a very self-indulgent way of answering your welcome, and provocative, pamphlets. For that, forgive me, but it's the deepest level take-up I have, because you have enlightened me upon something in my own practice. I want to describe the motivations that led me towards the word, 'Pearl', in <u>The Infant and the Pearl</u>, because they include many of the kinds of motivation you tease out in 'The Star' and 'The Tiger', and at some cost in personal emotionalism perhaps, deal with when the stars throw down their watery spears.[1]

In 1966, Jan was in labour with our first child, Kate, a home birth. So one snowy January night, we called the Cambridge city midwife service and at about midnight I opened the front door to a broad woman with a battler face who growled: 'I'm Pearl.' Her way of breaking the ice I suppose. I admired her very much.

Then, when my son, Tom, was alive I wrote a poem to him once.[2] Down Syndrome children make the inner lining of their mouth conspicuous, and I wrote, 'So my word, love, attaches to the lining of / your oyster mouth'. When he died, no-one except me wanted a funeral ceremony; everyone had perfectly good reasons (especially Jan), but I wanted a ceremony out of a sense of the equality between our lives. So we had this odd funeral where I was the only mourner and had to decide how long the whole thing lasted. In tandem with that wish, I wanted his death recorded in an orthodox way and so had inscribed in the crematorium book of remembrance those above words from my poem about him, a procedure that I would not have followed under any other circumstances and which, of course, I am now glad about.

Shortly after that time, early 1970, I started taking anxious note of Margaret Thatcher, then shadow education minister, because she was so dynamic and held views so far opposite to all I believed about Tom and equality. My novel, <u>The Harmless Building</u>, was impregnated with such thinking. She seemed like a counterpart to my own evil demon—that potentially very harmful exultance when we ignore the other person in our dazzlement at our own self-righteousness and zip. And I would cut her picture out of newspapers and stare at it.

One day, I was reading with Andrew at Dartington and John Hall told me that <u>The Harmless Building</u> reminded him strongly of the medieval <u>Pearl</u>, because of the way the dead child instructed the author.[3] With my half-educated background, I'd never read <u>Pearl</u>; so I immediately sat down to it and was entranced. Not least, my developing theories about the smallest details of prosody—in particular, the speed of sounds through consonants and the role of certain consonants (not just those identified linguistically) as semi-vowels under some circumstances—seemed to tie in with the effects created by alliteration in that poem. Allied to that, were the changing effects played

---

1 'when the stars [...]', Oliver interpolates language from Blake's 'The Tiger' (lines 17–18), discussed by Prynne in *STSW*, 22–35.

2 Oliver refers to 'Mongol in the Woods', from *Oppo Hectic* (*Kind*, 41). Oliver slightly misquotes his poem; the lines in question are printed as: 'So my / word, love, attaches to the lining of / his oyster mouth'.

3 John Hall (b. 1945), British poet. The copy of *Pearl* that Oliver first read was E. V. Gordon's edition (Oxford: Oxford University Press, 1953), lent to him by Hall in the 1970s (Hall to the editor, 28 July 2014). Oliver refers to Dartington College of Arts, Devon, where Hall taught between 1974 and 2016, during which time the College merged with University College Falmouth (2008) and relocated to Falmouth (2010–11).

through refrain repetitions, so that, for example, a sense of whiteness could be greatly intensified. And the extra linguistic role of such repetition, incidentally, seems to play closely in both with your earlier article on the phatic 'o' and this present work relating to motivated encoding.[1] Why should repetition cause such an effect, since the arbitrary linguistic code of the actual sentence doesn't change? Why should repetition of meaning intensify meaning and emotional significance? The answers are less simple than people suppose. (And why is repetition in a Blake song ('The Lamb') so right, whereas repetition in some imitator writing for children so obviously false, although there is no apparent difference in the way the arbitrary codes are used? My answer would be that, for Blake, the vividness of the vision doesn't change and so it imposes the repetition as by necessity. To invoke necessity, obviously, is to countermand the arbitrary.)[2]

Similarly, with rhyme; for I read your own remarks about this with considerable assent. My own sense of prosody implies:

If one human spirit at a particular life-moment (and context) should bring to mind a particular content (meanings, associations, emotional significance, etc.), arising, remembered, protended, pretended, etc., from past, present, and future, including bodily past, present, and future;

and if this should be accompanied by a particular moment in the interacting continuum of emotion;

and if this moment could be made to endure for ever;

then that particular human with all his/her characteristic vocal habits and qualities would wish to create the same sound for ever.

To put it absurdly, the instant would not have changed but would have endured.

I am, of course, talking about an ideal description whose Platonism you long ago identified, although I don't believe I am quite Platonic about it.

Well, rhyme is a repetition of the same sound but slightly changed within a small compass of time in which we have a small change of semantic, emotional, and experimental situation. The point about rhyme is evidently that the repetition of sound is not exact. The change in sound between rhyme A and answering rhyme A echoes (in that Popean sense) the change in situation within that small compass: it indicates how far things have changed, thus changing our impulse to utter the same sound— instead we utter a slightly different sound and the change reveals the change in our impulse. Rhyme probably 'springs to mind' as much because of this as by association in memory storage.

So these thoughts about prosody, not so different from yours, also motivated my thinking about the word, Pearl.

As soon as Margaret Thatcher came to power—and slightly before, during the politicking in the Spectator offices and so on— I became immensely worried about what was going to happen to Britain. No poets seemed to be taking on this precise subject

3 April 1993

1 'your earlier article', Oliver refers to 'English Poetry and Emphatical Language'.

2 Oliver's contrast between 'The Lamb' and 'some imitator writing for children' parallels the comparison developed by Prynne in *STSW* between 'The Tiger' and the nursery rhyme 'The Star' ('Twinkle, twinkle, little star').

matter quite that early on (I'm aware that you have taken it on throughout and it may be found easily in <u>The White Stones</u>, some poems of which were influential upon me). And there were dangers of becoming feeble if I adopted that weaker 60s poetical-political rant. In the 60s I had already experimented with non semi-vowel consonants used with semi-vowel effect, and was looking at Sanskrit poetry for models. Now, I decided that it would help me to move between political tonalities without rant if I could choose a highly formal prosodic rhetoric of some kind. Then the last piece of the jigsaw fell into place. Margaret in Greek means Pearl, and we may surely call it a false pearl of great price—and cost. The prosody of consonant repetition, rhyme, and refrain repetition exhibit many of the effects you are describing, with deepening of encoding. For satire, this has many bonuses: for example, if one is scornful, the scorn can be put into the refrain and deepened by repetition. Or a sense of wonder can be deepened in refrains. Alliteration, more subtly, can continue these effects because of the emotional resonance of consonants in the mouth and in the spirit. '... that fair face in fits / of aging ...' is not so far from Macbeth's greater use of the consonant and verbal stem.[1]

These, then, were all active concerns of mine that prompted me towards the medieval rhetorical forms of alliteration, and made me think even more earnestly about the speech of a handicapped child: its phatic meanings and the incorporation into those meanings of a wonderfully sunny spirit. (As you can imagine, during the early years of such an infant the parent agonises over how to help the child to speak. And I am terrifically affected by the fact that my younger daughter, Bonamy, has just become a junior assistant in a Westminster Hospital pilot programme which is examining similarities between different kinds of mental handicap in children, including language acquisition— which Bonny investigated for her undergraduate project.)

So to put this into a poem, Rosine, my muse of socialism in <u>The Harmless Building</u>, leads easily to the Rosy Pearl in <u>The Infant and the Pearl</u>. And the seed of that Rosy Pearl already lay inside the lining of Tom's mouth, as the child lies a seed in the lining of the womb. So the theme of childbirth can unite with that of the ignorant but blessed child. And, as I had desperately seen in 1970, this child is a touchstone by which to gauge politicians like Thatcher. Why don't we see that the most important question with any politician is the tone of what is said? Here is the very great danger of too great a trust in the arbitrariness of language: if the conventions can be mastered by a politician (as Reagan and his scriptwriters mastered them) you can get away with any non Pantagruelian shit. Politics, also, as my more recent <u>Penniless Politics</u> states, means nothing if it is not informed by the knowledge that we have been born to a brief life and soon die.

Whether this is an answer to what you wrote about anagrams, I don't know.[2] In these conversations, I always seem to talk more

---

1 Oliver quotes *The Infant and the Pearl* (*Kind*, 155).

2 Oliver refers to Prynne's discussion of Ferdinand de Saussure's research into 'verbal anagrams in the composition of classical literary texts' in part 2 of *STSW* (19).

self-indulgently than you do, referring more to my own projects. But I do know that there are no more important themes in poetry for me than these; and that we are touching upon them.

    Best,
        Doug

14 April 1994   61 rue Lepic
                                                                                           Paris

Dear Jeremy,

    We had a correspondence last year which you might well consider finished, since I have such a heavily personalised answer to the mysteries of your current prosody. I didn't mean things to go like that. Now I've been reading the Parataxis Winter issue.[1]

    You have always had very considerable influence on the younger post-Cambridge writers, of course, but perhaps never so much as now. It's as if the 'textual' school have suddenly realised how deeply all along you have been radicalising the authorial process. I suppose that, long ago, when I was concentrating upon Wound Response and came across 'some detecting mechanism must integrate right across that loop' I might have seen in your description of natural process a germ of your present notion of prosody.[2] In a way, I did. But I am not sure what, now, to make of this intense and detailed realisation of inner language in the minutest parts of the poetic line. Or the inner language may be buried there more deliberately, of course, in such a way that confutes our more compromised intentional notions. There is a considerable direction here, an arrow arc towards the avoidance of wrongness where that is centred in the liberalised poet as indulgence. Instead, you create at least the possibility of doing that sought-after thing in our poetic times, of truly opening the poem out to the infinitesimal and not-quite-personal determinations. Almost a getting-beyond the unconscious. That's a very fascinating inquiry, I've come to see in my clopping along way: for until I have taken an idea slowly into my emotions I'm never able to judge it. If then.

    When poetry is in the condition of principled experiment and advance, as I believe is true in your own case, I don't have questions but rather engagement.

    But I have this great fear in my own poetry, and you clearly share it. What if the traditional poor person hoves in sight and asks what I'm saying to the other rich people of the world like myself. I've come to think that we've had so much postmodernism that our culture is being helped to rot by it. So—as an experiment, perhaps, in drawing fire from very sophisticated poetic viewpoints—there's quite a simple step to restore a direct urgency of speech (this is not an alternative to any other kind of poetic inquiry, by the way, just a thing to do). It is to pass outside the western body and ventriloquise ourselves

1 *Parataxis: Modernism and Modern Writing* (1991–2001), journal edited by Drew Milne. The 'Winter issue' referred to is no. 5 (Winter 1993–4), which features poetry by Oliver ('The Herb') and Notley ('Folksongs') and correspondence between Prynne and Milne. For a complete contents list of numbers 1–10, see 'Parataxis: Modernism and Modern Writing', Drew Milne/Parataxis, accessed 30 October 2021, https://drewmilne.tripod.com/text/paracontents.html. Oliver's poem was published in *A Salvo for Africa* (Newcastle upon Tyne: Bloodaxe Books, 2000), 111.

2 Oliver slightly misquotes 'Of Movement Towards a Natural Place', from *Wound Response*: 'a detecting mechanism must integrate across that / population' (*Poems*, 223).

into the poor person; then we may look back at ourselves and see so much of what we're doing as futile and so much of what remains to be done as immensely urgent and simple, with ourselves as very heavily under obligation to at least [*do*] what we can. Oh, but this is simply old, charitable empathy! Well, it depends upon the direction of the attention: who has the right to the regard, as Marx of course knew. On some U.S. campuses just now, that move is regarded as rather disgusting, a sort of emotional intrusion on the life of the poor, which, if the regard is in the wrong direction, it perhaps is. But I sort of can't stand the emotional coldness in the self-righteousness of such middle-class niceties. Supposing one were simply to acknowledge the false consciousness in stepping outside one's western body, and yet do it? Perhaps, simply doing what Malcolm X recommended when asked what white people could do:

> Whites who are sincere don't accomplish anything by joining Negro organizations and making them integrated. Whites who are sincere should organize among themselves and figure out some strategy to break down the prejudice that exists in white communities. This is where they can function more intelligently and more effectively, in the white community itself, and this has never been done.[1]

And so too with world poverty and the allied threats. Well, who will dream up a strategy when all round us people are cleverly ruling all strategies out—this impasse you talk of where to raise any shout at all is hard enough? This other possible strategy presents itself then and it's crude indeed: to do what one is supposedly, out of cleverness, stupid for doing, and to do it because one may that way, at least, speak directly. But ... the dialectic ... this poet is doomed to get it wrong! Well, yes ... and yet to continue. My sense of that is that the dialectic will reassert itself in the—possibly quite hostile—criticism one's stupidity will arouse. Out of that hostility, spirit might rise. Is this shooting oneself in the foot and then into the air? I don't think that's quite your meaning: the intense radicalisation of the critique so as to create process, so that the shot will be a clear one, isn't it? That is, mightn't we just accept the subject-self as what others may criticise, because they <u>should</u> and above all the third world <u>should</u>? And then still carry on, unredeemed, deadly unredeemed in fact, not seeking profit, trying to damp down our sneaky prides as far as we can? Am I being theological? Not in the very least. It's as simple as one child has five apples and one child has one and the minute the child with five starts talking about anything else but the disparity you know he's avoiding the issue. And if he talks about the disparity and still doesn't give any apples back, at least there's no doubt about his selfishness and, who knows?, he might get ashamed.

One Adam Thorpe, reviewing me recently, scorned my use of the word, socialism, as simply outdated by world events.[2]

---

1 Oliver quotes Malcolm X, 'The Role of Young People'. *Malcolm X Speaks: Selected Speeches and Statements*, ed. George Breitman (New York: Merit Publishers, 1965), 221.

2 Oliver refers to Adam Thorpe, 'Narcissist in a Space–Time Continuum', review of *Three Variations on the Theme of Harm: Selected Poetry and Prose*, by Douglas Oliver, *Poetry Review* 83, no. 3 (Autumn 1993): 48–9.

This is the kind of shallowness I fear so much right now. It's like saying 'romanticism' has been defeated by 'classicism', as if either tendency—socialist or free market—could disappear from politics definitively: we would have solved everything if they could. The American hysterical self-congratulation about the Soviet Union's collapse was one of the more notable idiocies of our time, and we are now seeing it [*illeg.*] out with the dangerous Yeltsin at the dice box.

I don't know if you'll like the enclosed poem but that is, according to the foregoing rationale, a motive for sending it.[1] (I am hardly unaware, by the way, of the present regime in Malawi, but we may talk of Britain without mentioning its present damp incumbent regime.)

A moment to reiterate how thoroughly I am fascinated by your present direction, which—almost alone in contemporary practice—calls up all the questions that in this deliberately ignorant fashion I'm wrestling with. (Do you know Dominique Fourcade's highly abstract 'IL' (just out from P.O.L.), by the way, in which part of the prosody and thematic is carried on individual letters of the alphabet?[2] I have it in manuscript and gave up on trying to translate it.)

    Very best,
        Doug

[1] Oliver enclosed a typescript of 'A Salvo for Malawi' (*A Salvo for Africa*, 40–6).

[2] Dominique Fourcade (b. 1938), French poet. *IL* (Paris: Éditions P.O.L., 1994).

---

3 May 1994   17 Ferry Path
                                                             Cambridge

Dear Doug,

Your letter and the Salvo both arrived, and in between the usual frenzies here I have been thinking about them. What you say about the instigatory shedding of defences is indeed part of our discussion, and is made more complicated for me by some awkward shifts & turns in my own current position (i.e., 'position'). The main thrust of our divergence has mostly been not in that, but in what to do from where most intently we are. For me that rather simple idea excludes whole-body ventriloquism or culture-transplant, because I have uneasy feelings that a certain privilege can creep into the displacements by unavoidable inversions, the sanctimony of trying so hard to admit one's least amiable features. I rather think that one has to use the forms of intelligence that are active centrally in one's life, as hard as one can, and that self-borrowing can scarcely avoid unnoticed false notes or compensations. Put crudely, if we are too clever to be effectively unclever, then clever is what we must be. But that view is temperamental, not principled, I'd be the first to admit.

Yet more problematical is the substance of the underlying position ('position'). My acknowledgement of political dialectic has I think been more harsh than yours, since the construction of human and social feeling has seemed to me based on assumptions that comfort us without much matching to the experience of those to whom they are extended. I come in with a more schematic outlook, not altogether immune to certain forms which might be described as implicitly violent ones. This outlook sits very uncomfortably with my own practical experience, because what one learns from it may be not what one wants and hopes to learn; then one has to decide what if anything one has a right to ignore ('not enough data', or 'others have seen more, and interpreted differently', etc.). I have to think of China in this, because that's a major test for my sense of things, and my return there last summer shewed me more and more difficult questions. In these nuances of insight I have been able to learn almost nothing at all from the blandishments of those who have recited their own experiences: hysterical and doctrinaire and unverifiable, such as the boastful this-is-the-only-way-to-be-truly-human bleating of Orwell and his kind. I do not believe, for a start, that one could risk listening to such voices, even if some angelic warranty could be stamped upon them, guaranteeing 'truth'. Perhaps only those with nothing to say can tell me what I need to know.

But more and more I have come to notice (I mean, see clearly what once I half-saw) the oppression of power in a non-dialectical state. In utterly simplistic terms this compels me to ask what forms of political order can invest the dialectic process with a centrality so rooted that it cannot be shifted. I am not so idealistic as to imagine that all can have equal access to that central process, nor that it can always be deployed against those who contravene its rescript for their own individual or sectional ends. But it is not enough, for me, to contend that such a process is lodged permanently within a populace ('the people'), or verified and empowered by permanent human feeling ('the heart'), because both can be cauterised by false devices, and I have begun to grasp how utterly they can be replaced by exterior mimic forms from which the life force has been sucked out and wasted. I am not talking about freedom, here, since I am deeply wary of what prompts the use of that word, but of reality and reasonable completion; that a central process ought to work most especially for those who don't know how to work it or to get their hands on the levers.

To lay a helpless card upon the table, what I now have to ask is whether adequate defence against oppression isn't more important even than every other value: since values not adequately defended seem to yield so insidiously to those forms of inner rot within a system that disarm all remedy and confute awareness itself. If a system is ugly and stupid in all its incidentals but contains what may seem the least-easily-subverted mechanism to maintain awareness of oppression then it may have to be preferred. Or, one may reason that awareness may simply substitute for defence and remedy; but then the case shifts without really altering. For myself I am afflicted by an overwhelming Tolstoyan sentimentalism, but I realise that it doesn't have a good record. In China, the most stupendous sacrifices and feats of social bonding were largely thrown away, and the cost in oppression was unthinkable. I have a completely partial and distorted view of this, but it is based now more and more on personal experience, as I see what I see and struggle to understand it. It makes me feel terrible, I mean struck with a kind of terror about the defencelessness of what I most want and admire.

The sentiment is what I pursue nevertheless, and in this we run in a certain parallel; but not in my 'work', at all directly, as rather in my personal attempts to learn from what I see and do. Because the Chinese situation is so complex, hardly third-world and yet deeply impoverished within the terms of its own history, it is where I learn most. My contact with the advanced poets whom I have come to know there will soon be visible in the anthology of translations that's now in proof.[1] Certain individuals within that world lay out rather different stories: like the young professional calligrapher who is utterly dedicated to this infinitely subtle and powerful tradition that he knows the ordinary citizen now cannot read. What should he do — give it up? Open a whelk stall? He has a burning talent. He is surrounded by not-quite poverty. My one-time student Liu Xiang-jun was sent to teach in a totally backward provincial middle school, and last summer by means of a (for me) epic journey we together visited both his school and his birthplace. His parents are deeply rural peasants. I had never made such a trip before. It was utterly real, and of course utterly Tolstoyan. His school was a sink of envy and narrow-minded resentments, not just against me but against itself and in particular against the students. I tried hard not to believe this, but it was unmistakably so. The school was too unsophisticated even to try very hard to pretend otherwise. I saw with deep foreboding that this setup was entirely normal: in the cities and more enlightened townships I had seen brighter and more various situations, but out here in the backlands this was the rock-bottom reality.

Xiang-jun has just passed the graduate examination, at second attempt and after a protracted struggle, and this will lift him away into a university setting so that probably he will never have to go back again to this benighted graveyard of vanishing hopes. Why should he ever return? What could he do there? The engine of instinctual, formalised oppression is truly enormous. In one of the classes where I was grudgingly allowed to talk to the students, age about 15 or 16, I found that one of them had not been given an English name (they use them in their English lessons). So in response to his request I said that he should be Peter, that is, I named him. He said, now I shall be Peter for the rest of my life. As you will perhaps see, I cannot help myself in such things. Of course they had none of them ever seen a white man before, despite the years spent painfully learning that strange tongue. Xiang-jun for his part is good at English and deeply thoughtful, and we exchange a large volume of letters. To trade off for your Salvo I'll enclose a couple of recent screeds

---

[1] Prynne refers to *Parataxis*, no. 7 (Fall 1994), subtitled 'Original: Chinese Language-Poetry Group'.

from my side.[1] I know that what I write to him is didactic and moralising; as in Ruskin for example there is a note of contrived simplification which could easily be enough to make me wince into silence or brevity. But now that the channel works for him I will go on with it because thus it works for me, via his openness to our attempts at candour.

But even in his limited sense of the world so far he has faced squarely into oppression, and I have seen how it works and what it can do. Simple, age-old questions: how could I want him to go back to that school? How will it ever change if someone like him doesn't go there? It is stupid to say, I have stood in that classroom and I know with utter certainty how it is: both the literalism and the tokenism are pretty fatuous. And I like him too much to risk his being ruined by an experiment, one that on my side I've never thought to undertake. I'll say, that's because our diagram here squares onto the map of human reality quite differently, but of course that's not so. My best bet is to write as I do, knowing what I have seen and feeling the gap, knowing that the gap is something I have to bear because otherwise I would just fall into it. Soon I will have another, even flimsier booklet to send over. How interesting that we come to differ so much in the direction taken by work in hand, and that even so we can see clearly the impulsions shaping the directive. Thus we include our variant selves, without dishonour if possible and, if not, not.

Saluti:
J.

P.S. The mention of influence is of course painful because it for sure reminds me of oppression, even if its existence ought to be a prompt to commitment rather than to its means & ends; even that much gives me a lot of alarm. We are compelled to know what we know, and my knowledge is that deliberate ignorance is either not deliberate or not ignorant; maybe neither. Yet if that sounds grim, what about the pleasures of larking about, knowing that caring too much is not caring at all. Such thoughts make Dominique Fourcade's *IL* (which he has sent me) highly instructive and diverting, both together and each through the other's displacement.

---

[1] Prynne enclosed two letters to Liu Xiang-jun, of 6 October 1993 and 27 March 1994. These are printed in appendix E.

---

12 May 1994 61 rue Lepic
Paris

Dear Jeremy,

I was very glad you were able to reply so promptly and in detail on such important matters. Various kinds of attack are needed on the often inert body of our culture, and this is why I feel my own current poetry is both just part of a more overall thing I do and also cohabits quite happily with those few more experimental modes which genuinely share similar concerns. Particularly, we badly need your own further forays; and, so that there should be a certain voice around, I badly need to do what I'm doing.

As you must have been aware, it's rather agonisingly poignant to receive on the one hand a letter pointing out (what I know, of course) that 'a certain privilege' creeps into 'whole-body ventriloquism' or 'culture transplant' and that therefore this must be eschewed, alongside on the other hand two letters to Xiang-jun which live out the necessity for just such movements of heart in a real-life situation. A novel theory–praxis opposition? I could hardly have thought of a more apposite parable than your own of the stuck-in-the-mud situation for what I'm trying to do.[1] You get off the carriage; you are not authentic, but because you are a friend and not just a western teacher (read: 'westerner in general'), you have to help, get muddy, not become separated. Since you're wearing the wrong clothes, have the wrong muscles, and do not have to do this as part of your normal life, this is surely 'whole-body ventriloquism' and 'culture transplant' in one. As your affecting remarks to your student imply, it's the kind of right instinct that might change both yourself and Xiang-jun (given the role of teacher, apparently, in Chinese life). Also, it's a use of intelligence that I'd call utterly central to the situation, and indeed to western culture. (I'm discussing your statement that we must use the forms of intelligence that are active centrally in one's life.) Jumping into mud to help simply aces that other remark, 'if we are too clever to be effectively un-clever, then clever is what we must be'. Cleverness or un-cleverness doesn't much come into it: if anyone is trying to be 'clever' (and it's utterly understandable in a young man at such a trajectory in his development), it would be Xiang-jun in his embarrassment lest you should be trapped into an un-clever, rural situation. I question whether our national poetry can afford to leave out your kind of instinctual rightness. Similarly, with the instructional tone of your letters: it is not your normal tone of voice but is clearly the right tone—so are we to name that 'ventriloquism'? No: it's a proper human response: a voice called out of you as a westerner by the deeper needs of a young man in his culture. So do we need to put 'the heart' into quote marks?

Unfortunately, your experience is a very small moment lost in the incredible vastness of the Chinese problem—and I see there are increasing rebellious movements in the remoter villages, serious disturbances to rural order (if we are to believe American reports), and, in Dalian, strikes in foreign-owned firms, and elsewhere widespread strikes and 25% inflation.[2] Rather absurd to operate some Hollywood mental zoom in from the crinkly physical map of the nation down to the carriage in the mud, which is more like a moment of human feeling. Ah, but the zoom misses the carriage and, instead, finds a point-like source of disorder: your experience in the middle-school where the breakdown of dialectic is in minute but full operation, I gather. I vividly sense the claustrophobia of that and—amid such immensity

1 Oliver refers to Prynne's letter to Liu of 6 October 1993.

2 'American reports', Oliver refers to Steven Brull, 'With Inflation Rising at 25% Rate, Worries Over Social Stability Grow: Strikes in China Hit Foreign-Owned Firms', *New York Times*, 10 May 1994.

of the national power—the waste of a promising young life which returns to mere locale, gets sucked into its meaner, tiny thinking, and in trying to reform the home environment burns to mental ashes. If we were Christian we would admire the sacrifice, I suppose; in practical terms, we would have to look closely for the good of it. (And if a student can be named Peter for life who knows what rock he would turn out to be, says that Christian!) Further, I assume the origin of these national problems lies far behind the Cultural Revolution as such, but was in the nature of Mao's leadership from the beginning—the personal dominance of the dialectical process, accompanied by popular euphoria during the preliminary period of sacrifices. Power may corrupt as it will but a man and his close associates don't suddenly become monsters, as many an African country has sadly discovered. The great danger of so-called change of consciousness during a dialectical convulsion is the hypnotic self-righteousness that seizes crowds.

One response is to keep the dialectic true at every jointure. It certainly destabilises 'position'. But it, too, is a privilege in practical terms denied to the teachers at Xiang-jun's school; and cleverness is a privilege; and poetry protected from all criticism is; and the apparently disappeared pronoun is—the traveller who remains seated on the carriage becomes indistinguishably part of the carriage while the workers disengage the wheels. So too, the poet who remains inside the intelligence of his culture when even the dialectical process of that culture is protected against mud and impoverishment may, most radically, lose much valuable individuality as he/she tries to operate in utter dialectics. This, our utmost intelligence, can only hardly work because the dialectic itself is not an empty thing but is in its western forms so loaded already.

There's a tricky poetry that has emerged, not much readable except as exemplar that a certain process has been followed— that is, the creative idea that forms the poem is more important than the poem itself. The poem is read for the notion of its process, mostly. Your own poetry is not like this; it's a necessary work of tackling the innermost secrets of motivation. I do understand this and its connection with your life work (just possibly I may write something on the subject.[1]) So to your remark, 'clever is what we must be', I'd reply, 'It is clever not to forget the moment in the mud. It is clever not to forget that emotional tone is perhaps our best touchstone of the worth of what is said. Nothing is free of it. So it's a touchstone, too, of texts which refuse to own the emotional tones that they actually do have, or refuse to admit to the ambition that lurks behind that refusal. My favourite example is the colossal deafness of the U.S. people to the tone of Reagan (parody of sincerity laid upon speech-writer's parody of it laid upon the U.S. political codes of sincerity, and so forth), coming out of the mouth as arsenic-flavoured treacle: talk about post-modern!

---

[1] Oliver discusses 'process' and (among other poems) Prynne's *Her Weasels Wild Returning* (Cambridge: Equipage, 1994) in his essay 'Poetry's Subject', a revision of his 2 February 1995 Judith E. Wilson Lecture on Poetry at the University of Cambridge, published in *PN Review* 21, no. 7 [22, no. 1] (issue 105, September–October 1995): 52–8. A further revision was published in Philip Davies, ed., *Real Voices on Reading* (Houndmills, UK: Macmillan, 1997), 83–102.

12 May 1994

Sometimes, then, cleverness dictates that we should be unclever, jump in the mud, so that we may be justly criticised, and so that the privileged deficiencies in our emotional response should be evident to the disadvantaged. That privilege infects everything we do, even the utmost radicalisation of a privileged dialectic, as you know. But someone has to get off the carriage, so that people can see he's wearing the wrong clothes, has the wrong muscles, and so forth; but also see that he doesn't mind being laughed at as he tries to help, tries not to be separate in his clever weakness. Your 'helpless card' is also the card: 'whether adequate defence against oppression isn't more important than every other value'. It surely is, but only providing the disadvantaged (the 'weak') don't suffer too much in consequence—for this has been the great error of our century, an error so huge in its various manifestations that it shocks utterly. Viz: there has to be a wealth so that the disadvantaged don't, simply, die while things change. The politically self-conscious embargo against Haiti just now is not a clear benefit to that country (and my various journalist friends who are expert in Haitian politics often agree);[1] yet, surely, it is supposed to tackle the centre-point where the dialectic is hideously perverted (it actually affects the impoverished peripheries not the centre, and that's the trouble).

Poetically, therefore, while the central dialectic is being placed under constant challenge, there has to be this other voice. It's a sort of hot, electric thing to radicalise; all the more, we need humane warmth as our other voice, and I think this is where our dialogue begins.

To return to Xiang-jun: if he returned to home pastures and destroyed himself in the hopeless attempt to make an improvement, I could say nothing against it. Instead, I should think 'What integrity to be willing to deteriorate intellectually and even morally in the bid to save a small society! Countess Cathleen, surely!'[2] If, as he will do, he heads for more metropolitan roles (as I/you have done), then let him beware a more subtle corruption: that of thinking that a critique so highly developed that it is privileged counts more on the same human scale than the hopeless work in the hopeless school. Not for nothing were the teachers in that school envious. Their desperation casts a light upon rather a lot of contemporary poetry whose extremely enlightened political concern arises from textual fragments. As it is my own eavesdropping, I will not name the U.S. poet who can be seen at poetry readings taking down phrases into his notebook at random intervals.[3] I regard the avant-garde dilemma not with hostility but with sympathy and a sort of desperate hope. But this is not the dialectic escaped: the evaded 'I' has many subterfuges, and the deconstructed pronouns are (in the reformed Husserlian sense) not those of that natural attitude which, in fact, informs our real-world activities—therefore, the political problems are more easily 'solved' on some abstract plane.[4] The textual surface is apparently 'in the mud', but I'm

1 Oliver refers to the trade embargo against Haiti by the UN, begun in June 1993.

2 Oliver refers to the selfless eponymous heroine of Yeats's early play *The Countess Cathleen*, in which the Countess gives up her wealth and sells her soul to the Devil to save her tenants. Oliver may plausibly allude to Prynne's interpolation of lines from Yeats's play in 'Fool's Bracelet', from *Bands around the Throat* (*Poems*, 342).

3 'U.S. poet', Jackson Mac Low (1922–2004), as Oliver describes in a letter to Peter Riley of 11 October 1997: 'I've sat behind Jackson (Mac Low) at poetry readings and watched him jot down words and phrases as they wing through the air—presumably musical elements for his next composition: sonic play and stolen phrasings caught mid-flight—at least for the poems he writes in that way.' DOA, box 9.

4 'natural attitude', see p. 57n2.

12 May 1994

not sure the poem is. (The apparently established moves from Husserl to Heidegger to Derrida and beyond have never made me entirely happy: I don't think anyone has deconstructed the word, 'eidetic', properly, and Derrida, certainly, has reified the temporal question in Husserl in order to form his paradoxes.)[1]

In sharp contrast to that, I've come recently to your centre-fold sequence of 'Not-You' and, particularly, the way it condenses (in its 'part-motivations' you might say) the sonic modulations in the rest of the sequences in the book, so as to display its own catheses [sic] and yet catch at the ineffable, would-be said.[2] This is process: this is the missing trick, and it is given both by turn of the wrist and also by deeply moral principle, a driving-through, a wish-for, a buried optative that you may resist acknowledging, I don't know. Yet without the optative we have nothing worth.

I, if you like, have chosen just now to return to Xiang-jun's school in its forms of western culture, so that the envious may poke fun or be mean with some justice—and for me to do that aware of the corruptions involved. I'm not ignorant of the tonal errors I can't improve, for example; but I have mixed in student circles often enough to understand how cleaning up one's expression from tonal errors can be rather an unpleasant form of lying. Incidentally, I don't preclude a later return to the more experimental. I have grown tired, for example, of art galleries which show how a painter, having discovered a sellable image, doggedly works through its transformations, afraid to leave his/her trademark unexploited to the full. If Picasso was the most important instigator of the century's explosions of styles, then how refreshing to go to the Picasso museum and be reminded of his stylistic range. For my present work, I think of Philip Guston's figurative move, late-career, an example of which hangs on our walls here: the art-world regarded the move almost as a betrayal at the time.[3]

Michael Stone-Richards has been talking to me about the Dubourg translations.[4] It seems such a pity they are not published in French. I believe you are solicitous for the feelings of Dubourg's son and reluctant for any promotion until the situation is clearer. I was talking to Dominique Fourcade the other day and I hope you don't mind my having mentioned this matter. To my surprise, he knew nothing of the translations, could only dredge up the name of Bernard Dubourg as a painter whom he thought still alive; yet declared that if good translations existed and you approved of them they should certainly be published. In this, strangely, I have a wish to do the French poetry scene some good. Merely, if you thought it would be a good idea for me to call personally on Dubourg's son and he were reasonably within reach of me here, I would be glad to see how things lay. And I naturally hesitate even in intruding thus far because I know nothing at all about the Dubourgs and their emotional suffering recently, and so must be instructed.

      Very best,

           [unsigned]

12 May 1994

---

1 'eidetic', Oliver refers to the Husserlian terminology which designates the kind of phenomenology characterized by an interest not in 'concrete facts—even transcendentally purified ones—but in [the realm of] *essences*: in particular, in the necessary *a priori* structures and norms of any possible consciousness whatever'. The philosophical procedure which enables this reflection is the 'eidetic reduction'. Smith, *Husserl and the Cartesian Meditations*, 62, 133. Engagement with, and critique of, Husserlian phenomenology is a lifelong component of Derrida's work, but temporality and eidetic reduction are most closely addressed in *Le problème de la genèse dans la philosophie de Husserl* (Paris: Presses Universitaires de France, 1990); *La voix et le phénomène* (Paris: Presses Universitaires de France, 1967); and *L'écriture et la différence* (Paris: Éditions du Seuil, 1967).

2 See *Poems*, 392–3.

3 Philip Guston (1913–80), American artist. In a description of his and Notley's art collection in *Whisper 'Louise'*, Oliver mentions 'two entrancing late Philip Gustons which we eventually sold to help to send each boy [Anselm and Edmund Berrigan] to college' (246).

4 Michael Stone-Richards (b. 1960), British scholar.

17 June 1994   61 rue Lepic
Paris

Dear Jeremy,

   I'll take what I can, so far, of the dense meanings in the *Weasels*, especially, a resuming of certain themes playing into the male–female dynamic.[1]

   First, though, a run back (for this, too is in the *Weasels* spirit) at *Not You*, whose centre-fold poem I have been reading in the light of the 'Stars and Tigers' lectures—because that's where your side of our recent correspondence begins for me. In the centre-fold, your 'part-motivations' seem to have formed a meta-poem out of the sonic, lexical, emotional, and semantic hints provided from other poems in the sequence, so that a half-motivated, line-truncated set of poetic possibilities emerges like a will-of-the-wisp from what else has been written there. The poem does display such motivation almost as a 'proof' of your theoretical speculations: that's why the *Not You* poems are beautiful. The benefit ought to be a getting-beyond the worse sense of 'human', which, incidentally, leads to a puzzle in our human judgements—how do we know what has been achieved? What is curious is that, as we dip down into that world of sounds and meanings, a stern sense of moral discrimination seems to creep over us via a ghostly poetics. And that is distinctly new—it is some way beyond what still passes for 'experimentalism' (all that 1966–1973 stuff about decentralising the ego and so on).

   I bring that in because the new book can be read in a light that shines two ways: back on to the preoccupations in, say, *Wound Response*, and forward into the world of part-motivations, now arising in the heat of facing pronouns and its various analogies in kinds of process. If the centre-fold poem in *Not You* arises in that ghostly way I have described, then so do the poems in *Weasels* arise from the more general body of your work. I note, for example the repetition of role played by the words 'even' 'level' and 'mean' (semantic and statistical implication) in 'Attending Her Aggregate, Detour', and in 'Well Enough …'. I note 'morning light' 'blood' and the slope in towards event—these perhaps the two most Wound Responsish poems of the set.[2] In the stone-heartedness, the female pronoun takes a forward movement out of the pairing of shadow and sun, the blooded moment, and it is an onward-going; the male pronoun takes the backward step, and so the contrary arrows set up the momentary that is, however, lost, both necessarily and by fault—'a new track' or 'late to consult', and the two 'brought together' as 'a trial to go on', with deep punning on 'trial' and 'go on', which firstly yields event and assay and effort—becoming 'trail' later; secondly, acceptance and forward motion.[3] And I pick up that vocabulary you have made your own—the consequent 'loop' of loss and recuperation that has to be tackled, the spirit in which we must tackle it, 'gentle' and 'just'.[4] It's an essential good process in its flaws—'fruit' on the matching tree—and the repetitions of pronouns

---

[1] Oliver refers to *Her Weasels Wild Returning*.

[2] *Poems*, 413–14.

[3] Oliver quotes 'Well Enough in Her Riding After' (*Poems*, 414).

[4] Oliver quotes 'Well Enough in Her Riding After' and 'Then So Much She Did' (*Poems*, 414, 412).

in 'Then So Much She Did' match the 'here, here, here' in the attempt at unity of relation.[1] The 'well enough' in a later poem shows what we must live by, as we can, and as truly as we can, despite all the detours.[2] There's a great value set by you in the lovely word, 'candour', with all its pristine meanings so important—a lucent consciousness rather than a 'white'.[3]

More even than before we may follow the fortunes of the individual words through the sequence as if we were following a general progress in your work with pleasure: 'stone', 'band', 'throat', 'even' becoming 'evenly', 'blood'; or the financial analogies of 'debenture' and 'option'; or the Wound Response vocabulary of plants, horizon dynamics—'line', 'shadow' and 'light', and of biological-biochemical analogy too. Then: 'little pieces of the whole body / invented as lucid driftwork', taking up the slow drift' and reminding me of the *'anima tota in singulis membris sui corporis'* citation in 'Of Movement towards a Natural Place'.[4] It's like a re-gathering of your forces permitted by trust in your sense of motivation, an exact assembly of part of your army of words. I find that this description of your creative dynamic repeats the arrow-directions I have earlier distinguished: the assembly for the forward movements created in tandem with the backward recuperation of loaded words. This is probably a necessary step, so that the 'nothing should be lost' is impelled into the 'future that must be trusted'.[5]

I don't know whether I ever told you, but I made glottograph print-outs once of the dizaines used in 'Of Movement towards a Natural Place' because the poem so fascinated me.[6] I found a Miltonic kind of prosody, not unlike other glottograph recordings I made of parts of *Paradise Lost*. I was going to include a chapter on your poem in my prosody book Poetry and Narrative in Performance, but, in the end, kept with Milton himself so as to make an already difficult overall argument simpler for the reader. It's a music composed of subtlest repetitions and syncopations across long cadences, the cadences in your own work being kept going by constant finesse with line-breaks and by sentences that characteristically start mid-line. I could easily find the same elements at work in these douzaine stanzas. In 'Well Enough...', for example, my ear tells me of intonational matching like this—to take intonational pairs only:

'So far the slope drifts in' / 'Be gentle, be just, afoot trim' (very interestingly matched, because of the different internal truncation of the second one of the pair).

'often it does' / 'a trial to go on' (again interesting, because 'go on', through the pun 'take as sufficient for future action' or, alternatively, 'continue' can be stressed on 'go' or 'on' respectively, so that only the second alternative makes a close intonation match).

'often it does' / 'late to consult' (very Miltonic—compare 'hap may find' / 'prop so far' / 'storm so nigh' in *PL* IX, 420–33).

'Furnishing a new track' / 'trim ducting on a wave' (more inexact in its matching because the first little cadence is swung—

---

1 Oliver quotes and interpolates language from 'Then So Much She Did' and 'The Stony Heart of Her' (*Poems*, 412, 410).

2 Oliver quotes the title of 'Well Enough in Her Riding After' (*Poems*, 414).

3 Oliver quotes 'Well Enough in Her Riding After' and 'The Stony Heart of Her' (*Poems*, 414, 410).

4 Oliver quotes 'Well Enough in Her Riding After' and 'Of Movement Towards a Natural Place' (*Poems*, 414, 223). For details of the Latin phrase, see p. 65n2.

5 The phrases in quotation marks are Oliver's own.

6 Oliver refers to 'What the Plants Can Tell Us'. Oliver enclosed a copy of the chapter in a letter of 18 May 1986. See appendix C.

17 June 1994

'trimmmduct'—in the second, a swing created, I think, by the labial/dental movement from 'm' to 'd'.)

'the little pieces of the whole body' / 'firm up the same border edging' / 'following out her candour there' (as much the differences in intonation as the similarities are intriguing here).

So I could go on.
>   Very best,
>   Doug

Christophe Campos has just told me your reference is in. Thanks.[1]

---

19 June 1994 17 Ferry Path
 Cambridge

Dear Doug,
  Not so *accelerato* this time, as the exam hysteria climbed to its fatuous peak, and was compounded by my second year's stint as external panjandrum for the University of Hong Kong (which sheds a certain sideways light). But I need to return to the trade-off you observed between theory and practice in my last despatch, because of course I couldn't but guess you would take it so, as indeed in some kind of way perhaps it is. But also, perhaps it isn't. The mud fable pulls at me in just the way that you took it, but the cognisance that it represents (where knowing & doing have some kind of crossover attachment) does not translate into the full spectrum of self-agency except by extremely deep inflection. The fable works its effect by strong but hidden facets, chief among which is that I didn't stay there, for even a full day: it was a moment's absoluteness, under no challenge at all from or towards repetition. Primal events tap into the stock at primal level, and the effect is proportionately direct; but in my view it cannot simply trump the divaricated branches, because differences of level and application supervene. The moral impetus is so strong in part precisely because the outflow from it has to be mediated, into repeatable and mutable forms; because the politeness rules on the other side are of such elaborated pedigree as to make our niceties seem bowdlerised, and the simplification holds by exception what in normative conduct would just as simply collapse. Artefacts of first-time amazement have their chance of deeply pre-emptive survival, but I'd say not in that form, because they are anecdotes and they proclaim a rightness to which there is an equally right resistance (e.g., the Confucian view, as well as the post-colonialist one). 'Cleverness' by this token does and must come into it, as a burden and a responsibility, because in our own lives (or mine) the moral levers are connected differently to the springs of action and reflection, and to jump-start the engine leads right on to righteous simplification.
  The burden is otherwise. To ignore it would for me certainly be ventriloquism; not in the sense of lending a voice elsewhere

---

1 Christophe Campos (b. 1938), director of the British Institute in Paris, 1978–2003. Oliver wrote to Prynne on 11 June 1994 to let him know that Campos was putting his name forward for promotion to senior lecturer at the Institute, and that Oliver had named Prynne as a referee. Campos sent a formal request for a reference to Prynne on 1 June, and Prynne replied, 'with unqualified positive enthusiasm', on 11 June.

(which I have done and will, to Xiang-jun as best I can), but in the sense of taking in a voice to which my predicament allows me no commensurate access. The mud could kill Xiang-jun's father easily enough, and might still engulf him; but I am safe from it in that form, though 'on some abstract plane' I could equally lose too much of my balance to keep going. There are other tacit denominators which are also not common. The commonalty which so vividly appeals is compelling enough but I would never seek to utter it generally: not because it is not sufficiently general, but because it is too much so. Ergo, you shouldn't under-estimate my commitment to dialectic, not only from choice but from perceived necessity, since in a case like this the precursory vividness for sure cannot enter the field of expression in such sub-mediated form, even were I to supplicate hyper-ardently. It is not open to aspire towards a Franciscan abandon, as that would merely entail throwing over a full trellis of other responsibilities, including those to the current violence of obscurity and contradiction which make up the hurtled raft of where we are. Bitterly enough I acknowledge this, thus ruling out the jump to a simple example of truth beyond its level of simplicity (natural 'rightness'), because honesty tells me that to draw on that account head-on would just be mendacious, in effect if not by intent. It could be fully adopted into the demands of current recognition only by citation, by exemplarised or precedential over-trumping.

Furthermore, to adhere strongly to such self-instruction would almost certainly exploit its original with strongly distorting effect. I offered interpretation to Xiang-jun as also a kind of recompense, for at least part-threatening his sense of implicit order which may not be so negligible as the dynamics of ethical self-correction somewhat recklessly presume. The evidence of praxis perhaps ought to displace that of theory in quite another sense, as for example might be suggested by Feuchtwang: 'Giving priority to performance might describe processes of standardisation and control. These are processes of political culture and of cultural politics. They set up authority and identification with authority. In China, the identification of what is properly Chinese, and the means of claiming the authority to be so identified, have seldom in the long history of a unified polity been those of adherence to a dogma. "Belief" in the sense of adherence to a dogmatic proposition of what is held to be true, is a key problem of modern European, Western religion, theology and philosophy. It is not central in Chinese philosophical and religious authority and judgement' (Stephan Feuchtwang, *The Imperial Metaphor; Popular Religion in China* [London, 1992], pp. 8–9). For *dogma* substitute *conscience* or *individual conviction* equally; it is not so easy to snatch up a lesson in such way as to be confident (the 'feel-good' factor) that the community where you worked it out would be grateful to have its new interpretation superimposed upon the meaning previously supposed; or to be even half-confident that in some ideal order the new meaning would comprise an advance over the old; the more so when all the overt indicators seem strongly to suggest as much (well they would, wouldn't they).

Of course, as you say, the evaded and transferred first-person has many subterfuges, lots of them quite well known to me, and differently (also of course) to you. All of the above shorthand is meant as utterly person-specific. Furthermore, what is in question within our exchanges is clearly non-fundamental, being an issue of projective outwork and backflow rather than difference at source. That indeed doesn't make the discussion any less to the point; where the divergence is one of second-order praxis (that first-order ditto won't transfer directly across order-boundaries) there is special need to pay due attention to the critical margins in between. At one time I might have felt some twinges of bad faith in this kind of remonstrance on my part; but now I sense that much faith is thus bad on the grounds that only within a limited terrain can one elect to struggle towards an alternative. The mud fable works its force locally within my own world of action, where I do try to change what 'takes place' in order to clarify and understand my relation to it, by experimental candour; many of my poems also have a try at obliquely analogous experimental candour and will draw on every connection there is; but not by one-to-one matching, still less by causal promotion or retroflex. Appropriating the grounds for self-displacement and reduction is often the greediest manoeuvre just because of the dogmatic sacrificialism implicitly involved. What I held out to Xiang-jun was in fact learned by me from his world even more than from mine; but from his as of thirty years back, or more.

Yet in all this I don't disguise that a kind of large patch of feeling or moral sentiment or sense of elected agency does take up a space in consciousness and does have many offset but traceable effects there. What to say in one gallery or another, minding or not; going all out where one has skill and experience enough to shrug away worthless prevarication, but not fancying that such skill then transfers to all other fields of action. Some new vividness not infrequently works by unlocking a very old one, while biding its own time for what may come of it; all grazing the optative while seldom merely outright, except in wonderful flashes as from some windowpane when the sun is low. And for other cases & places, other voices, there's no doubt of that. '¿Tan malo es ser poeta? —replicó Preciosa. —No es malo —dijo el paje—; pero el ser poeta a solas no tengo por muy bueno.'[1]

J.

P.S. Regarding Bernard Dubourg's work the scene is still quite obscure. I have recently been in touch with Alexis, Bernard's son, but I still do not know where he is or how he is placed. For sure I should like some way to be found for Bernard's work to be better known, and not just in connection with my own productions;

---

[1] Prynne quotes Cervantes, *The Little Gypsy Girl*: "'Is it such a bad thing to be a poet?' asked Preciosa. 'It is not a bad thing', said the page, 'but to be a poet alone doesn't seem a good idea to me.'" *Exemplary Stories*, trans. C. A. Jones (Harmondsworth, UK: Penguin, 1972), 42–3.

19 June 1994

1 This letter appears to be a reply to a letter from Oliver not preserved in either archive.

2 'aggressive dissentience', Prynne likely refers to reviews in recent years that were critical of Oliver's poetry, including Adam Thorpe's review of *TVTH*, 'Narcissist in a Space–Time Continuum' (1993) (see Oliver to Prynne, 14 April 1994); and John Wilkinson's review of *Penniless Politics*, 'Hoodoo Bozo Talks That Rainbow Jive', *Angel Exhaust*, no. 8 (1992): 110–13. Wilkinson's review, whilst full of admiration for Oliver's work and poetics, nevertheless takes aim at what it calls *Penniless Politics*' 'cult of nature over culture, its cult of innocence and of a prelapsarian unity' (111). The review, especially its accusation of a racist 'epidermal fetishism' in the portrayal of Will Penniless's sexuality, prompted a correspondence between Oliver and Wilkinson that is preserved in Oliver's papers (DOA, box 10).

but I think that I must wait a little. If there is then a way forward, I'll be glad to call on you for some help. Oh, and in the matter of the Institut, they had already written to me, and I back to them, and indeed it's right and proper and doesn't require any alerts or trail-blazing in the least; a pleasure to try for a good outcome in its due sense.

5 September 1994[1]

17 Ferry Path
Cambridge

Dear Doug,

Well, I think we see our not quite parallel ways through the dust. It was always my point, in speaking of 'person-specifics', to refer to distinctly individual perceptions of risk and necessity and the certain need for variation. I suppose that I do conceive of internally contradicted enterprises, or those evidently off the rails; but (such things apart) it is not facile to speak of ethical style, and to recognise that even within a single lifetime there is room for many shifts which can nonetheless preserve a thread of purposeful mutation. I think and believe that when I describe some differences between our present positions I intend the account thus, i.e., descriptively; for sure I don't hold that there's some exalted upper layer of pure contemplation and, down below, the unprivileged scrapping in the street. I wouldn't pretend that my own practical spheres of action have taken me into large slices at every level; but the force of the blunt and the unavailed in narrow margins or none at all makes the grammar bite and even more so the inflexion. No love in rubber gloves!

In fact I surmise that you've had to square up to some aggressive dissentience recently, which means that you're accustomed to a guarded stance; but no jabs from this corner, because I know well that my own habit now is sharply altered from only a few years back.[2] I know too that what you have consistently said about the moment, that it may define a quantum difference from all that leads up to it, is beyond question true and indeed is true precisely there. We exercise a deep caution which is the structure of intelligent vicariousness itself, our passion for its limits as the focus which locates the central pulse; and then, by the skill of this living practice but right across its inmost grain, there are other moments of action and indeed of thought itself; even virtue *per se* isn't immune because, as we are allowed to know, the best habits too are habitual, and to act against the false is not yet acting right out truly. It is exactly necessary to advance to the danger spots, not because they are some kind of Sartrian test-rig but because they aren't. Prosody is such a powerful lens, and so often it has instructed me as I hold the pencil: when I go back to look at the page, line by line is the proof that a lot of fundamental effort will be required to understand what is written there. I suppose that we can say this to each other without seeming simply absurd: such moments have changed my life, not once but repeatedly.

Maybe something like that was the trigger to ponder the early Maoist texts, from the innocent (well, more so) first sketches of a theory of practice.¹ Much of that writing was adopted with gusto by fashionable intellectuals, who jumped at a path from the page to the rice-field without getting so much as a speck of mud on one's sleeve; you'll remember the *Tel Quel* grandiosities. But the essays on practice are very interesting, still, because they attempted a discourse so alien to their historic context; certainly at a 90° variance to the Feuchtwang dogma. The theory of practice is usually a way of recruiting what might be done into the arrays of speculative overview, binding the order of events into the form of a sanctioned precedent; it makes little difference whether conscience is in command, or tradition, and the Confucian ethic effectively conflated the two. Whereas here the experience of practice set the terms for the test of and by theory; the insight from effective action (individual acts) was to allow the construction of understanding as a method of perceiving material and social actualities. The very directions of the language process needed realignment, to bring about this simple but drastic upending of priorities. There must have been some of the awkward pedagogy we have spoken of before, in these 'little chats' and talk from above as if it was coming from below; there is no escaping the highly complex ideological construction of such a radicalised simplicity.

All of this is just remembered impressions, because I don't have the impulse at this moment to re-open my notes or to go back to the texts themselves. And what rises up in the mind is the way that any kind of urgency can be used to turn up the heat under very different kettles; what indeed sounded then like elementary virtue in homespun guise led away by tortuous spirals into outcomes more catastrophic than almost any others in the historical record, because they were in large measure self-inflicted, out of an idealism more dreadful than even the most barbarous tyranny. Every word of those essays now casts a deep and corrosive shadow, just as its immediate site within the paragraph was to seem altogether unshaded: not words but actions, not names but things! From such a retrospect the historically self-conscious reader might conclude that there is indeed always a shadow, even when the words on the page don't shew it and perhaps then more so than ever. But that's just to go right back to precautionary anticipation. And when Mao went in for prosody itself, it was the old forms that proffered the moment of newest ordeal: smash your cooking pots!

Meanwhile the Irish struggle seems almost as if it might be over, in the large-scale killing phase, and the pragmatics of this turnabout seem to hang from a profound fatigue, at the attrition of a stuck claim in a changing order.² Virtue here is sticking to your guns, and what Pound did to Propertius shewed that you get play with arms in a narrow bed precisely when, out there, Virgil is Phoebus' chief of police.³ The dialect does not permit

1 Prynne refers in particular to Mao's essays 'On Practice' and 'On Contradiction'. See Prynne to Oliver, 23 October 1991.

2 Prynne refers to the IRA ceasefire announced on 31 August 1994.

3 Prynne refers to, and interpolates a phrase from, Pound's *Homage to Sextus Propertius*: 'Upon the Actian marshes Virgil is Phoebus' chief of police, / He can tabulate Caesar's great ships.' *Personæ: The Shorter Poems of Ezra Pound* (London: Faber and Faber, 2001), 223.

5 September 1994

of a word like courage except in the wasted sense of not going back on a word already shunted out of the current lexicon. Or so it appears, like a liberty bodice on some primate torso.

Your final enquiry about the weasels almost suggests that some tunes go round and round like the hurdy-gurdy, even when the fairground has supposedly moved on several times. In fact the smart rodents are of hyper-recent origin, for all their throwback filiations.[1] It's hard to mind over reminding, since that's what mind is, or at least over this neck of the target practice. Put up a decoy and watch the feathers glisten: naturally, how to suck eggs.

  Saluti cari:
    J.

24 August 1996   21 rue des Messageries
                          Paris

Dear Jeremy,

I was pleased to have even a brief contact with you at the peculiar Picador reading some time ago.[2]

So much of my efforts go into keeping parenthood afloat in England and America that I tend to forget that I've been out of England now for 14 years. So it's surprising—pleasantly enough, though a little distancing—to see how the groupings have changed over the years and how influential your own work has been. I was glad about the Kinsella publication.[3] I've also been looking at the Reeve/Kerridge volume, which I take to be throwing down a marker that someone should do the thorough work on your poetry.[4]

This is bland enough, so I'm sharpening it up a bit by sending you these Celan/Heine poems, since they are so different from your own approach to such subject matters—different, in fact, from much that goes on by way of Celan scholarship.[5] (And I don't pretend to be a scholar in his poetry myself—I need dual texts to read most of the German.) I've never accepted any phrase such as 'the death of the lyric impulse' (even supposing it were possible) because, to me, that's the equivalent of the death of personal responsibility (notwithstanding all the problems that arise in that notion). I believe in working at self-transcendence from the problematic-inside out, not from the outside forces that create its possibility inwards to the centre that then vanishes. So I looked at those implications in two poets who stand much in contrast: the assimilator and clear lyricist in an old tradition and the unassimilated compacter of semantic units in a new tradition. Rightly or wrongly, with Celan I decided the most challenging thing in terms of his own poetry was to write directly and personally, which I think is possible without tiresome accusations of narcissism. His death, now, is a quarter of a century ago and the family will not be harmed by anything I can say, supposing anyone were interested enough to read it.

---

1 'smart rodents […] of hyper-recent origin', Prynne refers to the origin of the phrase 'Weasels Wild' in the title of his recent book: the F-4G Wild Weasel anti-air defence jets deployed by the US Air Force against Iraq in 1991.

2 Picador published the anthology *Conductors of Chaos*, edited by Iain Sinclair and featuring among its contributors both Oliver and Prynne, on 7 June 1996. There were three readings to promote the book in 1996: 22 June at The Spitz, Old Spitalfields Market, London; 23 June at Pig in Paradise, Brighton; and 1 August at Compendium, Camden Town, London. Oliver likely refers to the 22 June reading, which Prynne attended. Iain Sinclair, ed., *Conductors of Chaos* (London: Picador, 1996); Jeffrey M. Johnson, *The Works of Iain Sinclair: A Descriptive Bibliography and Biographical Chronology*, fascicle 4 (n.p.: Test Centre Books, 2019), 159–60, 166.

3 John Kinsella (b. 1963), Australian poet and editor. Oliver refers to the plans to publish Prynne's collected and expanded *Poems* with Fremantle Arts Centre Press and Folio (Salt), then in their infancy; the book was published jointly with Bloodaxe Books in 1999.

4 Oliver refers to N. H. Reeve and Richard Kerridge, *Nearly Too Much: The Poetry of J. H. Prynne* (Liverpool: Liverpool University Press, 1995).

5 Oliver enclosed typescripts of 'Forearms', 'A Little Night', 'Evening Descending Mauve: *Giséle Celan-Lestrange*', 'Crystal Eagle 1', 'Crystal Eagle 2', 'Walnut and Lily', and 'Twilight Flowers'. All except 'Forearms' were published, with minor variations, in Oliver's posthumous *Arrondissements* (Cambridge: Salt, 2003), 9–10, 13–17, 32–3, 35–6.

I'm perhaps repeating an earlier argument to you: that to see how responsibility plays into the language web is a task for some but it isn't the only task. Your own conceptions of deep subliminal motivations continue to interest me because it's just in that area (or as I would say, in the mysterious moments of performance of our lives) that there is much to say just now.

Very best, and please pass my regards to Sue, whom I haven't seen for so many years.
    Doug

16 January [1998][1]   21 rue des Messageries
                                                                 Paris

Dear Jeremy,

The *LRB* is going to publish the enclosed poem some time within the next few months, so I should send you a copy.[2] It's part of a series of short poems which come out of Paris's 13th arrondissement where a high-rise Chinatown has grown up within about 10 years—an extraordinary example of expatriate Chinese entrepreneurial skill cooperating with Asia, even with mainland China itself, while employing other-nationality Asians for its workforce.

I should mention I have a long poem which plays like a video game and therefore sets a 'trial' for the protagonist, a trial which is ultimately a puzzle about process.[3] I've inserted into it, with due acknowledgement, that quotation from *Her Weasels Wild* which fascinates me so much because it has such a highly-condensed accuracy about process from your own point of view:

> So far the slope drifts in, often it does. Furnishing
> a new track or late to consult, all the way brought
> together, a trial to go on.[4]

Evidently, I'd eventually need your permission to include it. If you felt you had to see the whole poem first I'd send it on but I hesitate to bother you with a 70-page read at what is probably a busy time of your year. You may recall I discussed these lines in my Judith E. Wilson lecture two years ago, which is going to be reprinted as a chapter in a Macmillan book this year, I think.[5]

(I don't normally keep referring to anyone else's work in my own poetry as I'm not a very multi-textual writer, but it seems I must have had these two topics of word order and of 'trial' on my mind.)

Gives me a chance to wish you the best for the year.
    As ever
        Doug

---

1 Oliver dates this letter 1997. Given the date of appearance of his poems in the *London Review of Books* (see below), the correct year is likely 1998.

2 Oliver enclosed a typescript of 'Money in Sunshine', dedicated 'for J. H. Prynne'; it was published, with 'Chinese Bridport', in the *London Review of Books* 20, no. 9 (7 May 1998): 6. *Arrondissements*, 41–2.

3 Oliver refers to 'The Video House of Fame', excerpted in *Gare du Nord* 1, no. 2 (1998): 43–4; 1, no. 3 (1998): 40–2; 2, no. 1 (1998): 42; 2, no. 2 (1999): 43–4; and published posthumously in full in *Arrondissements* (51–156).

4 Oliver quotes 'Well Enough in Her Riding After' (*Poems*, 414). Neither the excerpts of 'The Video House of Fame' in *Gare du Nord*, nor the complete published text in *Arrondissements*, include the quoted lines.

5 Oliver refers to 'Poetry's Subject'. For the lecture's publication history, see p. 152n1.

16 February 2000

21 rue des Messageries
Paris

Dear Jeremy,

For various precise reasons—many of them none of my business really—I was pleased that you spent some time with Anselm and Karen at your New York reception a couple of days back.[1] {Haven't seen the voting returns yet.}[2] The reasons that aren't my business have all to do with my admiration for Anselm, the good things I hear about Karen, and my feeling that contact with you would be very good all round: so let me leave those topics alone.

Personally, however, I've been wanting to write you a letter all year to say that the two highlights of the past poetic year have been for me the publication of your Folio/Salt <u>Collected</u> and the fact that you and Ed got together to give a reading before he died.[3] On both these matters I had a slight block in writing to say why I was so pleased; but I was so, tremendously.

It's clear to me that your <u>Collected</u> is the most important poetry book to come out for a long time and, last May or so, I'd been thinking of writing a general review of it for <u>Gare du Nord</u> which would have tried to explain the overall shaping processes that have driven through your poetry <u>since</u> that Routledge book.[4] This would have taken a lot of research but I feel that it's because no reliable identification of the various fils conducteurs exists (as far as I know) that much of the silliest hostility to your work creeps into the TLS and similar 'organs'—the Don Patersons and the Hugo Williamses.[5] Pin pricks no doubt, but energy-sapping.

As you know, my illness was then diagnosed: a double and strange obstacle. First, I heard a rumour that you yourself had been ill last summer, perhaps even with a prostate problem like me; but I became sort of inexorably immobilised, making further inquiries (let alone a fully researched article) impossible to follow through—the long-suffering Alice added most of my own correspondence and computer work on to an already formidable work load. At some point, surfacing briefly, I got in contact with Candice Ward about a possible article on you, of which more in a minute.[6]

But, another fix! When I was first diagnosed, my strongest initial reaction was {to ask myself} how I would shape up to the illness, most especially in terms of Alice, our four children, and our closest circles. Ten years ago in NYC I had transcribed a lot of interviews with HIV+ patients and rapidly became convinced that those who were most useful to their friends—and to their own health—didn't hesitate to call on the resources of their support networks so as to gain maximum strength and morale and also to help those really close networks to talk unabashedly to each other (most importantly in my case, my British and American families). Financial discussions were also important. So was humour!

---

1 Karen Weiser (b. 1975), American poet, married to Anselm Berrigan.

2 Oliver refers to the 1999 *New Yorker* book prize for which Prynne's *Poems* (South Fremantle, AU: Fremantle Arts Centre Press and Folio (Salt); Newcastle upon Tyne: Bloodaxe Books, 1999) was nominated, alongside books by David Ferry, Louise Glück (who won), John Koethe, and Sherod Santos. The prize ceremony was held in New York on 14 February 2000.

3 The reading to which Oliver refers (and which Prynne describes in his reply) took place on 2 August 1999 at the Arnolfini gallery in Bristol. Dorn reflects on the reading in an interview with Iain Sinclair conducted the following day in *Ed Dorn Live: Lectures, Interviews, and Outtakes*, ed. Joseph Richey (Ann Arbor: University of Michigan Press, 2007), 153–67 (167). The reading was reviewed by Phil Johnson in 'War, Cancer, and Other Ills', *The Independent*, 3 August 1999. Dorn died on 10 December 1999.

4 *Gare du Nord* (1997–9), journal edited by Oliver and Notley.
 'Routledge book', Oliver refers to Prynne's first published book of poetry, *Force of Circumstance and Other Poems* (London: Routledge and Kegan Paul, 1962), which remains uncollected in all editions of Prynne's *Poems*.

5 'fils conducteurs', Oliver puns on the title of the anthology *Conductors of Chaos*.
 'the TLS and similar "organs"', the most recent review of Prynne's work in the *TLS* was Roger Caldwell, 'The Flight Back to Where We Are', review of *Poems*, by J. H. Prynne, *Times Literary Supplement*, no. 5012 (23 April 1999): 27.
 Don Paterson (b. 1963), Scottish poet.
 Hugo Williams (b. 1942), British poet, journalist, and travel writer.

6 Candice Ward (d. 2010), American poet, academic, and editor.

I therefore took a deliberate decision to go public, at the cost of all sorts of desirable modesties. My overwhelming concentration has been to keep up our spirits as a family.

An unexpectedly unfortunate result was that if I happened to be out of touch with an old friend—who would have all the health news from such as Peter Riley anyway—I became 'shy' about writing in case it should be interpreted as a childish plea for compassion (which all along has <u>not</u> been my intent {health <u>has</u>}), from someone who had not yet written. I have <u>no</u> thoughts of that kind.

Your meeting Anselm gives me a chance at last to express my pleasure, to say how wonderful I think your book is, to felicitate you on reading with Ed (whom it must surely have heartened; as did, I expect, your remarks at the funeral hearten Jenny).[1]

And I can also raise this other question about Candice Ward and your Celtic runes. When I published <u>In the Cave of Suicession</u>, you sent me a copy of these runes, which I mounted and pinned up above my desk in Brightlingsea: they have been mounted above my desk ever since because I regard them as a good luck charm. Candice has now linked the runes with 'Glove Timing' on adjacent pages {in the 'Collected'} and suggested that <u>Gare du Nord</u> might be interested in the result.[2] <u>Gare du Nord</u> is not quite the format for close scholarly work of this kind—not least because I, as the more 'academic' of the two editors, at least in the British sense, am simply unable to carry out any background investigative research on her thesis. What we <u>would</u> like to do is reprint the runes along with her new translation, to make a separate work in the issue, (Runes reprinted by photocopy.)

I hope this is clear, as I'm slightly nodding out on a Duragesic pain patch. We'd obviously need two permissions: your own and Candice's; the runes are a great favourite of mine and often overlooked; so let me know what you think.

It was a proper sequencing to ask Anselm how Alice is doing, as my own progress comes in for quite enough attention. In all day to day matters except at the (increasingly rare) worse times, she has a harder time of it than I: she gets exhausted and it's a wonder we're not at each other's throats. Instead, she has helped me prepare my Bloodaxe proofs (<u>A Salvo for Africa</u>) and has enabled me to finish a double historical memoir.[3] Yet her own poetry continues down extraordinary pathways.

I'm aware that my current work doesn't fit many Cambridge preoccupations just now, but its motivations remain highly principled in my own terms and include intense loyalty to the cogency of your own work. I'm being influenced by the mid-turn in Philip Guston's work, actually.

Best,
Doug—forgive the general drugginess and the consequent need for white-out and interpellation.

---

[1] Jennifer Dunbar Dorn (b. 1945), married to Edward Dorn.

[2] See *Poems*, 244–5.

[3] Oliver refers to *Whisper 'Louise': A Double Historical Memoir and Meditation*. The book is dedicated: 'For Alice Notley / to whom my story / constantly returns.'

16 February 2000

13 March 2000

17 Ferry Path
Cambridge

Dear Doug,

Extremely good to receive your letter and to repair a lapse that seems not that but just an extension of what was it, the indirect free style, holding the line, because it's so clear from what you say that the connection is close and true. My flit over the ocean was a pretty daft thing, I didn't believe in any of the razz and didn't much care for it either; and yet I curiously did want to meet or hover with a few younger persons—the familiar fringe preference—and also get to see and study the Crawford Collection of Chinese painting & calligraphy at the Metropolitan Museum. And so it was that I met Anselm and Karen and a skein of visitants all amusing and in party mood and all eager, or was it that I was a little elevated from prolonged travel. Anyway as now you know (rapid grape-vine) I was pleased to talk with Anselm and sense that it did mean something notable to him, and I thought of you and I did take a certain trouble because I felt alerted to it and thus I know exactly why you wrote what you did and not more.

The bearing here I suppose must go far back and then re-express through a subsequent grafting. When Ed asked me to read with him I knew altogether why he wanted me to skip my usual reluctance, and that was entirely my reason to be glad in the face of mortal thoughts, because we would communicate in that public space by private admission that could be done in no other way. And so exactly it proved, he said things that only I could hear, and wept, and I asked him then to read 'Thesis' for me, to them, and he started out as if it had been written by some other person, and rediscovered it as he read and thus gave it back to me.[1] I suppose this sounds rather extreme, but so it was, because we wrote upon the tablets of memory. Then Keston Sutherland, who has been rummaging in the Storrs Archive, found a copy of 'The Ideal Star-Fighter' which had been latterly inscribed by Ed as a kind of witness or maybe testament, unseen and unknown by me, and all these years later this hidden unsayable script came home to roost and spoke as from a burning bush.[2] I'll enclose that for your eyes, because it communicates now across an unknowable distance that feels so close to home.

Crossing to Denver for the farewell was thus like a homing pigeon's dash, and only on the day of my arrival was I asked if I would do the rite myself. I had told Jenny's parents, and also Tom and Val, that I would stand in for them, but the speaking perch was uttermost for all that, I was glad I had not been asked earlier.[3] Since we were out on the shoulder of the Rockies and in the open air it was up to the very last possible that a snow blizzard would be upon us, so that no text of any kind was possible. That troop in attendance I conducted as if all ready for flight, I mean we all leaned into the moment and I wanted them to fly or at least see the flight of the great wing-span up ahead. Well,

---

1 Dorn's poem 'Thesis' was first circulated in *The English Intelligencer* in April 1967 and collected in *The North Atlantic Turbine* (London: Fulcrum Press, 1967). The poem was known to Prynne since its composition in December 1966. See Latter, *Late Modernism*, 100, 247n44.

2 Keston Sutherland (b. 1976), British poet. Prynne refers to the location of the Edward Dorn Papers at the Thomas J. Dodd Research Center, University of Connecticut Libraries, Storrs. Dorn's inscription on a copy of 'The Ideal Star-Fighter' (*Poems*, 165–6), a photocopy of which Prynne enclosed, reads:
when I received this, and still,
it was the most powerful
and forward motion energy
to myself—personally that
I had—the impetus was
unimaginable it was a time of
inestimable danger and derangement
there was no relief in sight &
this piece held the meniscus for a spell
JHP has always been the fucking light
for me—Edward Dorn in testimony 1988

3 'Tom and Val', Tom and Valarie Raworth.

maybe. But at least nothing was recorded, so the words went into the air and dissolved to nothing as I wanted. Who gives two drats about book reviews or snipes when men and mountains meet?[1]

I did feel a little strange about your illness, in part because every time I was bootlegged a telephone number for your new bedside signal-box it turned out that you had just a short while earlier been moved on, and I never caught up. I was myself going through some trouble, at a much reduced scale, and was in fact out of effective action for almost a year. Naturally one does reflect and make a few measurements. Since I was constantly about to be taken in and then was turned away, over and over, I thought about the reason for ration and graded share, in even more direct light. Of course I approved the constant re-calibration, supposing it to be that and not disorder, believing the NHS to be operating right by over and over not operating; but I was dismayed to be treated like a cypher in the clinics and finally had myself transferred to Barts after I had affirmed with total vigour not to be shuffled into a private warehouse.[2] It is hard to describe the florescence of ethical emotion that I associate with patienthood, but I have felt it before and I know deeply what it means, as for sure you do too.

Regarding the runes let me supply a gentle correction: you don't own a *copy*, you have the *original*, the only authentic single object which is the text at very first hand. I have only a photocopy taken from it, and it was from the photocopy that the published versions have been prepared. Indeed there is a Suicession link intricate with their origins, as the enclosed reminder of those days (which miraculously floated into my hand while I was looking for another thing) will testify; and several other ties buried a long way inside, wrapped in Anglo-Saxon newspaper like fish carved upon chips.[3] What will the glove connection have to offer, I wonder: not too much, it sounds at first guess like a loony loop. So far as printing her essay and translation is concerned, my only thought is that it would not be with even implied concurrence from me because I have no imprint to give and would not wish to seem to be doing so. I suppose I would need to give permission, and I suppose too that I don't care to see the texts or proofs up ahead because it's none of my business. If you care to usher this wacky project forth, that's quite enough for me: does this make sense at all?

I seem to be worked rather crazy over here, more and more, and when I want a morsel of time I have to drop everything in rather ruthless and scandalous ways, to snatch the moment. It is really good to be exchanging such accurate connection, now, because it confirms how reliable are the threads that matter. I do look forward to your Afrique Salvo, because as you know my oriental forays have roused me in some parallel determinations, indeed I again had to be careful in New York on the subject of Tibet so as not to upset the faithful, as *Triodes* would do for the

13 March 2000

1 'when men and mountains meet', Prynne interpolates a phrase from a couplet by Blake: 'Great things are done when Men & Mountains meet / This is not done by Jostling in the Street'. *William Blake's Writings*, ed. G. E. Bentley, Jr., vol. 2 (Oxford: Clarendon Press, 1978), 954.

For further details of Prynne's presence at Dorn's memorial, see Jennifer Dunbar Dorn's account in Dorn's *Collected Poems*: 'J. H. Prynne, who flew halfway across the world to attend Edward Dorn's memorial on 17 December 1999, presided over the interment of his ashes in the Garden of Knowledge at Boulder's Green Mountain Cemetery. The eulogy he gave extempore at the graveside went unrecorded, but fortunately, after the memorial and reception at the University of Colorado's British Studies room at Norlin Library, Prynne was interviewed by Joe Richey, a former student of Dorn's and the editor of *Ed Dorn Live*.' *Collected Poems*, ed. Jennifer Dunbar Dorn with Justin Katko, Reitha Pattison, and Kyle Waugh (Manchester: Carcanet, 2012), 938. A 'lightly edited transcription' of the interview is printed on pp. 938–41.

2 'Barts', St Bartholomew's Hospital, London.

3 Prynne's papers preserve a Gonville and Caius-headed filing card, a photocopy of which was evidently enclosed. On the recto is written: 'for Doug: W. T. Bartholomew, "Voice Research at Peabody Conservatory", Bulletin of the American Musicological Society, VI [on differing tonal timbres of vowels in singing]'. On the verso is written: 'Margot Astrov, "The Concept of Motion as the Psychological Leitmotif of Navaho Life and Literature", Journal of American Folklore, 63 (1950), 45–56 [on the shamanic Traveller & the primality of his Travel]'. A double-page spread photocopy of the embellished dedication page and '[p]ortrait of the inquirer' (*Kind*, 68) from the copy of *ICS* that Oliver sent Prynne in 1974 (see Oliver to Prynne, December 1974) is preserved in Prynne's papers with the card, suggesting that Prynne included copies of these in his letter as a further 'reminder of those days'.

Anglo-Irish if any were attentive enough to read it.¹ At least the French will not get to peruse *Pearls That Were*, since the supposed complete text of Pierre Alferi's translation in *Quaderno* dropped an extended clutch of poems off the end without a murmur.² Voilà, c'est tout.

But really when I was pruning the apple tree a few days back I knew that you cut back to the old wood and don't lean too far out from the ladder; these things one knows without knowing. 'Look into that closed room, the empty chamber where brightness is born!'³

    Saluti cari:

        J.

---

1 Prynne, *Triodes* (Cambridge: Barque Press, 1999).

2 Prynne, *Pearls That Were* (Cambridge: privately printed, 1999). Pierre Alferi (b. 1963), French poet and novelist. His translations of Prynne's work were published in *Quaderno, cahiers de poésie*, no. 5 (Printemps 2000). The complete text was published as *Perles qui furent* (Marseille: Éric Pesty Éditeur, 2013).

3 Prynne quotes section 4 ('In the World of Men') of *The Complete Works of Zhuangzi* (26).

APPENDIX A

Reviews from the *Cambridge News*

Douglas Oliver

PIONEER IN POETRY
10 August 1968

The achievements, already considerable, of a poetry movement many of whose impulses came from Cambridge, are in danger of being overlooked by the wider public. I hope that a new book by a Cambridge don who is one of the movement's leaders will have its deserved impact.

J. H. Prynne, a university English lecturer of Gonville and Caius, has established in his *Kitchen Poems* (Cape Golliard, 13s. 6d.) a quality of experiment and of technical advance which has not been equalled by an English poet for some years. It is clear why his work has been looked up to by the poets throughout the country whose movement centred on a Cambridge-produced news-sheet, now wound up, called *The English Intelligencer*, where the present poems first appeared.

The group have formed one of the very few points in this head-in-the-sand country where writers have not been afraid of the newest advances in New York and San Francisco. Prynne's work underlines that there is an English initiative to take—and that puts him way ahead of all those writers here who, incredibly, drag their stale, so-called free-verse rhythms about like sacred relics of a forgotten religion.

His is difficult verse, whose themes are too complex for short summary. Already the book has been called pretentious—though in a sense all search for fresh knowledge is necessarily so.[1] The strategy that is basic I take from the second poem, 'Die a Millionaire', which opens:

> The first essential is to take knowledge
> back to the springs, because despite
> everything and especially the recent
> events carried under that flag, there is
> specific power in the *idea* of it [...][2]

Thus far would be little more than a restatement of Wallace Stevens's main preoccupation. But for Prynne this is a starting point for honesty in a poetry that can take politics and economics into its strands.

He has an insight into the inflationary falsity of personal and political values that takes him beyond the Poundian conception of usury. His elegant, leftist philosophies are totally different

---

Oliver's journalism for the *Cambridge News* was extremely varied. Hired in the early 1960s to cover agriculture and general news—as he recounts in *Whisper 'Louise'*—by the end of the decade he wrote regular book reviews and ran his own 'Study' column, treating trends in contemporary theory with a sympathetic skepticism and reviewing the publications of the larger poetry presses as well as the books of the Cambridge-based poets with whom he fraternized. 'When the Signs Break Down', for example (*Cambridge News*, 11 July 1969, 11), reviews a volume of interviews with Claude Lévi-Strauss, sketching in the process an overview of the structuralist movement and assessing its value for 'the phenomenologists and the philosophers of the left'; 'A Formidable Figure' (on the same page) reviews John James's *The Small Henderson Room* (London: Ferry Press, 1969), and argues that James's work maintains 'a great awareness of the decadence of poetry as just a marginal activity, a concern that there shall be a real dialogue or a real community'.

The reviews reproduced here pertain only to Prynne's poetry. With Terry Eagleton's 1968 review of *Kitchen Poems* ('Recent Poetry', *Stand* 10, no. 1 (1968): 66–74 (72–3)) they constitute the first public assessments of Prynne's poetry of the mid- to late 1960s.

1 'pretentious', Oliver likely refers to Eagleton's review of *Kitchen Poems*, which begins by summarising the book as a 'deeply esoteric and intellectualist dissection of the metaphysics of neo-capitalism, done in an aridly unruffled Black Mountain style filtered through the thin and occasionally pedantic tones of English academicism'. 'Recent Poetry', 73.

2 *Poems*, 13.

from Pound, yet the aim is towards an analogous development of purity in the process.

It is a poetry which says—in part—that the imperfect knowledge of aims blinds us to our best courses. Purity of process requires that the names of these aims—themselves necessarily idealised, a hopeless quest—be uttered with this true knowledge and as a kind of prayer. Already I am in danger of reducing him to platitude. The hope remains that, with the habit of purity, the qualities we seek will return to us, to be emitted, finally outward, from the self.

The honesty of purpose here lives through the technique, too. A line in 'Sketch for a Financial Theory of the Self' reads:

> purity
> is a glissade into the last, most beautiful return.[1]

Prynne's verse-line is often itself a glissade, but an intricate one always subject to a masterly use of pause. Line-endings and beginnings are important clues to what he is doing, partly because of the way they make meaning stagger into the awkward and difficult entrances and partly as a clue to the glissade's return and departure. The fundamental rhythm underlying all speech is the difference between silence and not-silence (this is what makes the basic pattern on an oscillograph of poetry being read). In Prynne's verse the difference is under control in a way that is quite new.

This book contains only five poems. Ultimately it will prove one of British poetry's milestones with, fallen way back, some of the pop poetry which ignored questions of stamina, and some of the academic quietudes that set out with no energy to endure.

From the portentous atmosphere of these large-scale economic constructions Mr. Prynne shows in *Day Light Songs* (R. Beech Lane, Pampisford, 3s. 6d.) that he has considerable ability in handling the light lyric, too. This is a brief sequence of short songs in which a created landscape associates with the poet's creating breath. The poet and his lover fill with the landscape's brightness. The landscape pulses as though it breathes.

The process going on is not the pathetic fallacy, nothing so feeble as flowers that bow to someone's tread. It is an involvement of corporeal and natural imagery that reminds me of the intensity of William Blake's streams of bodies winding into the heavens.

Yet so light is the songs' texture that where, as occasionally, control slips small words like 'it', 'the', and 'to' become minutely obtrusive.

---

[1] Ibid., 20.

POETRY IN PAPERBACK
21 February 1969

Paperbacks from small presses are often the vehicle chosen by poetry's new directions, and the latest volumes from writers with Cambridge backgrounds deserve close attention.

I take J. H. Prynne's *Aristeas* (Ferry Press, 5s.) first because its complex title poem yields so many of the coordinates of the new direction. Arcane and literary though he at first seems, Aristeas speaks through Mr. Prynne directly to our time. A figure from Herodotus and other sources in the notes, this hero crosses in spirit a broad continent, which displays huge economic forces. The relationship between the poetic searching for value and economic needs that the spirit must honestly respond to is one of the central mobilisations in this poem of ant-like tribal movements across Asia.

A coherent prose 'explanation' of this poem is not too hard to establish, for those who like such things. I'll just say that a Greek, Aristeas, author of a real but lost poem, described a sort of shaman trance ('inspired by Apollo') in which his spirit travelled to the land of the Scythians and mythical lands beyond.

In Mr. Prynne's *Aristeas*, the shamanic trance brings large-scale economic movements of peoples like a map underneath the soaring spirit of the hero. The Scythians, who already appeared in the earlier *Kitchen Poems*, express the new nomadic and shamanistic culture as it usurps the pastoral. Then the pedants can track about among the symbols—the staff for the journey is the larch, centre-pole of the shaman tent and tree of the spirits. The smoke-hole is at the top of the tent, leading to the region of the upper spirits and the middle world of the journey (a very different project from Gary Snyder's 'Smoke-Hole' poem).[1] And so forth.

But a key phrase says:

> the spirit excursion
> was no more than the need and will of the
> flesh.[2]

And I do not need to carry my own attempt at exegesis further, for we have reached a description of what the poem itself displays as a parable of the quest for northern gold, for value. A prose passage about alchemy and metallurgy deepens the parable further into Marxian productive terms.[3] In another poem the paradox is balanced on a Hegelian pivot:

> we must mean the
> entire force of what we shall come to say.[4]

It is Mr. Prynne's own aim. His superbly exact diction is subject to the need and will behind the large-scale architecture of rhythms as the masonry grows. What at one level is considerable technical expertise at another is a richly humanising activity whose occasional archness we may therefore easily forgive.

---

1 Gary Snyder (b. 1930), American poet. His 'Through the Smoke Hole' first appeared in *Poetry* 106, no. 1/2 (April–May 1965): 120–2.

2 'Aristeas, in Seven Years' (*Poems*, 90–6 (92)).

3 Oliver refers to 'A Note on Metal' (*Poems*, 127–32).

4 'Star Damage at Home' (*Poems*, 108–9 (108)).

Appendix A

REWARDING POETRY
13 June 1969

First I tried reading the fifty-eight poems in J. H. Prynne's new collection at one sitting. It was like putting on athlete's shorts for a brisk run up Ben Nevis, and I ended up with a mild brainstorm.

But I was to learn that there's enough solid achievement in *The White Stones* (Grosseteste Press, 14s.) to establish this Cambridge don's work in the forefront of current English poetry. It is a book I shall have to be continually coming to terms with, one which costs me intellectual labour but repays it immensely.

We have to home on these poems with rigorous intent. For instance, a failure on my part to understand 'A Figure of Mercy, of Speech' cleared all at once;[1] and what had been bothering me fled like smoke between the trees of a river setting I had not before pictured clearly enough. All the fine discriminations the poem was making began to operate where before they had seemed, what they remain in part, a poise. Not to continue with a Prynne poem is to be falsely convinced it is unnecessarily difficult.

As for poise, take just the phrase:

> Which makes the thinning sorrow of flight
> the last disjunction, of the heart: [...][2]

I know very few who can match that combination of poise with emotional dignity and distinction (the perspective thins into the distance, the plane shrinks, individual lines of perspective thin; so the sense of loss thins with the very facts of departure).

The attempt is considerable to progress beyond narrowly deterministic notions of behaviour. On the one hand: 'Finally it's trade that the deep changes / work with';[3] but this develops to such phrases as:

>   there
> is this insurgence of form:
> we *are* more pliant than the mercantile notion
> of choice will determine [...][4]

The last statement is not to be made glibly; but when Mr. Prynne makes it in 'Moon Poem' I am dazzled by lustre.

There is a kind of imagery that is neither metaphysical nor quite phenomenological:

>   the thought
> dries off into the arch ready for it.[5]

That points towards an elegance that will be established even by the most organic and immediate utterance. And Mr. Prynne's work has always had an excellent characteristic—a rhythm within the almost spontaneous orders itself into a jagged page pattern. This is more structured than the usual mindless fear of

---

1 *Poems*, 39.

2 'Airport Poem: Ethics of Survival' (*Poems*, 38).

3 'In the Long Run, to be Stranded' (*Poems*, 47).

4 'Moon Poem' (*Poems*, 53–4 (53)).

5 'A Stone Called Nothing' (*Poems*, 120–1 (120)).

starting against the margin, yet a structure never quite regular because of its organic origin.

It is paralleled by a sense of pattern of form in behaviour (after I wrote that I found the phrase 'the strophic muscular pattern is *use*').[1] 'Again' is therefore a sacred word:

> With such
> patience maybe we can listen to the rain
> without always thinking about rain, we
> trifle with rhyme and again is the
> sound of immortality. We think we have
> it & we must, for the sacred resides in this;
> once more falling into the hour of my birth, going
> down the hill and then in at the back door.[2]

His key preoccupations are wide-ranging—some of them: time as a potential that must not be falsely or glibly pre-empted by behaviour; the dispersal of form as the condition of acquiring knowledge; and the influence of economic needs ('The city / is the language of transfer / to the human account').[3] There is also a signalling of the attempt to create values and the qualities left to us in that attempt which, as they enter our lives, are self-justifying.

It is the need to walk by impulse, blindfolded, to buy 'The stone called nothing',[4] a 'temporary nothing in which life goes on'.[5]

Mr. Prynne's weaker poems are, like those of many considerable poets, self-parody, for the tendency towards abstract language can shirk emotional difficulties and lead to monotony of tone.

But I would stake much on claiming the high merit of such poems as 'Aristeas, in Seven Years', which came out in a small edition a short while ago, 'Star Damage at Home' from the same book, 'Thoughts on the Esterházy Court Uniform', 'On the Matter of Thermal Packing', 'As It Were an Attendant', or 'Moon Poem'.[6] To think of *The White Stones* builds already patterns in my mind that do not eradicate. It is one of the best books of poetry for a long time.

---

1 'First Notes on Daylight' (*Poems*, 69).

2 'Thoughts on the Esterházy Court Uniform' (*Poems*, 99–100 (100)).

3 'In the Long Run, to be Stranded' (*Poems*, 47).

4 Oliver refers to 'A Stone Called Nothing' (*Poems*, 120–1).

5 'Questions for the Time Being' (*Poems*, 112–3 (113)).

6 *Poems*, 90–6, 108–9, 99–100, 84–6, 124–5, 53–4.

Prynne enclosed the following transliteration and 'literal rendering' of his rune poem, including the description of its composition, in his letter to Oliver of 6 September 1974. Both description and transliteration are excerpted from Prynne's pseudonymous correspondence with Edward Dorn, 12 July 1972; for the complete letter, see Katko, 'Regarding a Specimen', 43–4. Katko notes that the runes were written 'at Dorn's explicit request' in his letter to Prynne of 6 July 1972 (42, 46; hence, 'an inscription which we hope may suit your requirements'). The original correspondence with Dorn is held in the Edward Dorn Papers at the Thomas J. Dodd Research Center, University of Connecticut Libraries.

APPENDIX B

Transliteration of Runic Inscription

J. H. Prynne

Our rune-master has now prejected an inscription which we hope may suit your requirements. It is a gnomic amulet or avertive charm in the form of a solstice song. Its signification should by no means be revealed to the general public or to any profane person but for your eye here are (a) the transliteration into Anglo-Saxon, and (b) a literal rendering into pre-Nixon. Note that the single runes marked off by points from the longer sequences are grammalogues, that is, they stand for the meaning or name of the individual rune and are not alphabetic; and note also that triads of the same rune are incantatory formulae and do not 'signify' directly. The lines are numbered in each version according to the actual layout of the original.

(a) 1   bbb : alu (talismanic sign) : bbb : sefatorn : bbb : alu : bbb
     2   : : d (dæg) : ciserbeam · biþ · beobread ·
     3   beorhtlic : s (sigel) : : g (gyfu) : bean · beobearn :
         w (wyn) : :
     4   ėo (eoh) : bearu · deorc · beoþ · lifbeag : o (*ansuz/os) : :
     5   bbb : alu : bbb : sefatorn : bbb : alu : bbb

(b) 1   bbb : 'protection' : bbb : anguish of spirit : bbb :
         'protection' : bbb
     2   : : day : the cherrytree · is · the honeycomb (food of
         bees) ·
     3   bright-shining : sun : : gift : the bean · [is] the bee-child
         (child of the bee) : joy : :
     4   yew(-tree) : the grove · dark · is · the life-circlet :
         god/mouth : :
     5   bbb : 'protection' : bbb : anguish of spirit : bbb :
         'protection' : bbb

The central three lines might be roughly metaphrased thus: 'By day the cherrytree is the bright-shining honeycomb of the sun; by gift the bean is the child in joy of the bee; the dark grove of the yew-tree is the circlet of life, the mouth of the god.' The dialect shews a number of idiosyncratic features.

APPENDIX C

What the Plants Can Tell Us

Douglas Oliver

Methods so far developed can now be illustrated by applying them to the study of an individual modern English poem, whose versification presents special problems of analysis.[1]

J. H. Prynne's 'Of Movement Towards a Natural Place' has long interested me because its attitude towards spatio-temporal events, and to the human conception of them, is similar to those proposed elsewhere in this book.[2] From my own point of view, I should emphasise that what follows has nothing to do with so-called Black Mountain poetics; although Prynne has had associations in the past with some Black Mountain figures, he has always very much gone his own way.

He is a difficult, often rather obscure poet at a time when it is not very modish to be obscure; once understood, his work can prove rewarding. If one examines the ephemera of newspaper and journal reviews, one finds that his poetry has sometimes been dismissed by reviewers who think that confessing their own lack of understanding permits the arrogance of blind attack. But it has sometimes been stoutly defended by those who, understanding perhaps fitfully, have made his poetry's difficulty into a virtue, emphasising how it so interestingly creates a language surface (in the current, Frenchified sense), or how, in resisting monovalent interpretations of meaning, it enlarges the reader's potential of response. I am resistant to such defences. Obscurity is never a virtue; the difficulties in Prynne mostly result from a deliberate choice of writing method in which the emphasis is upon the act of writing itself.

I suppose I understand his poetry rather fitfully myself but the best way to restore a decent public discussion of Prynne's work is to insist upon the most bald and obvious role of its meanings. Without resorting to the author himself for explanation, we can often make more headway than at first reading we thought possible. I am going to risk fourth-form dangers of paraphrasing a poem to make my point, since there can be more human happiness in winning a sack race than some dull chess game.

Furthermore, his sense of prosody is organic and subtle, too subtle, it seems, for critics who have dogmatic attitudes towards what constitutes a line-ending; some of his line-endings are more like a hairline between one line and another than any kind of resting-place, although I think they are something other than arbitrary. Praising Prynne's work, the poet-critic Donald Davie once asserted that it made little difference whether certain lines

---

'What the Plants Can Tell Us' is a draft chapter originally intended for publication in Oliver's theoretical work *Poetry and Narrative in Performance* (1989) and sent to Prynne on 18 May 1986. The chapter is referred to in Oliver to Prynne, 18 November 1985 and 17 June 1994. 'What the Plants Can Tell Us' was cut from *PNP* for the reasons given in Oliver to Prynne, 17 June 1994. It refers to numerous points established or argued over the course of *PNP* and looks forward to others; these have been noted as fully as possible with reference to *PNP* (currently out of print) to provide some sense of the chapter's broader context.

The formatting of Oliver's own footnotes, indicated here by asterisks, have been silently emended according to the editorial principles of the present volume.

1 Oliver refers to the methods of recording and describing 'the music of poetry' developed across the first six chapters of *PNP* (vii). Central to Oliver's argument is the claim that poetic '"stress" and "duration" are paradoxical partners: it is inaccurate to speak of "duration" as part of stress; rather, stress is a notional "instant" when the duration of certain sonic elements in a line of poetry is perceived; moreover, the developing meaning and emotional significance of the line must play a part, too, in deciding how heavy we think the stress is. [...] Though notionally an instant, a stress is sited by the mind at some point during a syllable' (ix–x). In chapter 6, Oliver develops a 'hierarchy of units of sound in a poem, beginning with the notional "instant" (stress), extending through various units of duration, and ending with the form of the whole poem' (xi).

2 Oliver proposes a similarity between *PNP*'s emphasis on the spatiotemporal paradox of poetic stress and the way in which Prynne's poem describes the temporality of mind acts. Poetic stress is 'born in time, and in sound, meaning and emotion; but [...] also stands outside time in a sort of minor, eternal present, a trembling instant which half stands still' (*PNP*, 19). Prynne's poem, Oliver argues below, suggests that '[t]he mental instant [...] is like a horizon rim between night and day but a rim that both trembles with night and shines with day'.

* Donald Davie, *Thomas Hardy and British Poetry* (London: Routledge and Kegan Paul, 1973).

1 Emotion is discussed throughout *PNP*, but is the explicit subject of chapter 12, 'Emotion in Literary Response', in which Oliver clarifies the relationship between poetic stress and literary form: 'Poetry discovers a way to unify the time-scales of emotion, concept, and verbal music. It does so by transforming the emotion itself into a concept, a fiction' (*PNP*, 166). What is true of poetry is equally true for narrative fiction: 'Literary form fills the apparent "instant" of time with mental content, an operation which ought to be impossible and, in fact, is only achieved in a paradoxical way. But because the paradox is infinitely repeatable, literary form allows the reader to think he is sharing this "instant" with the imagined author of the text. Its full value appears when the text is activated by a performance, because in the repeatability of a shared mental experience lies the hope that we can enrich our perception and human sympathy' (*PNP*, xiii). This sense of emotional consonance is the very 'task of literary form' itself: 'to fill the instant with content from thought and conceptualised emotion, united through verbal music or narrative movement, so that the result is a permanent working model of experience' (*PNP*, 172).

were printed as poetry or as prose and, astonishingly, decided to print them as prose.*

Evidently, then, there is a problem with Prynne's prosody, which elsewhere in his book Davie analyses sensitively. For three reasons, it seems ideal to choose the poem, 'Of Movement Towards a Natural Place' from the 1974 book, Wound Response, for interpretation. This will enable me to underline the spatio-temporal assertions so far made, but in another mode, introduce my closing topic of emotion.[1] Finally, machine data can help us to find significant pattern in poetry that does not obey orthodox prosodic prescriptions, though I do not suggest that Davie would try to print this poem as prose.

Of Movement Towards a Natural Place

See him recall the day by moral trace, a squint
to cross-fire shewing fear of hurt at top left; the
bruise is glossed by 'nothing much' but drains
to deep excitement. His recall is false but the charge
is still there in neural space, pearly blue with a
touch of crimson. 'By this I mean a distribution
of neurons ... some topologically preserved transform',
upon his lips curious white flakes, like thin snow.
He sees his left wrist rise to tell him the time,
to set damage control at the same white rate.

What mean square error. Remorse is a pathology of
syntax, the expanded time-display depletes the
input of 'blame' which patters like scar tissue.
First intentions are cleanest: no paint on the nail
cancels the flux link. Then the sun comes out
(top right) and local numbness starts to spread, still
he is 'excited' because in part shadow. Not will
but chance the plants claim but tremble, 'a
detecting mechanism must integrate across that
population'; it makes sense right at the contre-coup.

So the trace was moral but on both sides, as formerly
the moment of godly suffusion: anima tota in singulis
membris sui corporis. The warmth of cognition not
yet neuroleptic but starry and granular. The more
you recall what you call the need for it, she tells
him by a shout down the staircase. You call it
your lost benevolence (little room for charity),
and he rises like a plaque to the sun. Up there the
blood levels of the counter-self come into beat
by immune reflection, by night lines above the cut:

Only at the rim does the day tremble and shine.

A full reading requires setting the poem into the wider meanings of Wound Response, a transitional book, marking a turning point from the gradual assembly of poetic positions in books up to and including Brass, to the increasing concentration upon biological and biochemical topics of Prynne's later work as he has taken a poetic microscope to those earlier preoccupations and, like Renard's 'Homme chez les microbes', explored new worlds lying within brain chemistry.[1] The best approach to Prynne's poetry is to read along the chronological sequence of composition; 'Of Movement…' will help to show where the earlier work was tending and provides some access to the difficult later work.

In Wound Response, a physical process, the causing of a wound to a physical body, such as a human body or a plant, becomes somewhat more than an analogy for mental process, especially in the sense of response to an emotional and intellectual 'wound'. Somewhat more than an analogy because Prynne's work would reach, if it could, beyond the language condition where sub-microscopic, biochemical events are mere metaphor for mental process to a condition where they more closely become a description of that process. Evidently, total success at this would 'solve' the body–mind question and I am not suggesting that Prynne's poetry aspires so high.

Linking a description of sub-microscopic events to mental events proposes an inner relation that is matched by an outward relation between human mental process and the external world it perceives, where the same sub-microscopic events determine process. That the phenomena of mind are but part of universal natural process has been, of course, one preoccupation of modernist poetry; in 'post-modernist' England, the tendency has more recently been not to question such matters too far but to aim instead for the well-made poem. We need well-made poems, but in the last decade, science has revitalised this micro-macrocosmological question, whose roots, of course, reach back beyond Renaissance and medieval world-views to classical times. The phenomenon of 'mind' is either born in or accompanied by physiological brain events whose laws arise fundamentally from sub-atomic circumstances. But mathematicians and scientists have had increasing success in relating mathematically events at sub-atomic level to the mathematics of the forces emerging at the presumed origin of the universe. The link between modern scientific viewpoints and a poetic conception of mind, with its Eliotesque 'instantaneity of creation', may be clearer if I say that one of the early analogues of 'Black Hole' theory was Edgar Allan Poe's odd tract, Eureka, in which he constructed a view of universal creation rather like the then avant-garde scientific theories of Laplace.* For Poe, a universe conceived on the model of poetic creation would start from a point-like origin and expand outwards until its originating energy was exhausted, whereupon it would collapse back inwards to the point, afterwards entering a spiritual condition. What Prynne's poetry has often sought to do is look at the sub-atomic, instead of the macrocosmic, and see if close analogies can be drawn between such events and the poetic act of mind.

[1] 'transitional book', for Prynne's reference to Wound Response as 'probably rather an interim text', and Oliver's enthusiastic designation of the work as 'transitional' in reply, see Prynne to Oliver, 6 September 1974, and Oliver to Prynne, 11 September 1974.

* E.g. the Black Hole theorists S. W. Hawking and G. F. R. Ellis reprint a 1799 essay by Laplace. *The Large Scale Structure of Space–Time* (Cambridge: Cambridge University Press, 1973).

Appendix C

This could get pretentious, but there is always a risk that poets will give up on the kind of task set for them by the great figures such as Dante. Particularly, the birth of the mind-act is one of poetry's primary subject matters, for, as I shall argue in my final chapter, in its notional moment of birth, language opens out to wider possibilities only imperfectly achieved in the actual writing-down of the poetic line.[1] For our own time, as I say, it will not exactly be an analogy between sub-atomic physiological events and mind-acts that this subject matter affords nor (since body–mind questions are intractable) a literal similarity; but, providing it keeps its humility, poetry can try to reach beyond analogy towards a kind of visionary-literal.

As a book, <u>Wound Response</u> starts with bodily and mental wounding. The bodily response to the wound has its quiddity: the unattainable 'instant' when the event occurs, deploying into wider responses as the wound takes effect, with the very first biochemical responses, then with the signals that mean pain to the mind, and eventually with the physical bruising. So too, the mental events have their quiddity, the 'instant' when the event occurs, the unattainable 'truth', that is, of the event in its birth, and then the deploying of this event into consciousness and into memory. If we may call a bruise a bodily pathology, then a pathology of mental experience is also possible—remorse and regrets which impair both language (hence Prynne's poetic interest) and future decision and action. One other thing before examining the poem: we shall see that Prynne, in this poem concerning the birth of an event and its deployment into space–time, refers to his wider investigations of on the one hand sidereal and on the other fixed-frame earthly space–time. I shall pull up somewhat short of those more grandiose themes, except to say that <u>Wound Response</u> looks beyond itself to larger considerations in Prynne's work where I follow him uncertainly.

The poem comes in the book at a stage where the bruising is spreading and the mind is casting back to the event in memory. The event seems to have caused psychological, and presumably physical, hurt. I do not think the poem is cold-hearted about this (despite that line about charity) but it keeps implying that the instant when the event 'happened' transcends the past of it, the anticipatory fears that led up to it, and also the future of it, the recollection in remorse. The more you live in the instant, the less you stay pegged down in fear as anticipatory or remorse and guilt as reflective, and the better you will act anyway. It is to this extent a poem about morality. My use of 'instant', here is evidently linked with my use of that term in discussing poetic stress, the notional point at which we assume the sound of the poem to 'happen'.[2]

We need the proper definition of a key word at the end of the second stanza, 'contre-coup'; it is an injury resulting from a blow suffered on the opposite side of the physical body or a part at a distance from the impact, e.g. a fracture appearing on the side of the skull opposite to that on which a blow fell.

---

1 In the closing paragraph of *PNP*, Oliver argues that '[a]uthor and reader create, through their own implied personification in the text, a special subjectivity—a perfecting of the emotional and semantic fields through a shared experience of space and time, owing to the mystery of artistic form. This process reveals what our everyday experience could be like if, when our emotions were real and not imaginary, our hearts and heads were in temporal consonance' (172). An apparent contradiction between Oliver's phrase 'imperfectly achieved' in the draft chapter and the final paragraph in *PNP* is resolved by attention to Oliver's point that the relative 'perfecting of the emotional and semantic fields' (compared with the paucity of such experience in everyday life) is itself indicative of the state of emotional and temporal consonance that constitutes 'what our everyday experience *could* be like' (my emphasis).

2 See p. 175n1.

Whatever this wound is, it is preceded by fearful anticipation, the hurt occurs (unconsciously) in an 'instant' of time including but transcending the fear and throwing a shadow into the future, so that the instant is double-valenced with past and future yet all occurs simultaneously; and then there is that contre-coup, the answering injury on the other side of the real impact. It is a pathology both of the flesh and of the mental processes. Prynne says that recalling an event by the moral trace it leaves for you is like that: it leads to a squint backwards at fear, the left-hand side of the verse-line, so to speak, the left-hand side of some scientific data about a physiological event—in short at the past. On the recall side of the event we gloss it, betray its real nature by saying it was 'nothing much'. Both sides of the reaction drain inwards, though, to the deep excitement of the moment of impact, the moment of hurt. We are close here to the Augustinian triple present, which I discuss in Chapter 9.[1] Recollection falsifies but the electrochemical charge the actual event wrought in us is still represented there by the bruise eventually and also in whatever way the neurons or nerve cells of our flesh retain a representation of our experience. Prynne quotes, like an external voice, a self-explanatory text; the text means that involved in the physical preservation of the event (compare memory) is some kind of transform or coding in a distribution of neurons whose topology, or, loosely, transformed pattern, will preserve the event's happening. (The mention of topology to explain the coding is in slight risk of dating scientifically but is sufficiently general for this not to be important.) The actual bodily and mental experience, this quasi-instant, leads to the transformation; for the truly poetic consciousness, looking back, the experience is a unity, a notional instant of hurt. From the experience we try to spring a genuine poetic language. The words freeze out from the unimaginable speed of the instant itself; a suggestion of the words to come is in this poem, the white flakes like thin snow on the lips, freezing out from the original excitement. Words already try to contain the hurt, control its damage, rather as when we console a child watching his first Dracula film and in a dark forest Dracula suddenly appears from behind a tree: 'It's all right; you can buy teeth like that in the joke shop.' So, almost in a joke, Prynne has the protagonist's left wrist rise to check him back into ordinary living, not into the excitement of the instant but into a view of the instant as always in the past of our ordinary sense of time and into the lesser time-scales of 'Oh, it was nothing much.'

'What mean square error' is an especially concentrated phrase. The second stanza's theme will partly concern the role of probability laws in interpreting biological phenomena: in this case, the wound's impact and its effect. Biologists, looking at events whose foundation is sub-atomic have to employ quantum theory. Probability theory, or the summing up of chances, rules quantum theory: a French Nobel Prize biologist, Jacques Monod, once claimed that organic process was fundamentally ruled by

[1] Oliver describes Augustine's 'triple present' in chapter 8 of *PNP*, applying it to his own formulation of poetic stress: 'How is it, [Augustine] asks, that we can measure the duration of the short and long syllables [in the Ambrosian hymn *Deus creator omnium*], since while they exist, in each present moment of their sounding, we have no knowledge of their duration, and after they have finished they no longer exist and it is only in memory that we can know for how long they have sounded? His answer is that it is in the mind that we measure times, by the establishment of a triple present—the past-as-present (memory), the present (attention), and the future-as-present (expectation). [...] [P]roviding we [...] call the present 'notional', emphasise that the triple present is itself held in memory, and acknowledge that logical difficulties will arise if we consider these questions abstracted from performance, St Augustine's is an appropriate formulation to apply to the performance of poetic stresses' (*PNP*, 109).

chance.[1] In probability equations it is often important to find the mean or average for the 'population' (or complete set of scores for the biological data studied), and some formulae require this to be squared. We get a packet of meaning out of Prynne's phrase through a play between whether it is a question or not. First, a straightforward point: 'What does an error mean if we square averages obtained from chance occurrences? Can an error happen by chance?' The stanza will go on to argue that there must be something else besides chance operating in organic processes and therefore, by extension, in mental processes; something like a purpose in nature, a natural 'detecting' mechanism that integrates the events measured in a biological population. But because of the pun on 'mean' (= 'signify' and 'average') we can read this ambiguously as a question not fully posed: what + average + square + error. The lack of question mark, and the curious syntax, make the words mysterious so that we reflect more deeply on each word's individual meaning. Prynne does not, of course, deny probability mathematics but makes the statistical method itself imply an error in our view of things, not an error in the method itself but an error if using the method seems to deny a driving force in natural processes that is not chance.

That is, he claims against biological studies of events in plants that the notional occurrence of an event transcends our description of it. In human, psychological terms, the excitement 'when' the hurt was caused had real significance; no doubt it translated a moment of will into practice and left behind a moral trace: it was not totally chance. If it were, if our decisions about how we act (which, just as plant growth, seem to depend upon minute electrochemical changes)... if those are pure chance at base then how explain this excitement that they give rise to? How could we be excited during a moment of experience if it is true that the event could just go either way, depending merely upon probabilities? It makes no emotional sense. 'Probable excitement' seems an oxymoron to me. Our will must be implicated: for the instant casts a shadow into the future; and, if I can just slip this in, so does a notional instant of poetic stress with its emotional charge, its mental 'detecting mechanisms', its expectancy, its intention, and its excitement.

To miss this and to look back on an event merely with remorse, is the linguistic and emotional pathology. Even 'blame' is without meaning if it is seen from the different time-scale of the event itself. To catch intention at its birth leads to the cleanest action; like nail varnish, remorse does not convincingly gloss over the 'flux link', the actual point at which the nail grows. I cannot explain 'Then the sun comes out', though I am aware the poem points outside itself to Prynne's other work on the effects of diurnal sequence upon bodily and plant process— he has, for example, four little books in sequence on diurnal themes.[2] Elsewhere in the book, we have a 'wounded' plant, the 'Little Musgrove' with cut-off roots, and its response to light

---

[1] Oliver refers to Monod's *Le hasard et la nécessité: Essai sur la philosophie naturelle de la biologie moderne* (Paris: Éditions du Seuil, 1970).

[2] Oliver refers to *Day Light Songs, Fire Lizard* (Barnet, UK: Blacksuede Boot Press, 1970), *A Night Square*, and *Into the Day*.

coming from a certain direction; we have discussions about 'plant-time'; and there may be analogous data concerned here too. But evidently the sun also relates to the fear of hurt at top left and is some kind of antithesis, perhaps symbolically considered the birth of consciousness or the birth of the next reaction; at all events, the right-hand side of the moment itself, its future leaning. The original hurt at this point starts to pass into numbness as the original moment dulls.

There is, says Prynne's last stanza, this moment that precedes the actual transformation of the event into the cognition represented by the nerve cell topology—that is the meaning of 'neuroleptic', nerve cognition, literally. The moment that precedes is that in which the time-scales are those of large- or sub-atomic space–times or of the large-scale notionally in the infinitesimal compass of the temporal instant. Ed Dorn's catchphrase has a certain celebrity:

> the inside real
> and the
> outsidereal[1]

that is, starry, that word in this last stanza. The real time we live by is the space–time of the outer universe, and the inner space–time lived through by the particles or whatever is fundamental in the sub-atomic worlds of flesh; and yet we also have the local-fixed-hour, Euclidean-space version of it that we construct down here on earth to serve our needs. Truly regarded, bodily space–time is like the old description of it by the medieval Christian philosophers or the neo-Platonists: the whole soul present in the individual members of the body. (As for 'granular', I'm assuming this refers to granulation tissue, which fills up the gap left by a wound. However, 'granule' has other scientific significance: for example, the granule cells of the hippocampus —a primitive part of the cerebrum believed to be important in the laying-down of memory traces—have been much studied because of their greater excitement of activity according to frequency of input. {also granular snow})

What is there in potential, if we could only place ourselves without fear and in full emotional risk at the disposal of the next instant when we shall act, is the possibility of getting actions right. The remarks about blame, lost benevolence and charity are not a denial of those virtues but a claim that ethics themselves freeze out from the real nature of the events we live through, where the dark and the light side of our mind-acts come into consonance, and we act rightly almost without knowing it, except that this is a paradox and we act rightly because we have trusted ourselves to do so (one reason why self-love is so necessary a prerequisite to moral behaviour). Then the hurt does not so much cast a moral trace into the future: rather the future is revealed as potential in the instant, like the shadow which is part of the cut.

[1] Oliver slightly misquotes the inscription to bk. 3 of Dorn's *Gunslinger*: 'The inside real / and the outsidereal'. *Collected Poems*, 499.

Themes of night and day now return. We have said that our mental acts have a dark side and a side which is like sunshine. According to our philosophical background these sides are variously named: the two faces of Janus; the past and future aspects of the present; the unconscious and conscious; in ego language, the subjective and objective; self–other; in the theory of J. Derrida (see footnote 13, Chapter 9) the ambiguity is called, precisely, the 'trace' and this may explain Prynne's use of the word... language keeps skirting round to describe mind acts whose genesis is so imperfectly understood.[1] The mental instant in its actual occurrence is not simply an empty interface between past and future. It is a unification of at least some past content into a mental event which is both sunlike and casts a shadow on the future. It is like a horizon rim between night and day but a rim that both trembles with night and shines with day.

Prosody

The ten-line stanzas usually have five-stressed lines, with one six-stressed (second line, third stanza) and others creating unusual effects through placement of articles and other small words at line-ends. There is occasional rhyme and half-rhyme, almost a couplet to round off the last stanza, and a final line of comment. This does not tell us much about how Prynne's prosody works.

In what follows, I must admit that the patterns that we find in fairly free verse forms cannot be related to meaning quite so confidently as they can in tightly metrical verse: that is a cost of free forms and a poet may agree to this cost in order to search for new rhythms. Furthermore, Prynne does not usually read his poems in public, so that the relationship between authorial speaking voice and written page might seem at first thought problematic. However, I argue throughout this book that meaning and intonation are necessarily related, whether in the flattest of ordinary conversation or in the most strict employment of metrics.[2] If the degree of ordering is high and a sense of rhythm strong we basically have poetic utterance—that is the only explanation of an organic and creative ordering. We may correctly make artificial stipulations, such as that poetry must be written in lines, whereas prose poems are not, but the basis of all distinction is the manner in which the language is born in the head and of this process we have a fairly infallible intuitive sense.

The elements of Prynne's versification that seem to give most trouble are that line-endings are often so fine as almost to disappear and that, if we fail to hear it as poetry, the rather academic tone reminds us more of cultivated conversation than of, say, the highest lyric tone. The conversational poetry of Wordsworth and Coleridge, however, because set into more orthodox metrical patterns, seems to give critics no trouble in comprehending its prosody. Examining the machine data discloses that Prynne,

---

1 Oliver's description of the Derridean trace appears in the fourth footnote to chapter 8 of *PNP*: 'The Derridean "trace" has much of the ambiguity about spatio-temporal relations of past, present, and future elements in linguistic experience that is required for my following discussion. But the language of Derridean deconstruction is too removed from our ordinary language and too inherently paradoxical about the interrelation of absence and presence ("the disappearance of truth as presence") to be *useful* in describing our everyday belief that we have just had a "present" experience of a beat in a poem' (*PNP*, 174n4). Oliver published further thoughts on the trace in relation to poetic stress and performance in 'More Than a Trace', *Scarlet*, no. 5 (September 1991), n.p.

2 Oliver makes this point across *PNP*, but esp. in chapters 3 ('Intonation Contours'), 4 ('Voicing Patterns and the Pace of Poetry'), and 12 ('Emotion in Literary Response'). In the latter, Oliver writes: 'There is [...] a necessary link in *any* given utterance between what is said and its intonation; language cannot avoid it and it is specific to performance' (*PNP*, 164).

like Milton, may work with syllable length, voicing, pause and intonation to set up internal repetitions and contrasts which bind the music together and may emphasise meanings.[1] Along with this, we shall find an interesting use of syncopation. I shall study the second stanza only; because the interpretation section was complicated I did not break it up with prosodic findings but shall now tabulate the latter, leaving it to the reader to refer them back to the interpretation. {(See Figs. xxi–xxxiv.)}[2]

(a) 'What mean square error'

Each word is fairly equal in length and pace to accentuate the ambiguity of the phrase already noted. 'Error' forms a double-syllable voicing pattern whose broken intonation differentiates it from the preceding words.

(b) 'Remorse is a pathology of
syntax'

The main effect here, apart from some repeated intonation contours, is the speed through 'is a pathology of' followed by a pause at the unusual line-ending. The speed contrasts with the length and rise–fall of the emotional word, 'Remorse', and the intonation drops in pitch for the technical words 'pathology' and 'syntax', so that the contrast between the emotional word and the more clinical analysis is affirmed. The effect is a syncopated unit whose following pause highlights the most surprising word, 'syntax', which, like a double drum tap, justifies the slightness of the line-ending on 'of'.

(c) 'panded/ /time/ /di/ /splay/ /de/ /pletes/ /the
/in/ /put/ /of/ /blame/'

The broken voicing patterns emphasise the slowness involved in an expanded time display, thereby miming the concentration upon the unusual condition of time. There is syncopation by reversal of syllabic duration, as shown, to throw emphasis on blame, which is again a surprising but emotional word and, like 'Remorse' takes a full duration to contrast with the scientific language. It is the syncopation that justifies the line-ending on 'the'.

(d) There are intonational and rhythmic similarities between:

'patters like scar tissue'
'cancels the flux link'

which are syncopated, and both refer to covering over the immediate point of pain. They form by contrast somewhat of an intonational triplet with 'First intentions are cleanest', which is rhythmically quite similar but whose greater

[1] The seventh chapter of *PNP*, which replaced the present draft chapter in the published book, considers lines from *Paradise Lost*. See *PNP*, 85–98.

[2] Oliver's figures comprise fourteen pages of glottograph read-outs, preserved in Prynne's papers. See p. 187 for figs. xxi–xxiii. For details of the machinary used, see p. 65n3.

definiteness is emphasised by a high pitch on 'First', since falling intonation contributes a sense of the definite. These syncopations may be reinforced by contrast, as here where the longer syllables of 'no paint on the nail' are in musical contrast to 'cancels the flux link', a contrast which underlines the negative comparison between covering over and the quick of the nail.

(e) 'Then the sun comes out
(top right)'

This creates a further syncopation, effectuated by a line break, this time to prepare for the longer durations that follow. 'Syntax', 'flux link' and '(top right)' are all double drum taps and the sharpness of '(top right)' prepares for a new movement in the analysis of time.

(f) 'and local numbness starts to spread'

The voicing patterns partly join together and the durations expand to express a numbed attention, which contrasts with the rhythm of 'comes out / (top right)'.

(g) 'nail', 'still', '<u>will</u>' form end-rhymes which can be tracked in the traces. The general effect is to throw emphasis upon the important word, 'will'.

(h) '/<u>Not will</u>/ /<u>but chance</u>/ /the plants/ /claim but/ / tremble/'

This is a rhythmic unit, internally half-rhyming 'chance' and 'plants' and, by pauses and linked pairs of short and long (separate) syllables, its pulses prepare for the weaker double-syllable voicing pattern on 'tremble' and so emphasises the difference between definite statement and doubt.

(i)   '/a/
/de/ /tect/ /ing/ /mechanism/ /must/ /in/ /te/ / grate/ /a/ /cross/ /that/ /popula/ /tion'

The broken voicing and quick tempo are expressive of the interpolated, technical information, an effect accentuated by the trivial words at the line-endings. The tempo is slower for the notion of 'detecting' because of the line break at 'a', which should I think be observed by a slight break in the voice; it is quicker for the notion comprised in 'integrate' and slower again at the end to form a rhythmically bounded unit, slow–fast–slow.

(j) 'it makes sense right at the contre-coup'

'it makes sense' shows the role of sibilance, for the unvoiced 's's can be prolonged, mid-word, and so can syllabic length generally, so as to increase our sense of deliberate statement. The intonation falls and the pause after 'sense' can be prolonged so as to throw more stress back on to that word. 'Right' creates syncopation with 'at the' to prepare for the exact syncopation on the word, 'con/ /tre/ / coup/', whose triple beat befits the whole sense of time past and future concentred on the present expressed in the poem, as already discussed. The word also gives us the image of a bruise appearing on the other side from a blow, the hard 'k' sounds making that beat sharper and the image of a blow more vivid. Of course, the word is in normal usage expressive but here is more so because caught up in the whole rhythm of the line, rounding off the syncopation in previous lines and expressive of the main meaning of the poem.

Tabulated like this, the various sonic repetitions and contrasts may seem less closely motivated than they are in the very tight working of Milton.[1] Evidently, a critic would make a mistake in applying to this versification criteria better suited for verse in abstract metrical form. Prynne's rhythms are more organic, in some respects free-form, like rhythmic conversation but too organised and fast in their changes and syncopations for that. It is not a neat exercise in 'Practical Criticism' to describe them; they have to be caught on the wing, in their cadences.

The description of the overall stanzaic structure with which I began the formal investigation can now be made more interesting. The three stanzas do not fit the pattern, 'before the wound', 'after the wound', and 'the wounding itself', because both the first two stanzas recall the wound's significance; nevertheless they suggest this pattern more subtly. In the first stanza 'top left' refers us to the moment before the wound happened, when there was anticipatory fear, and the second stanza introduces 'top right', the moment after the wound happened. These two stanzas concern the temporal 'pathology' of how we damp down vividness (in the case of pain, thank goodness!). Then the last stanza reflects on the nature of the moment itself. 'Contre-coup', the other side of the blow, is the word that pictures on the physical level the mental operations of anticipation, event and recall which the first two stanzas are discussing; it is centrally sited at the end of the second stanza. Its syncopation also hints at the three stages of blow-arriving, impact/wounding, and answering bruise on the far side of the wound. There has been much earlier syncopation to prepare for a small rhythmic climax on this central word. The pleasure this word gave was not comprehensible until I saw that 'contre-coup' catches up these already established

---

1 'One profitable approach to the music of Milton's poetry is to combine analyses of: his care in syntactical placement of key words; his management of syllabic pace; the incorporation of this movement and syntax into longer cadences organised into paragraphs of the sonorous measure; and the interaction of this with the poem as a whole' (*PNP*, 85).

syncopations and concentrates them into the three-fold nature of the response to event, the 'before', 'present', and 'after' that are all in a sense part of the event itself.

Following the word, 'contre-coup', comes a stanza which homes on the centre of the relationships of past and future, that is on the primary cognition of the event. (Prynne gives this three-phase cognition the Derridean word, 'trace'—see footnotes to Chapter 3[1]—but if this is the source the word is used with different temporal dynamics.) It is a cognitive moment: in the 'centre' the direct cognition of event and on both sides of the centre the moral elaborations, like the medieval Christian notion of the soul. We may remember, from Chapter 3, how St. Augustine associated his passive aspect of the triple present with an extension in the soul.[2] In this centre, space and time are paradoxical, what is self and not-self reflect each other. Then we see why there is a single line after the three stanzas. The three stanzas analyse the relations of past, future, and present; but the single-line coda unites them in the image of a horizon between night and day, between self and not-self, between present, on the one hand, and past and future on the other. It is like a horizon itself.

Providing we trust the free organicism of Prynne's rhythms, without doctrines about what a poetic line is and how it should end, we find that this is a tightly organised poem in which rhythms combine in an original way with meaning and emotional significance.

---

1 See p. 182n1.

2 '[Paul] Ricoeur [...] distinguishes the active and passive facets of Augustine's triple present. It is a double-facing triple present, triple in activity, triple in passivity. Augustine has a passive description of the present as an attentiveness along with impression-images in memory and sign-images in expectation. These are spatial expressions and therefore need another spatial expression in which they can remain, a space which may be thought of as distended, yet present. For Augustine this is the soul, considered under Ricoeur's passive aspect' (*PNP*, 109–10).

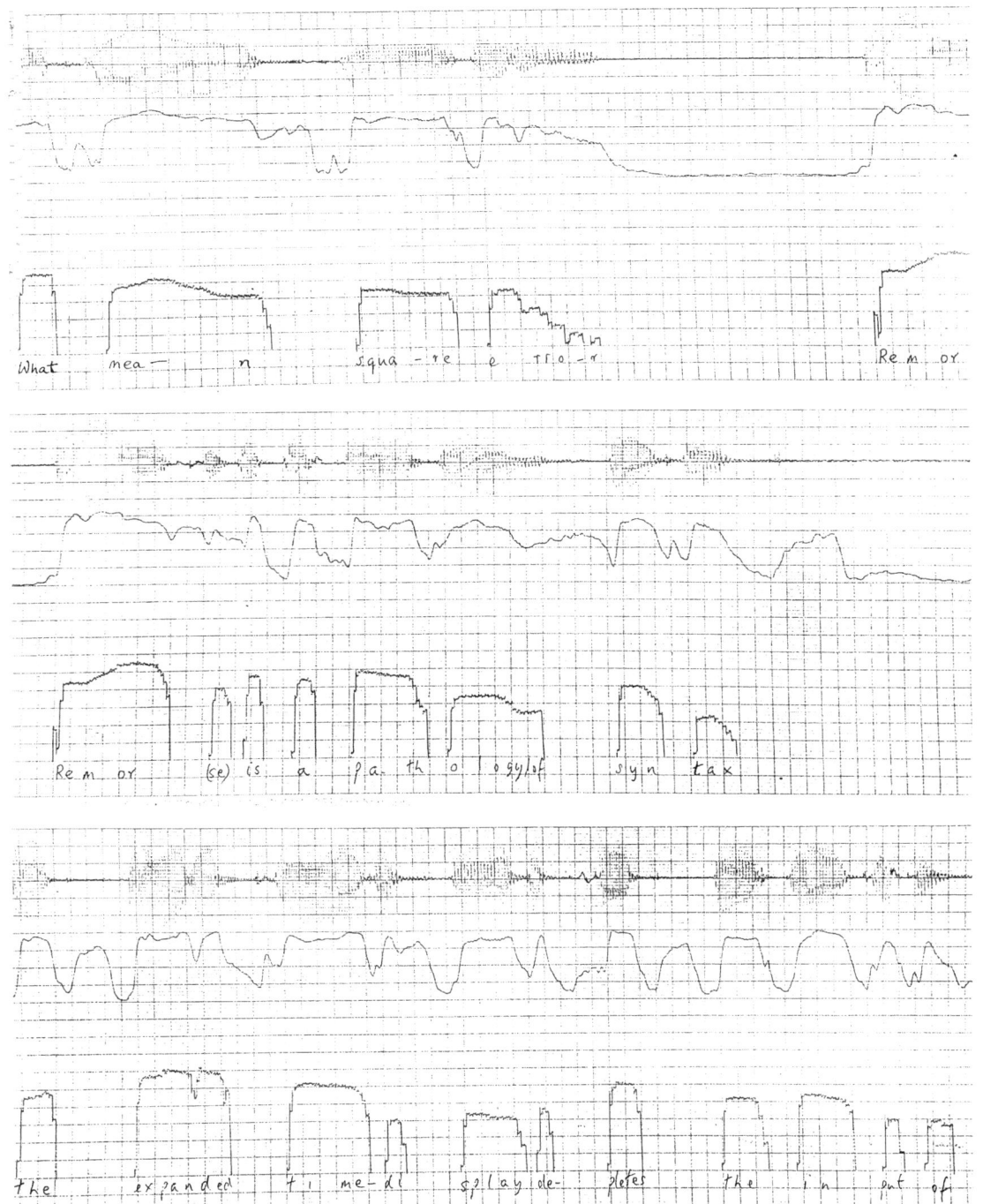

Figures xxi–xxiii from 'What the Plants Can Tell Us'.

APPENDIX D

Defunct Tokens: Review of Prynne's 'Marzipan'

Douglas Oliver

Oliver enclosed the following review in his letter to Prynne of 1 January 1991, though it was evidently written some time before this. Oliver first discusses 'Marzipan' in his letter of 2 June 1986. The opening paragraph's mention of 'the late 1980s' in retrospect suggests composition sometime in 1989 or 1990, making it near-contemporaneous with D. S. Marriott's review of *Bands around the Throat* in *Archeus* (1989). Prynne's 'Marzipan' was first published in Edward and Jennifer Dunbar Dorn's journal *Rolling Stock*, no. 10 (October 1985). See *Poems*, 347–8.

1 Oliver's review is reproduced in appendix A.

2 'Sketch for a Financial Theory of the Self' (*Poems*, 20).

The shortish poem, 'Marzipan', has been thirstily received by J. H. Prynne's readers in England. At least, so it seems to me in the US, where Mrs Thatcher remains the most admired world politician; the late 1980s required such a bitter draught, a poem castigating the enfeeblement of virtue which led to her party's re-election.

'Marzipan' deals in shadows and depletion, unenergetic inhabitants and <u>mores</u> seen in provincial landscapes of river banks, hospitals, and shopping marts, where a rigorous value has departed. It's as if some washing powder token—even one zero value—could satisfy all our meagre impulse, diminished to a wish for household peace, and as if that were a debating ground for politics:

> We poor shadows light up, again
> slowly now in the wasted province
> where colours fall and are debated
> through a zero coupon, the de-
> funct tokens in a soft regard.

This is a time when a ruling party faces a 'broken enemy', an opposition which it can toy with like a cat. What it offers instead is shopkeeping, with its seasonal rebates and conventional pieties:

>   Fortune
> rich in spoil, surfeit in pray.

When Prynne's voice becomes so direct it speaks out for a generation acerbic at their Britain fallen into carelessness about political rectitude and even about fundamental fairness.

Reviewing <u>Kitchen Poems</u> in 1968, I carried into my inner mind the strict economy of personal quality suggested in his 'Sketch for a Financial Theory of the Self'.[1] It was a quality so maintained ethically that it did not have to think acquisitively of the returns or gains of right action—'the star & silk of my eye, that will not return'.[2] It's a sadness for me to see the necessity for this later poem, 'Marzipan', where that same fierce ethic is set against a Britain whose neo-Conservative ruthlessness masks a desperate wish for comfort and unearned status. The ethical, magical, bright life remains of course—underground. A Baudelairean ennui might easily result, except that responsibility is placed squarely on the self as participant in the dreary political process:

>   to ask grace
>   at a graceless face it is our own
>   in the glass of dark recall […].

I don't know a contemporary poet better equipped to show this nation's loss of social heart, and loss also of outrage—that 'burning / powder' scraped from the heart, to use 'Marzipan's phrase. Marzipan, the lack of icing, I suppose: the poem shows most forcibly that settling for second best hides a deeper viciousness: comfort at the expense of others.

The poem leads us only half-suspecting through the narrow aspirations of neo-Conservative economy to an ending that makes a reader catch breath. The penultimate stanza ends:

>   The price
>   is right, <u>eau minerale naturelle</u>
>   from the hypermarket and thousands…

At this point we expect a final punch to the face of domesticised acquisitiveness. 'Thousands of what?' Some items from the stacked shelves perhaps? But there's a conceptual leap between this and the final stanza. '… thousands / Of feet of glacial sand'. And we are to find that our easy-osey attitudes of domestic politics now leap over into horror…

>   … and thousands
>
>   Of feet of glacial sand. Ten thousand
>   families in the mountains, starved
>   on mountain grass: and made me eat
>   both gravel, dirt and mud, and last
>   of all, to gnaw my flesh and blood.

I have a fancy that this stanza may become quite celebrated, for the extent of its leap seems entirely justified. Some third person account is being brought in, obviously, with typical Prynne allusiveness. In the third line, by syntactical ellipsis the external-view suddenly gives way to a pronoun shift and we are unsure who the 'me' is: it could almost be the poet, who is already representative of ourselves. An account of literal starvation is thus brought head-on into relation with the cosy world of a British electorate, whose complaining forms a background to the poverty of other nations. By deserved trope, the starvation is cast back upon us wealthy ones as our own, a starvation of right-acting. A danger of overstatement here, you might think: alas not.

The chilling 'No Song No Supper', with its frozen British landscapes a companion piece to 'Marzipan', is another reminder of our need for Prynne.[1] He remains one of the few to keep his song bright and frosty when the supper has gone stale. 'Marzipan' would establish a mark in the national conscience if it ever got out that far. Don't let these days pass without bearing witness.

---

[1] 'No Song No Supper' was first published as *Infolio*, no. 67 (3 April 1987). See *Poems*, 343–4.

Prynne's papers preserve at least five letters from Liu Xiang-jun and nine from Prynne to Liu, 1992–5 (MS Add.10144/500–1). Liu's letters were sent from Suzhou University and Guanyun County Middle School, Jiangsu, China. Prynne enclosed copies of the following two letters to Liu in his letter to Oliver of 3 May 1994; they are discussed at length in Oliver and Prynne's subsequent exchange (Oliver to Prynne, 12 May 1994, and Prynne to Oliver, 19 June 1994).

APPENDIX E

Letters to Liu Xiang-jun

J. H. Prynne

6 October 1993   Gonville and Caius College
                       Cambridge

Dear Xiang-jun,

Your welcome letter reached me this afternoon, and even though time is in frightfully short supply, here I am sending a completely prompt letter in return! In fact [*it*] is late at night, here, and I have just finished all the extra work caused by the arrival of all my students, and so I thought it would be very pleasant to send you a note.

Of course you are quite right to think about the 'carriage scene', because I too have thought about it, as you know. It is hard for me to explain fully what was meant by that scene, because for sure it had a lot of meaning. Very well I can imagine the response of those to whom you have told this story; what a shame that the honourable foreign visitor should suffer from so much inconvenience, and how he must think that our country is rather backward, to have such bad roads and such inefficient methods of transport. Maybe even, a little, just at first, your father felt like that; and perhaps, just for a few moments, you did too.

But my own reaction was entirely different! It was a cause of real happiness and satisfaction to me, to be so far from the official city world, and to see so closely the real life of the countryside. But to see is not completely to experience. When our driver was trying to choose the best track, as he steered his carriage between the ruts and the mud, I was looking over his shoulder and making the same choices in my mind. Mostly he was successful, and I could feel the skill which he had, as based on his own practice and his observant eye for hints about which way to go. He would make a choice and I would think, 'is that the right one?', and then, 'yes, it is', or 'well, maybe', or, 'I cannot see anything better'. Then, as the road got more difficult, his choosing became more difficult also, and sometimes I held my breath a little. I was not watching the scenery, or the white clouds in the blue sky, I was watching a small patch of road, and holding on to the bars so as not to be shaken to pieces. When he made his choice, which way to go, immediately we felt the jolts and the shaking which told us which ruts or holes in the ground had been struck by his wheels.

I could feel that he was doing his best, and working with full concentration; partly because he was a serious worker, trying to fulfill his responsibilities; partly because he did not want the visitor to suffer inconvenience; and partly because his carriage was important to him and he would suffer much if it was seriously damaged—his method of living would be affected. So, I could feel that he was quite relaxed but also quite anxious, and for this reason, I was the same. All of these things make up a very interesting kind of experience, because they are quite different from being just a foreign guest, being protected from 'inconvenience'. When the carriage got stuck in the mud, I scarcely thought about not helping him, and helping us, because we were all together in the same problem. If we stayed in the carriage, it would be too heavy to go forward. If we stood to one side, he would have to do all the work by himself, and he might not have enough strength to be successful. If you helped him (because you are a fellow-Chinese) but I did not (because I was a guest), we should be separated—just like your Headmaster who wants only Chinese scientists on the walls of his classroom! If everyone gets muddy then the mud is what joins each person to the same world, and to the same work. The mud is what makes the crops grow, and feeds the people; the rain which made the track difficult made the crops easy.

Of course, if we had taken bicycles, as we planned at first, then we should have had no problems, or not many of them. Instead, we took the carriage because that seemed to be 'more dignified' for the visitor. So, when the carriage met with obstruction I was in fact quite pleased, because that prevented the visitor from being separated from what would be the common experience of ordinary people: it took away the 'false dignity'. Watching each one of our moves on the track, I did not think, 'I am a visitor and the others are different from me'; I thought, 'shall we be successful' and 'which way shall we turn'. When we got stuck, almost I did not think for a single moment, but I jumped down at once because it was the natural thing to do. But, just a little, I did think, because I was quite glad of the opportunity not to think, just to do the natural thing. All of these thoughts, which I describe now, I had while we were pushing our carriage and trying to get free of the mud. By pushing the carriage I was talking to the driver, and he was talking to me, even though we could not at all understand each other's speech. And so I was talking to you through him, not in the English which you have learned, nor even in Chinese, but in the language of simple human effort and contriving a solution. And he in turn was talking through me to you, saying that it was not necessary to be anxious because the problems were simple and practical and could not be helped by thought. He could see that, if I was not 'anxious', then nobody in that little scene had any need to be anxious at all. Each of these messages we understood, because we acted on the basis of understanding them. I believe that this is why, on the return journey, he took us so far and without any worry about payment: because he did not feel any separation and so he trusted us not to cheat him.

When you are a foreigner, in a very distant land, it is difficult to have completely real experiences, because so many things do not happen directly; they have to be translated, carried across a sort of gulf which is the difference between one way of life and another. By closely observing and listening and watching, and by imagination and sympathy, you can make some crossings of this gulf. But sometimes you can cross it by instinct, by some task or experience which is completely common and fundamental— like being stuck in the mud! Also, that is the true secret of a good teacher; because when a student is stuck in the mud the teacher does not give instructions or watch to make an appraisal; he gets out and helps with the pushing, and gets muddy also, and then the students will believe that he is human and real and that he is a friend as well as a teacher. In that way the teacher will make the students real also, because they are not separated. Not all the time should a teacher do this, and when it happens it should not be too calculated; but it is part of an instinct which a person can learn to make good use of, and even little things at the right moment can completely change the life of another person. Already I think that you know this. He or she may even not understand what has happened, and they may quite quickly forget it; but it will be a little mark of reality and human connection in their experience, and it can have an effect for the whole of life.

And of course it is interesting that there was no danger, no risk to life or serious possibility of being hurt. When a challenge is harder and more dangerous, then maybe the definitions change also. Perhaps in some emergencies there is the chance that someone might be killed, or even the certainty that many people will be; perhaps in some terrible war or confronted by a great natural disaster. How will we behave then? That would not be an occasion when we could enjoy simple touches, and be happy to have natural human contact; instead, everything could be dark and terrible. But when such things happen, why does one person still try to help another? Because we have learned how to value our simple human nature, and I think we learn this by many little experiences, almost as if we are practising for life itself.

On all of our journeys this summer I could see very well that you were always a little bit anxious that we would get stuck in the mud, in a symbolic sense, and then you would be a little bit ashamed that you could not protect the foreign guest from being uncomfortable, or from forming a bad impression of your fellow countrymen. Of course I told you, all the time, that I did not react like that; but still, you did not find it quite easy to be really certain. Remember the Sunday train; I know that you were worried, not for yourself, but for me; and so, I was a little worried also, not for me, but for you! That is how, gradually, we learned, not to be worried at all for each other because of the difference, but to try to find a compromise because we were both the same. That is why I really was quite glad that we were 'unsuccessful'; because it was more interesting and more true to life to be 'stuck in the mud', and because each of us could finally see that the other person did not need to be anxious. Here, the 'driver' was the 'mud' itself! To be anxious in that way is a kind of human care-for-others, but it is the great enemy of the real. So, when the Confucian says that it is honourable to care for others, and the Taoist says that it is foolish to care even for oneself, I can begin to see the truth of both of these statements; and the real truth of them is to be found only in the mud! The backward is the forward, and the forward is the backward.

This is the end of my little essay about mud. It comes into this form because it is the result of a 'Night Vigil', maybe a little like that of Shen Zhou.[1] Soon I will write another letter, in which I will be more practical and give proper replies to your other points, about the photographs and so on. But just for the moment I hope that we have a good understanding, about just this one thing, which is almost big enough to be all things!

祝 好

骆 恩

[1] Shen Zhou (1425–1509), Ming dynasty Chinese painter. Prynne published a commentary on 'Night Vigil' in *Glossator: Practice and Theory of the Commentary*, no. 3 (2010): 1–15.

27 March 1994   Gonville and Caius College
                 Cambridge

Dear Xiang-jun,

Just as I was thinking about your long letter of 6th March, your extra-recent message arrived, with its truly *excellent* news. I am going to be a little cautious about expressing my opinion very strongly, because your mark on the Politics examination is quite important and could perhaps change the overall result. But, of course I do think that your high marks are extremely good and altogether well-deserved; you have really found out how to be a scholar, in the way that suits you best but with determination and method and concentration of mind. Naturally it is important to set a careful programme of preparation, and keep closely to it; but also you have to have the right spirit, with a good flow of ideas and an accurate control of fluent expression. And indeed you do have these qualities: I know! So, it is VERY GOOD NEWS, and it will be completely wonderful when you can tell me also that Politics haven't let you down.

In fact, as you know, I am very interested in politics; and for some time I have felt that the decline of knowledge, in contemporary China, about the dialectic of contradiction and the interconnection of opposites, leaves the pattern of political ideas and practices throughout your modern society in severe confusion and disorder. There seems to be a kind of simple laziness and selfishness in many areas of life, not only in how people behave but also in how they think about the problems of social behaviour within a co-operative community. Mostly, it seems, they prefer not to think at all! In defence of current practice it could perhaps be claimed that, in radical transition from one system to another, there is bound to be a period of uncertainty and experiment. But nowadays in China the study of politics, and of social practice as related to ideas and principles, seems to have dwindled to a mere formality. I think that this is a great loss and a great danger.

But certainly you don't need me to tell you this. I have many questions I want to ask, soon, about your next stage of study as a graduate student: when it will begin, and what you must do to get ready; but I save all that until you can give me the COMPLETE news. But also, even despite my restraint, you must know that I am filled with joy by your success, not because you have been lucky but because you have worked so hard and because it is deserved. I am sure that your family will be very proud of your progress.

Let me look back, now, to your previous letter, and to its very different mood. Even when you leave your current teaching position at the Middle School I think it will have taught you some very interesting lessons.[1] Looking from the outside at what you told me about the Examination-and-Instruction inspection I feel that I can interpret quite easily what happened to you. One of the very worst things about an institution where there are backward ideas and many members of staff who have suffered obstruction and disappointment is that there is rather little spirit of genuine co-operation and mutual encouragement. Senior people are suspicious of juniors, and resent the fact that the juniors are still lively and have natural instincts to experiment with new ideas and methods. In your case it was worse, because you were actively preparing to demonstrate your superior intellectual qualifications, by which if you were successful you would escape from the confines of that world and its repression. Quite instinctively, there was resentment against you: not modestly respecting your seniors, but preparing to jump right over their shoulders! All of the bad comments were concealed; partly because some people were a little ashamed of them, but partly also in order to retain the power of affecting your feelings and your future. During this time you were having to concentrate on two full programmes of work, for the school and for the examinations; and both the strain and the anxiety made you very vulnerable. People who use power against those around them have an instinct for when a person is vulnerable, and choose their effects carefully. At the same time, the vulnerable person is not able to see what is happening, and to strengthen his mood and work out a plan of tactical resistance, because stress makes this impossible.

I can well see, therefore, why you felt, and still feel, quite bitter. It would have been a fine thing, if the other teachers and officials there had been encouraging and supportive, and maybe had even offered to take a few of your classes or help with some marking; and if they had been truly pleased at your success. What is it that breaks down the instinct of human co-operation

---

1 'Middle School', Guanyun County Middle School, Jiangsu.

and support ('mutual aid', Kropotkin called it[1]), and replaces this with negative, selfish rivalry and persecution? While the unpleasant struggle rages, the true victims are those who are supposed to benefit from care and attention but who are just neglected and left out of the picture: the students. In a suspicious and resentful institute, everyone is too busy with rivalry and self-defence to have much real concern for the students; the Nanjing teaching students could see that for themselves, and so could you.

How does such a situation arise? I have a sense that it is rather common in your country at the present time, the bullying mentality and the habit of exploiting weakness by claiming power against the young or the vulnerable or those with any kind of new or independent ideas. Senior people or minor officials cling to their little bit of power, by using it against those who must submit to them or make requests for some kind of permission. In your very deeply anxious state of mind at the time you were profoundly affected by this experience, as you were also in that office where the official held your dossier and seemed to hold absolute power over your life. Do similar situations arise in my country, and if so are they prevalent and unchecked? What is the underlying reason? I persist in asking these questions because you should not allow this period of your life to scar your ideas about human behaviour; indeed, it's essential that you try to understand all this while it is fresh for you, rather than simply forgetting it. There will surely also be more personal setbacks ahead, and you must become strong enough to absorb them and keep a steady course, even by controlling your feelings if you have to.

Part of the phenomenon you have encountered is connected to a complex history of social attitudes and practices in your country's past. There is 'filial piety' and the Confucian habit of complete obedience towards those in authority. There is the long-standing modern backwardness of China's development, which puts strain on the old methods without discovering how to improve them; all the time there are urgent pressures to modernise but not enough resources and not enough ideas about how this is to be done. Then also there is what I referred to above: the decline in political organisation and in the shaping of social attitudes towards common values and purposes. During the middle part of this century and the decades following your country had a strongly shaped sense of priorities and methods, giving rise to discipline and shared commitments (even during very bad times); you did not have liberty in the western sense but you had co-operation and cohesion and some quite firm control over mere defensive individualism. What seems to have killed that is the Cultural Revolution, and then the get-rich-quick market socialism that has followed. The first of these left a whole generation scarred by injustice and persecution and abject misery ('humiliation' is your term: loss of spirit and destruction of self-esteem); the second has prompted a disordered and quite

1 Prynne refers to the work of the Russian revolutionary anarchist Peter Kropotkin (1842–1921), especially his *Mutual Aid: A Factor of Evolution*.

ruthless private individualism. When people and their families are threatened by rising prices and loss of employment stability, it seems inevitable that they will resort to individualistic remedies, taking more for themselves at the expense of a just distribution. Greed and fear are very closely related.

In consequence, this means that the institutions of public life are progressively neglected, as ambitious individuals prepare to leave the professions in search of their own separate opportunity. Serious commitment to new ideas and new resources begins to stagnate, just as the large state enterprises begin to look increasingly like fossils in today's economic markets. In the older idea of state enterprise, areas that were not yet much developed were given priority and support; but nowadays that practice is reversed, so that the successful become more successful and the backward are just left to look after themselves. Teachers are a notable example. Since schools are not directly productive in economic terms, there is reluctance to put high-pressure ideas or resources into their development. Teachers are by definition trained and qualified, with special abilities; and many of the bright ones are already leaving to 'swim in the sea'. But the ones who stay behind are resentful and disappointed, because they are in a backwater and they know it. The control structure is formed as a rigid hierarchy, bureaucratic and sluggish, with harshly defended status boundaries; the active intellectuals know that they are suspected of not being loyal to the system, and thus the payment and status of the entire profession will always be depressed. Those within the system who have given up their ideas and their commitment to positive thinking will be doubly resentful of those who still try not to give up, because they feel the implicit reproach against them and they wish to suppress it, by almost any means. Even during my few and brief visits to schools I could sense the atmosphere; one or two cases of genuine effort to keep a true spirit alive, the rest rather sullen and mechanical and rigorously bureaucratic.

We have a lot of this in the west, too; indeed, here in the college where I work. For myself I will never give in to it; but I have had the advantage of not having come from a victimised generation, within a social structure deeply wounded and a political tradition broken apart by contradictions no longer understood. The bullying mentality stays alive in cycles, each later cycle feeding off the results of an earlier one; those who are badly affected by bullying when young are much more likely to become bullies in turn, and thus to pass on the social malady; just as those who are victims of greed quite soon become the greedy ones. To break these cycles requires very strong intelligence and decisive, corporate action. It requires, finally, an accepted and supported concept of the individual's relation to the state and the state's duties to the individual, reflecting and reflected in the relations within the family and its successive generations. Forms of state control that give power to single individuals remove the dialectical structure that enables criticism and discussion to generate common values and unselfish support for them, and that enables a younger generation to develop from the ideas of earlier ones without provoking unrestrained enmity and suspicion. When such a system works it can bring very great benefits; but when it begins to go wrong there seems no easy way to control or rectify it. Then, bitterness and despair begin to set in, and then of course these attitudes will spread outwards and onwards through the cycle of such things. That's why I say that you must never give in to this mood, however bad everything may seem; everyone is vulnerable to cruel and unjustified attack, but if we become bitter we shall certainly sooner or later become cruel ourselves, even without realising it.

Really, I read your earlier letter with very close attention, and each part of your adventures I could visualise very clearly. Now, if you have truly escaped for the moment from that narrow and vicious world, you will be tempted to forget it completely, while still clinging to the bitter feeling. But you must take care to remember everything fully! Not so that you can have a later revenge, but so that you can watch out for these features in yourself. Those teachers envied but also hated all the books that you had, and I expect they thought that you were making a spiteful display of them, just to show how superior you were. Also, because you didn't really understand their suppressed chagrin I expect that you were in fact sometimes quite tactless. They could not bear your friendliness towards the students; your commitment to hard work; your contact with foreigners and your ambition to make progress. All this made them feel bad. There was a time when each of them tried to study and to be friends with books, but as they each became disappointed in their lives, and overwhelmed by struggle, they began to feel bitter against themselves, and they now cannot bear this bitterness; they transfer it against something (anything) outside. When they find a good target (fully three minutes late to sign your name!) they can hardly help themselves, because they have lost the ability to understand and control their own resentment. Then, when the good news arrives, they try to make amends by being friendly and admiring.

Well, here is a clear lesson for you, don't you think? I can comprehend their wretched behaviour, all too well, and of course I wouldn't excuse it at all. But also I remember that some terrible things happened to that generation; and now, what have they got to look forward to? Maybe they were once just like you are now. The drinking parties are a kind of way of making up for the resentment, while also fixing the cycle as a reality of social life, so that if the young learn how to bridge the gap they can be allowed into a relationship that both varies and also at the same time confirms the underlying structure. In Suzhou last summer I went to the official final party after the graduation ceremony for the post-graduate students; it was a very rigid example of mechanical drunkenness, rather hysterical and not very good-natured. Actually I think that the teachers on that campus also do not have a good atmosphere, and maybe the student of mine that has given up being a teacher there, almost as soon as he began, has found this out for himself.

I think that possibly you will feel that I am a bit cruel and negative, to spend so much time on your depressed letter, and to give less attention to the wonderfully good news that came afterwards. Perhaps I have been rather too outspoken, writing like this. What you said to the Nanjing students was a kind of joke, against yourself and your own sadness; it was a good lesson for them because it opened their eyes to reality, and to what is quickly forced upon those who begin with the best intentions. Were you leading them astray, you ask? Well, no, but for two reasons: the first is that you were warning them by giving them practical knowledge, not to be gained from their theoretical studies; but the second is, that you hoped they would not fully believe you, but instead would understand your mood which caused you to say what you did. But, even so, it is a little dangerous to be cynical, don't you think? Not because it would damage them, but because it might damage you. Ah well, how serious I am about such things! And what a difficult letter this will be for you, full of complex sentences and difficult words!

Next time we write there will be quite a different mood. I shall be able to give you some news about the proofs of the ORIGINAL collection, and you will be able to report on progress with the Afterword.[1] Also, you will have the final and complete information about graduate exams, and will be able to tell me everything about that and about what follows next. Spring will have come, and the whole world will be full of new warmth and optimism!

Until then:

祝好

龄恩

---

[1] Prynne refers to the anthology of translations published in *Parataxis*, no. 7, for which he wrote the afterword.

Bibliography

Ackroyd, Peter. 'Legislators of Language', review of *A Various Art*, ed. Andrew Crozier and Tim Longville. *The Times* (London), 3 December 1987, 17.

———. 'The New and the Novel', review of *The Harmless Building*, by Douglas Oliver. *The Spectator*, 5 January 1974, 15–16.

———, Victoria Glendinning, Robert Nye, Isabel Raphael, Woodrow Wyatt, Elaine Feinstein, Tim Heald, et al. 'Bringing the Year to Book…' *The Times* (London), 28 November 1987, 13–14.

Adams, Terry. *Bill Butler and the Unicorn Bookshop*. N.p.: Beat Scene, 2020.

Adorno, Theodor. 'On Commitment'. Translated by Francis McDonagh. *Performing Arts Journal* 3, no. 3 (Winter 1979): 58–67.

———, Walter Benjamin, Ernst Bloch, Bertolt Brecht, and Georg Lukács. *Aesthetics and Politics*. London: New Left Books, 1977.

Ælfric. 'On the Assumption of the Blessed Mary'. In *The Homilies of the Anglo-Saxon Church: The First Part, Containing the Sermones Catholici, or Homilies of Ælfric; In the Original Anglo-Saxon, with an English Version*. Vol. 1. Translated by Benjamin Thorpe. London: Printed for the Ælfric Society, 1844.

Alexander, Gavin, ed. *Sidney's 'The Defence of Poesy' and Selected Renaissance Literary Criticism*. London: Penguin, 2004.

Andrew, Malcolm, and Ronald Waldron, eds. *The Poems of the Pearl Manuscript: Pearl, Cleanness, Patience, Sir Gawain and the Green Knight*. Liverpool: Liverpool University Press, 2007.

Anselm. *St. Anselm's Proslogion*. Translated by M. J. Charlesworth. Oxford: Clarendon Press, 1965.

Associated Press. 'Double Designation: The 2 Faces of George'. *Newsday*, 30 December 1990, 4.

Astrov, Margot. 'The Concept of Motion as the Psychological Leitmotif of Navaho Life and Literature'. *Journal of American Folklore* 63 (1950): 45–56.

Bartholomew, W. T. 'Voice Research at Peabody Conservatory'. *Bulletin of the American Musicological Society* 6 (August 1942): 11–13.

Bayley, John. 'Tom Paulin's Radical Cheek', review of *The Faber Book of Political Verse*, ed. Tom Paulin. *The Guardian* (London), 29 May 1986, 22.

Beckett, Samuel. *Disjecta: Miscellaneous Writings and a Dramatic Fragment*. Edited by Ruby Cohn. London: John Calder, 1983.

Bentley, Jr., G. E., ed. *William Blake's Writings*. Vol. 2, *Writings in Conventional Typography and in Manuscript*. Oxford: Clarendon Press, 1978.

Bernard, Claude. *An Introduction to the Study of Experimental Medicine*. Translated by Henry Copley Greene. New York: Dover, 1957.

Berrigan, Ted. *The Collected Poems of Ted Berrigan*. Edited by Alice Notley with Anselm Berrigan and Edmund Berrigan. Berkeley: University of Los Angeles Press, 2007.

Bion, Wilfred. *Attention and Interpretation: A Scientific Approach to Insight in Psycho-Analysis and Groups*. London: Tavistock, 1970.

———. *The Long Week-End, 1897–1919: Part of a Life*. London: Free Association Books, 1986.

Birrell, Anne, trans. *New Songs from a Jade Terrace: An Anthology of Early Chinese Love Poetry*. London: George Allen and Unwin, 1982.

———, trans. *New Songs from a Jade Terrace: An Anthology of Early Chinese Love Poetry*. Harmondsworth, UK: Penguin, 1986.

Bleibtreu, John N. *The Parable of the Beast*. London: Victor Gollancz, 1968.

Boss, Medard. *Meaning and Content of Sexual Perversions: A Daseinsanalytic Approach to the Psychopathology of the Phenomenon of Love*. Translated by Liese Lewis Abell. New York: Grune and Stratton, 1949.

Broadbent, D. E., and L. Weiskrantz, eds. *The Neuropsychology of Cognitive Function: Proceedings of a Royal Society Discussion Meeting, Held on 18 and 19 November 1981*. Philosophical Transactions of the Royal Society of London: Series B, Biological Sciences 298, no. 1089 (1982).

Burnley, J. D. *Chaucer's Language and the Philosophers' Tradition*. Cambridge: D. S. Brewer, 1979.

Busoni, Ferruccio. *Sketch of a New Esthetic of Music*. Translated by Theodore Baker. New York: G. Schirmer, 1911.

Calder, John. *Pursuit: The Memoirs of John Calder*. Richmond: Alma Books, 2016.

Caldwell, Roger. 'The Flight Back to Where We Are', review of *Poems*, by J. H. Prynne. *Times Literary Supplement*, no. 5012 (23 April 1999): 27.

Celan, Paul. *Collected Prose*. Translated by Rosmarie Waldrop. Manchester: Carcanet, 1986.

———. *Gesammelte Werke in fünf Bänden*. Vol. 2. Frankfurt am Main: Suhrkamp Verlag, 1983.

Cervantes. *Exemplary Stories*. Translated by C. A. Jones. Harmondsworth, UK: Penguin, 1972.

Chancellor, Alexander. 'Notebook'. *The Spectator*, 1 March 1980, 5.

Char, René. *Œuvres complètes*. Paris: Gallimard, 1983.

Christensen, Peter G. 'Georg Groddeck's Defense of Homosexuality in *Das Buch vom Es*'. *Monatshefte* 85, no. 2 (Summer 1993): 198–210.

Chuang Tzu. *The Complete Works of Chuang Tzu*. Translated by Burton Watson. New York: Columbia University Press, 1968.

Coetzee, J. M. *Waiting for the Barbarians*. London: Secker and Warburg, 1980.

Crozier, Andrew. *Printed Circuit*. Cambridge: Street Editions, 1974.

———, and Tim Longville, eds. *A Various Art*. Manchester: Carcanet, 1987.

Darwin, Charles. *The Expression of the Emotions in Man and Animals*. London: John Murray, 1872.

Davie, Donald. *Thomas Hardy and British Poetry*. London: Routledge and Kegan Paul, 1973.

Davies, Paul. *The Mind of God: Science and the Search for Ultimate Meaning*. London: Simon and Schuster, 1992.

Debord, Guy. *Society of the Spectacle*. Translated by Ken Knabb. London: Rebel, 2005.

De Quincey, Thomas. *The Works of Thomas De Quincey*. Edited by Grevel Lindop. Vol. 2, *Confessions of an English Opium-Eater, 1821–1856*. London: Routledge, 2016.

Derrida, Jacques. *L'écriture et la différence*. Paris: Éditions du Seuil, 1967.

———. *Le problème de la genèse dans la philosophie de Husserl*. Paris: Presses Universitaires de France, 1990.

———. *La voix et le phénomène*. Paris: Presses Universitaires de France, 1967.

Dickens, Charles. *Great Expectations*. Edited by Margaret Cardwell. Oxford: Oxford University Press, 2008.

Dodds, E. R. *The Greeks and the Irrational*. Berkeley: University of California Press, 1951.

Donne, John. *Fifty Sermons, Preached by That Learned and Reverend Divine, John Donne, Dr in Divinity, Late Deane of the Cathedrall Church of S. Pauls London. The Second Volume*. London: Printed by Ja. Flesher for M. F. J. Marriot and R. Royston, 1649.

———. *Poems, by J.D. with Elegies on the Authors Death*. London: Printed by M. F. for Iohn Marriot, 1633.

Dorn, Edward. *Collected Poems*. Edited by Jennifer Dunbar Dorn with Justin Katko, Reitha Pattison, and Kyle Waugh. Manchester: Carcanet, 2012.

———. *The Cycle*. West Newbury, MA: Frontier, 1971.

———. *The North Atlantic Turbine*. London: Fulcrum, 1967.

———. *Songs: Set Two—a Short Count*. West Newbury, MA: Frontier Press, 1970.

———. *Twenty-Four Love Songs*. San Francisco and West Newbury, MA: Frontier Press, 1969.

Duncan, Andrew. 'In a German Hotel'. *Ochre*, no. 6 (ca. 1979): n.p.

———. *Threads of Iron*. Bristol: Shearsman, 2013.

Dunning, T. P., and A. J. Bliss, eds. *The Wanderer*. London: Methuen, 1969.

Eagleton, Terry. 'And the Poetry He Invented Was Easy to Understand', review of *W. H. Auden: The Critical Heritage*, ed. John Haffenden, and *Auden: A Carnival of Intellect*, by Edward Callan. *Poetry Review* 73, no. 4 (January 1984): 60–1.

———. 'Recent Poetry'. *Stand* 10, no. 1 (1968): 66–74.

Edelen, Dominic, and Albert Wilson. *Relativity and the Question of Discretization in Astronomy*. Berlin: Springer-Verlag, 1970.

Eliot, T. S. *Collected Poems, 1909–1962*. London: Faber and Faber, 2002.

———. *The Use of Poetry and the Use of Criticism: Studies in the Relation of Criticism to Poetry in England*. London: Faber and Faber, 1933.

Feuchtwang, Stephan. *The Imperial Metaphor: Popular Religion in China*. London: Routledge, 1992.

Fielding, Henry. *Tom Jones*. Edited by Sheridan Baker. New York: W. W. Norton, 1973.

Fisher, Seymour, and Sidney E. Cleveland. *Body Image and Personality*, 2nd rev. ed. New York: Dover, 1968.

Fónagy, Ivan. *La vive voix: Essais de psycho-phonétique*. Paris: Editions Payot, 1983.

Fraser, Robert. *Night Thoughts: The Surreal Life of the Poet David Gascoyne*. Oxford: Oxford University Press, 2012.

French, Lloyd, dir. *Dirty Work*. Beverly Hills, CA: Metro-Goldwyn-Mayer, 1933.

Freud, Sigmund. *The Standard Edition of the Complete Psychological Works of Sigmund Freud*. Vol. 11, *Five Lectures on Psycho-Analysis, Leonardo da Vinci and Other Works*. Edited and translated by James Strachey. London: Hogarth, 1957.

Friedman, Milton, and Anna J. Schwartz. *A Monetary History of the United States, 1867–1960*. Princeton, NJ: Princeton University Press, 1963.

———. *Monetary Trends in the United States and the United Kingdom: Their Relation to Income, Prices, and Interest Rates, 1867–1975*. Chicago: University of Chicago Press, 1982.

Funkhouser, Linda Bradley. 'Acoustic Rhythm in Randall Jarrell's "The Death of the Ball Turret Gunner"'. *Poetics* 8, no. 4 (August 1979): 381–403.

Gardner, Ernest. *Fundamentals of Neurology*. Philadelphia: W. B. Saunders, 1947.

Geschwind, Norman. *Selected Papers on Language and the Brain*. Dordrecht, NL: D. Reidel, 1974.

Glucksmann, André. *Les maîtres penseurs*. Paris: Grasset, 1977.

Gonda, Jan. *The Character of the Indo-European Moods: With Special Regard to Greek and Sanskrit*. Wiesbaden, DE: Otto Harrassowitz, 1956.

Gordon, E. V., ed. *Pearl*. Oxford: Oxford University Press, 1953.

Graves, Robert. *The Greek Myths*. Vol. 1. Harmondsworth, UK: Penguin, 1955.

Groddeck, Georg. *Das Buch vom Es: Psychoanalytische Briefe an eine Freundin*. Leipzig: Internationaler Psychoanalytischer Verlag, 1923.

Halliday, Michael. *Intonation and Grammar in British English*. Janua Linguarum, Series Practica 48. The Hague: Mouton, 1967.

Hawking, S. W., and G. F. R. Ellis. *The Large Scale Structure of Space–Time*. Cambridge: Cambridge University Press, 1973.

Hazlitt, William. *Liber Amoris: or, The New Pygmalion*. In *The Complete Works of William Hazlitt*, vol. 9, edited by P. P. Howe, 95–162. London: J. M. Dent and Sons, 1930–4.

———. 'On Locke's Essay on the Human Understanding'. In *The Complete Works of William Hazlitt*, vol. 2, edited by P. P. Howe, 146–91. London: J. M. Dent and Sons, 1930–4.

———. 'On Paradox and Common-Place'. In *The Complete Works of William Hazlitt*, vol. 8, edited by P. P. Howe, 146–56. London: J. M. Dent and Sons, 1930–4.

Heidegger, Martin. *Being and Time*. Translated by John Macquarrie and Edward Robinson. Oxford: Blackwell, 1962.

Hendry, David F., and Neil R. Ericsson. 'Assertion Without Empirical Basis: An Econometric Appraisal of *Monetary Trends in … the United Kingdom* by Milton Friedman and Anna J. Schwartz'. In *Bank of England Panel of Academic Consultants: Panel Paper 22*, edited by R. C. O. Matthews, 45–101. London: Bank of England, 1983.

Hodgson, Phyllis, ed. *The Cloud of Unknowing and the Book of Privy Counselling*. London: Early English Text Society, 1944.

Hopkins, Jasper. *A Concise Introduction to the Philosophy of Nicholas of Cusa*. Minneapolis: University of Minnesota Press, 1978.

Hume, David. *An Enquiry Concerning the Principles of Morals*. London: Printed for A. Millar, 1751.

Husserl, Edmund. *Cartesian Meditations: An Introduction to Phenomenology*. Translated by Dorion Cairns. The Hague: Martinus Nijhoff, 1960.

Huxley, Francis. *The Invisibles: Voodoo Gods in Haiti*. New York: McGraw-Hill, 1966.

James, John. *The Small Henderson Room*. London: Ferry, 1969.

———, Tom Philips, and Andrew Crozier. *In One Side and Out the Other*. London: Ferry, 1970.

Jefferies, Richard. *After London; or, Wild England*. London: Cassell, 1885.

John, E. Roy. *Mechanisms of Memory*. New York: Academic Press, 1967.

Johnson, Jeffrey M. *The Works of Iain Sinclair: A Descriptive Bibliography and Biographical Chronology*. Fascicle 4. N.p.: Test Centre Books, 2019.

Johnson, Phil. 'War, Cancer, and Other Ills', review of Edward Dorn and J. H. Prynne (poetry reading), Arnolfini, Bristol, 2 August 1999. *The Independent* (London), 3 August 1999.

Katko, Justin. 'Regarding a Specimen of Palaeobotanic Epigraphy: J. H. Prynne's Runic Fertility Prayer'. *If A Then B*, no. 1 (2010): 42–60.

———. 'Relativistic Phytosophy: Towards a Commentary on "The *Plant Time Manifold* Transcripts"'. *Glossator: Practice and Theory of the Commentary*, no. 2 (2010): 245–93.

Kenny, Anthony. *Will, Freedom and Power*. Oxford: Basil Blackwell, 1975.

King, M. A. '*Bands around the Throat*, J. H. Prynne, Racial Capitalism: Thoughts/Directions'. *Jacket 2*, 1 December 2021. https://jacket2.org/article/bands-around-throat-j-h-prynne-racial-capitalism.

Kristeva, Julia. *Revolution in Poetic Language*. Translated by Margaret Waller. New York: Columbia University Press, 1984.

Kropotkin, Peter. *Mutual Aid: A Factor of Evolution*. New York: McClure Phillips, 1902.

Lacan, Jacques. *Écrits: The First Complete Edition in English*. Translated by Bruce Fink. New York: W. W. Norton, 2006.

Laertius, Diogenes. *Lives of Eminent Philosophers*. Translated by R. D. Hicks. Vol. 2. Cambridge, MA: Harvard University Press, 1925.

Lardreau, Guy, and Christian Jambet. *L'ange: ontologie de la revolution*. Vol. 1. Paris: Grasset, 1976.

Latimer, Hugh. *Selected Sermons of Hugh Latimer*. Edited by Allan G. Chester. Charlottesville: University Press of Virginia, 1968.

Latter, Alex. '"Beyond the Path Itself": Archive and Text in the Correspondence of Bernard Dubourg and J. H. Prynne'. *The Cambridge Quarterly* 50, no. 3 (September 2021): 261–78.

———. *Late Modernism and* The English Intelligencer. London: Bloomsbury, 2015.

Lawson, Andrew. 'Becoming Bourgeois: Benjamin Franklin's Account of the Self'. *ELH* 87, no. 2 (Summer 2020): 463–89.

Leavis, F. R. *Reading Out Poetry and Eugenio Montale—a Tribute*. Belfast: The Queen's University of Belfast, 1979.

Leech, Geoffrey N. *Towards a Semantic Description of English*. London: Longman, 1969.

Lehmann, Winfred P. *Proto-Indo-European Syntax*. Austin: University of Texas Press, 1974.

Leslie, R. F., ed. *The Wanderer*. Manchester: Manchester University Press, 1966.

Liu, Wu-chi, and Irving Yucheng Lo, eds. *Sunflower Splendor: Three Thousand Years of Chinese Poetry*. Garden City, NY: Anchor Books, 1975.

Locke, John. *An Essay Concerning Humane Understanding*. London: Printed for Tho. Basset, 1690 [1689].

Long, Michael. Review of *Brass*, by J. H. Prynne. *Cambridge Review* 93 (19 November 1971): 62–3.

Loots, M. E. *Metrical Myths: An Experimental-Phonetic Investigation into the Production and Perception of Metrical Speech*. The Hague: Martinus Nijhoff, 1980.

MacSweeney, Barry. *Just 22 and I Don't Mind Dyin': The Official Poetical Biography of Jim Morrison, Rock Idol*. London: Curiously Strong, 1971.

Mailer, Norman. *Ancient Evenings*. Boston: Little, Brown, 1983.

Malantschuk, Gregor. *Kierkegaard's Thought*. Edited and translated by Howard V. Hong and Edna H. Hong. Princeton, NJ: Princeton University Press, 1971.

Mandel'shtam, Osip. *Selected Poems*. Translated by David McDuff. Cambridge: Rivers, 1973.

Mao Tse-tung. *An Anthology of His Writings*. Edited and translated by Anne Fremantle. New York: New American Library, 1954.

Mason, Russell Ellsworth. *Internal Perception and Bodily Functioning*. New York: International Universities Press, 1961.

Massu, Jacques. *La vraie bataille d'Alger*. Paris: Plon, 1972.

Matasović, Ranko. 'Latin *paenitet me, miseret me, pudet me* and Active Clause Alignment in Proto-Indo-European'. *Indogermanische Forschungen* 118 (2013): 93–110.

Mayer, Bernadette, Barry Alpert, and Dick Miller. 'Bernadette Mayer—an Interview'. *The World*, no. 29 (April 1974): 76–84.

McKeon, Richard, ed. and trans. *Selections from Medieval Philosophers*. Vol. 1, *Augustine to Albert the Great*. London: Charles Scribner's Sons, 1930.

Merleau-Ponty, M. *The Phenomenology of Perception*. Translated by Colin Smith. London: Routledge and Kegan Paul, 1962.

Mirbeau, Octave. *Le jardin des supplices*. Paris: Bibliothèque-Charpentier, 1899.

Monod, Jacques. *Le hasard et la nécessité: Essai sur la philosophie naturelle de la biologie moderne*. Paris: Éditions du Seuil, 1970.

More, Thomas. *Utopia*. Translated by Paul Turner. Harmondsworth, UK: Penguin, 1965.

Morris, William. *News from Nowhere*. Boston: Roberts Brothers, 1890.

Mottram, Eric. 'The British Poetry Revival, 1960–75'. In *New British Poetries: The Scope of the Possible*, edited by Robert Hampson and Peter Barry, 15–50. Manchester: Manchester University Press, 1993.

———. 'Rencontre avec William Burroughs'. *Les langues modernes* 59, no. 1 (Janvier–Février 1965): 79–83.

Murdoch, Iris. 'The Idea of Perfection'. In *The Sovereignty of Good*, 1–45. London: Routledge and Kegan Paul, 1970.

Needham, Joseph. *Science and Civilisation in China*. Vol. 5, *Chemistry and Chemical Technology*, pt. 2, *Spagyrical Discovery and Invention: Magisteries of Gold and Immortality*. London: Cambridge University Press, 1974.

Nietzsche, Friedrich. *On the Genealogy of Morals*. Translated by Douglas Smith. Oxford: Oxford University Press, 1996.

Nock, Arthur Darby. 'Religious Attitudes of the Ancient Greeks'. In *Essays on Religion and the Ancient World*, vol. 2, 534–50. Oxford: Clarendon Press, 1972.

O'Hara, Frank. *The Collected Poems of Frank O'Hara*. Edited by Donald Allen. Berkeley: University of California Press, 1995.

Oliver, Douglas. '3 Works by Doug Oliver'. In 'European Edition, no. 2'. Special issue, *Chicago* (February 1974): n.p.

———. *Arrondissements*. Cambridge: Salt, 2003.

———. *The Diagram Poems*. London: Ferry, 1979.

———. 'Diagram-poems'. *Ochre*, no. 4 (n.d., ca. 1978): n.p.

———. 'Douglas Oliver, 1937–'. *Contemporary Authors Autobiography Series* 27 (1997): 241–61.

———. 'Even Poets Can Have Beliefs about Poetic "Stress"'. *Grosseteste Review* 12 (1979): 12–32.

———. 'A Formidable Figure', review of *The Small Henderson Room*, by John James. *Cambridge News*, 11 July 1969, 11.

———. 'Four Poems'. *Ambit*, no. 5 (Summer 1960): 13–15.

———. 'From *Second-Rate Deity*'. *Gare du Nord*, no. 1 (1997): 9–13.

———. 'From *The Video House of Fame*'. *Gare du Nord* 1, no. 2 (1998): 43–4.

———. 'From *The Video House of Fame*'. *Gare du Nord* 2, no. 1 (1998): 42.

———. 'From *The Video House of Fame*'. *Gare du Nord* 2, no. 2 (1999): 43–4.

———. 'Fundamental Frequency Studies as a Preliminary to the Literary Criticism of Poetry'. *Journal of Phonetics* 11 (1983): 1–35.

———. 'Importantly'. *Sesheta*, no. 4 (Winter 1972/1973): 4–5.

———. *The Infant and the Pearl*. London: Ferry Press (for Silver Hounds), 1985.

———. *In the Cave of Suicession*. Cambridge: Street Editions, 1974.

———. *Islands of Voices: Selected Poems*. Edited by Ian Brinton. Swindon: Shearsman Books, 2020.

———. *Kind*. London: Agneau 2 / Allardyce, Barnett, 1987.

———. 'Money in Sunshine'. *London Review of Books* 20, no. 9 (7 May 1998): 6.

———. 'More Than a Trace'. *Scarlet* 5 (September 1991): n.p.

———. 'On J. H. Prynne's "Of Movement Towards a Natural Place"'. *Grosseteste Review* 12 (1979): 93–102.

———. *Oppo Hectic*. London: Ferry, 1969.

———. *Penniless Politics*. London: Hoarse Commerce, 1991.

———. *Penniless Politics*. Newcastle upon Tyne: Bloodaxe Books, 1994.

———. 'Pioneer in Poetry', review of *Kitchen Poems* and *Day Light Songs*, by J. H. Prynne. *Cambridge News*, 10 August 1968.

———. *Poetry and Narrative in Performance*. Houndmills, UK: Macmillan, 1989.

———. 'Poetry in Paperback', review of *Aristeas*, by J. H. Prynne. *Cambridge News*, 21 February 1969.

———. 'Poetry's Subject'. *PN Review* 21, no. 7 [22, no. 1] (issue 105, September–October 1995): 52–8.

———. 'Poetry's Subject'. In *Real Voices on Reading*, edited by Philip Davies, 83–102. Houndmills, UK: Macmillan, 1997.

———. 'Rewarding Poetry', review of *The White Stones*, by J. H. Prynne. *Cambridge News*, 13 June 1969.

———. *A Salvo for Africa*. Newcastle upon Tyne: Bloodaxe Books, 2000.

———. 'Tailpiece from *The Video House of Fame*'. *Gare du Nord* 1, no. 3 (1998): 40–2.

———. 'Team Leader'. *Sesheta*, no. 4 (Winter 1972/1973): 6–7.

———. *Three Variations on the Theme of Harm: Selected Poetry and Prose*. London: Paladin, 1990.

———. 'Voicing Patterns as One Key to the Pace of Poetry'. *Journal of Phonetics* 12 (1984): 115–32.

———. 'When the Signs Break Down', review of *Conversations with Claude Lévi-Strauss*, by Georges Charbonnier. *Cambridge News*, 11 July 1969, 11.

———. *Whisper 'Louise': A Double Historical Memoir and Meditation*. Hastings: Reality Street, 2005.

———. 'The Woman Who Was Too Tall'. *Infolio*, no. 47 (14 November 1986).

———, and Peter Riley. Correspondence. DOA, box 9.

Olson, Charles. *Collected Prose*. Edited by Donald Allen and Benjamin Friedlander. Berkeley: University of California Press, 1997.

———. *Human Universe and Other Essays*. Edited by Donald Allen. New York: Grove Press, 1967.

———. *The Maximus Poems*. Edited by George F. Butterick. Berkeley: University of California Press, 1985.

Oppenheim, A. Leo. 'The Interpretation of Dreams in the Ancient Near East, with a Translation of an Assyrian Dream-Book'. *Transactions of the American Philosophical Society* 46, no. 3 (1956): 179–373.

———. 'New Fragments of the Assyrian Dream-Book'. *Iraq* 31, no. 2 (Autumn 1969): 153–65.

Parke, H. W. *The Delphic Oracle*. Oxford: Basil Blackwell, 1956.

Patch, Howard Rollin. *The Goddess Fortuna in Mediaeval Literature*. Cambridge, MA: Harvard University Press, 1927.

Pattison, Neil, Reitha Pattison, and Luke Roberts, eds. *Certain Prose of The English Intelligencer*. 2nd rev. ed. Cambridge: Mountain, 2014.

Percy, Sholto, and Reuben Percy [Joseph Clinton Robertson and Thomas Byerley]. *The Percy Anecdotes: Original and Select*. 20 vols. London: Printed for T. Boys, 1820–3.

Pfefferkorn, Kristin. *Novalis: A Romantic's Theory of Language and Poetry*. New Haven, CT: Yale University Press, 1988.

Plato. *Plato's Phaedrus*. Translated by R. Hackforth. Cambridge: Cambridge University Press, 1952.

Plutarch. *Moralia*. Translated by F. C. Babbit. Vol. 5. Cambridge, MA: Harvard University Press, 1936.

Poe, Edgar Allan. *Eureka: A Prose Poem*. New York: Geo P. Putnam, 1848.

Pound, Ezra. *The Cantos of Ezra Pound*. London: Faber and Faber, 1964.

———. *The Translations of Ezra Pound*. London: Faber and Faber, 1953.

Prynne, J. H. *Aristeas*. London: Ferry, 1968.

———. *Bands around the Throat*. Cambridge: privately printed, 1987.

———. *Brass*. London: Ferry, 1971.

———. 'China Figures', review of *New Songs from a Jade Terrace: An Anthology of Early Chinese Love Poetry*, trans. Anne Birrell. *Modern Asian Studies* 17, no. 4 (1983): 671–88.

———. *Day Light Songs*. Pampisford, UK: R Books, 1968.

———. 'English Poetry and Emphatical Language'. *Proceedings of the British Academy* 74 (1988): 135–69.

———. *Fire Lizard*. Barnet, UK: Blacksuede Boot, 1970.

———. *Force of Circumstance and Other Poems*. London: Routledge and Kegan Paul, 1962.

———. 'From a Letter to Douglas Oliver'. *Grosseteste Review* 6, nos. 1–4 (1973): 152–4.

———. *Her Weasels Wild Returning*. Cambridge: Equipage, 1994.

———. 'Highest Tender'. *Collection*, no. 7 (Autumn 1970): 24–6.

———. *Into the Day*. Cambridge: privately printed, 1972.

———. *Jie ban mi Shi Hu*. Cambridge: Poetical Histories, no. 22, 1992.

———. 'A Letter to Andrew Duncan'. *Grosseteste Review* 15 (1983–4): 100–18.

———. 'Marzipan'. *Rolling Stock*, no. 10 (October 1985).

———. *Marzipan*. Cambridge: Poetical Histories, no. 2, 1986.

———. *News of Warring Clans*. London: Trigram, 1977.

———. *A Night Square*. London: Albion Village, 1973.

———. 'The *Night Vigil* of Shen Zhou'. *Glossator: Practice and Theory of the Commentary*, no. 3 (2010): 1–15.

———. *Not-You*. Cambridge: Equipage, 1993.

———. *The Oval Window*. Cambridge: privately printed, 1983.

———. *The Oval Window*. Edited by N. H. Reeve and Richard Kerridge. Hexham, UK: Bloodaxe Books, 2018.

———. *Pearls That Were*. Cambridge: privately printed, 1999.

———. 'Perles qui furent'. Translated by Pierre Alferi. *Quaderno, cahiers de poésie*, no. 5 (Printemps 2000): n.p.

———. *Perles qui furent*. Translated by Pierre Alferi. Marseille: Éric Pesty Éditeur, 2013.

———. *Poems*. Edinburgh: Agneau 2, 1982.

———. *Poems*. South Fremantle, AU: Fremantle Arts Centre Press and Folio (Salt); Newcastle upon Tyne: Bloodaxe Books, 1999.

———. *Poems*. Hexham, UK: Bloodaxe Books, 2015.

———. *Stars, Tigers and the Shape of Words*. William Matthews Lectures. London: Birkbeck College, 1993.

———. *Triodes*. Cambridge: Barque, 1999.

———. *The White Stones*. Lincoln, UK: Grosseteste Press, 1969.

———. *Word Order*. Kenilworth, UK: Prest Roots, 1989.

———. *Wound Response*. Cambridge: Street Editions, 1974.

———. 'Write-Out'. *Infolio*, no. 40 (25 August 1986).

———, and Charles Olson. *The Collected Letters of Charles Olson and J. H. Prynne*. Edited by Ryan Dobran. Albuquerque: University of New Mexico Press, 2017.

Quirk, Randolph, Sidney Greenbaum, Geoffrey Leech, and Jan Svartvik. *A Comprehensive Grammar of the English Language*. London: Longman, 1985.

Reeve, N. H., and Richard Kerridge. *Nearly Too Much: The Poetry of J. H. Prynne*. Liverpool: Liverpool University Press, 1995.

Renard, Maurice. *Un homme chez les microbes: Scherzo*. Paris: G. Crès et Cie, 1928.

Rexroth, Kenneth. *American Poetry in the Twentieth Century*. New York: Seabury, 1973.

Rheingold, Howard. *Virtual Reality*. London: Secker and Warburg, 1991.

Richey, Joseph, ed. *Ed Dorn Live: Lectures, Interviews, and Outtakes*. Ann Arbor: University of Michigan Press, 2007.

Rindler, W. 'Visual Horizons in World-Models'. *Monthly Notice of the Royal Astronomical Society* 116, no. 6 (December 1956): 662–77.

Ritter, R. M., ed. *The Oxford Manual of Style*. London: BCA, 2002.

Sartre, Jean-Paul. *Qu'est-ce que la littérature?* Paris: Éditions Gallimard, 1948.

———. *'What is Literature?' and Other Essays*. Cambridge, MA: Harvard University Press, 1988.

Scalapino, Leslie, and Ron Silliman. 'What/Person: From an Exchange'. *Poetics Journal*, no. 9 (1991): 51–68.

Schilder, Paul. *The Image and Appearance of the Human Body: Studies in the Constructive Energies of the Psyche*. London: Kegan Paul, 1935.

Screech, M. A. *Rabelais*. London: Gerald Duckworth, 1979.

———. *The Rabelaisian Marriage: Aspects of Rabelais's Religion, Ethics and Comic Philosophy*. London: Edward Arnold, 1958.

Seuren, Pieter A. M. 'Negative's Travels'. In *Semantic Syntax*, edited by Pieter A. M. Seuren, 183–208. London: Oxford University Press, 1974.

———. *Operators and Nucleus: A Contribution to the Theory of Grammar*. Cambridge: Cambridge University Press, 1969.

Silliman, Ron. *The New Sentence*. New York: Roof Books, 1977.

Sinclair, Iain, ed. *Conductors of Chaos*. London: Picador, 1996.

Skinner, Quentin. *The Foundations of Modern Political Thought*. Vol. 1. Cambridge: Cambridge University Press, 1978.

Smith, A. D. *Husserl and the Cartesian Meditations*. Abingdon: Routledge, 2003.

Smith, Adam. *Wealth of Nations: Books IV–V*. Edited by Andrew Skinner. London: Penguin, 1999.

Snyder, Gary. 'Through the Smoke Hole'. *Poetry* 106, no. 1/2 (April–May 1965): 120–2.

Spicer, Jack. *The Collected Books of Jack Spicer*. Edited by Robin Blaser. Los Angeles: Black Sparrow, 1975.

———. *My Vocabulary Did This to Me: The Collected Poetry of Jack Spicer*. Edited by Peter Gizzi and Kevin Killian. Middletown, CT: Wesleyan University Press, 2008.

Steiner, George. *Language and Silence: Essays 1958–1966*. London: Faber and Faber, 1967.

Stevens, John. *Music and Poetry in the Early Tudor Court*. London: Methuen, 1961.

Stevenson, Robert Louis. *Lay Morals and Other Papers*. London: Chatto and Windus, 1911.

Stora, Benjamin. *Algeria, 1830–2000: A Short History*. Ithaca, NY: Cornell University Press, 2000.

Stratton-Porter, Gene. *The Keeper of the Bees*. Toronto: S. B. Gundy, 1925.

Thom, René. 'Topological Models in Biology'. *Topology* 8, no. 3 (July 1969): 313–35.

Thorpe, Adam. 'Narcissist in a Space–Time Continuum', review of *Three Variations on the Theme of Harm*, by Douglas Oliver. *Poetry Review* 83, no. 3 (Autumn 1993): 48–9.

Turner, Fred. *From Counterculture to Cyberculture: Stewart Brand, the Whole Earth Network, and the Rise of Digital Utopianism*. Chicago: University of Chicago Press, 2006.

Turner, Victor W. *The Ritual Process: Structure and Anti-Structure*. London: Penguin Books, 1969.

Updike, John. *The Coup*. New York: Alfred A. Knopf, 1978.

Vaughan, Henry. *Poetry and Selected Prose*. Edited by L. C. Martin. London: Oxford University Press, 1963.

Verlaine, Paul. *Selected Poems*. Translated by Martin Sorrell. Oxford: Oxford University Press, 1999.

Vermeule, Emily. *Aspects of Death in Early Greek Art and Poetry*. Berkeley: University of California Press, 1979.

Vesalius, Andreas. *De humani corporis fabrica libri septem*. Basileae [Basel]: Ex officina Joannis Oporini, 1543.

Vignolo, L. A. 'Auditory Agnosia'. In *The Neuropsychology of Cognitive Function: Proceedings of a Royal Society Discussion Meeting, Held on 18 and 19 November 1981*, edited by D. E. Broadbent and L. Weiskrantz. Philosophical Transactions of the Royal Society of London: Series B, Biological Sciences 298, no. 1089 (1982): 49–57.

Whitehead, Alfred North. *Science and the Modern World: Lowell Lectures, 1925*. New York: New American Library, 1925.

Wilkinson, John. 'Hoodoo Bozo Talks That Rainbow Jive', review of *Penniless Politics*, by Douglas Oliver. *Angel Exhaust*, no. 8 (1992): 110–13.

Woolf, Douglas. *Ya! and John-Juan*. New York: Harper and Row, 1971.

Wordsworth, William. *The Prose Works of William Wordsworth*. Edited by W. J. B. Owen and Jane Worthington Smyser. Vol 3. Oxford: Clarendon Press, 1974.

Wren-Lewis, Simon. *The Role of Money in Determining Prices: A Reduced Form Approach*. Treasury Working Paper 18. London: H. M. Treasury, 1981.

Wright, Patrick. 'Rodinsky's Place', review of *White Chappell: Scarlet Tracings*, by Iain Sinclair. *London Review of Books* 9, no. 19 (29 October 1987): 3–5.

Wyatt, Thomas. *Collected Poems*. Edited by Joost Daalder. Oxford: Oxford University Press, 1975.

X, Malcolm. *Malcolm X Speaks: Selected Speeches and Statements*. Edited by George Breitman. New York: Merit, 1965.

Young, Hugo. *One of Us*. London: Pan Books, 1993.

Zeeman, E. C. *Catastrophe Theory: Selected Papers, 1972–1977*. Reading, MA: Addison-Wesley, 1977.

Zeldovich, Ya. B., and I. D. Novikov. *Relativistic Astrophysics*. Vol. 2, *Stars and Relativity*, translated by Eli Arlock. Chicago: University of Chicago Press, 1971.

Zhuangzi. *The Complete Works of Zhuangzi*. Translated by Burton Watson. New York: Columbia University Press, 2013.

Index

Ackroyd, Peter, 116, 116n2
Adorno, Theodor, 118, 118n3
Ælfric, 62, 62fig
Alferi, Pierre, 168, 168n2
Allen, Donald, 103n4
Ambit (periodical), ixn2
Andrew, Malcolm, 88n2, 89n6
Andrews, Bruce, 118n7
Angel Exhaust (periodical), 160n2
Anselm, Saint, 65, 65n2
Aquinas, Thomas, 65, 97–8
Archeus (periodical), 122n1, 188n
Aristotle, 109, 109n2, 140–1
Artaud, Antonin, 30, 30n4, 115
Astrov, Margot, 167n3
Auden, W. H., 52, 52n3, 86n6
Augustine, Saint, 65, 80–1, 81n1, 179n1, 186, 186n2

Barnes, William, 139
Barnett, Anthony, ix, 25n1, 55, 55n1, 61, 102, 102n1, 103, 108n3, 116
Bartholomew, W. T., 167n3
Bataille, Georges, 136, 136n6
Bayley, John, 101, 101n3
Bean News (periodical), 49n3
Beckett, Samuel, 54, 83–4, 118, 134
Benjamin, Walter, 118n2
Bernard, Claude, 26
Bernstein, Charles, 118n7
Berrigan, Anselm, 107, 107n4, 108, 122–3, 154n3, 164, 164n1, 165–6
Berrigan, Edmund, 107, 107n4, 108, 119, 122–3, 154n3
Berrigan, Ted, 106n4, 107n4
Betjeman, John, 31n2
Bion, Wilfred, 53, 53n3, 113–14, 114n1, 117
Birrell, Anne, 75, 75n2, 76n2
Blake, William, 73, 74n2, 89, 89n5, 128n3, 142n1, 143, 143n2, 167n1, 170
Blanchot, Maurice, 136, 136n6
Blaser, Robin, 76n1
Bleibtreu, John N., 44n5
Bliss, A. J., 52
Boccaccio, Giovanni, 65
Boss, Medard, 115, 115n2
Brand, Stewart, 132n1
Brecht, Bertolt, 118, 118n2
Britten, Benjamin, 113
Brull, Steven, 151n2
Bruno, Giordano, 37
Burliuk, Vladimir, 70fig
Burnley, J. D., 87–90, 95
Burroughs, William S., 58, 58n2, 61, 65
Bush, George H. W., 121, 123
Busoni, Ferruccio, 64, 64n1
Butler, Bill, 31n2
Byerley, Thomas. *See* Percy, Reuben

Calder, John, 31n2
Caldwell, Roger, 164n5
Cambridge Evening News (periodical), 25n3
Cambridge News (periodical), ix–x, 25, 25n3, 169–73
Cambridge Review (periodical), 32, 32n4
Campion, Thomas, 86n4
Campos, Cristophe, 157, 157n1
Castle, Barbara, 96
Celan, Paul, 35, 35n4, 45n3, 115, 162
Celan-Lestrange, Gisèle, 102n3
Cervantes, 159n1
Chamberlain, Greg, 96n2, n3
Chancellor, Alexander, 64n1
Char, René, 114–15, 115n1
Chaucer, Geoffrey, 56, 56n2, 87–8, 90, 108
Chicago (periodical), 106n4
Chomsky, Noam, 35, 37
Cicero, 56n2
Cleveland, Sidney E., 26
Clinton Robertson, Joseph. *See* Percy, Sholto
The Cloud of Unknowing (anon.), 84n1, 93n1
Coetzee, J. M., 132, 132n3, 134, 134n1, 136–7
Cohn, Ruby, 83
Coleridge, Samuel Taylor, 182
Collection (periodical), 30n2, 42n1
Conductors of Chaos (anthology), 162n2, 164n5
Conquest, Robert, viii
Coué, Émile, 44
Coventry Evening Telegraph (periodical), 26n3
Crozier, Andrew, ix–x, 25n1, 28n2, 31, 40n3, 47, 48fig, 70, 85n2, 112, 112n1, 116, 142
Crozier, Jean, 85
Cushion, Percy, 103
Cutler, Anne, 64n2

Daalder, Joost, 66n7
D'Annunzio, Gabriele, 83
Dante, 88n3, 94n3, 97, 178
Darwin, Charles, 140, 140n8
Davie, Donald, 175–6, 176n*
Davies, Paul, 137n6
Davies, Philip, 152n1
Debord, Guy, 127, 127n4
Dempsey, Michael, 31
Deng Xiaoping, 126
De Quincey, Thomas, 114, 114n1
Derrida, Jacques, 76n1, 154, 154n1, 182, 182n1
Descartes, René, 27n1
Dickens, Charles, 81n4
Diderot, Denis, 100
Diederich, Bernie, 96n3
Dodds, E. R., 45
Donne, John, 25–6, 53, 65

Dorn, Edward, xiv, xvi–xvii, 28, 31, 31n5, 32, 35, 37, 42, 42n2, 49, 49n3, 50n1, 107n1, 107fig, 164, 164n3, 165, 165n1, 166, 166n1, n2, 167n1, 174n, 181, 181n1, 188n
Dorn, Jennifer Dunbar, 107n1, 107fig, 165–6, 167n1, 188n
Dryden, John, 140, 140n3
Dubourg, Alexis, 154, 159
Dubourg, Bernard, 84n5, 101n1, 130, 130n1, 131, 135, 154, 159–60
Duncan, Andrew, 70, 70n2, 74
Dunning, T. P., 52
Duvalier, Jean-Claude, 96, 96n2

Eagleton, Terry, 86n6, 169n
Edelen, Dominic, 35
Einstein, Albert, 34
Eliot, T. S., 50n1, 64n3, 103, 114n1
Ellis, G. F. R., 177n*
Empedocles, 47, 47fig
The English Intelligencer (periodical), ix–x, xiiin1, n2, xvi, 25, 25n1, 166n1, 169
Ericsson, Neil R., 81, 81n2
Etheridge, Dick, 64n1
Étiemble, René, 139n3

Favorinus, 47, 47fig
Ferry, David, 164n2
Feuchtwang, Stephan, 158, 161
Fichte, Johann Gottlieb, 139n4
Ficino, Marsilio, 65
Fielding, Henry, 115, 115n3
Fisher, Seymour, 26
Fónagy, Ivan, 140, 140n5
Foucault, Michel, 76n1, 134
Fourcade, Dominique, 147, 150, 154
Franco-British Studies (periodical), 84, 84n5
Franklin, Benjamin, 59, 59n1
Fraser, G. S., viii
Frege, Gotlob, 80–1
Freud, Sigmund, 29n1, 58–60
Friedman, Milton, 81, 81n2
Fuller, Roy, 103
Funkhouser, Linda Bradley, 70, 70fig
Furmston, Suzanne, 45n5. *See also* Prynne, Suzanne

Gardner, Ernest, 28–9, 35
Gare du Nord (periodical), viii, 119n3, 137n5, 163n3, n4, 164–5
Gascoyne, David, 74, 74n1
Geschwind, Norman, 53–4
Ginsberg, Allen, 77, 77n2
Glossator (periodical), 193n1
Glück, Louise, 164n2
Glucksmann, André, 57
Gödel, Kurt, 33
Gonda, Jan, 53
Gorbachev, Mikhail, 109

204

Gordon, E. V., 142n3
Goya, Francisco, 118
Graves, Robert, 44n4
Groddeck, Georg, 52, 52n3
Grosseteste Review (periodical), xvii, 26n2, 62, 62n2, 70n2, 78, 80, 80n1, 85
Grosseteste, Robert, 80, 80n1
Guston, Philip, 154, 154n3, 165

Hall, John, 142, 142n3
Halliday, Michael, 73, 73n1
Harding, Adrian, 131
Hardy, Oliver, 106
Harwood, Lee, 30n2, 31, 31n7
Hawking, S. W., 39, 41, 177n*
Hawkins, Ralph, 70n2
Hazlitt, William, 82, 82n4, 86n5
Heaney, Seamus, 72, 79
Heidegger, Martin, xv, 41n2, 154
Heine, Heinrich, 162
Hendry, David F., 81, 81n2
Heraclitus, 32n3, 37
Herder, Johann Gottfried, 139n4, 141n2
Hermaeus, Ammonius, 141
Herodotus, 171
Hill, Geoffrey, 135
Hitler, Adolf, 61, 115
Hoyle, Fred, 33
Hsiao Kang, 76n2
Hughes, Janet, 38n4. *See also* Oliver, Janet
Hume, David, 114, 114n2
Hussein, Saddam, 121
Husserl, Edmund, xv, 57n2, 153, 153n4, 154, 154n1
Huxley, Francis, 57, 57n1

Infolio (periodical), 102n3, 105n2, 189n1
Ingham, Charles, 70n2

Jakobson, Roman, 140
Jambet, Christian, 57
James, John, ix–x, 25n1, 26, 28, 28n2, 30n2, 39, 40n3, n4, 41, 47, 48fig, 61, 63, 169n
James, Wendy. *See* Mulford, Wendy
Jarrell, Randall, 70, 70fig
Jefferies, Richard, 86, 86n2
Jiang Qing, 127, 127n3
Jian Song-qing, 125
John, E. Roy, 45
Johnson, Phil, 164n3
Jolicoeur, Aubelin, 96n3
Jordis, Christine, 74n1
Joseph, Keith, 85, 85n4

Kafka, Franz, 118, 118n2
Katko, Justin, 34n1, 35n3, 41n5, 42n2, 174n
Kenny, Anthony, 52–3, 53n5
Kerridge, Richard, 162, 162n4
Kierkegaard, Søren, 49n1, 57, 57n1, 99
King, M. A., 107n2
Kinnock, Neil, 89, 92, 96, 107
Kinsella, John, 162, 162n3
Koch, Kenneth, 33
Koethe, John, 164n2
Kristeva, Julia, 141, 141n4
Kropotkin, Peter, 195, 195n1

Lacan, Jacques, 76, 76n1
Laertius, Diogenes, 47, 47fig

Lane, David, 96
Langland, William, 88, 113n1, 129n2
L=A=N=G=U=A=G=E (periodical), 118, 118n7
Laplace, Pierre-Simon, 177, 177n*
Lardreau, Guy, 57
Larkin, Philip, viii
Latimer, Hugh, 136, 136n1
Latter, Alex, xiiin2, 25n1, 130n1, 166n1
Laurel, Stan, 106n2
Lawson, Nigel, 84, 84n2
Leary, Timothy, 65
Leavis, F. R., 64, 64n3, 65
Leech, Geoffrey N., 42
Lehmann, Winfred P., 51, 53n2, 55
Leonardo da Vinci, 29
Leslie, R. F., 52
Lévi-Strauss, Claude, 46, 169n
Lewis, Wyndham, 53n4
Liu, Wu-chi, 124n2
Liu Xiang-jun, xiv, 149–50, 150n1, 151, 151n1, 152–4, 158–9, 190–8
Lo, Irving Yucheng, 124n2
Locke, John, 82, 82n3
London Review of Books (periodical), 113, 113n4, 163, 163n1, n2
Long, Michael, 32n4
Longuet-Higgins, H. C., 64n2
Longville, Tim, xvii, 80n1, 112n1
Loots, M. E., 79

Machiavelli, Niccolò, 120, 120n4, 122
MacLean, Paul, 36n2
Mac Low, Jackson, 153n3
Macrobius, 56, 56n2
MacSweeney, Barry, 31, 31n7
Mailer, Norman, 104n3
Major, John, 126, 127n1
Malantschuk, Gregor, 57n1
Malherbe, François de, 83
Mallarmé, Stéphane, 141n4
Mandel'shtam, Osip, 45–6, 46n1
Manilius, Marcus, ix
Mao Tse-tung, 124n3, 126n1, 152, 161, 161n1
Marriott, D. S., 122, 122n1, 188n
Marvell, Andrew, 116
Marx, Karl, 146
Mason, Russell Ellsworth, 26
Massu, Jacques, 136n5
Maxwell, James Clerk, 39
Mayer, Bernadette, 45, 45n1
McCambridge, Mercedes, 38, 38n4
McKeon, Richard, 80n1, 81n1
Melville, Herman, 45n3
Merleau-Ponty, Maurice, 26, 28
Milne, Drew, 145n1
Milton, John, 84, 85n1, 156, 182–3, 183n1, 185, 185n1
Mirbeau, Octave, 136, 137n5
Monod, Jacques, 35, 179–80, 180n1
Montaigne, Michel de, 58
More, Thomas, 141n3
Morier, Henri, 72, 72n1
Morris, William, 86, 86n2
Mottram, Eric, viii–ix, 58, 58n2
Mozart, Wolfgang Amadeus, 111n1
Mulford, Wendy, ix, xvii, 25n1, 38n1, 39–40, 40n4, n6, 41, 44–5, 61, 63, 106n4

Murdoch, Iris, 27, 29

Nashe, Thomas, 129n2
Nasr, Said Husain, 42
Nasr, Seyyed Hossein. *See* Nasr, Said Husain
Needham, Joseph, 38n1, 42
Nerval, Gérard de, 115
Nicholas of Cusa, 37, 37n1
Nietzsche, Friedrich, 32n3
Nixon, Richard, 174
Nock, Arthur Darby, 42
The Norman Hackforth (periodical), 30n2, 33n5
Notley, Alice, viii, xvii, 106, 106n4, 107, 107n1, n4, 107fig, 114, 118n5, 119, 119n3, 120n1, 121n2, 122–3, 129n1, 131, 134, 145n1, 154n3, 164, 164n4, 165, 165n3
Novalis, 139, 139n4, 141, 141n2
Novikov, I. D., 28n1

O'Brien, Conor Cruise, 120n2
The Observer (periodical), 84, 84n3
Ochre (periodical), 53n1, 70, 70n2
O'Hara, Frank, 28, 28n2, 30
Oldfield, Steve, 105n2
Oliver, Douglas, works by:
  Arrondissements, 162n5, 163n3, n4
  'Before Suicide', ixn2
  Boxing novel, 48n2, 49, 49n3, 65
  'Central', 53n1, 62
  'Chinese Bridport', 163n2
  'Crystal Eagle 1', 162n5
  'Crystal Eagle 2', 162n5
  'Dance It', ixn2
  'The Diagonal is Diagonal', 136n4
  The Diagram Poems, xv, xvfig, xvi, 53n1, 55, 62, 62fig, 66, 66n3, 106n4, 136, 136n4
  'Dr. Dee and the Angels', 25n2
  'Evening Descending Mauve: *Gisèle Celan-Lestrange*', 162n5
  'Even Poets Can Have Beliefs about Poetic Stress', 62, 62n2, 63, 64n2, 65, 66, 66n5, 70, 78, 78n2
  'Forearms', 162n5
  'A Formidable Figure', 169n
  'Fundamental Frequency Studies as a Preliminary to the Literary Criticism of Poetry', 65n3, 66–74, 78, 78n1, 79, 79n3
  The Harmless Building, xii–xiii, xv–xvi, 26–31, 37n1, 38n4, 44, 44n3, 76n1, 88n1, 116n2, 142, 144
  'The Herb', 145n1
  'Illustrations', 25, 25n4
  'Importantly', 53n1
  'Indian Sequence', 25n2
  The Infant and the Pearl, 66, 66n2, 82–100, 102, 108, 142–4
  In the Cave of Suicession, xvi, 38–45, 47, 47n3, 54, 54n2, 59, 106n4, 165, 167, 167n3
  Islands of Voices: Selected Poems, viii
  'An Island That Is All the World', 42n2, 49n3
  'Jain Sequence', 25n2, 25n4
  'Jealous Mother', 25n2
  Kind, xvii, 25n2, 42n2, 55n1, 116n2

Oliver, Douglas, works by (*continued*):
'A Little Night', 162n5
'Maradevi and Her Torture Gardens', 137n5
'Maradevi and Marudevi', 137n5
A Meeting for Douglas Oliver and 27 Uncollected Poems, xvii
'Money in Sunshine', 163, 163n2
'Mongol in the Woods', 142, 142n2
'More Than a Trace', 182n1
'One Man and His Dove', ixn2
'On J. H. Prynne's "Of Movement Towards a Natural Place"', 62, 62n2, 63, 65, 84–5
Oppo Hectic, x, 25n2, 28, 38n4, 142n2
'The Oracle of the Drowned', 108n2, 113–14, 114n1
'The Ordeal of Conversation', ixn2
'P.C.', 53n1
Penniless. See *Penniless Politics*
Penniless Politics, 123, 123n4, 129–30, 138, 144, 160n2
'Pioneer in Poetry', 25n3, 169–70, 188
Poetry and Narrative in Performance, xviin2, 64n2, 65n3, 84–5, 85n1, 103, 103n4, 108n3, 117, 117n1, n2, n3, 119, 119n2, 140n6, n7, 141n3, 156, 175n, n1, n2, 176n1, 178n1, 179n1, 182n1, n2, 183n1, 185n1, 186n2
'Poetry in Paperback', 25n3, 171
'Poetry's Subject' (1995), 152n1, 163, 163n5
'Poetry's Subject' (1997), 152n1, 163, 163n5
'Rewarding Poetry', 25n3, 172–3
A Salvo for Africa, 145n1, 165, 167
'A Salvo for Malawi', 147, 147n2, 149
'Sampler (Dr. John Dee)', 25n2
The Second-Rate Deity, 137, 137n5
'Team Leader', 53n1
Three Variations on the Theme of Harm, 146n2
'Twilight Flowers', 162n5
'"u", "je", "r", "r", "im", "a", "finally"', 30n3, 31, 31n4
'The Video House of Fame', 163, 163n3, n4
'Voicing Patterns as One Key to the Pace of Poetry', 65n3
'Walnut and Lily', 162n5
'What the Plants Can Tell Us', 84–5, 85n1, 156, 156n6, 175–87
'When I Was in Bridport', 38n4
'When the Signs Break Down', 169n
'Whirlwind', 30, 30n3
Whisper 'Louise', xvii, 76n1, 137n5, 140n5, 154n3, 165, 165n3, 169n
'The Woman Who Was Too Tall', 105n2
Oliver, Janet, 38n4, 106n4, 107, 142
Oliver, Tom, xi–xiii, xvi, 42n2, 142, 144
Olson, Charles, x, xiv, xv, xvii, 32n3, 103, 103n4, 119, 119n2
Oppenheim, A. Leo, 41
Orwell, George, 148
Orlovsky, Peter, 77, 77n2
Ovid, 56
Owen, W. J. B., 83
Palgrave, F. T., 112
Parataxis (periodical), 145, 145n1, 149, 149n1, 198, 198n1

Parke, H. W., 45
Pascal, Blaise, 139n3
Patch, Howard Rollin, 97, 97n2
Paterson, Don, 164
Paul, Saint, 25
Paulin, Tom, 101, 101n3
Pausanias, 43
Pearl (anon.), 82, 86, 86n3, 88, 88n2, 89, 89n6, 91, 96, 142, 142n3, 143
Percy, Reuben, 104n2
Percy, Sholto, 104n2
Petrarch, 65
Pfefferkorn, Kristin, 139n4, 141n2
Philips, Tom, 28n2
Piaget, Jean, 30
Picasso, Pablo, 60, 154
Plato, 53, 53n4, 140, 140n6
Plotinus, 65
Plutarch, 38n1, 39, 39n2, 43
PN Review, 112, 112n2
Poe, Edgar Allan, 177
Pope, Alexander, 64n3, 65, 65n3, 73, 140, 140n2
Porter, Peter, 77
Pound, Ezra, xv, 52, 52n2, 75–6, 95, 97–8, 105, 161, 161n3, 169–70
Propertius, Sextus, 161
Prynne, J. H., works by:
'Again in the Black Cloud', 43
'Airport Poem: Ethics of Survival', 172
Aristeas, 25n3, 171
'Aristeas, in Seven Years', 171, 171n2, 173
'As It Were an Attendant', 173
'Attending Her Aggregate, Detour', 155
Bands around the Throat, 106–9, 111–13, 122n1, 153n2, 188n
'The Bee Target on His Shoulder', 41, 42n1, 43n5
'The Blade Given Back', 28, 28n1, 33, 33n5
Brass, 28, 30n2, 32n4, 33n5, 41–2, 42n1, 177
'China Figures' (1983), 75–7
'China Figures' (1986), 75n1
'Concerning Quality, Again', xiii, xiiin1
Day Light Songs, 25n3, 170, 180, 180n2
'Die a Millionaire', 169
Down Where Changed, 62, 62fig
'English Poetry and Emphatical Language', 117, 117n1, 119, 119n4, 143, 143n1
'An Evening Walk', 28, 28n1, 33, 33n6
'A Figure of Mercy, of Speech', 172
Fire Lizard, 180, 180n2
'First Notes on Daylight', 173
'Fool's Bracelet', 106, 113n2, 153n2
Force of Circumstance, ix, 164, 164n4
'Fresh Running Water', 106
'Glove Timing', 165, 167
Her Weasels Wild Returning, 152n1, 155–7, 162, 162n1, 163
'Highest Tender', 42n1
High Pink on Chrome, 48, 48n4
'The Ideal Star-Fighter', 166, 166n2
'In the Long Run, to Be Stranded', 172–3
Into the Day, 28, 28n1, 32–3, 43, 45, 45n3, 180, 180n2
Jie ban mi Shi Hu, 128n4, 131, 131n1
'The Kirghiz Disasters', 30, 30n2, 33n5

Prynne, J. H., works by (*continued*):
Kitchen Poems, xii, 25n3, 32, 48, 128n2, 169–71, 188
'Landing Area', 45, 45n4
'Lend a Hand', 106
'Marzipan', 101, 101n1, 106, 122, 122n1, 124n2, 188–9
'Massepain', 101n1
'Melanin', 43, 43n3
'Moon Poem', xiii, xiiin2, 172–3
News of Warring Clans, 48–55, 61, 61n1
A Night Square, 31n6, 180, 180n2
'No Song No Supper', 106, 106n3, 112, 112n4, 189, 189n1
'A Note on Metal', 43, 43n5, 171, 171n3
Not-You, 136–7, 154–5
'Of Movement Towards a Natural Place', xvii, 43, 65, 65n2, 81, 99, 99n2, 145, 145n2, 156, 156n4, 175–87
'On the Matter of Thermal Packing', 173
The Oval Window (1983), xv–xvi, 79, 79fig, 80–2
The Oval Window (2018), 80n1
Pearls That Were, 168, 168n2
Perles qui furent, 168n2
'Pigment Depôt', 43
'The *Plant Time Manifold* Transcripts', 42–3, 45, 45n2
Poems (1982), 55n1, 66, 66n1, 70n1, 79, 164n4
Poems (1999), xvii, 162, 162n3, 164–5
Poems (2015), vii, xvii, 164n4
'Questions for the Time Being', 173
'Rates of Return', 106
Rune poem, 42, 42n2, 44, 47–8, 165, 167, 174
'Sketch for a Financial Theory of the Self', 128, 128n2, 170, 188, 188n2
'Star Damage at Home', 171, 173
'Stars, Tigers and the Shape of Words', 139, 139n4, 140–5, 155
'A Stone Called Nothing', 172–3
'The Stony Heart of Her', 155–6
'Then So Much She Did', 155–6
'Thoughts on the Esterházy Court Uniform', 173
'Tortrix', 70n2
Triodes, 167–8, 168n1
'Viva Ken', 33, 33n5
'Well Enough in Her Riding After', 155–6, 163, 163n4
The White Stones, xii, 25n3, 45n5, 144, 172–3
Word Order, 117–19, 135–7
Wound Response, xvi–xvii, 28n1, 38n1, 40–5, 47, 47–8, 80, 99, 145, 145n2, 155–6, 176–8
'Write-Out', 102, 102n3, 105, 105n2, n3, n4
Prynne, Suzanne, 45, 45n5, 47n3, 50, 61, 119, 163

Quaderno (periodical), 168, 168n2
Quirk, Randolph, 113

Rabelais, 140, 140n6, 141
Racine, Jean, 83
Rainey, Ma, ix
Raworth, Tom, 105, 105n2, 166
Raworth, Valarie, 105, 166

Reagan, Ronald, 109–10, 144, 152
Reeve, N. H., 162, 162n4
Renard, Maurice, 177
Rexroth, Kenneth, 66, 66n6
Reynolds, Oliver, 84n3
Rheingold, Howard, 132n2
Rhodes James, Robert, 92, 92n2, 96n1
Richards, I. A., 185n2
Richey, Joseph, 164n3, 167n1
Ricoeur, Paul, 186n2
Riley, Denise, 106n4
Riley, Peter, x, xii, xvii, 30n2, 49n3, 76n1, 153n3, 165
Rilke, Rainer Maria, 64
Rindler, W., 42
Rivière, Jacques, 30, 30n4
Robinson, Derek, 64n1
Rolling Stock (periodical), 188n
Romer, Stephen, 79
Royet-Journoud, Claude, 79
Ruskin, John, 150

Salan, Raoul, 136, 136n5
Samedi, Baron, xiv, 57
Santos, Sherod, 164n2
Sartre, Jean-Paul, 136n6, 139n3
Saussure, Ferdinand de, 144n2
Scalapino, Leslie, 128n1
Scarlet (periodical), viii, 119, 119n3, 120, 120n1, 121, 121n1, 122–3, 123n3, n4, 182n1
Schilder, Paul, 26, 28
Schmidt, Michael, 112n2
Schutz, Alfred, 36
Schwartz, Anna J., 81n2
Schwitters, Kurt, 120n1
Screech, M. A., 140, 140n7
The Seafarer (anon.), 52, 52n2
Seneca, 87–8
Sesheta (periodical), 53n1
Seuren, Pieter A. M., 42, 47
Shakespeare, William, 91, 91n1, 98, 98n1, 99n1, 103, 103n3, n4, 119, 119n2, 144
Shelley (family), 44
Shelley, Percy Bysshe, 86n5, 105
Shen Zhou, 193, 193n1
Sidney, Philip, 95, 108, 108n5
Silliman, Ron, 104, 104n1, 118n7, 128n1
Sinclair, Iain, 113n4, 162n2, 164n3
Skinner, Quentin, 97, 97n3
Smith, Adam, 85n4, 94, 94n4, 109, 109n1
Smyser, Jane Worthington, 83
Smythies, J. R., 45
Snyder, Gary, 171, 171n1
The Spectator (periodical), 64n1, 116n2, 143
Spenser, Edmund, 89, 89n7
Spicer, Jack, 33, 33n3
Spinoza, Baruch, 37
Steiner, George, 114, 114n3, 115
Stendhal, 105
Stevens, John, 113n3
Stevens, Wallace, 169
Stevenson, Robert Louis, 57–60
Stone-Richards, Michael, 154
Stratton-Porter, Gene, 44
Sturm, Nick, 119n3
Sun Tzu, 120, 122
Sutherland, Keston, 166

T'ang Yin, 124, 124n2
Tennyson, Alfred, 139
Thatcher, Margaret, 92, 92n2, 101n2, 107, 107n2, 109, 120–1, 142–4, 188
Thom, René, 30, 32, 32n5, 33–4, 34n1, 35–7
Thorpe, Adam, 146, 146n2, 160n2
The Times (periodical), xv, 62n2, 84n2, 85n4, 96n3, 104, 116n2, 120n2, 120n5, 127n1, n6
Tin-tin, 125
Tolpuddle Martyrs, 139, 139n2
Tupamaros, xv–xvi, 136n4
Turner, Fred, 132n1
Turner, Victor W., 46
Tzarad (periodical), 30n2

Updike, John, 104

A Various Art (anthology), 111–12, 112n1, 113, 116, 116n2, 117
Vaughan, Henry, 46, 46n2
Verlaine, Paul, 114n1
Vermeule, Emily, 66
Vesalius, Andreas, 25
Vignolo, L. A., 70
Virgil, 103, 161

Waddington, C. H., 45
Waldman, Anne, 108
Waldron, Ronald, 88n2, 89n6
Walker, Sarah, 82
The Wanderer (anon.), 52, 56, 56n1
Wang Hongwen, 127n3
Ward, Candice, 164–5, 167
Ward, Dunstan, 84, 84n5
Wei Chuang, 124n2
Weiser, Karen, 164, 166
Wheale, Nigel, xvii
Whetstone, Keith, 25n3
Whitehead, Alfred North, 116n1
Whorf, Benjamin Lee, 55
Widdowson, Henry, 73, 73n2
Wilkinson, John, 160n2
Williams, Hugo, 164
Williams, Shirley, 92, 92n2, 96, 110
Wilson, Albert, 35
Wilson, Angus, 54
Wilson, Harold, 85n4
Wilson, Mary, 31n2
Woolf, Douglas, 28, 31
Wordsworth, William, 83, 99n1, 112, 182
Wren-Lewis, Simon, 95
Wright, Patrick, 113, 113n4, 117
Wyatt, Thomas, 66, 66n7, 67–74, 86, 86n1, 88

X, Malcolm, 146, 146n1

Yao Wenyuan, 127n3
Yeats, W. B., 153n2
Yeltsin, Boris, 147
Young, Hugo, 85n4

Zeeman, Christopher, xv, 35, 35n1, 36, 36n2, 37
Zeldovich, Ya. B., 28n1
Zhang Chunqiao, 127n3
Zhuangzi, 135, 135n2, 168n3